Power and Conflict in Russia's Borderlands

Power and Conflict in Russia's Borderlands

The Post-Soviet Geopolitics of Dispute Resolution

Helena Rytövuori-Apunen

I.B.TAURIS
LONDON • NEW YORK • OXFORD • NEW DELHI • SYDNEY

I.B. TAURIS
Bloomsbury Publishing Plc
50 Bedford Square, London, WC1B 3DP, UK
1385 Broadway, New York, NY 10018, USA
29 Earlsfort Terrace, Dublin 2, Ireland

BLOOMSBURY, I.B. TAURIS and the Diana logo are
trademarks of Bloomsbury Publishing Plc

First published in Great Britain 2020
Paperback edition published 2021

Copyright © Helena Rytövuori-Apunen, 2020

Helena Rytövuori-Apunen has asserted her right under the Copyright, Designs and Patents Act, 1988, to be identified as Author of this work.

For legal purposes the Acknowledgements on p. x constitute an extension of this copyright page.

Cover image: A column of Russian armoured vehicles on the Rokskiy tunnel on the border with Russia as they leave South Ossetia, August 23, 2008.
(© Dmitry Kostyukov/AFP/Getty Images)

All rights reserved. No part of this publication may be reproduced or transmitted in any form or by any means, electronic or mechanical, including photocopying, recording, or any information storage or retrieval system, without prior permission in writing from the publishers.

Bloomsbury Publishing Plc does not have any control over, or responsibility for, any third-party websites referred to or in this book. All internet addresses given in this book were correct at the time of going to press. The author and publisher regret any inconvenience caused if addresses have changed or sites have ceased to exist, but can accept no responsibility for any such changes.

A catalogue record for this book is available from the British Library.

A catalogue record for this book is available from the Library of Congress

ISBN:	HB:	978-1-7883-1143-4
	PB:	978-0-7556-3599-3
	ePDF:	978-1-7883-1693-4
	eBook:	978-1-7883-1692-7

Typeset by Integra Software Services Pvt. Ltd.

To find out more about our authors and books visit www.bloomsbury.com and sign up for our newsletters.

For Osmo

Contents

List of Illustrations	ix
Acknowledgements	x
Note on the Transliteration	xi
Introduction: Russia's Deep Borders in the Making	1
Part One Russia's Encounters with Georgia and Its Faltering Ways in the International Community	27
1 Conventional Rules and the Habitual Experience in the Justification of the War in August 2008	29
2 The 'Last Resort' Solution and the Experience of the Recurrent Violence	39
3 The Long and Winding Way to Decision	51
4 Russia in Georgia: Unhappy Policies and the Misfortunes of the Time	61
Part Two Dealing with Divided Moldova: Failed Resolution and Russian Policies of Vertical Power	69
5 The Political Split: Towards a New Future with Old Lines of Division	71
6 Historical Background of the Political and Cultural Split	83
7 Russia's Policies to Settle the Conflict over Transnistria	89
8 After the Kozak Plan	111
9 Prepared for Either Way: Strengthening Vertical Ties and Social Integration	121
10 Gagauzia and the Quest for Guarantees of Autonomy by Regional Powers	133

Part Three Nagorno-Karabakh: Leverage for Controlling Russia's
Deep Border Arrangements with Armenia and Azerbaijan   137

11 The Failed Policies of the Past and the Complexity of
the Contemporary Conflict   139
12 Russia's Settlement Policies in Karabakh: The Centrality of
Diplomatic Efforts   149
13 The Delicate Equation: Russia's Policy Arrangements with
Armenia and Azerbaijan   165
14 Nagorno-Karabakh and Its Precarious Relative Stability   189
15 Moscow's Main Thrust and Its Alternative   199

Conclusion: Russia's Deep Border Practices in Its
Post-Soviet Borderlands   203

Notes   242
Bibliography   309
Index   321

List of Illustrations

Figures

1 The three dimensions of the study	16
2 The *pragma* of Russia's Deep Borders	204

Maps

1 Georgia and Russia's borderland regions in the Caucasus (illustration by Ilkka Janatuinen; used with permission)	49
2 Moldova and its disputed regions (illustration by Ilkka Janatuinen; used with permission)	84
3 Nagorno-Karabakh in regional context (illustration by Ilkka Janatuinen; used with permission)	157

Acknowledgements

The present book was started in the context of the research project Proactive Conflict Management at Post-Soviet Deep Borders, funded by the Academy of Finland at the University of Tampere (2012–16). This financial support has enabled the long-term focus required by the subject at hand. I deeply appreciate the institutional support of the Faculty of Social Sciences at the University of Tampere and thank the Faculty's service staff and my colleagues at the Tampere Peace Research Institute (TAPRI) for providing an excellent environment for my work. I owe my gratitude to colleagues whose work contributed to this research project: Vadim Romashov, Helle Palu and Andrei Roumiantsev at the University of Tampere for their assistance over many years, and Michael Roush, Diia Gvazava, Marikki Rieppola and Joshua Rose at the same university for their assistance in gathering data during the various phases of my research, as well as Ilkka Janatuinen for the digital illustrations. Steven Parham did the language-editing, and his critical eye was invaluable in finalizing the different chapters. I am also thankful for the support and constructive criticism of Tomasz Hoskins and Tom Stottor at I.B. Tauris, and I am honoured to have this opportunity to contribute to this publisher's tradition of promoting the study of Russia and the former Soviet Union. Nayiri Kendir's kind assistance and the concluding steps with David Campbell further contributed to the pleasure of working with I.B. Tauris/Bloomsbury. I also owe my gratitude to two anonymous external reviewers for their comments and advice in processing the manuscript. Besides the students at my home university, the University of Tampere, I am thankful for the immediate resonance provided by students at the Moldova State University and the Yerevan State University in regard to my work. My family, the entire generational lineage from my parents Irene and Matti Juhani to my daughter Natalia and son-in-law Tapio, has made me aware of how fortunate I am to have a home that supports my explorations. I dedicate this book to my husband Osmo, whose knowledge and understanding of the historical subtleties of Finnish–Russian relations have so often inspired my reflections about the borders discussed in this book. This work has been written for all those who wish to learn about the complexities of world politics and the processes that underlie post-Soviet conflicts and the efforts to resolve them.

Note on the Transliteration

This book makes extensive use of Russian-language sources. In transliterating the Cyrillic to the Latin script it uses common journalistic practice for well-known names of persons and places, but otherwise follows the Library of Congress system without diacritical signs other than the Russian-language soft and hard signs, which are marked, respectively, with ′ and ″.

Introduction: Russia's Deep Borders in the Making

Argument for the study of frozen conflicts and Russia's borders

Often, Russia's security interests are left aside when the post-Soviet frozen conflicts in Abkhazia, South Ossetia, Transnistria and Nagorno-Karabakh are discussed as resolution processes in peace expert communities. And all too often, the attention given to Russia's security interests in these conflicts in discussions of its foreign and security policy does not go beyond a common emphasis on geopolitical conflict with the United States and NATO. The aim of this book is to present a wider and sharper perspective by examining how borders – understood here not only as linear but also zonal in nature – come into being through Russia's policies and action in these conflicts, and how these processes take place in interplay with its security interests and its relation to the normative international community. It asks how such zonal borders, which will be called *deep borders*, come into being with a variety of policy arrangements – both formal-institutional and non-formal and habitual – and in which different ways the legitimacy of this action is argued in Russia's official international communication and domestic discussions. *Deep borders* set our eyes on the complexity of a variety of Russia's border-making processes which cannot but elude us should we remain focused merely on the borderlines between states. They are 'deep' because they use the historical dividing lines in the frozen conflicts in the construction of zonal borders and, consequently, affect these countries' entire society. They create 'borders' because they extend and consolidate the geographic area in which Russia can develop its presence in multiple ways – militarily, politically, economically and culturally – that serve its policies within the wider regions of these conflicts. Deep borders are not by any means specific to Russia. However, Russia has a history and a tradition that makes them a prevalent feature in its practices and, moreover, aligns it on a collision course with the international normative community. Because the idea of a modern state with linear borders applies only superficially to Russia, using this perspective for the criticism of Russia also must remain superficial: it misses the core point about Russia itself. This argument is not merely about gaining a wider perspective of understanding; it is also about not missing the opportunities to solve conflicts with Russia and about acquiring the ability to take up proactive action in their prevention.

Abkhazia, South Ossetia, Transnistria and Nagorno-Karabakh are geographically small conflict spots left behind by the dissolution of the Soviet Union, which was a remarkably peaceful process when we consider the size of the territory and the large number of nationalities involved. In addition to these conflicts, the civil war in Tajikistan (1992–7) and the Chechen wars (1994–6 and 1999–2000), in which the active insurgency phase continued until 2009, were major violent struggles related to this process. Whilst the frozen conflicts of the 1990s could be considered as 'remnants' of the Soviet era, the deteriorating relations between Russia and the West, and especially the conflict which flared up in Ukraine in spring 2014, imbued them with new meaning: they became sensors and indicators of Russia's 'intentions' and 'strategies' not only in post-Soviet regions but in world politics in general. The war in Ukraine, a larger country by far than any of the older conflict areas and strategically situated on the Black Sea, boosted interpretations among Western observers that Russia was trying to usher in yet another, protracted frozen-conflict situation – and this time in outright rejection of international norms. Russia's annexation of the Crimea in March 2014 as well as its continued support of the separatists of 'Donbass' (*Donetskii bassein*, the basin of the Don River) in eastern Ukraine was argued to provide evidence of such intentions, and innumerable studies were conducted that focused on questions over the Kremlin's strategy and the intentions of President Vladimir Putin.[1]

The study in the present book grows out of an intellectual tiredness with the hasty conclusions that so often accompany observations of Russian policies. To know the workings of other people's minds shall always remain a complex task of interpretation. Unfortunately, the 'shortcut' of reasoning that has often been taken by policy analysts in Western think tanks is to presuppose intention by using rough historical analogies in order to construct continuity between past events and the future. The Russo-Georgian war in August 2008 stirred up Cold War-style interpretations by arguing Russia's expansionist geopolitical and neo-imperialist motives; and the annexation of the Crimea five and a half years later was seen to reconfirm these ideas. The argument that also often appears is that Russia uses proxy conflicts to project its great-power aspirations, in other words that the pursuit of power in relation to other major powers constitutes the main driving force of its actions. Such assumptions typically underlie the arguments which stress that the Western response must be to 'roll back and contain' Russia,[2] and that Russia's elites have something akin to an instinctive need to preserve the country's formerly dominant position and influence in the former Soviet republics.[3] Inspired by pragmatism, the present book argues that we can know about an agency or an actor – Russia and, in fact, any thing that exists – through the regularity of action that it shows or which relates to it and consequently gives it a pattern.[4] This pattern is not a regularity of behaviour. Instead, it tells about the way in which Russia's policies and action in the frozen conflicts are 'being patterned' with some 'basic' courses of action which vary in the interactive policy processes of the spatial geographic and temporal contexts of the different conflicts. This book traces these courses of action by using a variety of source materials, including official policy documents and news data from the Russian Federation as well as the states and regions directly involved in the conflicts. The period under consideration covers the entire post-Soviet era, from the years of the gradual dissolution of the Soviet Union in the late 1980s until the summer of 2018. Additionally, the discussion of the various conflicts includes excursions to explore their roots and background during the Soviet decades and, where pertinent, even earlier.

The idea of the book can be encapsulated in three key concepts: deep borders, vertical power and international community. *Deep borders* is an analytical perspective which is meant to deepen the shallow view of Russia that we are offered when we remain focused on the concept of the modern state territorially defined by its linear borders. Although the concept of borders in the multidisciplinary study of borders is more diverse than a simple focusing on those territorial lines that separate states, it is a field of study closely related to the problems of border management (i.e. issues about 'porous' and 'leaking' borders) and hence leads in a direction that is rather different from the present book. Research on borders over the past two decades has been motivated by the question of how a state border is evaded or contested by the transborder networks of non-state agents connected through family origin and livelihood practices as well as by insurgent activity, political mobilization and criminal economic organization. However, the problem of how agents of the state also engage in policies and practices that extend their control of geo-space into other states and, as a consequence thereof, fuse borderlines which, in established international practice, are the boundaries of sovereignty has not been paid sufficient attention. The question about deep borders which claim control of some territory or geo-space beyond internationally recognized borderlines between states can fill this lacuna in research.[5] Deep borders may be about forward defence, economic resources and cultural and ideological influence, and their visible signs may range from flags and other symbolic markers to major physical structures, such as military bases. They are 'deep' when they make it possible for one state to establish its presence in another state and to consolidate such a presence with the argument that it has legitimate reasons to oversee that those sections of the population to which it is connected ethnically or due to a long historical relationship can maintain the life practices which sustain this connection. The border is 'deepened' through the positive response aroused in the other country by such arguments – a response showing that the voices in both states speak in unison. In some parts of the world, religion is the connection that makes the borders between states appear artificial and 'shallow', easy to travel across in mind in comparison to the deep borders created by varying modes of religion. The Saudi–Iranian rivalry, which in Yemen and elsewhere in the Middle East uses the historical division between Sunni and Shi'i Muslims, is an example of this latter type of border. Where the modern state is deeply rooted, ideas about *lingua franca* (a common cultural sphere based on language) remain only as faint vestiges of an imperial past. In Russia the connection to transboundary communities on the bases of the Russian language and its Orthodox Christian religion are important symbols of its power-character. However, they must be seen in the more comprehensive context of its aspiration to re-establish its power in the Eurasian region and also to find ways of being part of Europe. Consequently, its deep borders significantly differ from those deriving from the expansionist mission which is typical of fundamentalist religious and radical political agendas (such as the goal to spread a Wahhabist interpretation of Islam or Communist ideology). Deep borders can take many forms, and strict classifications make little sense because they are in constant transformation. By drawing attention to the practices that express the specific historical experience in states, they enrich the study of international relations, which largely concentrates on studying the institutions that harmonize the practices of states.

Although the centrality of borders to Russia is one of the 'classical' themes on Russia and relates closely to the study of Russia as a continental power, this has remained a topic isolated from the study of frozen conflicts.[6] The previous focus on Russia's borders has also greatly contributed to the tendency to romanticize Russia by emphasizing its unique geographic features as a country of great width in terms of its Eurasian landmass and the openness of this space with the vast steppes in the South and the marshlands to the West; in a similar vein, the rugged Caucasus range of mountains is noted to make the control over territory extremely difficult. Whilst it would be hard to disagree with the observation that the sheer size of Russia, as the world's territorially largest country, and the length of its borders is part of the historical dilemma that makes this country so sensitive about its border areas, the focus in the present book is in fact more specific. It asks how the post-Soviet security condition established by the Belovezh Accords of December 1991, which agreed that the former Soviet republics should be independent states, helps us to make sense of Russia's policies in the frozen conflicts. The condition brought about by the dissolution of the Soviet Union is a 'dilemma' against the backdrop of the tradition of Russia as a continental power which has built itself by establishing relations of association in mutual political conditionality with other political entities, both small and large, and in this way possesses borders that are zonal and flexible instead of being merely the borderlines of the modern state.

Whereas 'deep borders' conveys a historical idea about Russia, *vertical power* tells about the characteristic features of corresponding practices. In the Russian tradition, vertical power is logically and historically related to the 'power vertical': a hierarchical command structure in which the spheres of 'competence' have not been defined by law. A single centre of power – the Moscow Kremlin – can potentially deal with 'everything' – all party, parliamentary, and personnel issues' without questions being raised about the legitimacy of such interference.[7] Because Moscow's relations with former Soviet subjects after the dissolution of the Soviet Union were reorganized by the rules of horizontal international relations (relations between formally equal states), it became problematic to apply such verticality as a direct command structure. The new frame of interstate relations has ruled out a direct command structure (a 'power vertical') and made military coercion an infringement on sovereignty. Consequently the use of power became much more indirect, and goals could be achieved through mutually conditional political relationships. Thus, the means of vertical power discussed in the present book are different in relation to the rules of formal equality (horizontal international relations) that pertain to treaty-based relations between sovereign states as well as universally accepted diplomatic conventions, and they also are different from direct coercion by military means or through the application of other repressive force.[8] Whereas these notions offer general starting points for the discussion of the means of vertical power, the means adopted by Russia have their own specific features. They are typically political 'trusting relationships', which build ties of loyalty through reciprocal obligations and expectations of benefit. Although individual instances of such relationships no doubt exist in both Moscow's relations with the former Soviet republics and their separatist regions, the systematic cultivation of such relationships is a specific 'vertical' means of Russian diplomacy and foreign policy which traditionally serves to promote stability and continuity rather than change in Russia's immediate geographic environment. Russia's vertical power in the separatist regions is manifested in a wide variety of practices which extend the authority of the Russian state over entire groups of people; such practices include granting large numbers of people citizenship and social benefits that normally belong to only Russian citizens, and they also include preferential economic treatment and cultural policies which draw the separatist regions into close cooperation with Russia, despite objections and protests by the state which is internationally recognized to exercise authority over these regions.

The tension between the horizontal and vertical international relations provides an analytical point of departure to examine the discord between Russia and the Western states over the position that Russia should assume in the post-Soviet space. The third concept, *international community*, asks how Russia, through its action in the frozen conflicts, participates in the assessment of the normative rules and practices that make this community. Whilst Russia has consistently emphasized that it follows the rules of the international community, the question about the interpretation of these rules has frequently been a source for disputes in its relations with Western states. The concept of the sovereign state illustrates how a perspective already defines the conclusion: fully convincing in its own logic, we are led to the conclusion that Russia's annexation of the Crimea in March 2014 is a criminal act. A more comprehensive interpretation which avoids such predefinition must not justify the annexation but it does help us to see a normative dimension of more complexity than that conveyed by the rules of horizontal international relations. Issues become more complex when they are considered in the light of Russia's historical concern over its borders. The question about a historical Russian connection in the conflicts and the significance of the fact that many small nations and ethnic groups have a pattern of relying on Russia to protect them from the dominance of an unacceptable 'parent state' or other regional power become important when the enquiry, as in this book, is about how Russian policies attempt to solve the tension between the rules of horizontal international relations and vertical practices. Russia's vertical policies repeatedly provide various forms of economic support to the separatist regions, where it also proclaims the right to defend its citizens. Whilst Russian policies are seen in the West as being ever bolder and more definite in character, the experience in Russia is that Western states are not prepared to listen to its concerns.[9]

Deep borders, vertical power and international community provide analytical points of departure by means of which this book seeks to look beyond the stalemated normative encounters between Russia and the Western states. By looking at the variety of practices (action and policies) from the vantage point of a time perspective which spans three decades and never forgets the prior, Soviet history of the conflicts, we become able to avoid simple projections of continuity, which appear when we interpret past occurrences in the light of our knowledge about present events and, conversely, force the past to predict the future. Seeing the past in the present ('Munich 1938' in the case of Russia's annexation of the Crimea, for example) and limiting to some present-day perspective our understanding of the possible developments that existed in the past (by arguing, for example, that it was the resolve of the United States and other Western states to stay firmly on the side of Georgia which, in August 2008, prevented Russia from rolling its tanks all the way to Tbilisi) succeeds only to lend legitimacy to the reasoning that Russia must be contained because it *will* try to expand its territory and influence, or at least constrained and made to realize that non-compliance with the norms and rules of the Western international community would be harmful to Russia. Such argumentation fails to understand how Russian policies intertwine with local interests and why (and with which concrete goals in view) decision-makers in Moscow pursue certain policies, and how these policies emerge in interaction with other states – with both those in the region and the external powers active in the region. A study of the complexity and regularity of Russia's policies and action questions the image of Russian tanks that, by way of analogy to the Soviet scenario, roll for the purpose of the expansion of territory or of spheres of influence. Tanks may well roll, but the important question is how such policy outcomes emerge from the interactive policy situations of world politics and leave aside other alternatives which also exist as options ('variants') for policies and action.

Reference points in the study of frozen conflicts and Russian policies

By speaking of 'frozen' conflicts this book does not suggest that these conflicts have been 'cooled down' in the sense that violence would have been eliminated. Dov Lynch correctly argues that the term in this sense is misleading because it downplays the dynamic developments of these conflicts, including the violent incidents that have occurred ever since the ceasefire regimes were set in place between 1992 and 1994.[10] Violence still simmers especially in Nagorno-Karabakh, where gunfire across the Line of Contact monitored by the OSCE occurs frequently and kills several tens of people every year, and where a few days' war flared up in early April 2016. While I fully agree with Lynch on this point, the usage of the term 'frozen' in this book has a different focus. My interest is about the policy mechanisms of 'freezing' and the political goals they serve in Russia's practices to settle these conflicts. The process includes both disputed issues which, in the eyes of the participants to the peace process, are negotiable within existing legal frameworks, and deep-rooted problems with seemingly non-negotiable issues (conflicts) that are resistant to resolution.[11] Because the ideal consensus, which the term 'resolution' presupposes in conflict resolution literature, cannot be assumed in the present study, 'settlement' is the best term to describe the content of the process; in the present study 'resolution' is used to refer to the peace process in general. 'Settlement' is the term which also best translates the Russian equivalent term (*uregulirovanie*) in international political and diplomatic practices.[12] Dispute and conflict settlement refers to a wide scope of policies meant to maintain peace and stability and does not necessarily include a plan for a conflict's final resolution.

The resolution processes of the post-Soviet frozen conflicts, like also Russia's security interests and policies in these regions, have been of continuous interest to researchers, and the author of the present book is not the first to notice that very little attention has been paid to their interplay in connection with the long-term goals that Russia pursues in the geographic proximity of its formal state borders. In most cases the study of these conflicts, as Matthew Sussex points out, is overshadowed by the more global problematic of terrorism, energy issues and the contest for allies.[13] The focus in the present book is similar to Sussex's edited collection (2012) in the sense that it rests on Russia's interests in its own immediate geostrategic environment. However, from this point forward our argumentative trajectories are very different. Sussex's focus lies on conflict in the post-Soviet space and the forms that the different conflicts can take in the future; and the frame of his discussion is global and seeks comparisons with separatist conflicts in South Asia and elsewhere in the world. He asks how some theoretical concepts (e.g. 'regional hegemony' and 'regional security complex') could appear to fit together with the factual reality in the regions, whereas the present book is motivated by pragmatism and starts with analytical concepts. It also wishes to advance beyond such generalizations which argue, for example, that Russia attempts to maintain a sphere of influence on the former territory of the USSR.[14] 'Sphere of influence' reveals nothing of the goals of policies or of the ways in which they are pursued. Instead, it is an indirect, symbolic expression for arguing that the pursuit of power over geo-space exists as a given thing, i.e. it is a concept which 'naturalizes' such a pursuit, suggesting that it exists as a drive or an innate inclination.[15]

In the politicized practices of international relations it is not uncommon to look at the actions of the 'adversary' party as an expression of some pre-given substance or property, inherent nature or a steady inclination – and in this way leave aside the entire question of the responsibility that belongs to the logic of the field as constituting mutually interactive *relations*.[16] By no means do I argue that the Kremlin is inhabited by benign spirits; rather, I argue that such a point of departure is misplaced in the study of international relations. It differs only insignificantly from notions of an 'axis of evil' and the pursuit of expansionist power in the sense that it, too, holds superficial assumptions of 'essence'-like features, which in a modern, image-creating rhetoric invoke archaic ideas about an ontology of substance as the 'ultimate' reality.[17] The discussion of Russian policies, in particular, is an empirical domain where assumptions about an 'inner substance' persist, and attitudes are maintained that pretend to know what Russia will do (if not obstructed), as if this could take place independently of what other states and international actors do.[18] The wish to avoid concepts which predefine actors' goals and intentions is the reason why the present book also does not use the term 'protracted' conflict to refer to the conflicts mentioned above. While the immediate meaning of the word is trivial in that it suggests that a conflict, for some reason, is long-lasting, it is also a term in a specific discourse on strategy. It borrows from Mao Zedong's revolutionary tactics and presumes that the Kremlin has a 'hidden' strategy to 'wear out the enemy'.[19] This 'field tactics' metaphor is context-bound and too simple when the question is about an encounter which is argumentative and discursive and which involves not only coercive, but also collaborative, means to produce desired outcomes. Moreover, to presume that there is a conscious, long-term strategy that spans the flux of events surrounding the dissolution of the Soviet Union clearly ignores the historical context of a time when Moscow, on a number of occasions, did not wish to hear or care much about these conflicts.

In the present book, Russia's long-term interest is a matter of enquiry and not an *a priori* assumption, and the pursuit of power is not synonymous with the intent to establish domination over territory. Instead, it is demonstrated by a capability to control outcomes of events in specific situations. Because Russia has striven to be not only a regional great power and a major player in world politics but also a member of the international community, its habitual ways of controlling political outcomes and justifying its own military, economic and cultural presence in the former Soviet republics have collided with the conventional discourse of the Western community of states. Russia's continuous support of separatist regions in Georgia, Moldova and Azerbaijan contradicts the rules of interstate relations, which prioritize the inviolability of internationally accepted state borders. The next chapter discusses Russia's dilemma in post-Soviet border security; a dilemma which exists to the extent that Russia is considered a continental power instead of one that follows the idea of an 'ordinary' state which defines the domain of its authority by means of its formal state borders. This dilemma is manifested in Russia's deep border policies in the frozen conflicts and cannot be ignored when we want to make sense of Russian policies and action in these conflicts in a more comprehensive manner than is allowed by the argumentation which derives its strength from the normative duality that lies at the heart of legal norms and which distinguishes between legal and illegal action.

Russia's dilemma in post-Soviet border security

As Dmitri Trenin points out, the drastic transformation of the Soviet state structures brought about in Russia by the dissolution of the USSR had many features which were different in historical comparison to the breakup of imperial structures elsewhere. In Russia, there was no modernized nation state that could lay the basis of the power of the state and be left as the 'solid rump' once the former imperium was cut into pieces; furthermore, colonized regions were immediately adjacent to its landmass rather than overseas.[20] In regard to the Chechen wars we may expand on Trenin's notions and state that such regions even existed inside the newly established boundaries of sovereignty. Thus, at the same time as aspiring to maintain its status as a global power, post-Soviet Russia also struggled to hold together its territorial unity. Because the internal borders within the Federation and the external borders introduced to replace former administrative lines were initially not very different from each other, it also became possible for insurgent groups especially along the southern borders (and most notably in the mountainous Caucasus regions) to establish connections across the new formal lines of sovereignty. This political situation aggravated the border problems inherited by Russia as the Soviet Union disintegrated, and it left the Kremlin with a dilemma: When the Belovezh Accords in December 1991[21] established relations between the former Soviet republics as relations between formally sovereign states, security around Russia's borders came to depend on the collaboration of friendly and predictable neighbours. The basic question that Moscow's policymakers were left with concerned the kinds of arrangements needed in order to maintain stability outside Russia's formal borders of state sovereignty and the matter of how to prevent the new states along its borders from joining another military bloc – NATO – which Russia sees as its traditional security threat.

A large number of Russian military installations had remained in the new independent states, and whilst some of them were closed down, others were negotiated to stay operative or to be relocated in the region. In many cases the political question also included significant economic interests and continued access to markets and raw materials which, in the fields of defence and energy, often were strategic in nature. It also included issues of changes in the cultural environment and the future political rights of the initially 25–30 million ethnic Russians who had been stranded in diaspora and had become minority populations outside the borders of the Russian Federation. Very soon after the Russian Federation was established, decision-makers in Moscow started to emphasize that Russia's security interests and elements of its society were intertwined with what they considered Russia's 'Near Abroad' (*blizhnee zarubezh'e*).²² In February 1993 President Boris Yeltsin announced to a domestic Russian audience that the time had come for authoritative international organizations such as the UN 'to grant Russia special powers as guarantor of peace and stability' in the region of the former Soviet Union.²³ This was the time when a ceasefire was in place in Moldova yet could be maintained in neither Georgia's separatist regions nor Nagorno-Karabakh; the civil war in Tajikistan was in full swing and was threatening to dissolve the border that had been built as a Soviet outpost on the Afghanistan marches. The United States and NATO were developing ties with Georgia, Azerbaijan and Uzbekistan. Russia had invited the UN and the CSCE (the predecessor of the OSCE) to participate in the resolution processes, but its policy was to hold the strings of political settlement in its own hands. Simultaneously the main direction of its policies remained oriented to the West, and its resources were limited and policies uncoordinated due to internal rivalries between the ministries of defence and foreign affairs.²⁴ It took more than a decade for Moscow's decision-makers to articulate Russia's interests in post-Soviet areas which had not joined NATO and the European Union and to start formulating foreign policies specifically focused on the former Soviet republics. In 2015, when Russia's relations with the West were strained over the conflict in Ukraine, experts in Moscow concluded that the 'post-Soviet space' had 'emerged as a top priority for Moscow on the international arena'. Russia now focused on this space as 'the first and most important "circle"' of its foreign policy.²⁵ In the South Caucasus and in Central Asia, as well as in those parts of formerly socialist Eastern Europe that had not joined the European Union, bi- and multilateral arrangements were developed to enable Russia's forward defence and to connect these countries through Eurasian economic integration projects led from Moscow. In these arrangements the multilateral and bilateral forms of cooperation provide mutually supportive structures, and the flexibility (and sometimes confusion) that this brings is further increased by the many networks, institutional as well as personal, which were inherited from the Soviet decades. From the outset, the fact that former Soviet party elites in many cases remained in power created the circumstances for building mutually conditional political relationships with Moscow. The leaders of the new states were expected to ensure peace and stability in the region so as to meet Russia's security needs; in exchange they gained political support and economic benefits that were helpful in consolidating their own political power.

These post-Soviet relationships are based on mutual expectations about joint benefits and reciprocal obligations. Such individualized institutional and personal relationships are very different from the idea of the universal rules of international relations, which are about relations between all sovereign states considered formally equal. They are an integral part of Russia's historical constitution as a power and manifest in the institutional speech of 'special' relations with 'mutual trust' and 'friendship'. This historical context of policies is ignored when, for example, Russian policies toward the former Soviet republics are described as neo-imperialist and it is argued that Russia uses a strategy of 'blackmail' in its energy trade and other matters with these countries. Although Russia's dominant position in this relationship is obvious, such arguments unveil only part of the story as they fail to see how political elites in the former Soviet territories are able to negotiate the relationship and how it is that they can use the tensions created in Russia's relations with the West to bargain for specific economic benefits. The former Soviet republics discussed in the present book all provide some examples. Next, I argue that the types of practices which Russia's post-Soviet border-security dilemma makes actual in the present day are an integral part of its historical development as a power, and that this feature can be recognized through the habitual practices represented by language.

Russia's long-standing ways of building power through association

Russia's focus on bilateral alliances, strategic partnerships and 'special' relations of political friendship tells about a habitual way of building its power through association. Historically, the Russian state has expanded by building relationships of association in which loyalties have been exchanged for protection. Whilst this is a common imperial practice, the Russian tradition has specific features which are mediated in the language that is employed. The Russian word for 'state', *gosudarstvo* – from *gosudar'*, the great sovereign, *tsar'*/czar (Caesar)[26] – refers to the *authority* of government in the sense of the *sphere of the sovereign*. *Gosudarstvo* as the sphere of the sovereign is very different from the notion of sovereignty as the domain under a state's law and the constitutional approach based on this notion.[27] It entails a historical idea of the state that, in the study of international relations, perhaps has its closest equivalent in Martin Wight's notion about 'a power', thereby providing a contrast to the contemporary, institutions-centred notion of a 'state'.[28] Because sovereignty in the Russian historical sense does not have the connotation of a legally bounded territory, there exists no 'external sphere' of a state's influence in contrast to a clearly bounded 'internal' sphere of its territorial sovereignty. The internal/external dichotomy, which is constitutive of the idea of sovereignty as the legal sphere of competence of the modern state, does not apply in this historical logic of practice. Instead, the sphere of the sovereign can be expanded by building political relationships based on reciprocal obligations and a mutual understanding of the benefits of such a relationship.[29] The party under Moscow's protection was expected to recognize Moscow's dominant position in the relationship, and Moscow in exchange was expected to acknowledge the privileges of local elites and thus to allow local autonomy in matters that did not concern the sovereign. In other words, the logic of *gosudarstvo* was not to extend the sovereign's power by extending Moscow's own rules of social organization over local populations. The empire marked its presence by building fortresses and extracting resources (in form of taxation and natural resources). Betrayal and failure to obey were severely punished, often by slaughtering whole populations. However, the tendency to read this history in the light of wars of imperial expansion has served to obscure the specific non-military features by which Russia has built its power and fought against the expansion of other powers in its southern and western border zones as well as deep within its core areas.

In the modern day these historical features of Russia's power, among other things, help us to better understand how Russia's external relations in the post-Soviet space are in line with its internal relations within the federation, i.e. the extremely accommodating concept of federalism, which in the 1990s meant flexible relations of federal subjects with the central power within the formal boundaries of a single state. After Boris Yeltsin had told the Soviet subjects in the late summer of 1990 to take 'as much sovereignty' as they could 'swallow' – that is, autonomy in relation to Moscow in the envisioned new Russia – the federation, which was established eighteen months later, was left adrift, plagued by constant negotiations over power-sharing with those of its subjects that had the capacity to be self-reliant, such as energy-rich Tatarstan.[30] President Putin resumed policies to reconstitute the state by introducing laws through which the central government extended its authority over federal subjects.[31] He also tightened Moscow's vertical control structures through political parties and security agencies. In Russia, like also in the Soviet Union, this vertical dimension of power, which is a hierarchical command structure logically opposed to the constitutional approach based on legally defined spheres of competence, creates an internal connectedness beyond the formal structures of administration. Its existence clarifies for us why the possibility to increase autonomy and even to strive for the separation declared by Yeltsin can so quickly prove to be only nominal, as Putin's policies have demonstrated. Although Russia under the presidency of Vladimir Putin has emphasized the direct command structure at the expense of its more subtle forms, it is those subtler elements that prevail in international relations with former subjects where formal equality has now become the necessary frame of relations.

The tradition of vertical power, which fuses the boundary between the internal and the external, is the distinctive feature of Russian power and helps us to make sense of its relations with the former Soviet subjects which participate in its security cooperation and remain economically integrated with Russia. Consequently Russia's means to control the areas in the proximity of its borders are very different from those of the European Union, which expands its frontiers on the basis of policies that emphasize institution-building based on the Union's identity as a political value community. Russian decision-makers, politicians and experts argue that a long, shared history, together with geography, has intertwined economic and security interests, and that the mutual interest of Russia and its neighbours consequently justifies Russia's continued presence beyond its formal state borders. It must be noted that the model of the Soviet Union, which in relation to the Russian historical tradition was built on 'imported' Western values, was based on a universal political ideology and therefore presents a contrast to this historical tradition. Although a duality of formal structures and actual power was the pervasive feature of also Soviet life, this contrast of concepts becomes clear from the 'anti-ideological' position through which Russia distances itself from Soviet tradition.

Because ideological legitimization for Russia's presence in other countries no longer exists, the question about the specific Russian connection in conflicts outside its formal borderlines has become unavoidable. Therefore we must ask what it is that Moscow's policymakers argue that they protect in the conflict regions as *Russia's own* – as its people or possession, and what it is that in each case makes them Russia's concern. Due to the fact that in Russia the internal dimension is more important than the external dimension, decision makers find themselves unable to ignore the fate of ethnic Russians abroad.[32] However, the connection is not limited to Russian and Slavic and, today, even Orthodox Christianity factors; it also includes historical relationships of protection which, in Russia, are considered to be in the 'sphere of its responsibility' to the region. These relations have their historical source in the tsar's direct relation to the people (by bypassing the institutions of the government), which is an important element in the legitimacy of authoritarian rule and manifests itself in Russia's historical great power (*derzhava*) tradition. The implication in the present day is that the denial of the legitimacy of the vertical relations of power, which in Russia's relations with former Soviet subjects within the post-Soviet networks of cooperation continue to complement formal state relations, is equivalent to denying Russia's status as a great power in the regional context: in other words, it is to put it in the form of an 'ordinary' state measured by its ability to meet the ideals of democracy and modernity – a form to which its practices do not easily bend. The recognition of Russia's historical border security problem also helps us see why it is that Russian policies in the post-Soviet space, as its representatives repeatedly highlight, have such an emphasis on being 'defensive' rather than 'offensive'. Whilst they show an aim to establish regional stability and a secure environment around the Russian Federation,[33] the policies designed to realize this general objective also have different, and sometimes even offensive, policy 'variants' (or options).

Focus and structure of study

The question that has motivated this study can now be summarized in one sentence: How are Russian deep borders, which are zonal and extend beyond linear state borders, created, consolidated and curtailed through the processes taking place around the settlement of the frozen conflicts, and in which ways do these outcomes emerge in the interplay of the rules of horizontal international relations and the means of vertical power to control developments and policy choices? The analysis focuses upon three facets of this process. First, it examines Russian policies and action in the specific conflicts, and does so with a particular eye to the practices of conflict settlement that bring together instances of action. Second, it asks how the borders set up or pursued in this way also represent something more than is suggested by their immediate relation or denotation. This symbolic relation can be about some anticipated recurrence of events or a regularity of developments – the threat of an increase in international terrorism, the strengthening of NATO's presence in proximity to Russia, etc. Whereas some conflict events and border-making practices represent (or symbolize) types of developments *for* Russia, others are more directly *about* Russia. The latter of these notions means that something about Russia itself is at stake in these conflicts and the borders they create. The loss or change associated with specific events and practices is considered to have such significance that something qualitatively important about Russia itself is lost or changed. In the pragmatist logic of interpretation that inspires the present study, this means that the factual events and instances of action have 'iconic' significance for Russia.[34] In other words, they can be understood as having 'existential' significance for Russia. The significance of specific conflicts for Russia's deep borders is never to be found in just one or another of these kinds; rather, the question is how strong the 'existential' connection is and wherein each conflict's symbolic significance lies. The third facet emerges from the tension between horizontal and vertical international relations and brings to focus the various courses of action and the discourses which are used to legitimize them in international and domestic Russian (decision-making and media) contexts and tell about Russia's participation in the normative international community. It brings into focus the interplay of action and discourse in which vertical relations are legitimized in various ways by the formal rules between sovereign states. The treaties and other contractual relations concluded by Russia with both Abkhazia and South Ossetia following its recognition of their independence in August 2008 present some examples. The question about the 'combination' of horizontal international relations and vertical power, which breaks, evades or eludes this logic of practices, elucidates the specific feature of the power that Russia uses to control policy outcomes in the frozen conflicts. Figure 1 summarizes the various dimensions of the study.

Figure 1 The three dimensions of the study.

Inspired by the idea of *pragma* as a pattern-ness that anticipates the future, this book examines how the Russian borders beyond its formal state borders emerge in such processes through the arrangements to settle the conflicts in specific ways. Examined in the wider perspective of Russia's deep border arrangements, these arrangements are sets of practices, both military and political, and they include explicit policies as well as more implicit habitual practices that mark directions of security policy. Military alignment or close military cooperation with external powers, neutrality in some sense of the term and retaining ethnic and other ties with Russia or a state aligned with Russia are policy directions which appear in the disputed regions in different combinations, and they often do so within the formal borders of only one state. The question of interest to this study is how these different policy outcomes relate to Russia's deep border policies, and how they do so in a patterned way. This pattern is not about a grand strategy or a conscious plan. In the etymology of the word, 'pragma' is the habitual 'business being done' – past and anticipatory – in the processes of its recurrence, where policy outcomes depend on the interactive contexts of international relations. Ignoring the interactive nature of international relations is to ignore history, and it is only through the study of long-term developments that we can reach conclusions about the patterns of practices. Because the conflicts in Georgia, Moldova and between Azerbaijan and Armenia were closely connected with the processes of the dissolution of the Soviet Union, Russia was from the start embroiled in a situation where its capability to control them in a coordinated way was foiled. Consequently, it was not until the arrangements to end the periods of war in these conflicts were in place that Russia was able to start developing a military presence through which it would be able to better exercise control over these conflicts and to ascertain its own political weight in the international efforts to resolve them. The next section discusses the different ways in which the ceasefire agreements (concluded between 1992 and 1994) enabled Russia's military control of the disputed regions and, as a consequence, strengthened its position in negotiating a political settlement in the conflicts in ways that would take its own interests into account.

The ceasefire agreements: Russia's efforts to establish military control of a political settlement

During the first half of the 1990s the interest in the UN to develop regionally based peacekeeping created a favourable political climate for Russia's efforts to negotiate the ceasefire agreements. In Tajikistan's civil war (1992–7) Russia, with the backing of the UN, was able to successfully prepare the ground for the negotiations which led to the Peace Accords of 1997. In this Central Asian country Russia backed the forces that represented continuity in relation to the former Soviet republic, and in this case the political border around which the war revolved was relatively clear: the goal was to hold the country together and to maintain it as a secular republic vis-à-vis the region's Islamic states and the influence of the Taliban to the south.[35] In the frozen conflicts Russia has contrarily supported separatist opposition forces against the governments of former Soviet republics and, at the same time, sought to maintain relations with the governments in question. In all cases (barring Moldova) the ceasefire that Russia actively helped to negotiate in these conflicts remained shaky and needed to be repeatedly re-established.

In Georgia, it took a few years (1992–4) for the ceasefire to take hold. In South Ossetia, the ceasefire was first agreed in June 1992. There, Russia's military presence was based on a two-tier structure which entailed a trilateral format for joint peacekeeping forces (JPKF) with the conflict parties (South Ossetia being represented by troops from North Ossetia) and a joint control commission (JCC, in which both North and South Ossetians participated). From the point of view of Russia, this structure was ideal in the sense that the JPKF was under Russian command, whilst the CSCE (OSCE since 1995) monitored the ceasefire in the frame of the JCC and in this way brought international legitimacy to the operation. The ceasefire in Abkhazia was far more difficult to negotiate and remained ambiguous in its structures of authority. Based on agreements made during 1993–4, a joint trilateral control group was established and the peacekeeping operation, in which Russia predominated from the start and until its end in August 2008, was put under the mandate of the Commonwealth of Independent States (CIS). In the Western states the CIS peacekeeping was expected to work in a way which kept it accountable to the UN Observer Mission (UNOMIG), yet this cooperation failed to function as intended. Although Russia had agreed to the UN mission, from the very start it objected to any clear subordination of its peacekeepers, which operated under a nominal CIS mandate, to the global organization. The ambiguity of the international arrangements undermined the legitimacy of the peacekeeping operation in Abkhazia. In South Ossetia Russia's control was based on the relatively clear structure of the arrangements, but in this case the predominance given to Russia in these arrangements was unacceptable in Georgia and contributed to the ultimate failure of the ceasefire agreement in August 2008.

Unlike in South Ossetia, where Russia's ability to maintain control over military issues followed from the formal arrangement, in the case of Transnistria this is the practical result of its close cooperation with the separatist region's peacekeeping contingent. When the ceasefire was set in place in July 1992, a trilateral peacekeeping force was established so as to include Russia, Moldova and Transnistria under rotating command, but Russia, together with the separatist region, agreed to provide a two-thirds majority of the number of troops. The JCC was designed to include all three parties and, in addition, Ukraine, which since 1998 has participated in the peacekeeping mission by deploying military observers.[36] The case of Nagorno-Karabakh is entirely different from both Georgia and Moldova due to the fact that no peacekeeping mission could be established after the ceasefire in May 1994 because of Azerbaijani and Western opposition to the dominant role that Russia pursued in the constitution of the mission. Instead, a mutual deterrence of conventional forces has prevailed across the Line of Contact established by the ceasefire and monitored by the OSCE since March 1995.

As this book argues (in Parts One, Two, and Three), the conflicts in the three different regions are mutually very different and, in spite of similarities in Russia's policies, the political settlement which it pursues in each case is dependent on the political circumstances in the wider region. Because the pattern of ends and means – the goals in the settlement and the goals that may be intermediary within the resolution process – undergoes constant change in the interactive constellation of world politics, it makes more sense to look for a pattern of action in all of its variation rather than to attempt predictions on what will happen in one conflict on the basis of analogies drawn from another conflict. The next section sets the study in this book on the path of this argument by pointing out that it would be misleading to interpret any of the already decades-long post-Soviet frozen conflicts in the light of more recent developments such as the annexation of the Crimea in 2014 and, following the same train of thought, to use this as a model to predict the future.

Similarity and difference in the frozen conflicts

In the referendum held in the Crimea on 16 March 2014, 95.5 per cent of voters (who were predominantly ethnic Russians) reportedly supported joining the Russian Federation.[37] A declaration of formal independence followed the referendum, and within two days the peninsula, which since 1992 had existed as an autonomous republic of Ukraine, was annexed by Russia and converted into two federal subjects – the Republic of Crimea and the Federal City of Sevastopol – on the basis of an accession treaty, which Russia's Federal Assembly ratified in only three days, i.e. by 21 March 2014. Whilst Moscow's decision makers in the case of the war with Georgia in August 2008 reasoned that the recognition of the independence of Kosovo by the Western states earlier that year had created a precedent, which under certain circumstances allowed for the prioritization of the principle of national self-determination over that of intact borders, the annexation of the Crimea almost six years later could not use similar reasoning as political justification. The annexation of Crimea, which (unlike Russia's military intervention in Tskhinvali) could not in any way be reasoned as a 'last resort' to physically protect any part of the population in the region, in effect erased the requirement of specific circumstances and made the principle of self-determination a norm that could be applied for political purposes. Russia declared that it was protecting the human rights of its citizens and also the entire Russian-speaking population in the Crimea, and that this had become necessary due to the unconstitutional change of government which had brought anti-Russian nationalists to power in Ukraine a few weeks earlier in

February.[38] This reasoning not only antagonized the Western international community but also confounded the norms that had been thought to be applicable in the post-Soviet space. While Russia's attempt to emphasize the principle of self-determination was welcomed in Armenia, where this norm legitimized support for the self-proclaimed Armenian-populated Artsakh Republic (Nagorno-Karabakh), it caused frustration in most other former Soviet republics, especially in Kazakhstan, which has a large Russian-speaking and ethnically Russian population along its northern borders.

Although the annexation of the Crimea does make plain the dilemmas experienced by Russia both internally and externally, a number of features make the Crimean Peninsula exceptional amongst the frozen conflicts; amongst these are the presence of Russia's Black Sea naval base, which prior to annexation had been Russia's largest military base outside its own territory and which since the late eighteenth century had guaranteed its access to both the Black Sea and the Mediterranean, Russia's long history of interaction with the region and the questionable legitimacy of Nikita Khrushchev's donation of the peninsula to the Ukrainian SSR in 1954. Khrushchev's gift was a symbol of contemporary close Soviet relations, but four decades later it had evolved into a grave conflict between two different approaches, one emphasizing Ukraine's sovereign authority over the territory of the Crimea, and the other its historical and treaty-based obligations to recognize the region's strong ties with Russia. Finally, the fact that a solid majority of the population (58–60 per cent of the peninsula's total population of 2 million) prior to annexation were Russian speakers and in the referendum supported the idea of the region becoming a part of Russia cannot be ignored – despite Russia's active use of such conditions in its attempts to legitimize the annexation. None of these features pertain in Nagorno-Karabakh. In Transnistria the historical justification for rejoining Russia is strong in a region that, since the end of the eighteenth century, has had no other relation of belonging to a larger state formation. However, although the present-day appeal of *Novorossiia* (with historical reference to the *guberniia* established in 1764 on the Black Sea coast of present-day Ukraine) is locally significant, Transnistria does not have a military, historical and cultural value in Moscow that in any way would be comparable to the Crimea on the Black Sea. The same conclusion holds for Abkhazia, a coast that is contiguous with the Crimean Peninsula, even if this region is not without strategic significance for Russia.

This brief discussion already shows that thinking that the annexation of the Crimea would represent the latest development in a series of events and signpost the way for the future would be to impose similarity as a model. In this book the tridimensional interpretation of the various conflicts provides a starting point which uses similarity to unfold difference. Each thematic question (see Figure 1, page 16) unfolds as a question about the interpretation of ('existential') experience, factual relations and the conventions (discourses) in which experience is communicated and action legitimized. Due to the nature of experience (which is never the 'same', only similar), all dimensions are not present to an equal degree or impact in the interpretation of the different conflicts. Because reality is considered to be 'dynamic', using a theory framework with predefined parameters of comparison (i.e. the idea of comparative research) would be to impose a concept upon this reality.[39] Instead, the pragmatist way followed in this book is to examine the different conflicts in terms of the features that can be abstracted from the individual conflict events and give them their distinctive 'faces' in the tridimensional thematic of the study. The discussion of each conflict starts with a focus on its distinctive 'face', i.e. the thematic dimension that dominates the conflict and provides the basis for discussing the two other thematic dimensions. In my opinion this is a better way because it enables us to gain a wider and a more nuanced understanding of the Russian policies relating to these conflicts and the possibilities that exist for alternative courses of action.

In Part One of this book, Russia's policies and action in Georgia's separatist regions generate questions for the examination of Moldova's conflict with Russia over separatist Transnistria (in Part Two). The discussion of the two conflicts in the two parts of the book, respectively, opens with emphasis on two different thematic dimensions in the study. While Georgia's separatist regions became a symbol of Russia's troubled relations with the Western international community after August 2008, in Moldova the question of how Moscow can affect developments outside the formal processes of the government – i.e. use its vertical power in a series of issues that range from elections and the organization of popular votes to pension support and energy subsidies in Transnistria – is the thematic dimension that dominates the conflict. Our third focus, Nagorno-Karabakh, is very different from either of these conflicts. It never hosted a Soviet military base and its society does not have any habitual basis for considering a future in close connection with Russia. However, Russia is continuously present there through the support – military, political and economic – that Moscow provides to Armenia. The characteristic feature of this conflict is that it is an important 'regulatory lever' of the peace and stability that Russia seeks to maintain in the South Caucasus, where its overall goal is to develop military and economic cooperation. Although Nagorno-Karabakh out of all our three conflict areas is the border which has least to do with Russia's formal borders, it is an illustrative example of the complexities of Russia's deep borders in their wider regional context. The next chapter discusses the positioning of this pragmatism-inspired study and relates it to previous research on not only the frozen conflicts but, more generally, on Russian policies and international relations.

Positioning beyond rationalist and romanticist assumptions

It is an academic research convention that the task of all research is chiefly to establish and challenge a concept. In the study of politics and international relations concepts and interpretations emerge from the processes of politics, which are the empirical domain of the study. In my opinion the remedy to politicization and avoiding the threat of corruption through one's object of research is not to choose a more 'scientific' attitude but to be aware of the workings of conventionalist interpretations and to attempt to challenge these. The pragmatist interpretation of Russia in this book is critical of the trivial 'realist' (or, rather, quasi-realist) approach which assumes that Russian policies contain a pre-given rationality for territorial expansion.[40] It is similarly critical of the romanticist thinking that accords grand uniqueness to Russia. Notions about Russia's specific geography and historical experience often lead to a deplorable emphasis on a collective mentality and collective-psychological fear about being threatened and 'encircled' by other powers. The argument that the emphasis on a 'Slavic brotherhood' outside Russia's state borders – a new pan-Slavism – is Russia's *revanche* in connection with its 'defeat' in Europe is but one example of how ideas of Russia's geographic and cultural uniqueness result in quasi-psychological framings.[41] Although mystification of historical experience ('primordialist' interpretation) and assumptions about an inherent (pre-given) substance ('essentialism') have been the targets of much criticism in the academic field of international relations, the study of Russia remains an area largely yet to be upset by such critical winds.[42] Instead it has remained an area in which trivial realism operating with 'spheres of interest' and the like retains a tight grip. The mainstream discussions in the academic study of international relations (neorealist discussions and their constructivist criticism) have concentrated on the traditional task of building a political theory of the 'international system'.[43] Due to this type of focus there exist only few studies that actually apply the argument according to which systemic qualities are produced in interactive processes (an argument which neorealist and constructivist approaches both emphasize) to the examination of Russia's relations with Western states. However, there are important exceptions to this dearth, which I now briefly outline.

One such noteworthy exception is Vincent Pouliot's research (2010), which asks why the promise of the immediate post–Cold war era, that is, the expectation that a security community could develop and come to incorporate Russia within a community of common security interests with the Western states, did not evolve despite the avoidance of direct confrontation and the prevalence of normalcy in diplomatic communication.[44] Pouliot argues that the answer cannot be found in what Kenneth N. Waltz calls 'unit properties' but that instead study needed to focus on relational issues. He shows how the change of Russian policies has emerged as a reaction to NATO's eastern enlargement. The broad picture is that the Kremlin has uncapped existing domestic pressures and let those representing a harder line towards the West influence policies as a result of disillusionment over Western recognition of its interests and perceived status in international politics.[45] Pouliot explains this phenomenon by means of social theory and applies Pierre Bourdieu's concept of 'hysteresis' (conduct prompted by a mismatch of disposition and position). This point of departure, although it is relational, provides the interpretation of the practices (NATO–Russia relations) with a theoretical frame derived from a discourse external to the interpretation proffered by the agents' own significations. The analysis of the logic of practicality, which succeeds in showing the results of interactive conduct, is in the end imbued with a theoretical concept borrowed from fashionable social theory. The study shows the 'story of a missed opportunity' but does not shed light on those Russian practices which could help us to understand the Russian response in order to reassess policies for the future.[46]

Nevertheless, Pouliot's basic insight in the need to focus on the interactive processes of world politics is continuously relevant to the study of Russia's relations with the West. Observers and politicians conversant with these relations and Russian policies know habitually that Russia's reaction to confrontation is to harden its measures and that the annexation of the Crimea had much to do with the direction that Western policies had taken in Europe, including the 'ring of friends' which the EU was developing through its European Neighbourhood policies in a way that increased its geopolitical tensions with Russia.[47] The present book shares Pouliot's methodological point of departure in that it also argues for a 'practice turn' that reverses the traditional, still basically idealist logic ('from ideas to practice', Anne L. Clunan's *The Social Construction of Russia's Resurgence* is an example of this approach) to the study of how practices shape the world and its meaning. In other words, instead of approaching 'practice' as the process in which ideas are realized, and instead of assuming that 'identity' shapes practices, our approach argues that agency (and consequently identity) *is* all that it (recurrently) *does*. Russia, like any other thing that is part of the reality that we experience, 'exists' not in its presumed substance – the given interests of the state, Russian culture and 'soul', and similar ideas – but in the regularities of its action (being). Thus the question of what Russia 'is' in the frozen conflicts is equivalent to what it 'does' in these conflicts, and the anticipatory notion of its *pragma* tells about its basic interests.

Pragmatism emphasizes that all search for new knowledge begins with an irritation of the mind through some conventional 'truth'. This I have done above when I explained some of my dissatisfaction with the prevalent interpretations of Russian policies in Western political, policy-research and academic discourses. Deep borders, vertical power and international community as the normative community of rules and expectations are concepts which relate the present study to previous research on frozen conflicts and Russian policies. Whilst pragmatism recognizes that concepts and discourses (linguistic and social conventions) are a constitutive part and a precondition of all communication, it also directs our attention to the factual and existential dimensions of experience ('proven' events and their significance as the experience which is different in relation to other experience). In this way, it sensitizes us to the predominance of theoretical *a priori* and predefined conceptual frameworks in the practices of research. In the sense of epistemic attitudes and methodological approaches, the interpretation of experience in its three dimensions – quality (difference), factuality and the conventions of communication – offers an alternative to theory-centred research as well as to the empiricist approach based on the dichotomization of theory and fact.[48]

Much of the previous literature to which the present study relates has already been mentioned. Although a large number of studies and reports have been written on the frozen conflicts, on the one hand, and Russian security and foreign policy, on the other hand, it is difficult to pinpoint antecedents in the literature. In the more specific sense of studying Russian policies in these conflicts, the predecessors of the study at hand are, above all, some works on Russian peacekeeping operations published in the second half of the 1990s. A book edited by Lena Jonson and Clive Archer discusses the general problems of peacekeeping, its supposed efficiency in terms of results and legitimacy, and its legitimacy in terms of international law encountered by Russia in its transformed role in Eurasia.[49] Their book, which appeared shortly after the ceasefire agreements in the frozen conflicts were put in place, discusses Russia as a 'newcomer' in peacekeeping activities. Another study to be mentioned is Dov Lynch's critical study of Russian peacekeeping policy towards the CIS.[50] Lynch notes that Russia adopted regionally and functionally differentiated policies in order to prioritize the Russian engagement vis-à-vis collective CIS policies.[51] While this is arguably true of the details of the arrangements, for example the different ways of engaging regional actors and acquiring an international mandate, the analytical point of departure in the present book is rather different: it looks for similarities (and differences) of practices on the more general level of policies' basic elements.

The researcher's mind, of course, is not a clean slate. Moreover, to pretend that we can interpret empirical phenomena without some prior notions or social conventions is merely yet another version of the dichotomy of the theoretical and the empirical which pragmatist interpretation seeks to overcome. My interest in Russia and its borders has been prompted by my experience of life in Finland, the European Union's outer border with Russia with a 1,340-kilometre-long borderline, in a country that has an earlier history as an autonomous part of tsarist Russia (1809–917) and, during the Cold War, had a role in the Soviet Union's border security arrangements, although it was never a part of the Soviet Union nor a member of the Warsaw Pact. From 1947 until 1991 Finland was part of the forward-defence area of the Soviet Union. This was based on a treaty of Friendship, Cooperation and Mutual Assistance as well as Finland's neutrality (regarding which Moscow and Helsinki did not share the same interpretation). Although the question of how this foreign and security policy was to be defined was highly contentious between the two countries, the positive circumstances of the time meant that joint military exercises were never even organized. After the dissolution of the Soviet Union, Finland abandoned its previous policy of neutrality and adopted the position of a militarily non-aligned country. This country became gradually integrated in NATO cooperation and, since 2016, it also intensified its military cooperation with the United States on a bilateral basis.[52] Although it is not a formal member of NATO, the territory of Finland is nowadays effectively a part of NATO's defence system through these two mutually integrated frames of cooperation. Through the cooperation arrangements which frequently entail joint military exercises in Northern Europe, it has become part of the extended border zones of the United States and NATO. The post-Soviet conflict areas discussed in the present book are very different from the problems which Finland encountered with the Soviet Union, and the present-day relations between the two countries are even less suited to comparison. In Finland, external circumstances over the past two centuries have enabled the development of a relatively homogenous society, and this has helped the country to survive throughout disintegrative processes in its history. However, although a comparison in terms of a common framework does not make sense, the Finnish experience of the problematic neighbourhood with Russia provides a point of departure for our questions. Such 'primacy of practice' (as opposed to the primacy of concept in theory-driven research) induces us to enquire what it is that is different in the 'new' encounter (the post-Soviet conflicts) and sets us upon a path of research. The interplay of the similarity and difference of experience makes us aware of how our own 'existential' knowledge gives significance to observations which may challenge conventional ways of knowing.[53] It does not give us any privileged position for 'knowing', but it does sensitize us to the all-too-easy way of adopting understandings about Russia from the discourse produced in other countries. It is a positioning which provides us with an alternative to authority and social convention as the grounds for knowing. In the next pages (Part One) of this book, this means examining Russia's actions in Georgia in 2008 from a perspective of experience that is wider than the one commonly centred on identifying Russia's violations of the rules of the international community of states.

Part One

Russia's Encounters with Georgia and Its Faltering Ways in the International Community

1

Conventional Rules and the Habitual Experience in the Justification of the War in August 2008

> *The right of nations to self-determination cannot justify recognition of Kosovo's independence along with the simultaneous refusal to discuss similar acts by other self-proclaimed states, which have obtained de facto independence exclusively by themselves.*
>
> – Statement of the Chamber Council of the Federation Council and the Council of the State Duma of the Federal Assembly of the Russian Federation concerning the consequences of the self-proclamation of independence by the territory of Kosovo (Serbia), 18 February 2008.[54]

In its war with Georgia, Moscow attempted to play according to the rules of the international community of states but also to 'boomerang back' the norms and principles set up by the United States and NATO together with the EU in their resolution of the conflict over Kosovo. The United States and the EU had paved the way for the recognition of Kosovo's independence by arguing that Kosovo was *sui generis*, of 'its own kind', i.e. that it should be treated as a singular and special case which would not constitute a precedent for other cases. On the basis of the Ahtisaari plan and with strong support from the United States, Kosovo's independence came into being in February 2008, initially with a status which was reminiscent of a trusteeship area in the old terminology of the League of Nations.

Russia argued that South Ossetia, just like Kosovo according to Western states, was a special case: The many years in which the conflict had been on the international agenda showed that it could not be resolved in any other way than by a final separation from Georgia. It claimed that it was its intervention alone in August 2008 that had prevented ethnic cleansing.[55] The two kinds of arguments that, according to Western states, had made Kosovo *sui generis* were emphasized to be even more applicable to South Ossetia. First, the more formal condition of referenda demonstrating that its people clearly wanted independence from Georgia had been fulfilled. Shortly after the formal dissolution of the Soviet Union, on 19 January

1992, South Ossetia had held a referendum on independence and becoming merged with North Ossetia on the Russian side of the international border between Russia and Georgia. The majority of the people residing in the region had shown their support for these ideas. (However, what these references to earlier history elide is that by this time the majority of the pro-Georgian population had already departed from South Ossetia.) Russia also reminded its international audience that on 19 November 1992, the South Ossetian Assembly voted to secede from Georgia and to join the Russian Federation. Second, Russia explained its military intervention by arguing that Georgia's action in August 2008 showed that independence was the only way to escape from the cycle of violence that had developed over the past decades. In South Ossetia large-scale violence had occurred during 1989–92, in the years of the dissolution of the Soviet Union – several years before Kosovo (1998–9). At that time President Yeltsin tried to negotiate a resolution with Eduard Shevardnadze, who had come to power in Georgia with Moscow's help. In August 2008, President Mikhail Saakashvili was accused of repeating the type of bloodshed reminiscent of the effects of the 'Georgia for Georgians' policies of late President Zviad Gamsakhurdia in 1991–2.

Accused of breaching Georgia's sovereignty, Russia explained that throughout the post-Soviet period it had recognized the sovereignty of Georgia and, prior to August 2008, seventeen years had been spent in a joint peacekeeping mission. The Georgian government's attack in Tskhinvali on a civilian population which it considers to be the country's own citizens *de facto* undermined Georgia's sovereignty and integrity, and Russia could not act in any other way but to try to prevent the escalation of the conflict through its military intervention.[56] Russia argued that its actions were intended to prevent its peacekeepers from encountering the kind of situation in which the Dutch contingent had found itself in Srebrenica – not to be able to prevent mass killings on an ethnic basis.[57] Should the Russian peacekeepers have run away, like 'some peacekeepers ran away from Srebrenica'? Russia's Ambassador to the UN Vitaly Churkin enquired at the session of the UN Security Council on 10 August 2008.[58] Later that month (26 August 2008) President Medvedev explained to the BBC:

> the aggression and genocide unleashed by the Saakashvili regime have changed the situation. Our main mission was to prevent a humanitarian disaster and save the lives of people for whom we are responsible, all the more so as many of them are Russian citizens. We therefore had no choice but to take the decision to recognise these two subjects of international law as independent states. We have taken the same course

of action as other countries took with regard to Kosovo and a number of similar problems.⁵⁹

'Aggression' and 'genocide' were terms in a political 'blame game'. They were not words with which Russia was able to legitimize its military intervention towards the international community. Although the final conclusion of the Independent International Fact-Finding Mission on the Conflict in Georgia was that Georgia had started the war, this did not justify Russia's actions in the eyes of qualified international opinion.⁶⁰ Russia had used the term 'genocide' with reference to the events in the Tskhinvali area during the first days of the war.⁶¹ However, the mere fact that the Georgian military had attacked Ossetians, members of another ethnic group, in the conflict area did not suffice to make this attack genocide, a term which presupposes systematic and intentional action to make extinct a population defined on basis of its ethnicity. Instead, this conflict was about the control of territory. Confronted with such criticism, Russia was left only with the argument that genocide had occurred during the previous, acute phases of the Georgian–Ossetian conflict of the early 1990s, and that it was *about to occur* again: therefore, Russia presented its action as being 'about preventing genocide'.⁶²

The reference to the responsibility to save lives resonates with Russia's initial, failed attempt to reactivate the UN principle of the Responsibility to Protect as justification for its military intervention. According to this principle, states have the responsibility to protect their populations from genocide, war crimes, ethnic cleansing and crimes against humanity. If they 'manifestly failed' in this, the international community was to take action through the mechanisms of the UN Charter.⁶³ The thin line of reasoning offered by Russia for the validity of this justification was that it immediately, as soon as the violence started on the evening of August 7, had requested the UN Security Council to call for a ceasefire and, therefore, had appealed to the right authority. In other words, it had hoped to gain *ex post facto* authorization for its intervention from the Council. This had been the case with the Council's approval of the ECOWAS peacekeeping intervention for cease-fire monitoring (ECOMOG) in the civil wars in Liberia in 1992 and in Sierra Leone in 1997. However, the crucial difference was that Russia had simultaneously launched a war on its own. In the debates of the Security Council Russia in vain sought the acknowledgement of the other members of the Council for its interpretation that Georgia was an 'aggressor' against its own people and that Russia's intervention was justified in order to prevent a humanitarian catastrophe and even genocide.

When the role of the UN had been discussed earlier in the first decade of the twenty-first century, Russia's position was that 'responsibility to protect' adds little (if anything) to already existing norms and that it, in fact, erodes these norms by being instrumentalized so easily for political purposes. Russia's argumentation showed some variation but the starting point remained consistently the same: only humanitarian intervention based on an endorsement by the UN Security Council was permissible.[64] Russia's position was articulated in the discussions of the International Commission on Intervention and State Sovereignty which, in response to the concerns that had been raised by UN Secretary General Kofi Annan in 1999 and again in 2000, examined the 'responsibility to protect' as an international obligation. These discussions were continued in connection with the High-level Panel on Threats, Challenges and Change, through which Annan a few years later sought to activate international opinion for reinforcing the global organization's authority.[65] The report of the first-mentioned project (*The Responsibility to Protect*, 2001) provides six criteria for the justification of military intervention (i.e. a just war): right authority, just cause, right intention, last resort, proportional means and reasonable prospects.[66] Because it had initiated a war alone, Russia failed on the first point. The military mobilization and the geographic scope of the action, which included parts of Georgia outside the separatist regions and destroyed Georgian military infrastructure and materiel, again were considered clearly 'disproportionate'. This was the evaluation of the situation made by US president George W. Bush immediately after the Russian intervention.[67]

The Kremlin and the Ministry of Foreign Affairs (MFA) explained that Russia's use of military force – which they referred to as a 'peace-making',[68] 'peace enforcement' and 'peace coercion' operation[69] – had been the last resort necessary in order to prevent the escalation of a humanitarian catastrophe. This catastrophe was argued to have left more than two thousand people dead, most of whom were Russian citizens, and to have caused a major refugee problem not only for Georgia but also for Russia in its republic of North Ossetia-Alania.[70] Humanitarian catastrophe, a term which refers to a great magnitude in the loss of lives or the number of people whose living conditions have dramatically deteriorated, arguably described the situation during and after the five days of war.[71] However, the question remains whether the magnitude would have been less had Russia not mobilized for military intervention. When it did so, it also heightened the moment for secession; and this, in turn, increased the strength of the argument that this move was a 'last resort' and an immediate 'remedial' solution to long-lasting violence following the example set by Kosovo.[72]

Towards the end of August 2008 Russia's reasoning about the humanitarian grounds had resulted in legal and political entanglement. Making reference to a United Nations General Assembly Resolution, which on the occasion of celebrating the 25th anniversary of the organization in 1970 had declared the principles of international law on friendly and cooperative relations between states (UNGAR 2625), Russia maintained that President Saakashvili himself had undermined the territorial integrity of Georgia. Moscow now reminded that in accordance with the 1970 declaration 'every State has the duty to refrain from any forcible action which deprives peoples of their right to self-determination and freedom and independence'. Russia argued that Saakashvili had demonstrated his inability to comply with 'the principle of equal rights and self-determination of peoples', which requires that a government must represent 'the whole people belonging to the territory'.[73] However, this argument, which, at best, could be considered customary international law, remained weak in any legal sense. Russia began to emphasize a very traditional principle as the basis for its action: the United Nations Charter Article 51, that is, the right to individual or collective self-defence.

Whilst collective self-defence was not logically a viable frame for explaining action (because South Ossetia was formally a part of Georgia), it was possible to refer to individual self-defence: Russia pointed out that its peacekeepers and civilian citizens had been attacked. When the war started and the Georgian troops rolled in, twelve Russian peacekeepers had been killed, some of them by their Georgian counterparts. However, it was not only members of the military who were Russian citizens in Georgia's secessionist regions. Half a decade before the war, Russia had started to hand out Russian passports in large numbers throughout Georgia's secessionist regions. The passport policy became an indirect way to tell the people of South Ossetia and Abkhazia that Russia was prepared to defend them. By the summer of 2008 almost the entire population of South Ossetia (40,000 out of the 45,000 who were left in the war-torn region in 2008) had Russian passports. The corresponding figure in Abkhazia during the same time was 150,000 out of 200,000.[74] Russia explained the passport policy by referring to humanitarian reasons: because they felt threatened in Georgia, it was important for South Ossetians to be able to affiliate with their kin and to be able to run their practical affairs and connect with family in North Ossetia-Alania on the Russian side of the border. Likewise in the case of Abkhazia Russian policymakers and experts argued that the population had been thrown into military conflict and that it was Russia's moral obligation to help them.[75] For the population of these regions possession of the passport of the former fatherland – Russia as the successor state of the Soviet Union – was also natural. In South Ossetia and Abkhazia owning a Russian passport became general practice prior to the introduction of the separatist regions' own identity papers.

This passport policy is a modern version of the historical relationship of protection offered by Russia to smaller ethnic groups who have wished to escape the domination of their 'parent states' or other regional powers. It is a way to build vertical relations by supporting a group of people within another state, and to do this in such a manner that claims to be justified in terms of horizontal international relations: The ethnic groups under Russia's protection become Russian citizens, which Russia has the right to protect even beyond its formal borders. However, in this particular case self-defence was not a plausible explanation, because Russia's operation in this sense had been 'disproportionate'. Russia ultimately conceded to the view that its war in South Ossetia had been a humanitarian intervention. Its reasoning remained weak against the criticism that, in fact, it was precisely the kind of demonstration of the unilateral use of force which the responsibility to protect was meant to avoid. In March 2009, Chairman of the State Duma Committee for International Affairs Konstantin Kosachev emphasized that for Russia the August war was a 'humanitarian mission' to protect people in dire need of protection. In comparison to the Kosovars, whose case evoked sentiments of solidarity in many countries, in South Ossetia in August 2008 there was 'simply nobody to protect them'. Kosachev repeated President Medvedev's argument of August 26, saying that the only way to save these people was to recognize the regions as subjects of international law.[76] In the discussion, which continued until the next spring, Russia explained its point in relation to established principles of international law: While the respect for the sovereignty and territorial integrity of states remains the fundamental principle of international law, the right of nations to self-determination prevails over this in only one case: when a people are threatened with physical extermination and the only way to save them is to establish a separate state. The rule that was articulated in this way left the possibility of its application contingent on the political context. How can it be known that it is 'the only way' when one cannot sit and wait for 'Srebrenica' to occur? Russia's answer to this problem is that in South Ossetia such a case was based on what *could be expected as an event in the future and what could be assumed as the intentions of the Georgian leadership.*

Wayward reasoning against the background of history

Russia's argumentation concerning Abkhazia followed lines in that it claimed that Abkhazia would be next on Saakashvili's agenda. When Georgia denounced the agreement on the presence of the Russian peacekeeping mission in Abkhazia and declared them occupying troops on 13 August,

Russia reacted by arguing that the Russian withdrawal would mean a collapse of the entire fragile arrangement to safeguard peace in Abkhazia. A statement of the Russian MFA on 13 August concludes:

> Thus, in case of the realization of the absurd demand of Mikhail Saakashvili to end the peacekeeping operation in Abkhazia the region risks getting bogged down even deeper in the quagmire of crisis brought on by the unhealthy ambitions of the present Georgian leadership. Such a scenario is categorically unacceptable for the peoples inhabiting the region. It is fraught with new bloodshed, with new thousands of refugees and with a widening of the humanitarian catastrophe.[77]

Following the line of argument that the Western states had used in the case of Kosovo, Russia's Ministry of Foreign Affairs argued that Abkhaz opinion had to be taken into account. However, Russia also needed to avoid the impression that it had now accepted NATO's use of force in the war between Serbia and Kosovo in 1999. This resulted in extremely detailed arguments about how Georgia failed to offer conditions under which South Ossetia and Abkhazia could exist, and that this was in spite of the fact that the concessions required from Georgia were less onerous than those that had been demanded of Serbia. Foreign Minister Lavrov added to the discussion by pointing out that while Belgrade never broke Security Council Resolution 1244 (June 1999), Tbilisi failed to fulfil its obligations under the peace deals (agreed on between the Georgian central authorities and South Ossetia and Abkhazia in the early 1990s).[78] Arguments about how Mikhail Saakashvili's crimes exceeded those of Slobodan Milosevic and how civilians had been attacked were brought up. The State Duma participated in the debate in support of Russian policies. Following the model of The Hague Tribunal for Yugoslavia, a group of representatives suggested establishing a tribunal to track the events in South Ossetia.[79] Russia accused Western countries of using 'double standards'. 'Our colleagues said more than once that Kosovo was a *casus sui generis*, a special case. But in that case, we can also say that South Ossetia and Abkhazia are also *sui generis*,' President Medvedev remarked in an interview in August 2008.[80] Dmitry Rogozin, then Russia's NATO envoy, re-emphasized points that had not been forgotten from the wars in the Balkans and the Middle East: If NATO had been able to bombard Belgrade in 1999 and the United States to intervene in Iraq in 2003 there should be no negative reaction to Russia's 'disproportionate' use of force, which destroyed Georgian military capacity and in this way prevented its use against the civilian population.[81] By emphasizing that the Western states could not logically take a line of action and subsequently prevent other states from following suit, Russia sought to undermine the justification of their action under what was argued to be the 'right cause' and also to ward off accusations of 'unilateralism'.

Domestic discussion in Russia over the use of military force against Serbia by NATO forces had intensified sentiments about 'Slavic unity'; yet for the makers of foreign and security policy this affiliation based on culture and history was about far more than that: it was about Russia being part of Europe. The emphasis in Western states that Kosovo was a 'European' conflict in Russia's view circumvented the interests of Serbia and consequently also excluded Russia. One decade later, this defeat was turned into a victory. If Kosovo could be presented in this way, then, in the same way, South Ossetia and Abkhazia were issues closely tied to Russia's interests about stability and security in the South Caucasus region. On August 8, the date of the mobilization to confront Georgian troops, President Medvedev explained: 'Russia has historically been a guarantor for the security of the peoples of the Caucasus, and this remains true today.'[82] The fact that the two disputed regions were conflicts which flared up after the dissolution of the Soviet Union – a state which Russia in the legal sense succeeds – was claimed to leave Russia with a special moral responsibility. Foreign Minister Lavrov argued that the basis for the pursuit of self-determination in Abkhazia and in South Ossetia was the same as it had been in Georgia, that is, the law of the USSR from 3 April 1990, and that all three had been building their own bases of statehood ever since they left the Soviet Union.[83] What this meant was twofold: the state borders of Georgia had not in any final way been agreed upon in the Belovezh Accords of December 1991, and history was to be brought up in order to question Georgia's authority in the issue.[84]

In the years following 2008, only Venezuela, Nicaragua and Nauru recognized South Ossetia and Abkhazia as independent states; and by 2019 only one more state – Syria in 2018 – had joined this group of states.[85] Most members of the Commonwealth of Independent States had reason to fear separatist problems of their own, and changing the rules of the borders agreed upon in the Belavezhskaia Pushcha in December 1991 seemed like a way to provoke instability. Although Russia's fellow-members in the CIS did not follow Russia in recognizing the independence of South Ossetia and Abkhazia, they refrained from objecting to Russia's interpretation which clearly undermined the legitimacy of Georgia's actions and argued that 'the actions of the Georgian armed forces in South Ossetia have created a humanitarian disaster' (Statement of Representatives of the Inter-Parliamentary Assembly of the CIS, 17 August 2008). The conclusion of the Independent International Fact-finding Mission on the Conflict in Georgia more than one year later (on 30 September 2009) found that Georgia had started the war on the night of August 7–8 but that Russia's reaction was

Justification of the War in August 2008   37

'disproportional'; this permitted Russia to hail the findings with satisfaction as it considered it to provide support to its argument that it had been Georgia that acted as the aggressor.

On the day of the report's release, the Russian Ministry of Foreign Affairs commented on the report's conclusions by remarking that 'it is difficult to imagine otherwise, if one recalls the content of Order No. 02 to the chief of staff of the 4th infantry brigade of Georgia's armed forces'. The statement cites the Georgian order: "The task force shall carry out a combat operation in the Samachablo (South Ossetia) region and rout the enemy within 72 hours. Georgia's jurisdiction shall be restored in the region."[86] Later, in August 2012 after Vladimir Putin had resumed the Russian presidency, he confirmed the intelligence already unofficially released before that showed that the plan for a war against Georgia had been prepared as early as in late 2006 and authorized in 2007.[87] Although military preparations are not equivalent to plans meant to put into operation, they clearly reveal that such a situation was foreseen as a possible development of events.

Russia's recognition of the independence of Georgia's secessionist regions in August 2008 seemed like an abrupt turn away from its previously uncompromising emphasis on intact borders, which had formed the line of thinking only months before when Russia warned that the recognition of Kosovo's independence would open up a 'Pandora's box of similar cases'. By doing so it had told about the options of its own policies.[88] A revision of this traditional approach was gathering strength in popular and expert discourses, and this opinion subsequently served to support official policy once events in Kosovo prompted such a turn. In contrast to the argumentation that justifies military intervention in terms of the normative conventions of the international community of states, the background of the domestic discussion lies in habitual experience. This is knowledge which emerges 'naturally' from immediate, first-hand experience and seems self-evident to its interlocutors. In other words, although the discussions outside Moscow's expert circles are little acquainted with a concept such as the Responsibility to Protect, the idea that Russia has geographic areas of responsibility outside its formal borders is recognized as part of Russia's history. Russia's own kind of 'responsibility to protect' ethnic groups who have remained loyal to it and asked for its protection has a deeper historical sense that involves understanding how the ideas of the centuries-old tradition of building the multinational state through relationships of association appear in contemporary practices. A modern meaning can easily be attached to Russia's 'responsibility to protect' in connection with the political argument that Georgia in August 2008 was close to being a 'failed state' because of its attacks on the civilian population. Although the state of affairs in Georgia did not lend support to this argument for international audiences, it resonated with the Russian tradition of imperial protection, which the Soviet state had provided for smaller ethnic groups who were helpful in the central administration's attempts to balance the nationalist ambitions of larger groups. This point places the Russian argumentation discussed above within a more comprehensive context. It reminds us that even political speech intended to be politically manipulative cannot be appreciated as merely instrumental if it, at the same time, is meant for an audience. As many philosophers of language have pointed out, the words used need to have some resonance with an audience's experience in order for that audience to be receptive.[89] In Russia, military intervention enjoyed not only popular approval but also strong support. This gap between the international, Western-led argumentation and Russian domestic opinion explains much about the roughness of Russia's attempts to justify its actions to the international community. Recognizing this tension is also helpful in identifying the possible 'variants' of policies available to Russia's decision makers.

2

The 'Last Resort' Solution and the Experience of the Recurrent Violence

In addition to 'humanitarian catastrophe', Russian policymakers and diplomats also used another term that was rather less specific about numbers: humanitarian tragedy.[90] 'Tragedy' is not a term that in diplomatic vocabulary entails specific action consequences. It imparts a historical narrative of the fate of a people under repression and trapped within a recurrent cycle of violence. Tragedy, due to a fatal flaw, is unsolvable; and so it is with South Ossetia's and Abkhazia's co-existence with Georgia, according to the Russian argumentation mobilized to support Moscow's policies in the aftermath of the war in August 2008. Because 'tragedy' identifies an inevitable but regrettable development it was well suited to explain why Russia had 'no other way': the violence witnessed in the early 1990s was predicted to recur; and to recur with the strength and magnitude of nothing less than 'genocide' – a term that is politically charged in the historical memory of ethnic groups and nationalities in the Caucasus. 'Genocide' had been the term used in June 1992, in the statement on South Ossetia by Ruslan Khasbulatov, the Chairman of the Russian Supreme Soviet, at a time when Russia was in the process of trying to broker a ceasefire in the conflict which had flared up in violence in late 1989.[91] The term then was intended less as a description than a way to tell Tbilisi that a ceasefire was necessary. The violence that had flared up in spring 1991 between Ossetians and Georgians and continued for more than a year had resulted in about 1,000 casualties. The number of Ossetians who at that time fled across the mountains to North Ossetia on the Russian side was as high as 100,000, and more than 20,000 Georgians became internally displaced in Georgia. In the war in August 2008 these figures were 35,000 and 17,000, respectively; the latter number included the entirety of the region's Georgian population.

The violence and disruption of the past decades repeated the historical experience of the flux of power in the period of the Russian Empire's collapse. In 1918–20, immediately prior to the region's conquest by the Red Army in February 1921, large-scale violence had occurred in the Ossetians' rebellion against the Menshevik Georgian Democratic Republic. In these events at least 5,000 Ossetians were killed and over 13,000 starved or died in epidemics. The Russian Empire had expanded into the Caucasus over the course of the first six decades of the nineteenth century and gained control of the entire region in 1864; however, the Ossetians had not been among those groups who resisted Russia's predominance. Historical memories of their suppression by larger groups, Georgians amongst them, are part of Ossetian self-identification. The depravations of that period were such that it was not difficult to later label them as 'genocide', although evidence in the modern legal sense remains controversial. However, power relations were changing, and protection and loyalty could turn into unreliability and oppression. During its expansion into the Caucasus, Russia had not only presented an alternative to Georgia's regional dominance, but it also on many occasions had allied itself with Georgia in suppressing smaller peoples. It follows that there exists no uncontroversial way for Russia to revive historical memory in the region in order to justify its actions today. Next, I argue that while both Abkhazia and South Ossetia have a historical pattern of relying on Russia in their struggle against Georgia these two cases differ greatly from each other. For the Ossetians, Russia mainly represents protection, whereas the relationship of the Abkhaz with Russia is rather more ambiguous in nature.

The Abkhaz and the Ossetians: The historical relationship with Russia

The principality of Abkhazia (Apkhazeti) was annexed to Russia by a manifesto of Tsar Alexander I in 1810 following several decades of petitioning by Abkhaz princes for Russia's protection. However, after Russia's Caucasus Wars ended in 1864 Abkhazia was put under Russia's direct military control in the Sukhumi Military District. The principality was abolished, half of the population left and Abkhazia was repopulated by Russians and people from other parts of the Caucasus region. After 1917 Abkhazia became part of the short-lived Democratic Republic of Georgia, which existed from May 1918 until February 1921 and was led by Social Democrats (Mensheviks).[92] Independent Georgia, which was supported by Germany, had softened its earlier, uncompromising attitude and assented to the autonomous position of Abkhazia just before the Bolshevik victory in February–March 1921. Bolshevik rule tried to woo Abkhazia to its side by similarly giving it the status of a Soviet Socialist Republic (SSR) in May 1921. However, by December 1921 this status was specified to exist in a 'contract of alliance' with Georgia.

One year later, in December 1922, Abkhazia along with Georgia entered the Transcaucasian Federation, which lasted until 1936. In February 1931 Abkhazia's status as an SSR associated with Georgia by treaty was reduced to the status of an Autonomous Republic (ASSR) within Georgia. After Stalin's rule Abkhaz intellectuals and elites repeatedly – in 1956, in 1967, and in 1977 – protested against Georgianization and went as far as appealing for the region's incorporation into the Russian Soviet Federative Socialist Republic. The idea was directly rejected in both Moscow and Tbilisi but by 1979 Moscow had used large sums of money to keep the Abkhaz content with their status.

Historically, the Abkhaz have always considered themselves as a separate, north-western Caucasian ethnicity, although they have also been in temporary alliances with Kartvelians (Southern Caucasians or Georgians) and, in particular, with Mingrelians and Svans. This sense of a distinct identity forms the background for the pursuit of greater symmetry with Georgia in a contract-arrangement derived from their early Soviet experience.[93] The separatist problem resurfaced when the People's Forum of Abkhazia appealed to Gorbachev in 1989 to allow Abkhazia to remain under Soviet rule at a time when Georgia was actively advocating independence from the Soviet Union. The violence that erupted into war in August 1992 – two years after Abkhazia had declared sovereignty – was preceded by a proposal by Abkhaz leaders over a federative arrangement with Georgia, but which Georgia ignored while it awaited Russian assistance to crush the separatists. At the same time the situation was becoming increasingly complex for Russia. In the immediate aftermath of the dissolution of the Soviet Union the Abkhaz cause for independence had gathered the sympathies of a large number of small ethnic groups throughout the Caucasus. The Adyghe, other Circassian groups and also Chechens supported Abkhazia's independence. The militant Confederation of Mountain Peoples, which was formed in Nalchik in Kabardino-Balkaria in autumn 1990, actively recruited volunteers and mercenaries to support the separatists' cause. These groups participated in the violent mobilization and war of 1991–2 in support of Abkhaz independence and in order to oppose Russia's predominance in the region.

In comparison to the Abkhaz, Ossetians in Georgia have a much stronger habitual, life-world connection to Russia, which in their case is based on a similarly long but less conflictful history in connection with Russia.[94] Ninety per cent of all Ossetians live on the Russian side of the border. The population of South Ossetia was about 70,000 in 2007; as opposed to this North Ossetia had about 700,000 inhabitants. When the Red Army conquered the region, the Ossetians were divided between Soviet Russia and Soviet Georgia. South Ossetia became an autonomous region (*oblast'*) within the Georgian SSR in

April 1922 and was included within the Transcaucasian Federation during 1922–36. Communal conflict in Georgia became embedded through Stalin's decision to include in the autonomous *oblast'* of South Ossetia not only its historical mountain region but also parts of a plain inhabited by non-Ossetian ethnic groups in Georgia and to make Tskhinvali, in which the majority of inhabitants were not Ossetians, its capital. In the Soviet political puzzle of nationalities, the division of the Ossetians between Soviet Russia and Georgia was instrumental for constraining a sense of ethnic unity and nationalism in Georgia. Leaving independence-minded Abkhazia within Georgia had the same purpose, but whilst Ossetia was split into two parts, Abkhazia had already become a mixture of ethnicities decades earlier, under the reign of the Russian Empire.

South Ossetians started arming themselves after violence flared up in November 1989, when a Georgian demonstration in Tskhinvali was blocked by the Ossetians.[95] This demonstration was organized in order to support the actions of the Supreme Soviet of the Georgian SSR that declared as illegal South Ossetia's attempts to change its status from being an autonomous region (*oblast'*) within Georgia to an autonomous republic. This status followed the model of North Ossetia, which since 1936 had been an autonomous republic within Soviet Russia (the Russian Soviet Federated Socialist Republic). In June 1990, North Ossetia declared its status as part of the Soviet Union in order to distance itself from the emergent new Russia. The South Ossetians boycotted elections for the Georgian Supreme Soviet and organized a vote for their own parliament. On 20 September 1990, they followed the line of conduct adopted in North Ossetia and proclaimed South Ossetia's status as a democratic republic within the Soviet Union. In December the Georgian SSR Supreme Soviet responded by a decision to abolish South Ossetia's status as an autonomous *oblast'* altogether and, consequently, as a separate administrative unit.[96] Tbilisi declared a state of emergency in South Ossetia – which now was called the Tskhinvali Region or also referred to by its historic Georgian name, *Samachablo* – and troops from the Georgian and Soviet Ministries of the Interior were sent to control the violence and disorder. South Ossetia was placed under Tbilisi's semi-military administrative control, and an economic blockade was imposed on the region so as to enable Tbilisi's full control. In January 1991, Gorbachev responded to Tbilisi's actions by a decree which ordered the withdrawal from South Ossetia of all 'armed formations' except the troops of the Soviet Ministry of the Interior. The decree, already an obsolete document because the Union was dissolving, called for compliance with Soviet law and protection of the rights of its citizens in the region. In March 1991, when the fighting in the separatist region was in full swing, Georgia refused to participate in the Union-wide referendum on the preservation of the Soviet Union. In the next month, in April 1991, Georgia declared independence from the Soviet Union and accused Moscow of supporting the separatists, who could use weapons from the Soviet army and draw manpower from volunteers in the North Caucasus regions and the ethnically non-Georgian parts of Georgia.

In Georgia nationalist sentiment pervaded the country, and those who had committed atrocities against Ossetians were left to go unpunished. Zviad Gamsakhurdia's presidency ended in a coup in January 1992, and Eduard Shevardnadze took his place as the acting chairman of the Georgian State Council the following March (Shevardnadze was formally elected as president in 1995). In June 1992, there was little other choice for Shevardnadze but to abide with the ceasefire in South Ossetia because another front of war had been opened in Abkhazia. In Abkhazia the Russian Ministry of Defense (MD) continued to support the separatists whilst the Ministry of Foreign Affairs (MFA) and President Yeltsin were negotiating cooperation with Shevardnadze. Two months after the third ceasefire (following the first in September 1992, and the second in May 1993) was signed for Abkhazia in late July 1993, and a Joint Control Commission to settle the conflict and trilateral monitoring groups agreed in it already were established, the separatists moved to capture Sukhumi. The Abkhaz capital became the site of a massacre that left several thousand civilian people dead; 50,000 (mostly Georgians) left Abkhazia. A new ceasefire was agreed in December 1993, against the backdrop of Georgia's agreement to join the CIS. Russia strengthened its military cooperation with the Georgian government, whereas its military support for the rebels became more indirect and covert. In a new ceasefire on 14 May 1994, the three parties were able to agree on cooperation with the CIS peacekeeping mission (five Russian battalions, i.e. some 2,500 troops) in conjunction with the UN Observer Mission (UNOMIG). The rebels adjusted the lines of control after the ceasefire was in place, and the new cycle of violence showed that the backing of the international community for the peacekeeping arrangements had become urgent.

For reasons that relate to the differing histories of South Ossetia and Abkhazia in terms of their specific relations with Russia, it was much more natural for Moscow's policy in August 2008 to invoke the notion of 'genocide' – the suggestion that a magnitude of atrocities that could be called genocide was *about to recur* – with reference to South Ossetia than in reference to Abkhazia, which was only vaguely referred to in such argumentation. Whereas Abkhazia was independence-minded and ethnically heterogeneous, for Ossetians South Ossetia had in fact remained a transboundary community of North Ossetia (North Ossetia-Alania since 1994[97]) on the Russian side. The population had remained loyal to Russia, the Soviet Union and, before that, to the Russian tsars, who had provided support against the oppression by Georgian landlords of this ethnic group that spoke a language remotely related to Persian.[98] Since the collapse of the Soviet Union North Ossetia on the Russian side of the border has reclaimed its historical role as the bastion of Christian Orthodox Russian civilization in the largely Muslim North Caucasus.[99] In 1993 North Ossetia recognized South Ossetia's independence – a move that was possible in the early 1990s when Yeltsin encouraged regions to increase their autonomy. The solidarity shown then, as well as during the conflict in 1989–91 and the war in 2008, has its historical foundation in the axis of cooperation that was established in 1917, when the Ossetians sided with the Bolsheviks against the Georgian Mensheviks. The dissolution of the Soviet Union and the rise of nationalism in Georgia reignited this historical conflict. When Gorbachev's tanks crushed a peaceful demonstration in Tbilisi in April 1989, they also prepared the ground for strengthening nationalist tendencies in Georgia and thereby further polarized the historical conflict between Ossetians and Georgians, which erupted into violence half a year later.[100]

This is the background against which the notion of an imminent threat of 'genocide' facing the Ossetians could easily invoke the concerns of the majority of Russians, for whom Russia's greatness is connected with its capability to protect those who are affiliated with it. As a consequence, in 2008, like also in the 1990s, it was mainly Georgia that was accused in Russia for the violence that had left thousands dead and forced hundreds of thousands to flee.[101] Due to its different features and different relationship with Moscow, Abkhazia does not mobilize popular solidarity in the same way in Russia. Moreover, a detailed argumentation similar to the one applied to South Ossetia in 2008 would also prove more problematic for the reason that the number of victims in the atrocities that had occurred during the time when Russian peacekeepers had already been stationed was much higher in Abkhazia, both in relative and in absolute terms. According to Georgian sources almost 300,000 of Abkhazia's Georgian residents were 'ethnically cleansed' by the Abkhaz with Russian military support during 1992–3.[102] However, although Russian peacekeepers did allow the Abkhaz rebels to extend their lines of control, developments were not always in their hands. During the acute phase of the war (1992–3) about 1,000 Russian civilians were killed and 30,000 of the total of 70,000 Russians in the region fled. The passport policies that Russia activated in Abkhazia already before 2008 are one indication of Moscow's wish to return to Abkhazia. Other indications of this desire include the fact that Russia never fully abandoned its base in Gudauta, Abkhazia, after the other Russian bases in Georgia were closed down in 2007. The situation that NATO in September 2006 offered Georgia an 'Intensified Dialogue' status to serve the country's membership aspirations made it important in Moscow to maintain its presence in Abkhazia; at the same time the low-profile attached to Gudauta as a 'training centre' still left space for rapprochement between Tbilisi and Moscow. The geopolitical moment was rapidly intensifying, but there was a deeper historical sense that kept Russia involved in Georgia. The idea of the multinational entity of the state had not disappeared with the Soviet Union because it developed centuries before it. Consequently it was natural to think that the conflict could be resolved through the negotiations between Moscow and Tbilisi.

The failure to establish the Moscow-Tbilisi relationship

In the early years of the Russian Federation public opinion in the country, which was mainly expressed in the State Duma and the media, was divided over how Russia should respond to the pursuit of greater autonomy by Russian speakers stranded in newly independent states by the dissolution of the Soviet Union as well as by non-Russian ethnic populations with a historical relationship of protection from Russia. The new state borders had abruptly revealed the simplistic assumptions of the Soviet-style approach, which depoliticized protest and rebellion by designating those who participated in such activities as 'hooligans' and criminal groups. The war that began in Transnistria in March 1992 prompted questions about the role and responsibilities of Russia in other conflicts that had started with the dissolution of the Soviet Union. In April 1992 – at a time when the violent conflict, which had flared up in South Ossetia in November 1989, continued unabated – *Nezavisimaya Gazeta* deplored that Russian authorities remained 'oblivious' to the problems in South Ossetia whilst they showed solidarity with the Transnistrian cause. This attitude was seen to derive from the then-novel foreign policy that enabled Russia to defend the rights of citizens of other countries but only when they were diasporic Russians. Consequently South Ossetia, the newspaper argued, had not managed to provoke an 'ecstasy' similar to Transnistria among the Russian authorities.[103] Unlike the residents of Transnistria, Ossetians were unable to generate feelings about 'Slavic unity'; hence, in Moscow's official language the conflict was termed 'Georgian-Ossetian'.

After the signing of the ceasefire agreements of 1992-4, Russia remained unable for years to determine which part of Georgia – the central government in Tbilisi or the separatist regions – could more reliably become the basis for the political and military stability it needed in the hinterland of the North Caucasus and in order to maintain its presence on the coast of the Black Sea.

On the one hand this uncertainty was largely due to the strong nationalist tendencies and anti-Russian sentiments that were driving Georgian politics, and on the other hand because of a lack of coordination in Moscow's policies. In the period between the Soviet Union's dissolution and Georgia's 'Rose Revolution' of November 2003, the main line of Russia's policy on Georgia was to prevent the country from disintegrating and to help develop its military so that it could constitute a strong defence zone in the South Caucasus along the border with Russia's North Caucasus. The broader policy goal was to build up cooperation in the frame of the Commonwealth of Independent States (CIS), which in December 1991 had been set up to replace the Soviet Union. As a result of these intertwined goals, Georgia's secessionist regions were used to apply pressure on Tbilisi in order to gain favourable conditions for Russia's military presence and to induce Georgia to participate in the collective CIS cooperation.[104] In the early years of the Russian Federation, about 15,000 members of the Russian military (including border guards) were stationed on Georgian territory. The main Soviet bases were located in Akhalkalaki near the Turkish border (the base for Russia's 62nd Division) and in Batumi on the Black Sea; in addition, strategic air fields were maintained in Gudauta in Abkhazia and in Vaziani near Tbilisi. The heavy military presence in Georgia gave Russia the initial impetus to supporting the secessionist regions and meant that such support was instrumental in the more comprehensive frame of negotiations. Such policies, which kept Georgia weak, were outlined by General Pavel Grachev, who led the Ministry of Defense (MD) during 1992–6. The Ministry of Foreign Affairs (MFA), which at that time was led by Andrei Kozyrev, whose policies initially were supported by President Yeltsin, contrarily believed that an internally strengthened Georgia, politically unified and a participant in the cooperation within the CIS frame, would be a solidifying zone of Russia's southern border.[105] The policies of these two ministries were somewhat better coordinated from 1993 onwards after the Russian government decreed a division of labour in which the MD was to control the ceasefire and the MFA was to coordinate the resolution process with the UN and other international organizations.

The sectoral policies of the two ministries increased the power of the State Duma, which, although many representatives were sympathetic to the cause of the secessionists, was reluctant to see Russia becoming militarily involved in favour of one or the other side. This was an opinion that called for non-interference except in extreme conditions. Expressing a similarly cautious line for policies *Moskovskiye Novosti* emphasized in June (1992) that although 'Russia can and must stop the genocide of the South Ossetians', 'the decisive use of military force is a last resort, one that is capable only of freezing the conflict, not of resolving it'.[106] When Abkhaz separatists moved to capture Sukhumi in mid-September 1993 (after the ceasefire of the preceding July), Russia was both unable and unwilling to prevent it. One day after the ceasefire was broken, the Duma remained unready to accept a proposal by Defence Minister Grachev to deploy two peacekeeping missions in Abkhazia.[107] It was both reluctant to give the executive branches a free hand to use the country's scarce resources and sympathetic to the cause of the Abkhaz rebels. The latter attitude reflected the idea that Russia's greatness was connected with its capability to protect those who were affiliated with it, and consequently it was mainly Georgia that was blamed for the violence that had left thousands dead and hundreds of thousands on the move.[108]

In the next spring the State Duma also refused to ratify the Treaty on Friendship, Good Neighborliness and Cooperation, to which Yeltsin had given a personal boost by visiting Tbilisi in February 1994 in connection with its signing. This was a major blow to the possibility for developing cooperation with Georgia. Starting from the time when the ceasefires had been signed for South Ossetia (in June 1992) and for Abkhazia (in July 1993), the Georgian leadership and parliament expected Russia to provide substantive assistance in building up the armed forces and its cooperation and assistance in ending the separatist conflicts. It also expected support in improving its shattered economy. Georgia joined the CIS in late 1993 and thereby met Moscow's expectation in agreeing to its Charter, the economic union and the Collective Security Treaty, which had been concluded in Tashkent in 1992. Likewise, agreements were prepared on extending the period of Georgia's hosting of four Russian military bases (strategic air fields in Vaziani near Tbilisi and in Gudauta in Abkhazia, the port in Batumi and the base for Russia's 62nd Division in Akhalkalaki in southern Georgia) for twenty-five years. In continuation of a Soviet pattern, the headquarters of Russia's Transcaucasus Group of Forces remained in Tbilisi. In addition the cooperation that was to enable the stationing of Russia's border guard on Georgia's Turkish border was on track.

Because Georgia had made these concessions despite the fall of Sukhumi to the separatists, the refusal by the State Duma in Moscow to ratify the treaty was a major disappointment in Tbilisi. In addition to enabling the Kremlin to equip the Georgian army – that is, something that the Duma did not wish for the Kremlin to be able to do – the treaty would have provided a frame for sector-specific economic cooperation. Consequently the Duma barred the Kremlin and the ministries of defence and foreign affairs from carrying out the negotiated 'deals' that would have tied the parties together in mutual benefit and strengthened Russia's presence in Georgia. A major stumbling block in the Tbilisi–Moscow relationship was also that the Russian MD insisted on securing Russia's military presence in Georgia (as per the agreement on an extended period for the bases) before military equipment could be delivered to Georgia. In early 1994 Pavel Grachev, Russia's Minister of Defense, stated that Russia wanted to maintain three military bases in Georgia within the framework of the CIS and the CSTO, and that this would be a precondition for Russia's assistance in holding the separatists at bay.[109] Against the backdrop of Georgian experiences with being repeatedly betrayed over Russia's purported assistance in controlling the rebels, Tbilisi's priority was to receive the military equipment without such preconditions. By spring 1996 it was clear that the Georgian parliament had refused to ratify the agreement, which had been signed in September 1995 by Shevardnadze and Prime Minister Viktor Chernomyrdin, on the twenty-five-year lease of the Soviet-era bases in Akhalkalaki, Batumi, Vaziani and Gudauta.[110]

Céline Francis concludes that the Russian and Georgian ministries of defence were able to agree in an annex to the treaty they had signed earlier in March that the restoration of Georgia's territorial integrity was a precondition for the treaty to come into effect.[111] This annex was missing from the final version, which Shevardnadze was pressured into signing at a time when the Kodori Valley remained the only area in Abkhazia under Tbilisi's control. The reasons for this change were no doubt complex and connected to questions over whether the ministries of defence actually had the authority to prepare such a treaty; nevertheless the circumstances of the time, as Francis also emphasizes, cannot be ignored. The Chechen war had rapidly escalated into a threat that could inflame the wider North Caucasus and create spillover effects in the Krasnodar Territory (*krai*) and its Black Sea coast (see Map 1, page 49). Russia had already let the rebels in Abkhazia consolidate their position; turning against them now would have brought Russian soldiers into a direct military encounter with them. Committing itself to supporting Georgia could also have increased mobilization against Russia by a large number of the 'Mountain Peoples' in the North Caucasus, including the Adyghe, other Circassian groups and the Chechens.[112] The first Chechen war (1994–6) was ignited only a few months after the ceasefire had been negotiated for Abkhazia, and the Chechens were seeking to solidify their republic by building connections with smaller ethnic groups in the South Caucasus, including with the Abkhaz. The uncertainty caused by these developments coincided with a period when Russia's military reform had come to nothing and its resources, both military and political, were scarce for action on several fronts simultaneously. At the same time Georgia, where Shevardnadze enjoyed little domestic support, appeared as a very uncertain ally. Shevardnadze was unable to control the situation on the ground, and Georgian paramilitaries such as the Forest Brotherhood and the White Legion

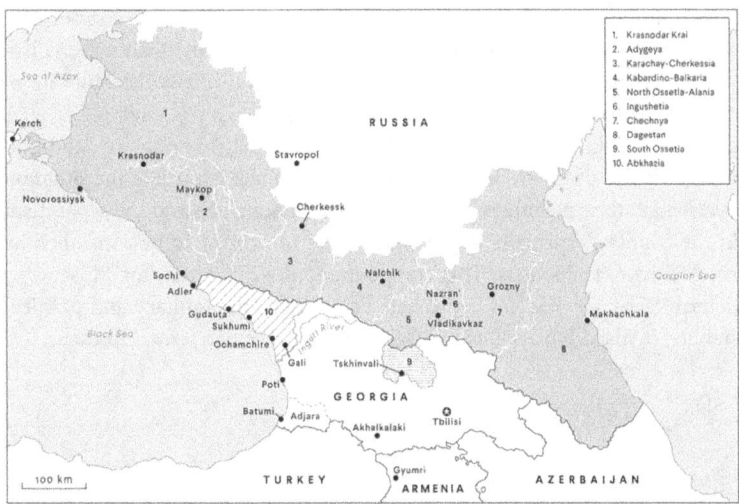

Map 1 Georgia and Russia's borderland regions in the Caucasus (illustration by Ilkka Janatuinen; used with permission).

were able to repeatedly attack and sabotage the Russian forces. This, in turn, increased the weight of the opinion of the Ministry of Defense in Moscow.

In Tbilisi Shevardnadze's position entailed a dilemma from the very moment that he was brought to power with Russian support in March 1992. The goal was to diminish the influence of the Zviadists, the supporters of the nationalist-minded first president Zviad Gamsakhurdia, who was ousted in December 1991 in a coup that resulted in the seizing of power by Georgia's military council in January 1992. From Moscow's point of view, the personage of Shevardnadze became a means to control Georgian nationalism, and Shevardnadze in turn was induced to make concessions and collaborate because of the separatist threat. Like this he was able to stay in power, but this also undermined his position in Tbilisi. Whilst he and his supporters in Georgia expected Russia to help them to restore Georgia's territorial integrity and then stay out of Georgian politics, their need for Russia's support to keep the Zviadists under control did not simply end. This vertical relationship based on mutual expectations about reciprocal obligations and shared benefits failed to create a positive dynamism that could generate a political 'friendship' of trust and good neighbourly relations in the Soviet-style tradition. The conditions remained implicit and ambiguous, and the expectations about mutual trust evaporated and were replaced by an increasing sense of mutual betrayal. Russia's political puzzle in the North Caucasus was too complex for Moscow to control with the scarce resources at its disposal in the 1990s; and Georgian nationalism was too strong in its anti-Russian undercurrents to allow the building of a political condition of mutual 'friendship' as a basis for solving Georgia's separatist conflicts. It was not possible for either Yeltsin or Shevardnadze to overcome this problem because neither of them had control of the situation over which they negotiated. Both Georgian nationalism and the separatism in the country, especially in Abkhazia, were too strong to be controlled by the Moscow–Tbilisi axis. This compounded the difficulties for Moscow to determine which policies could best bring about the military and political stability it wished to establish in Georgia and the wider South Caucasus.

3

The Long and Winding Way to Decision

Before autumn 2008, the core issue of Abkhazia's conflict with Georgia was about confederal relations, which the Abkhaz Supreme Soviet proposed in June 1992. The Georgian leadership under Shevardnadze did not see this as a basis for negotiations, and in the following months the Abkhaz Supreme Soviet unilaterally declared the 1925 Soviet Constitution as the basis for establishing Abkhaz–Georgian relations on a treaty basis.[113] As the fighting erupted in a new cycle of violence the Abkhaz secessionists' government fled to Gudauta, which at that time was the only ethnically Abkhaz-populated area. After Abkhaz combat victories in 1993, Shevardnadze conceded to Russian demands in 1994 for a ceasefire that would effectively separate Abkhazia from Georgia proper on the Inguri River. Now Georgia accepted Russia's suggestion about a federal arrangement as the basis for the negotiations, provided that it included no right of secession. The lack of a right to secede or change its status unilaterally corresponded to the status of the ASSR within the Georgian SSR. From late 1994 onwards Russia, which at that time already dealt with the war in Chechnya and now had this reason to lean towards a policy that saw a unified Georgia as a way to create stability in the South Caucasus, closed the Russian–Abkhaz border and pressured the Abkhaz to accept a federal formula similar to the treaty between Russia and Tatarstan.[114] A loose federal or confederal solution would have enabled Russia to control Georgian politics from the inside, and in the bilateral relations of the two countries it could have linked withdrawal of Russian support for the separatists with allowing a Russian military presence in Georgia. Francis notes that the discussion about a federal solution had begun in the immediate aftermath of the Soviet Union's collapse, at a time when both parties were relatively open to new ideas.[115] However, the window of opportunity soon closed when no preliminary agreement could be found on many issues, the toughest of which were citizenship and defence. Within the Abkhaz leadership some kind of federative arrangement had been under consideration as late as autumn 1993, but by the following autumn this was discarded.[116] Although Russia avoided committing itself to supporting the government in Tbilisi against the separatists, the independence of Abkhazia was not an option that was entertained by the Kremlin. In connection with the fragile accord reached by Moscow with Shevardnadze in 1993-4, this Abkhaz goal was designed from the outset as a means to pressure Tbilisi.

Above it was already described how the cooperation between Tbilisi and Moscow started to crumble as soon as it had been restored after the ceasefire was in place for Abkhazia in May 1994. In Moscow the State Duma did not ratify the treaty that would have enabled Russia to help in building up the Georgian army and economy, and in Tbilisi the parliament withheld the ratification of the agreement which would have provided Russian troops in Georgia with a legal status and confirmed the existence of Russian military bases in Georgia. Ending the support of the separatists was the necessary element in repairing relations with Shevardnadze, yet Russia was unable to do this at a crucial moment in the bilateral relationship because this would have opened an extremely complex battlefront for it at a time when the Chechen war was accelerating. Even if Russia by the end of 1993 restored the official channels of interstate relations along the Moscow-Tbilisi axis in its communications about the separatist issues, it also continued to support the separatists, and it did so in order to press Georgia to cooperate on issues relating to Russia's security interests, bilaterally in relation to the Russian military bases and multilaterally in the CIS frame.[117] In March 1994 the Russian government set up the Special Caucasus Border District (*Kavkazskii osobennyi pogranichnyi okrug*, KOPO), the purpose of which was to both control the Russian border in cooperation with Georgia and Armenia and organize joint control of these countries' external borders with Turkey and Iran, which Russia considered as its strategic borders.[118] By spring 1997 Georgia had adopted a law which confirmed the goal that the Georgian state would assume full control of its borders within two years. In the light of this principled goal it was no surprise that Tbilisi refused a request that came from Moscow one and a half years later – after Vladimir Putin had been appointed Prime Minister – to use the territory of Georgia in the second Chechen war.

As it gradually became obvious that Russia could not in agreement with Georgia through the territory of Georgia defend its own territorial unity, its response was to do nothing to prevent the diplomatic warfare which occurred around a number of issues and to allow the Abkhaz forces, who had demonstrated their unyielding attitude with the fighting that had erupted in the security zone in May 1998, to make advances as they decided. The Abkhaz forces had crossed the Inguri River with tanks in order to prevent the guerrilla operations from the Georgian-populated Gali district in Abkhazia permitted by Georgia; and Georgia accused Russia of allowing the Abkhaz to breach the ceasefire agreement by entering the zone with heavy weaponry.[119]

Georgia sharpened its policy by emphasizing that if the Russian peacekeeping under the CIS mandate could not help it regain territorial integrity, it would quit the membership – it did so in autumn 2008, but withdrew from the CSTO already in 1999. The Abkhaz in turn remained consistent in their demands: they were not prepared to accept anything less than relations based on 'equality' with Georgia. In December 2000, when the second Chechen war unfolded, Moscow claimed that Russian territory was threatened by terrorist infiltration from Georgia and imposed a visa regime on Georgia. Its exemption of Abkhazia and South Ossetia from this treatment, which was without precedent in Russia's policies in the CIS area, was a clear sign that priorities had now changed.[120]

Although Moscow's relations with Tbilisi had deteriorated already by early 1995 when it became clear that Tbilisi could not count on Moscow's support in suppressing separatist activity and the two years that followed had made it evident to both parties that building the relationship had failed, Russia's policymakers did not decide to abort their efforts because they still considered the situation to be in flux as long as the possibility existed that the Georgian regime could change. The diplomatic efforts – which were given the priority over military options after Evgenii Primakov became foreign minister in January 1996 – aimed to keep all options open by emphasizing that the two parties – Tbilisi and the secessionist government in Sukhumi – needed to give their consent before decisions could be taken to effectively change the situation. Russia's symmetrical treatment of the parties, which had been built into the ceasefire arrangement, was in this way institutionalized as a part of the negotiating mechanism of trilateral meetings between Moscow, Tbilisi and the separatists. Russia's indirect support of the separatists at the time when the ceasefire agreements were negotiated had helped to improve the separatists' positions, and Russia's symmetrical treatment in the negotiations achieved the same in the political resolution process. Because the relationship between Moscow and Tbilisi had disintegrated, Russia was unable to do anything except press ahead with the process of withdrawing its regular military units and obsolete equipment as had been agreed in the OSCE frame. By 2002 Russia had withdrawn the main part of its forces from the Gudauta base in Abkhazia in accordance with the requirements of the OSCE Istanbul summit (1999). It closed its base at Batumi in the Autonomous Republic of Adjara by the Black Sea in 2007, one year ahead of the schedule agreed in 2005. Earlier in 2004, Moscow had withheld support to the regional government and had not objected to the re-establishment of Tbilisi's control in that region. With the exception of the Gudauta base maintained for the peacekeepers' 'training purposes' under the CIS mandate, the closure of all bases outside Abkhazia was completed by 2007. In parallel with the reorganization of its military presence in the South Caucasus and shifting its weight to Armenia, even in early 2007 Russia was offering Georgia a deal that included the withdrawal of Russian troops and its assistance in the resolution of the conflicts in Abkhazia and South Ossetia in exchange for Georgia's non-alignment, supported by a legal obligation for Georgia not to employ third-country forces in the territory once the Russians had left.[121] However, this window of opportunity closed with the diplomatic confrontations and mutual accusations of the support of insurgency and separatism across the border.

Five years earlier, in 2002, the so-called Train and Equip Program had brought the US military to Georgian territory. Shevardnadze had turned to the West already in 1995 when the concessions made by Georgia to Russia had failed Georgia to regain control of Abkhazia and South Ossetia, but the 'Rose Revolution' in November 2003 provided this tactical turn with new meaning and set the course for the country's political future. After the 'Rose Revolution' brought to power Mikhail Saakashvili, who was elected president in January 2004, the presence of a new leader initially signified the opportunity for a fresh beginning in Moscow's relations with Tbilisi. However, events such as the closure of the Ergneti market near Tskhinvali soon signalled that the conflict with the Ossetians would worsen, and Saakashvili's vague promises about autonomy failed to bring any positive results. South Ossetia turned down Saakashvili's suggestions about reconciliation in a referendum in November 2006, which confirmed that independence remained the region's goal. Abkhazia was already functioning as a de facto state – that is, it was capable of performing the basic functions of a state within the territory under its control – and a new president, Sergey Bagapsh, had been elected in October 2004 to replace the ailing separatist leader Vladislav Ardzimba. Against the backdrop of these developments and the sense of failure and mutual betrayal in Georgia–Russia relations, it was not difficult in Russia to mobilize support for the idea of its responsibility to protect small populations which historically had been under its imperial care after Georgia launched an attack on Tskhinvali in August 2008.

Writing in 1998, Dov Lynch predicted that a Russia wishing to isolate itself from separatist conflicts in Georgia would pull out from Abkhazia and concentrate on picking up the pieces in its relations with Georgia.[122] Indeed, had Russia permitted Abkhazia's independence in 1998, this would have been a major sign of weakness towards both Georgia and the other former Soviet republics. Russia would have demonstratively betrayed Georgia and accordingly undermined its position in the CIS cooperation frame that it was trying to develop. Such a move would also have been a clear sign of weakness in relation to its own separatist problems in the North

Caucasus. In 1999 another round of war, this time lasting for a decade, had erupted in Chechnya and spread to the neighbouring republics. However, a crackdown on separatism in Georgia would also have been problematic because this would have contributed to polarizing the situation in the wider Caucasus region. The least problematic policy available was to bide time and thereby to keep both options open, i.e. to maintain relations with the regions functioning as de facto states and with Tbilisi. During this period it mattered little to Moscow that Georgia signed a strategic partnership with neighbouring Azerbaijan to open up cooperation in the energy sector in order to reduce its dependence on Russia; this was still cooperation between CIS members. But during 2005–6, when a Partnership for Peace liaison officer was agreed between NATO and Georgia and the IPAP (Individual Partnership Action Plan) mechanism established, Russia became concerned over NATO's plans in Georgia. The caesura came when Georgia, together with Ukraine, adopted an agenda for NATO membership. In the light of such institutional developments Russia could no longer afford to wait for a friendlier regime in Tbilisi.

After the NATO Bucharest summit in April 2008 had offered Georgia and Ukraine a path towards membership, the presidential administration in the Kremlin sent a letter to the Abkhaz and South Ossetian leaders; soon afterwards a decree was signed which allowed the Russian government and governmental sectors to begin establishing official institutional relations.[123] Earlier, on 6 March 2008, a few weeks after Kosovo's declaration of independence and its recognition by three permanent members of the UN Security Council – the United States, the UK and France – Russia formally lifted the sanctions which had been imposed on economic interaction with Abkhazia by decision of the Commonwealth of Independent States (CIS) in 1996. This signalled a political turning point, although Russia had not in fact been following the CIS decision. Russian actors, the Orthodox Church among them, had provided humanitarian assistance to the separatist regions since the early 1990s, but in the year prior to the August 2008 war Russia intensified a coordinated effort to start bringing the secessionist regions into its trade, business and logistic networks and continued to offer passports to the Abkhaz and South Ossetian populations. Because 'humanitarian' in the Russian-language practice is not limited to altruistic concerns and the morals to protect human life but also includes broadly humanistic interest and, most generally, refers to relations which are not formally state-authorized, much space is left for a wide range of cooperation.[124] This kind of cooperation facilitated the integration of Georgia's separatist regions with Russian communities across the border already years before summer 2008.[125]

Setting up quasi-states: Vertical power in an interstate fold

> We only care about the destinies and interests of people. Their right to life is the loftiest among human rights and the first among European values, of which there is so much talk going on. Now Abkhazia and South Ossetia can normally, full-fledgedly develop, having been denied this by the constant threat of use of force on the part of Tbilisi.
>
> –Foreign Minister Sergey Lavrov, 'On the Caucasus Crisis and Russia's Ukrainian Policy', published in Russian in the Ukrainian weekly *2000* (Kiev), no. 38, 19–25 September.[126]

In the 2008 war, Abkhazia and South Ossetia ceased to be the controversial means through which Russia controlled Georgia's role in regional security. Instead, they became the solution to Russia's intractable border security dilemma in relation to Georgia and were established as militarily fortified zones that secured its deep borders in the South Caucasus. Shortly after the violence had started on 7 August 2008, Abkhaz separatist forces used both air force and ground troops to drive the Abkhaz government-in-exile out of the Upper Kodori Valley, where it had persisted since 2006 as a clear sign of Georgia's resolve to retake Abkhazia. Once the ceasefire, which was negotiated with the assistance of the OSCE and the EU, was in place, Russia on 26 August 2008 recognized the independence of Abkhazia and South Ossetia. An Agreement on Friendship, Cooperation and Mutual Assistance was concluded equally with both new quasi-states[127] on 17 September 2008. These treaties laid the basis for the interstate frame of relations in which these entities have been integrated in Russian military cooperation and regional development with a wide range of sector-specific treaties. The bilateral treaties abolished barriers to economic interaction (including obstacles to property rights in either country), established the Russian rouble as the sole currency and double citizenship with the Russian passport as a practice,[128] and stipulated that Russia would henceforth control the coordination of foreign policy and do this in relation to its defence policy.

When Abkhazia in August 2008 declared its sovereignty and proceeded to promote its independence, it also asked to be included in the Russian Federation as an 'associate member'. The Constitution of the Russian Federation (1993) does not allow for such a status, and bilateral association is an anomaly in relation to the collective security and the multilateral economic cooperation pursued through the Collective Security Treaty Organization (CSTO) and the Eurasian Economic Union (EAEU) and its predecessors (i.e. the Customs Union of Russia, Belarus and Kazakhstan and the Eurasian Economic Community). However, the Russian practice of building and solidifying the multilateral frames of cooperation with its bilateral arrangements leaves space for such a 'variant' of association. For Abkhazia and South Ossetia bilateral cooperation with Russia is a matter of survival as far as wider international recognition cannot be gained even within the multilateral cooperation led by Russia. However, whilst the formal frame is bilateral, the huge discrepancy in size alone has the consequence that establishing cooperation with Russia practically means cooperation with Russia's regions. Consequently the two de facto states in their formally 'horizontal' form are vertically structured in relation to Moscow. Since autumn 2008, the horizontal form has enabled the development of a vertical relationship that has made these de facto states into 'external members' or close associates of the Russian Federation. As this structure is being strengthened, they become more and more quasi-states: dependent on Russia in the sense of both their territorial jurisdiction and the material resources required to perform the domestic functions of a state.

A sign of such a structure is that the Russian Federation's official representation in Sukhumi and in Tskhinvali came to include not only diplomatic missions but also the Russian President's special representatives. Whilst an embassy is a sign of official relations, the Kremlin's envoy is a sign of presence and that the entity in question belongs to the administrative sphere of the central power in Moscow. By decision of President Medvedev in March 2012 the governor of the Krasnodar Territory (*Krasnodarskii krai*), Aleksandr Tkachev, became the Special Representative of the Kremlin in Sukhumi, and the leader of North Ossetia-Alania was given the same position in Tskhinvali. The Kremlin's appointment of its own 'governors' for the newly established political entities follows the model of the administrative measure from spring 2000, which created presidential envoys (Plenipotentiary Representative of the President of the Russian Federation) for defined groups of federal subjects. This reform was explained to be necessary for overseeing the implementation of the Russian Constitution throughout the country. Appointing such envoys also for the two nominally independent states is a sign of vertical power within the horizontal fold and, more specifically, it is a sign of the continuity of a historical relationship of subordination and protection. Simultaneously, the fact that the appointed officials represent neighbouring regions served to set the two de facto states within the frame of regional cooperation instead of emphasizing their connection with Moscow and thus contributed to the course of making them quasi-states.

The regional frame of integration is similarly emphasized by the arrangements of economic assistance, which are coordinated by the Ministry of Regional Development.[129] Given the asymmetry in size, this frame of reference for the de facto states is logical in running administrative affairs. It also reveals just how much the formal interstate relations are packaging that holds vertical relations of control and subordination. Vertical power is effective in a number of ways in the domestic political arena of the two small de facto states through the structural condition that the two entities' political existence and economic survival are entirely dependent on Russia's military presence and economic cooperation. In 2016, more than 60 per cent of Abkhazia's state budget was estimated to be sustained by Russian government assistance.[130] Abkhazia's main economic assets are the tourist industry, which is in dire need of investment to renew the decrepit infrastructure, and citrus fruit and wine exports. In the regional context mutual cooperation is developed specifically with the Crimea, for whose construction industry Abkhazia provides gravel and inert material. The region's economic dependence on these industries has made it subject to severe criticism for ecological reasons.[131] South Ossetia, which has few prospects for any exports, has carried out a process of legislative and economic harmonization with Russia. One of the first measures to prepare for the integration of its administrative structures was to harmonize the wages of officials to meet the general level of Russia's North Caucasus Federal District.

Based on agreements in April 2009 Abkhazia and South Ossetia agreed that their border control on the borders with Georgia would be realized jointly with Russia for the following five years. The peacekeeping missions, which at certain times had backed the secessionists' advance, were transformed into joint border-control forces. In March 2015, President Putin and the South Ossetian president Leonid Tibilov signed a Treaty of Alliance and Integration, which abolished the institutional procedures of a state border between Russia and South Ossetia in the frame of a 'single space'.[132] In April 2016, Tibilov confirmed that South Ossetia was preparing a popular vote on joining the Russian Federation. By this move (which at the time of writing has been postponed, the initial plan was to organize the vote in summer 2016), South Ossetia is likely to formally join the family of its 'twin-sister' – North Ossetia-Alania – from which it had initially been separated by Soviet administrative structures. On its territory some 1,500 Russian border guards will oversee the Russian Federation's border with Georgia.

In contrast to South Ossetia's treaty on 'alliance and integration', Russia and Abkhazia signed and ratified an Alliance and Strategic Partnership Treaty in January 2015. Based on this treaty, Abkhazia's participation in the integration processes of the former Soviet subjects occurs on the initiative and with the assistance of the Russian Federation. Abkhazia's initial request to become an 'associate member' in the Russian Federation is realized through the creation of jointly controlled outer borders and the harmonization of its economy and social sector with Russia's North Caucasus Federal District. In its treaty frame this arrangement is much like the confederation that Abkhazia had sought with Georgia, but in this case 'equality' is clearly only formal in nature due to the differences in size and resources. The diplomatic language of 'friendship', 'mutual trust' and 'good neighbourliness' is a sign of a formal 'horizontality', and good relations between Russian representatives and the president and his cabinet members are guarantees for the continuity of policies. Simultaneously, in Abkhazia just like in South Ossetia, Russia has adopted a policy of not forcing the local governments to choose its candidates but instead settling with 'second-best' options, although obstacles have been created for those not approved by Russia.[133] By avoiding a practice of visibly promoting its own favourite candidates Moscow has increased local rulers' legitimacy and thus also eased its own relations with the political entities it has helped to create.

The establishment of bilateral military relations has enabled the stationing of Russian military bases in the new entities and, in this way, solved the problem created by its withdrawal from Georgia. In Abkhazia Russia's seventh military base – 7th Krasnodar Red Banner Order of Kutuzov and Red Star military base stationed in the Gudauta and Ochamchira districts, respectively – took up operation on the basis of Russia's agreement with Abkhazia signed in September 2009, and its troops became a part of the Maykop brigade stationed in Adygeya.[134] The military command structure of this base, and likewise the base in South Ossetia, was subordinated to the headquarters of the Southern Military District in Rostov-on-Don.[135] An agreement on 'a joint Russian base on the territory of the Republic of Abkhazia' was concluded on 17 February 2010. In August 2010 Russia announced that the Gudauta base would host long-range missiles, and by 2013 the seventh military bases in Gudauta and Ochamchira were furnished with a full range of forces – air, ground and naval equipment. The total number of the troops there amounted to a division, that is, about 4,000 troops. The base includes a battalion of BM-21 'Grad' MLRS (Multiple Launch Rocket System) and a regiment of strategic air defence missiles (S-300PS).[136] Missiles with a range that can reach any target in Georgia were soon also introduced in the fourth military base in South Ossetia. This base, which has compounds in Java and in the vicinity of Tskhinvali, is equipped with multiple rocket launchers (Smerch) and a battalion of missiles (Tochka-U) capable of causing heavy infrastructural damage. The troops at the fourth base in South Ossetia are motorized infantry brigades and calculated to number over 3,000. This equipment is mainly intended to deter possible attacks by conventional forces from the Georgian side. Like the S-300PS stationed in Gudauta, Tochka-U are also technically fitted to allow the instalment of nuclear warheads.[137] However, the significance of this fact is more political than military because Russian strategic missiles can easily reach Georgia from the Russian side of the border (the 58th Army in North Ossetia-Alania).

4

Russia in Georgia: Unhappy Policies and the Misfortunes of the Time

Georgia reportedly started the war, but it was NATO's advances in Georgia and Russia's own failures to come to terms with Georgia which generated the war. Russia's failures, again, had much to do with its weakness during the 1990s and the brittleness of its southern borders. Paradoxically, it was the ethnically and politically multifactional groups of the 'Mountain Peoples' who ultimately derailed the troubled Russia–Georgia relations. During a crucial period in the mid-1990s they tied Moscow's hands by supporting Abkhaz independence. Consequently, the quasi-independence gained through the war in 2008 by Abkhazia and South Ossetia was not the settlement prioritized by Russia; instead, it was a political 'last resort'. In August 2008 Russia solved its post-Soviet security dilemma in relation to Georgia through arrangements that re-established its vertical power in an interstate relations format by recognizing the independence of the separatist regions. The Geneva talks, which started their first rounds in November 2008 on the basis of point 6 of the ceasefire agreement negotiated by the OSCE, EU and Russia to end the war of the preceding August, froze the conflict at a new level. The talks, which include Russia, Georgia, Abkhazia, South Ossetia and the United States, and in which the UN, the OSCE and the EU act as co-chairs, are politically incapable of discussing a resolution. Instead, they concentrate on solving specific problems – such as enabling economic and social interaction across the present de facto borders, providing humanitarian assistance and preventing violent incidents – in order to accommodate the situation that has developed since separation in August 2008. Yet, the problems which directly derive from the conflict – the question of the return of more than 200,000 people ('internally displaced persons', of whom more than one-third had fled to Georgia before August 2008) and an agreement on the non-use of force – cannot be dealt with in the present structure of the conflict. Because Georgia refuses to make formal agreements with its regions, and because Russia emphasizes the importance of agreeing about the non-use of force in such a format, the only way to maintain negotiations and prevent undesirable developments is to concentrate on politically low-priority humanitarian issues.

The approach of institutionalizing the conflict and concentrating on practical issues in the situation that pertains is common in international conflicts, and the negotiations which Russia supported between Tbilisi and Abkhazia during earlier phases of the conflict also display these features. In these last-mentioned negotiations representatives of Georgia and its separatist regions were invited to rounds of negotiations in Moscow and in Sochi, and working groups were established to solve specific problems, including the tens of thousands who had fled the violence and settled elsewhere in Georgia and in Russia.[138] The difference here is that while these earlier negotiations, which had some success during the second half of the 1990s, were a way for Russia to retain control over an unpredictable situation, the Geneva negotiations are about the 'residual problems' following Moscow's resolution of the problematic situation. When South Ossetia joins the Russian Federation, the residual character of the issues will be even more manifest and there is little that the normative international community will be able to do about these conflicts as long as the larger one of the two de facto states, Abkhazia, remains dependent on Russia – and this will be the case for as long as it lacks international legitimacy as a state.

Preparing the ground for setting new rules

Although Moscow's decision makers can make seemingly abrupt turns in policies, such turns also require preparation for their political backing in the State Duma to ascertain the popular support necessary to increase legitimacy domestically as well as the justification of Russian policies outside the country. Because in Russia official 'civil society' is largely organized and led by the Federal Assembly through institutions such as the Civic Chamber (*Obshchestvennaia palata*), these discussions are an important sign of the range of policy options envisioned by Russian policy makers. The State Duma has served as the main forum at which delegations from the separatist regions and de facto states have been able to communicate with official Russia. In December 2006, parliamentary delegations of the 'Republic of Abkhazia, the Pridnestrovskaia Moldavskaia Respublica and the Republic of South Ossetia' in a joint declaration called upon the international community to recognize their independence based on the results of the referenda of the respective regions ('nations') and the principle of self-determination. The declaration was given in the frame of the Commonwealth for Democracy and Rights of Nations (also known as the Community for Democracy and Human Rights), which had been established earlier that year and already agreed in

2001. This community of unrecognized de facto states includes the three aforementioned entities as well as Nagorno-Karabakh. In June 2007, all four de facto states issued a further joint declaration in which they took note of 'a new model of conflict settlement in Serbia and Montenegro, Cyprus, Kosovo and other conflict zones'. The declaration made reference to the 'will of the people of Abkhazia, Nagorno-Karabakh, Transnistria and South Ossetia' as demonstrated in popular referenda and emphasized the need to resolve these conflicts by peaceful means and by constructing a system of guarantees with international legal and economic arrangements for post-conflict settlement. Guarantees for the security of peoples and human rights were also requested.[139] By demonstrating the 'will of the people' and emphasizing their adherence to international norms, the de facto states seek to bolster legitimacy for the recognition of their independent existence.

Later in March 2008 – after Kosovo had declared independence in February – the State Duma adopted a Declaration on the policy of the Russian Federation in relation to Abkhazia, South Ossetia and Transnistria.[140] The declaration proposed that President Putin and the government should search for a sovereignty option for Abkhazia and South Ossetia and that this might ultimately result in the recognition of their independence. The declaration, which had been prepared by Duma Speaker and then-chairman of the United Russia Party Boris Gryzlov, emphasized that Russia should take this step immediately, if Georgia continued to actively work for its accession to NATO. During the preceding weeks, speeches were recorded in the Duma in support of a policy according to which the recognition of the independence of the two breakaway regions would serve the purpose of establishing a buffer zone (*bufernaia zona*) in case Georgia joined NATO. It would enable a military agreement between Russia and the two regions and, on this basis, permit the fortification of Russia's forces on the spot in case Georgia resorted to aggression.[141] Against this background, it did not come as a surprise in Moscow when later in May, as the conflict between Georgia and its breakaway republics became more and more aggravated, the Ministry of Defense ordered troops in Abkhazia and South Ossetia to act as the situation demanded.[142] The peacekeeping operation had been transformed into a more heavily equipped peace-making concept already months before the war. However, although Russia had started to reformulate the rules to follow, according to its own explanations, Western policies in Kosovo, it was not until Georgia started to use open violence in Tskhinvali that these rules were played out. The atrocities that could be reported provided Russia's military intervention with clear domestic support in spite of the fact that the war itself was deplored. The 'voice of the people', which had been expressed in the repeated referendums in the regions and their appeals to Moscow, could then be emphasized; the way was paved for a quick turn of policy in favour of the principle of self-determination under the specific circumstances that had unfolded and away from the policy of emphasizing the intact borders of sovereign states.

The problem that Russia might be manoeuvring itself into a trap by playing by old rules while NATO continued its approach towards its borders was building up over the period of two decades. Russia prepared its own policies for a possible need to change the rules by planning the course of action it took in August 2008 as one possible 'variant' (option) of policies. In the Russian foreign and security policy experts' journal *Russia in Global Affairs* Ivan Kotlyarov argued in autumn 2008 that lives could have been saved in the war in August had Russia aired its statement at an earlier date (it did so on 8 August) that the Russian army would protect the people of South Ossetia. Had it done so Saakashvili may have had second thoughts.[143] Russia, in fact, had sent this message through its passport policies, which had encouraged especially the Abkhaz population to acquire a Russian passport. It had used such vertical policies but refrained from articulating any statements, which could have discouraged Georgian decision makers. Later, in 2014 in Ukraine, Russia followed the line of policy suggested by Kotlyarov. Already before the acting President Oleksandr Turtshinov on 11 April declared that the occupation of government buildings in the cities of eastern Ukraine would be resisted by all forces, Russia had announced that it would defend the occupiers, whose cause was emphasized to be no less legitimate than that of the Maidan protesters in Kiev some weeks earlier. This airing of intention was confirmed by President Putin's statement of 17 April 2014, which, based on the decision of the Federation Council, announced that Russian troops could be ordered to enter Ukraine if needed, as well as by Foreign Minister Sergey Lavrov's remark in an interview a few days later to the effect that this need could rise if 'the interests of Russians have been attacked directly, like they were in South Ossetia for example'.[144] The fact that Putin later softened this policy as a positive gesture towards the West does not diminish the significance of such signs, which tell about the range of possibilities considered in Moscow as well as about the space available for quick decisions in the Kremlin.

Concluding remarks and further questions

The presence of Russian troops under a peacekeeping mandate, together with the Soviet military infrastructure that was in place in Georgia until 2007, consolidated Russia's predominant position in its negotiations with

Georgia and made it possible to shift the axis of collaboration from the secessionists to Tbilisi and back. Simultaneously the diplomatic approach, which since the late 1990s had emphasized the need to have voices of both conflict parties at the negotiation table, enabled Moscow to avoid definite commitments. From the point of view of Tbilisi, the policy which avoided definite commitments undermined any possibility of trust. After almost two decades of a troubled relationship, Saakashvili became a very clear symbol in Moscow of an unfriendly neighbour and traitor who invites a rivalling military power to Russia's border in a region where the Russian state is under threat of being crumbled apart from within. Rules were then reversed and the two de facto states became Russia's primary, state-level relations, whereas relations with Georgia after August 2008 were maintained by making this country a locus for 'people-level' contact. President Medvedev announced that 'Russia has always been and continues to be attached to centuries-long traditions of good neighborly relations and camaraderie with our friends, the Georgian people.'[145]

From Russia's perspective, the question of Georgia's future was from the start a question about the stability of its own borders and the development of security cooperation in the CIS frame. The protection of borders in the sense of historical spheres of habitual cooperation and collaboration for security purposes – the borders envisioned by the CIS cooperation agreed in December 1991 – is not easily made legitimate through the norms of the modern international community. At the point of collision in 2008 the situation, where Saakashvili could represent the 'tyrant' who resorted to aggression against his own people and, according to Russia, thereby undermined the territorial integrity of his country, served to remove Russia's normative problem in starting the military intervention. Although this could easily resonate with sentiments of solidarity with the smaller peoples of the Caucasus still held in memories of a not all-too-distant past by many in Russia, the same argumentation could not satisfy the universalist criteria of international community. 'Genocide' in its context-free (universalist) sense is a matter of magnitude and systematic nature of action, whereas Russia had argued from its own experience of the violence that had pertained in previous phases of the conflict. In the light of the universalist criteria of criminality, it was illogical to summon figures from the past as evidence for a present case, especially when previous violence had been sporadic and part of the disruption caused by dismantling Soviet structures; they were not of Saakashvili's making. In Russia's argument, they were not *yet* so, because Saakashvili was seen to repeat the harsh nationalist-minded suppression of small nations and ethnic groups remembered from Gamsakhurdia's times and earlier.

In Russia's diplomatic communications, the seemingly context-free argument about necessity ('the only possibility', 'the last resort') intertwined with a sense of historical privilege and duty. Once the ceasefire had been agreed, President Medvedev argued at a press conference with Germany's Chancellor Angela Merkel on 15 August 2008 that the Ossetians and Abkhaz were only able to trust the Russian peacekeepers and that this was the case because of their previous experience. The events of the last fifteen years had shown them that 'the Russian peacekeepers are the only force able to protect their interests and often their very lives'.[146] Thus, only Russian troops had the position to offer *locally acceptable security guarantees*; a circumstantial factor that other states were to take into account. Medvedev also reminded the world that when Kosovo rejected the participation of peacekeepers under UN mandate and asked for peacekeeper units formed on the basis of a special European Union mandate, this request was met.[147] Russia refused to accept Kosovo's independence as a special case but made it a rule for the consideration of similar cases. This rule was ultimately not about self-determination but about the possibility of using this principle to consolidate its border zone, and to try to do this justifiably, with a moral sense of the 'right' and, moreover, to try to do this legitimately within the frames of the accepted rules of the normative international community.

In hindsight, Russian decision makers, politicians and experts have celebrated Russia's 'victory' – and Putin's personal resolve as then-prime minister – in being able to 'draw a line' in front of NATO.[148] Such arguments, which claim that Russia's actions in August 2008 were about strategic relations between great powers, demonstrate a politically instrumental 'bias of the present' in the interpretation of the series of events that led to the war. Saakashvili and NATO, together, were the match that lit the fire once the conditions were there (Georgia's attack on Tskhinvali) to justify it, but the material that was so easily ignited was made of the instability and insecurity of Russia's borders in the entire Caucasus region and along the Black Sea coast. Georgia is directly on the Russian borderline, and it is located in the region where Russia's internal and external security is more intertwined than anywhere else. During the first decade of this post-Soviet conflict, Moscow remained unconvinced that Georgia, which was torn by nationalism and separatism and lacked economic resources for development and strengthening its own military forces, could become a country strong enough to contain these tensions. Later on it also became clear that Russian peacekeeping (as formulated in the MFA by Foreign Minister Andrei Kozyrev and implemented by his successor Evgenii Primakov) did not provide a working interim solution in Georgia's political climate of nationalism. But whilst the separatists were instrumental in pressuring Georgia by affecting

Moscow's relations with Tbilisi, Moscow's wavering policies frustrated Georgia, who instead invited the United States and NATO to offer to train Georgia's military and jumpstart its modernization. NATO entered the scene as a side product of failed Russia – Georgia relations – with the result that it, in 2008, became Russia's acutest problem with Georgia.[149]

Five years after the war Russian experts could argue: 'Only massive supplies of modern equipment to Georgia from NATO member states could change the situation' so that Georgia could militarily threaten its separatist regions and their supporter, Russia, who by now had newly established military bases in Abkhazia and South Ossetia.[150] By 2013 Russia's military weight in the region had shifted towards Armenia and Abkhazia. Although Abkhazia after August 2008 needed to drop its earlier goal of becoming a neutral, demilitarized republic, such hopes are still actively maintained in Russia in regard to Georgia. In an interview given by President Medvedev on 26 August, on the day Russia recognized the independence of South Ossetia and Abkhazia, he re-emphasized that if NATO did decide to open its membership plan to Georgia, Russia 'will not be happy, of course, and this certainly would increase the tension'.[151] In the military sense the relationship between the two countries had become such that a military-political analyst in Russia could argue: 'Any normal person understands that Georgia will be able to return to them [the separatist regions] only in the event of the collapse of Russia as a state. Unfortunately, this option cannot be ruled out, but its realization does not depend on Georgia. If Russia survives, Abkhazia and South Ossetia never and under no circumstances [will] return to Georgia.'[152] The argument that the two small political entities are part of the constitution of Russia means that they are not merely symbolic signs of Russia's power outside of its borders but signs of Russia's own survival or demise. In this sense, they are iconic signs of the solidity of Russia's borders and the unity of the country. By setting up the two quasi-states and tying them closely to the cooperation of its own regions, Russia has solved its border security dilemma with Georgia through institutional arrangements which firmly consolidate its deep borders inside Georgia's internationally recognized borders. These borders are 'deep' because the bilateral arrangements which Russia has made with the two separatist regions following the war in August 2008 interlock Russia's efforts to secure stability on its state borders with the long-term struggle of the Ossetians and the Abkhaz for greater independence from Georgia. They institutionalize the historical relationship of collaboration and protection which Russia has had especially with the Ossetians but also with the ethnically diversified population in Abkhazia. Although the two quasi-states have strong symbolic significance for Russia's capability to avert the threat of NATO's direct presence on the other side of Russia's border, they have deeper, 'existential' significance as part of Russia's efforts to avert the threat of crumbling borders.

Although Transnistria, in 1992, was a more burning issue for Moscow than South Ossetia at that time, it later came to exemplify the conflict, which, out of all the 'frozen' conflicts, was imagined to be the easiest to resolve. In Transnistria, which does not share a border with Russia, Russia's interest about border security is not as acute as it is in South Ossetia and Abkhazia. The following chapters in Part Two of this book ask what is it that keeps Russia so deeply interested in this small piece of land and seek an answer to this question by identifying the course charted by Russia's settlement policies in this country. Because the developments in the conflict in Moldova are very different in comparison to the issues in Georgia's separatist conflicts after autumn 2008, Part One and Part Two do not unfold the three themes of the study with the same points of emphasis in their discussion. Instead of beginning with a discussion of Russia's problems in trying to legitimate its action towards the international community (which is the starting point in Part One), Part Two begins with an examination of the complex political and historical relations through which Moldova is connected to Russia while it also seeks closer relations with the West. As Moldova's 'external' relations with Russia are interlinked with the political and cultural conflicts inside the country, this focus also leads the study to examine the historical dividing lines and legitimacy issues which these dividing lines actualize as Moldova's future is being discussed in its domestic and international contexts. The initial emphasis of the specific features of each conflict makes it possible to avoid interpretations where the discussion of one conflict defines the form of the discussion of another conflict. This makes it possible to avoid *a priori* assumptions, such as the notion of Russia's 'legitimacy problem', which goes together with the principled normative idea of international relations as being relations between sovereign states and, consequently, entails a theoretical *a priori* not in harmony with the pragmatist approach of this book.

Part Two

Dealing with Divided Moldova: Failed Resolution and Russian Policies of Vertical Power

5

The Political Split: Towards a New Future with Old Lines of Division

The Transnistrian Moldavian Republic (*Pridnestrovskaia Moldavskaia Respublica*, PMR) declared independence on 2 September 1990. It is active in organizing international conferences in which researchers and practitioners from Russia, Ukraine, South Ossetia, Abkhazia, Nagorno-Karabakh and the PMR are convened in Tiraspol to develop their mutual cooperation and to support the aspirations of the four separatist regions to be recognized as sovereign states. A major conference organized for the PMR's 20th anniversary in 2010 called upon the UN and emphasized that the PMR's creation was based on the free will of the population to realize its right to self-determination.[153] In a referendum held in December 2001, 98 per cent of Transnistrian voters were reported to support independence. In another referendum arranged in September 2006, voter turnout was reported to be 97.1 per cent; and 94.4 per cent of the votes were cast in support of Transnistria's 'independence and subsequent free entry into the Russian Federation'.[154] In reference to these figures, Tiraspol has demonstrated its 'own voice' in reconfirming its plans to pursue independence with the goal of joining the Russian Federation. However, although the self-styled 'the will of the people' has been demonstrated by the local authorities in Transnistria even more consistently than in the case of the Crimea, where annexation to Russia was legitimized by a single referendum organized in March 2014, Russia has chosen to let the situation persist. It has signalled its support by recognizing the legitimacy of the 2006 referendum in a resolution in the State Duma only weeks later (on 6 October 2006) but refrained from showing direct political support to the pleas of Transnistria's politicians and activists.[155]

In the Republic of Moldova, which the PMR considers another state, the parliamentary elections of April 2009 brought to an end eight years of communist rule. Before this, Moldovan politicians in power had looked mainly eastward, and most were party functionaries from the Soviet times. In autumn 2009 a new liberal coalition government formed by the parties in the Alliance for European Integration began to pursue Moldova's integration with the European Union. Moldova's policy experts soon discovered common ground with the opinions in the Union which argued that Moldova could become the model country for demonstrating the success of the Eastern Partnership policy, which the Union had launched that spring. Although it was obvious that Moldova's road to Europe would be burdened with deep-cutting reforms, the country with only 3.5 million people (4 million including Transnistria) was considered a tiny piece to integrate into the EU, especially in comparison with its neighbour Ukraine (42.5 million people). Unlike Belarus (the third Eastern European country targeted by the EU's Partnership policies), Moldova had set itself on the road to Europe, and in comparison with Georgia (which was included in the Eastern Partnership policies along with Armenia and Azerbaijan), it was both geographically and culturally closer to Europe. However, while Chisinau's liberal policymakers applauded the historic opportunity offered by the European Union and carried through a significant number of the reforms in just a few years, they failed to do two crucial things: to eradicate corruption in the political system and to renew the judicial sector.

In late autumn 2014, after Moldova's liberal governmental coalition reconstituted itself following elections in November and gained confirmation for the path it had taken by signing the Association Agreement with the EU in June, the coalition was embroiled in a large-scale corruption scandal. The disappearance of a sum exceeding US$1 billion – amounting to 12–20 per cent of Moldova's GDP – from the country's three largest banks destroyed the idea of Moldova as the 'model state' for European reforms and evoked the image of Moldova as a 'mafia state', a 'capture state', in which the state is a source for elites to gain resources.[156] In January 2016, the Democratic Party led by Vladimir Plahotniuc, an oligarch-businessman, assumed governmental power and a less controversial person, Pavel Filip, became the prime minister. The following year saw Igor Dodon, the leader of the Socialist Party, in the president's office. The political field was reorganized for a new battle about controlling the legislative body (the parliament), and this was done with three different agendas: the European integration promoted by the Liberal Democratic Party and its allies in the liberal coalition, the argument of the 'centre-right' Democratic Party that Moldova has to cooperate with both Russia and the EU, and the policy of the Socialist Party that Moldova must altogether annul the agreement with the EU and, instead, join the Eurasian Economic Union.[157] In this flux of events the EU could do little other but to tighten its purse strings and to re-emphasize the necessity of reforms in the judicial sector and public administration. When the Moldovan parliament in July 2017 changed the electoral code from the proportional system to a combination of this system and a uninominal system (i.e. single-mandate territorial constituencies), the Union gave its support to Moldova's liberal political forces who were the losers in the new system.[158] However, although Moldova seems to be changing rapidly from Brussels' point of view, the change in Moldova is not so abrupt. During the past two to three years frustrations had already grown over the Union's European Neighbourhood Policy (ENP) that promised 'more for more' yet without providing institutions – in other words, without providing Moldova with a tangible and reliable long-term perspective for membership in the foreseeable future.[159]

From the start Moldova's path to Europe was additionally burdened by the problem of Transnistria,[160] which has strained its entire existence as an independent state. Although Moldova's liberal coalition government in September 2009 immediately signalled its determination to bring to an end Transnistria's separation and, among other measures, established the office of a deputy prime minister with a dossier for reintegration,[161] the fact that the country was split into two state entities, one *de jure* and the other *de facto*, was an insurmountable obstacle in the country-wide implementation of the reforms required in principle by the EU–Moldova agreements. Although Transnistria has since 2006 been able to benefit from a series of schemes of trade preferences with the EU on the basis of special agreements, it has approached them as temporary trade arrangements and kept them separate from its clearly announced political goal to join Russia and develop economic cooperation with the Eurasian Economic Union.[162] Consequently, the European Union's attempts to facilitate the closing of the divide between the 'right bank' and the 'left bank' of Moldova – the areas controlled by the Republic of Moldova and the de facto state of the *Pridnestrovskaia Moldavskaia Respublica* (PMR), respectively – have been very little successful even if they have brought economic and social benefits to the population on both sides of the Dniestr River.

The political momentum of 'Europeanization' in the EU's Eastern Partnership policies has left very little space for understanding how such project in a country like Moldova brings to the forefront the issues relating to social and cultural lines of division. When the EU opened negotiations on the Deep and Comprehensive Free Trade Area (DCFTA) with Moldova in 2012, José Mañuel Barroso, the President of the European Commission, visited Chisinau. Barroso addressed the two thousand guests in the National Palace by emphasizing that the Moldovan people are European and 'belong to our family of nations'.[163] The country's efforts to implement a series of reforms were rewarded when he announced that an agreement on the liberalization of the visa regime could be signed earlier than expected, and that it could be signed together with the agreement on association and free trade at the EU's Eastern Partnership summit in Vilnius in November 2013. At that time less than 40 per cent of the population in 'right-bank' Moldova supported the policy that would lead the country to join the EU, while 60 per cent supported closer economic cooperation with Russia (in 2017, the last-mentioned figure was 57 per cent).[164] Chisinau's liberal forces, and Barroso as well, were painfully aware that the burden of the economic reforms might quickly turn the political tide and bring the Communists back to power.

However, the relation between agents and agenda is more complicated in the political rivalries in Moldova. The political direction towards the European Union had been adopted already under the previous regime, during the rule of the communist president Vladimir Voronin (2001–9).[165] The liberal forces who took power in 2009 considered this earlier phase to have been 'façade integration' and argued that while some formal criteria required by the EU had been fulfilled, substantive reforms, especially in the key sectors of political power, justice and home affairs, had failed to materialize.[166] Following a pattern typical of many post-Soviet leaders, Voronin had addressed both the East and the West in order to gain economic resources. Ideologically, his path was nationalist and 'centre-left'. After the liberals took governmental power in summer 2009 the Communist Party started to emphasize the need to maintain Moldova's sovereignty and independence in the light of the European Union's influence in the country. Because Moldova is a predominantly agricultural country without any significant modern infrastructure, it has little possibility to sustain itself economically without international trade. Thus, arguing against closer integration with the European Union means proposing integration with the organizations led by Russia – the CIS (Commonwealth of Independent States), the Customs Union established between Russia, Belarus and Kazakhstan in 2010, and the Eurasian Economic Union, which, prior to its inauguration in January 2015, existed as a plan to further develop this cooperation.

The argument of the President of the European Commission in Chisinau in 2012 appealed similarly to the Moldovans' sense of independence, although the whole point was sharply opposed to Voronin's: Political association and economic integration with the European Union, Barroso said, was 'a path which is intrinsically linked with another fundamental choice the country has made twenty-one years ago, that of being a fully independent, democratic and free nation'.[167] This political rhetoric argues that the Western organizations and institutions, in their expansion into the area of the former Soviet Union, in themselves signify democracy, the independence of the state and the freedom of the people. Barroso emphasized that the reforms, which require sacrifices from the population, are 'necessary for Moldova to fulfill the promises of its independence and to provide for its citizens the perspective of a better future'. He greeted his audience in the Moldovan language, which is essentially the same as the Romanian language, saying that this Latin language makes him 'feel at home' in the Republic of Moldova.[168] In the separatist conflict that started in September 1990 with the declaration of independence of the *Pridnestrovskaia Moldavskaia Respublica* and led to an internal war in spring 1992, language had been the element that (in 1989) ignited the conflict; and language has remained the main symbol of the country's cleaved identity. Barroso's speech went straight to the heart of this cleavage between 'Romanizing Moldova' and its Russian-language speakers.

As it later turned out, the political Association Agreement, which includes the DCFTA, was initialled in Vilnius in November 2013. It was signed in Brussels in June 2014 and ratified by the Moldovan Parliament only five days later. The DCFTA was implemented in September, ahead of its ratification by the European Parliament in November. The Agreement entered into force on 1 July 2016, based on a decision taken in May by the EU Foreign Affairs Council. Over the course of this process Moldova's domestic political field was transformed, although the lines of division remained unchanged. The discredited liberal parties (whose leading figures were Vladimir Filat and Mihai Ghimpu) were replaced by the Action and Solidarity Party (led by Maia Sandu) and the Civic Platform Dignity and Truth (led by Andrei Nastase), whereas in the pro-Russian wing Igor Dodon's Socialist Party took the place previously held by the Communist Party. The Socialist Party assumed the image of the opponent of both the 'Unire' movement (which favours some degree of unification with Romania) as well as the 'oligarchs', amongst whom it included both Plahotniuc and Filat.[169] In order to better understand the political and historical context which makes Moldova a 'cleft country' – to use Ivan Katchanovski's description of Moldova with the Huntingtonian term – this book will next discuss Moldova's complex position between Russia and the EU and the history that to this day divides the two banks of the Dniestr River.

Changing ties of political friendship

In the aftermath of the Russia–Georgia war of August 2008, Russia consistently signalled that the way in which it had concluded the separatist conflicts in Georgia was not part of its agenda for Transnistria (and also not for Nagorno-Karabakh). In spring 2009, two months before the elections that were to change governmental power in Moldova, Foreign Minister Sergey Lavrov emphasized in Chisinau that a comprehensive political accord 'must certainly rest on the fostering of trust and economic ties'.[170]

Russia reconfirmed its willingness to work for a political solution but also emphasized that the comprehensive approach that it promotes requires a sustained effort to maintain good economic relations. The message was that the development of economic cooperation with Russia and the CIS is expected to take place simultaneously to the advances that Moldova makes in its approach towards the EU. At that time, the Russian market consumed 48 per cent of Moldova's wine production and compensating markets were not in sight for this key export sector in spite of the fact that it is the focus of efforts to modernize Moldova's agriculture with the support of European financing institutions. A few years later, in 2013, the revenues from the migrant labour force (more than 400,000 people) in the Russian Federation constituted about 15 per cent of the GNP, and more than half of this labour force was assumed to be working in Russia illegally.[171] Moreover, the country's total dependence on energy deliveries from Russia has decreased only marginally,[172] and Transnistria's debt for Russian gas is an issue on the political agenda of reintegration. In 2010, when this debt exceeded US$2 billion, Gazprom began legal proceedings against Moldovagaz – of which it owns 65 per cent – over the US$300 million in unpaid gas bills, most of which were believed to stem from gas sent to Transnistria. Although a deal could be negotiated about this last-mentioned part (agreed to be Moldova's responsibility), it is a small portion in relation to Transnistria's debt, which by 2017 had risen to US$6 billion.[173] During their six years in power (2009–15, with six different prime ministers) Moldova's pro-European parties were not able to significantly alter the country's structural economic dependencies on Russia.[174]

Economic ties with Russia are not only structural but also habitual, and they are maintained through a shared culture and personal relations between political decision makers. When the Communist Party left government in 2009, its members started to describe the new parties in power as pro-Romanian and anti-Russian. However, it was with these new power-holders that Moscow now began to develop ties, and the 'Moscow card' still had relevance in Moldova's domestic political rivalries. Upon his return from Moscow in May 2010 Moldova's Acting President Mihai Ghimpu reported on his discussions with President Dmitry Medvedev by revealing that they 'not only spoke, but also drank and ate'.[175] The statement about the amicable atmosphere does not tell about the personal relations between the Russian president and the leader of Moldova's Liberal Party who after the re-elections in July 2009 became the Speaker of the Parliament and was chosen as Acting President a few weeks later. Instead, it is part of institutional policymaking and suggests negotiating in an environment of trust which, together with friendship, is a code word in Moscow for good relations between countries. A trusting relationship in this sense is a mutually conditional political friendship and means that the parties are prepared to be sensitive about the interests of the other party and do not take advantage of each other's vulnerabilities.[176] In this vein, failed expectations must entail some kind of 'punishment', such as withdrawal of support and setting up 'problems' to obstruct action. During the first two post-Soviet decades the vulnerabilities in the bilateral relationship affected mainly Moldova because of its economic dependence on Russia. However, as a consequence of the new political situation created by the re-elections of July 2009, Russia also became diplomatically vulnerable to a political unfriendliness resulting from negative use of the 'Russia card' in Moldova's domestic politics. The political gestures of Mihai Ghimpu show how relations with Russia in Moldovan politics are a positive resource as well as a strong negative identification. Unlike his predecessor Vladimir Voronin, Ghimpu stayed away from the Victory Day celebrations in Moscow in May 2010. Earlier that spring Moldova's new regime had established a committee to study and evaluate the damages resulting from what was called the 'Soviet occupation': they estimated this to amount to US$27.8 billion, a number that corresponded to that presented by the Baltic States. When the Federal Consumer Protection Service (*RosPotrebNadzor*) began to screen 'substandard' Moldovan wines in May, this act was widely considered as a political response to Moldova's demand for compensation for the damage caused by the Soviet Union.[177] The culmination in Moldova's new ideological distancing from Russia came in June, when Ghimpu decreed the date of 28 June as the 'Day of Soviet Occupation' on which mourning ceremonies would take place annually. The decree was meant to commemorate the Soviet invasion of eastern Romania and three quarters of present-day Moldova in 1940 (then based on the deal made in the Molotov–Ribbentrop Pact of August 1939) and to demand the withdrawal of Russian troops from the 'Transdnestr province'.[178] The Communists of the opposition took the question of the competence of an acting president to undertake such measures to the Constitutional Court, which annulled the decree within two weeks.

The symbolic action in the first years of liberal rule which demolished the signs of respect for the common history with Russia not only strained relations with Moscow but also tore apart the ruling coalition from within and deepened the political and social split of the country into pro-Romanian and pro-Russian parts of the population.[179] The political split was reflected in the presidential elections in autumn 2010, which resulted in yet another stalemate in the Moldovan parliament.[180] Marian Lupu from the Democratic Party became a second acting president, and it was not until March 2012 that the Parliament was able to elect Nicolae Timofti as a compromise candidate between the government parties and the political opposition. The permanent internal crisis and discord increased the influence of external factors, and both Russia and the EU – in terms of the values they symbolized and the financial support they provided – served as resources in the internal rivalries between the different political parties. Simultaneously the government was able to reinvigorate inter-governmental relations with Russia and started ministerial-level preparations to sign a programme on cooperation for the following three years (2011–13). Vladimir Filat, prime minister for four years (September 2009–April 2013) and the representative of the Liberal Democratic Party, was initially greeted as a 'pragmatic man' with whom political confrontation could be avoided and who would develop economic cooperation based on mutual benefits. In March 2010 the new Moldovan government ratified the Concept of the Further Development of the CIS, which Voronin had signed in 2007, and this was accomplished with the aid of 53 votes from the previously 'anti-Russian' governing majority; the Communists, who at this point of time were in the political opposition, however refused to participate in the discussion led by the liberal coalition. Although Prime Minister Filat emphasized that political relations with Russia were to be based on mutual trust and that the concept of strategic relationship, which Moscow proposed as the frame of the relationship, applied to the relations between the two countries, he also explained that the reason for such policies was to pursue 'balanced' policies in order to facilitate Moldova's path towards the EU.[181] The amenable political atmosphere and working economic relations that Chisinau was prepared to maintain with Russia did not indicate a willingness to engage in more substantive cooperation, and it definitely did not mean that Chisinau was prepared to negotiate a solution to the Transnistrian conflict on Russia's conditions.

Moldovans' deep desire for change was the thrust which the liberal parties were able to use in the elections of 2009, and it also was the thrust that their political opponents were able to use in the wake of the popular protest that these parties faced over the corruption charges. Now, if we consider 'change' not in terms of the change represented by the replacement of one ruling party's (or party coalition's) political programme by another but, instead, approach it from a wider perspective that focuses on the way in which political change takes place in a country divided by constant political rivalry, we are able to recognize continuity beneath superficial change. A movement away from the liberal right to the political centre and left, which from the liberals' point of view may look like a move 'back' ('backward'), is not a singular event but an episode in a longer process. It is under such conditions that we understand how it is that Moscow has built its axis of cooperation in Chisinau in two ways: on the one hand, it has supported the pro-Russian opposition parties who represent themselves as the forces of change and, on the other hand, it has simultaneously cooperated with the centrist political forces which, in the government, represent continuity and stability. Already during the liberal coalition government (2009–14) the Democratic Party (formerly Democratic Agrarian Party) became the basis on which Russia built a working relationship with Chisinau. When this party became the leading government party in July 2015, it demonstrated the intention to actively maintain a friendly political relationship which, from Moscow's point of view, is the kind of political context in which a solution to the conflict over Transnistria can be actively sought. A new three-year humanitarian cooperation programme, which includes measures to support the Russian language in Moldova, was welcomed in Moscow as a sign of a direction which could also solve the problems which Moldova's Association Agreement with the EU had brought in trade relations with Russia.[182] The Democratic Party's centre-right political orientation emphasizes the need to maintain relations with both Russia and Western states in much the same way as did the centre-left rule of the Communist Party during 2001–9. It is important to see this continuity even if Moldova, after the Maidan events in Ukraine in late autumn 2013, has become a battleground for geopolitical rivalries in terms of the indirect influence exerted by both Russia and Western states and, as a consequence, has an external environment very different from that of the 2000s.

The Communist leadership 2001–9

From early spring 2001 until summer 2009, the Communist Party had full control of Moldova – the president, the parliament, the government and also the main sectors of business and key positions in the judicial system. The party gained governmental power with policies that openly proclaimed its pro-Russian stance and its activity in the government focused on establishing bilateral contractual relations with Moscow. When power changed hands in 2009, about one hundred and sixty agreements existed on the governmental and inter-departmental levels. However, this did not mean that the Communist Party and President Vladimir Voronin, a former Soviet Interior Ministry general, could be said to have served Moscow. Voronin's communism was not a Soviet-type ideology but a nationalist line of policies, as is often the case with communist parties in the former Soviet republics, and he had a serious conflict with Russia: Transnistria. In 2003 the Kremlin appointed a special representative, Dmitri Kozak, to negotiate the settlement of the conflict over Transnistria. In the last hours before the intended signing ceremony in November of that year, Voronin rejected the negotiated agreement because of domestic opposition and Western pressure. The failure of the agreement, which had been expected to lead to a breakthrough in the conflict, was a major diplomatic humiliation for Russia and caused it to freeze its relations with Chisinau for several years. One year later, that is, in the year before the parliamentary elections of 2005, the Communist Party made a full U-turn in its foreign policy and, contrary to the preferences expressed by Voronin during his presidential campaign, it decided to keep Moldova out of the Russia–Belarus Union. Moreover, the Communist Party did not favour the privatization and the economic modernization programmes that were required from the point of view of the prospects for either European or Russian-led integration. During Moldova's parliamentary elections of 2005 Russian state-controlled media openly supported Voronin's political opponents, first and foremost the party alliance 'Our Moldova' and the mayor of Chisinau, Serafim Urekian. Unlike in the era of the Soviet Union, a communist party was no longer automatically the 'privileged partner' in the political power vertical, and new lines of friendship were pursued.

Moldova's relations with Russia reached a nadir in March 2006 when Russia, which at that time imported 60–80 per cent of the wine produced in Moldova, imposed a ban on Moldova's wine and selected agricultural products. In 2006 (and likewise in 2013 and 2014) Russia justified its heavy-handed policy by claiming that serious impurities had been discovered in Moldovan products.[183] In Moldova this was interpreted to be a response to a series of customs regulations introduced by Moldova, among them a Moldovan–Ukrainian agreement made in 2006 that required goods from Transnistria to show certificates issued in Chisinau.[184] In February 2005, Voronin's administration had signed a three-year Moldova–EU Action Plan, and in November of that year Moldova and Ukraine had agreed to accept the European Union's Border Assistance Mission (EUBAM) on the Ukraine–Moldova border, which includes Transnistria's 453-kilometre-long borderline with Ukraine.[185] Additionally, in August 2005 the Moldovan government had issued a decree on the regulation of traffic, by means of which it intended to overwrite the PMR's system of rules and regulations for enterprises in Transnistria. When this decree entered into force in March 2006, Ukraine, where Victor Yushchenko had risen to the presidency in the wake of the 'Orange Revolution' (November 2004–January 2005), supported the Moldovan measures by controlling the transactions of Transnistrian economic agents at its border and by increasing the pressure on these enterprises to register and pay taxes in Chisinau. As a result of these coordinated measures Transnistria became totally dependent on Russia's economic support. This 'trade war' had already started in early autumn 2001, when Moldova adopted a new policy which deprived Transnistria of the right to use its customs seals in export-import operations. In spring 2006 Russian media described the chain of events that related to the customs regulations as an 'economic stranglehold' over Transnistria. Russia supported the PMR in its protests against the 'economic blockade' which, it was argued, was causing a 'humanitarian disaster' and 'humanitarian catastrophe' in the region. Four years later, after the presidency had changed in Ukraine and presidents Viktor Yanukovich and Dmitry Medvedev were about to meet in Kiev on 17 May 2010, the rumour was spread that the border would be opened and the 'economic isolation of Transdniestria' would come to an end. The Tiraspol leadership hailed this as a sign of support.[186] Such measures were not mentioned in the joint declaration of 17 May of the two presidents on the resolution of the conflict in Transnistria;[187] however, a set of measures that impacted the economic transactions across the border were adopted in order to clearly make the point that Moldova's attempts to control economic flows through administrative measures in Chisinau could not be effective without the cooperation of both the PMR and Russia.

The embargo set by Moscow on Moldovan wine products, other agricultural and meat products during 2006–7 had severe effects on Moldova, which has little industrial infrastructure other than in Transnistria. By the beginning of 2010 Moldova was able to restore only 12 per cent of its previous share of the Russian market. When the wine embargo was reintroduced in 2013, it explicitly excluded Transnistrian companies. Chisinau's relations with Moscow had already been restored before Voronin's rule ended in summer 2009 (in 2006 Putin and Voronin met for the first time since late autumn 2003), and in spring 2009 Voronin could bring back from Moscow a 'gift' of 50,000 tons of Russian fuel to be distributed as 'humanitarian aid' to farmers to facilitate the sowing of crops that spring. In June, Voronin was promised a US$500 million loan from Moscow, but the sum soon shrank to 150 million and was no longer mentioned as the events relating to Moldova's re-elections the following month unfolded. After the election, in autumn 2009, the financial support promised by Moscow was very small in comparison with the US aid which began to flow in as a sign of support for the new government's European policies and cooperation with NATO.

Eight years of communist rule did not achieve much in terms of settling the conflict over Transnistria. It was not until April 2008 that Voronin met with Smirnov for the first time since 2001, and the meeting in Bender was a fiasco: Smirnov presented him with a draft Treaty on Friendship and Cooperation, which, already revealed by its title, meant recognition of the independence of Transnistria. Voronin's liberal opponents strongly believed that entering into these direct discussions with Tiraspol was a grave mistake by Voronin. In late April 2011 Smirnov invited Prime Minister Vladimir Filat to pay an 'official visit' to the Transnistrian Moldovan Republic, and Filat's reply through the media was that he was unable to pay an official visit to his own home country. The stalemate in the efforts to bridge the political chasm could only reinforce the historical lines of division which underlie the conflict as well as strengthen the social basis that Russia claims in its role as mediator and 'guarantor' for peace in Transnistria. The next chapter discusses the establishment of these historical lines of division in the region's geopolitical transformations over the course of two centuries.

6

Historical Background of the Political and Cultural Split

The border of present-day Transnistria with the area under Chisinau's control (see Map 2 on page 84) roughly corresponds to the western border of the Moldavian Autonomous Soviet Socialist Republic (MASSR), which was created in 1924, as well as the frontier set in a Russo-Ottoman agreement in 1792. With only a few exceptions, the area under the rule of the self-declared PMR has never been part of historical Bessarabia (the area which in contemporary Moldova is the 'right-bank' of the country) or the medieval principality of Moldova.[188] The exceptions are a number of villages and the city of Bender (Bendery),[189] which in the ceasefire agreement of July 1992 was placed under joint administration. The largest part of the 4,163-square-kilometre area controlled by the PMR has been connected to Russia and the Soviet Union ever since 1792.[190] It was then that the Dniestr River became the frontier which it still, today, represents: a geographic line that marks the political and cultural contrast between the 'right' and 'left' banks of the Dniestr.[191] This historical background explains why the 'left bank' (Transnistria) lacks the habitual ground for implanting Romanian cultural influences, the key symbol of which is the Romanian language. 'One cannot make our people live differently [...] We have Slavic roots; we will always be with Russia,' the self-proclaimed republic's leader Igor Smirnov declared in September 2010, when the Pridnestrovian Moldavian Republic celebrated its 20th anniversary.[192] Although such arguments serve political purposes, they cannot be addressed to Transnistrians without containing an appeal to this people's historical experience.

The Russian Empire extended its power from the Dniestr (Dniester) to the Prut River in 1812 as a result of a Alexander I's victory over the Ottomans in the region. The Empire gained control of the medieval Moldavian principality (roughly the area of present-day 'right-bank' Moldova, plus parts of Romania) and, along with the southwestern part of present-day Ukraine's Odessa region, these areas became the province (*guberniia*) of Bessarabia (Basarabia in Romanian[193]). Bessarabia remained within the Russian Empire until its collapse in 1917.[194] As a part of the transformations that followed the

Map 2 Moldova and its disputed regions (illustration by Ilkka Janatuinen; used with permission).

First World War, which in Europe included the dissolution of the Austro-Hungarian Empire, the Moldovan Republic was declared in Bessarabia in February 1918.[195] In 1920, the Parliament of the new republic decided to join the Kingdom of Romania, which already in 1859 had started out as a personal union between the western parts of Moldova and Valakia (southern Romania) and (from 1881 until 1947) had evolved with the aim of creating a 'Greater Romania'. After the First World War, 'Greater Romania' under the rule of the Kingdom of Romania grew to include not only Eastern Moldova (Bessarabia) but also Transylvania and Bukovyna (an area to the west of Moldova and divided between present-day Romania and Ukraine). The Soviet Union never recognized Romania's right to a region that was a former Russian province. In March 1924 Soviet authorities declared the narrow strip of Ukrainian land on the northeastern bank of the Dniester River to be the Moldavian Autonomous *Oblast'* and, seven months later in October, its status was elevated to the Moldavian Autonomous Soviet Socialist Republic (ASSR) within the Ukrainian Soviet Socialist Republic (SSR).[196] In this way, the Transnistrian strip of land was made into the territorial basis for the re-acquisition of Bessarabia.

Soviet authorities actively promoted the view that the Moldavian people were a separate nationality with an identity and language distinct from the Romanian language. Soviet administrative practices utilized the existing nationalist mood that opposed Romanian influences, but the frame in which this took place was Soviet-Russian, and a Cyrillic-based alphabet was institutionalized for writing the Moldovan language.[197] Cyrillic was extended to the 'right bank' after the Second World War, when the areas of Bukovyna and Bessarabia (in addition to the region between the Dniestr and the Prut rivers as well as the southern part of the Odessa region) were taken away from Romania and annexed to the Soviet Union by Soviet troops in June 1940 on the basis of the Molotov–Ribbentrop pact of August 1939. The Moldavian Soviet Socialist Republic (Moldavian SSR) was proclaimed on 2 August 1940, and the Transnistrian region, which in 1924 had been established as the Moldavian ASSR, became a part of it. Soviet control over the region was interrupted between June 1941 and August 1944 by Romanian rule (in alliance with Germany). After the Second World War Moldova was led by a communist party that was an integral part of the Communist Party of the Soviet Union. Moldovan nationalism did not disappear in this period but was, instead, developed as a cultural counterforce to Moldova's Romania-affiliated nationalism, and its main vehicle was the Moldovan (Romanian) language written in the Cyrillic alphabet.[198] The 'national' identity promoted in the PMR today – 'Moldavism' – is a contemporary incarnation of this multinational identity discourse from the Soviet era.[199] Its modern emphasis of cultural tolerance can be traced back to the policy of the tsarist Russia to treat the Romanian, Moldovan and Ukrainian populations under the common rubric of *rossiianye*, inhabitants of the empire. In the present time the broad picture is that Russians, Ukrainians and Moldovans each constitute roughly one third of Transnistria's 555,000 residents. In the region, which historically is a transit area, bio-ethnic dividing lines are mostly fused, and therefore the main marker of this identity is language.

Until the perestroika movement was launched in Moscow in the mid-1980s, Moldova's leaders represented the eastern parts of the country or came from other areas of the Soviet Union. The western part, where nationalist sentiments were stronger and intertwined with Romanian nationalism, did not have much of a voice.[200] Among the new political figures introduced during the perestroika years was Mircea Snegur, who became the first president of independent Moldova. The Popular Front, which was supported by the electorate on the right bank of the Dniestr River, evolved during the 1980s and became an influential, nationalist-minded force in parliament in the elections of 1990. The new political sentiments soon erupted over the issue of language. In August 1989 (i.e. two years before the declaration of independence) the Supreme Soviet of the Moldavian SSR adopted Moldovan, which is so close to Romanian that it is often called 'Romanian', as the sole official language and returned to the Latin alphabet. In the 'left-bank' region there was no equivalent movement; the electorate there supported strike committees and the United Council of Workers' Collectives instead.[201] The economic difference between the agricultural 'right bank' and the development of the 'left bank' as an industrial area strengthened the political and cultural differences between the two. The leadership of Transnistria's enterprises were connected to Moscow even when the region's administrative connections disappeared.[202]

In 1987 Igor Smirnov, who later took the position of president in Transnistria and remained in this position until December 2011, was allegedly sent to Moldova from Moscow to help generate a movement that would counterbalance the nationalist sentiments burgeoning in Chisinau. During the break-up of the Soviet Union speculation spread that Moldova might join Romania (just like the Bessarabian part of it had done in 1920); as a consequence, on 2 September 1990 five districts on the eastern bank of the Dniester River declared an autonomous republic of their own – the Dniestrian Moldavian Soviet Socialist Republic. A few months before this, in June 1990, the local 'red-directors' corps' had initiated a 'free economic zone' that was intended as a basis for pursuing the region's own economic interests. Chisinau refused to recognize the newly declared zone. In August 1990 a number of districts in southern Moldova, which were populated by the Turkic-speaking Orthodox Christian Gagauz, had declared the creation of the Gagauz Soviet Socialist Republic. The Gagauz have a historical background which makes their pro-Russian attitudes part of their identity. Under Romanian rule (1920–40, and June 1941–August 1944) the Gagauz were among the most impoverished groups, but they had benefitted much from the Soviet policy of mass education and economic development. In the decades after Bessarabia became part of the Russian Empire (in 1812), the Gagauz, who were descendants of a Turkic tribe, were resettled from today's eastern Bulgaria (then under Ottoman rule) to Orthodox Bessarabia, where they found protection under the rule of the Russian tsar.[203]

On the first days of September 1991, shortly after Moldova had declared state sovereignty on 27 August and only three months before the official dissolution of the Soviet Union, the PMR Supreme Soviet (*Verkhovnyi Sovet*) claimed independence from Moldova and thus reconfirmed the de facto secession declared in September one year earlier. It also voted in favour of making the region a part of the Soviet Union. It adopted a separate constitution and other institutions of independence, and it was claimed that its independence was confirmed in a referendum on 1 December. The decision makers of the new PMR argued that the legal basis for independence was the Soviet Constitution and its specification by a law from April 1990 which gave not only the republics but also the autonomous regions and similar distinct territories within the Soviet republics the right to secede from and to enter into a union state as independent subjects in the case that larger republics refused to sign such a union treaty.[204] Consequently, the PMR claims to have separated from Moldova at a time (September 1990) when the country had not yet declared independence; and it attempted to re-integrate with the Soviet Union at a point in time when that state structure had ceased to exist de facto.[205] Like also Abkhazia and Gagauzia, Transnistria voted for the maintenance of the Soviet Union in the March 1991 All-Union referendum on the future of the Soviet Union.[206] In Moscow the leaders of these regions were part of the conservative forces that supported the failed coup attempt in August 1991.[207] The Soviet Union was looked upon as a frame which would protect these smaller entities against the emerging regional power aspirations that were stirring up old rivalries in the region. Even today, the existence of Transnistria and Gagauzia is presented as a 'small people's' resistance to neighbouring nationalism (Romanism) that can survive only with the 'fraternal' help of Russia.[208] During the 1990s, when ideas about Soviet and Russian greatness were in tatters, the construction of such an identity was problematic; as opposed to this, the Russia–Georgia war (2008) and the annexation of the Crimea (2014) were seen in these regions as signs of Russia's recovered greatness. In Transnistria these events invigorated hopes that the region could also finally be able to join together with Russia. Amongst the Gagauz they increased the hope that this ethnic population, which on the brink of war in autumn 1991 had negotiated for itself the status of an autonomous territorial unit within the Republic of Moldova, could with Russian support find its way through the complexity caused by Moldova's European advances.[209] The next chapter discusses how Russia, through its policies and action since the early 1990s, has built for itself a position that enables it to provide this kind of support.

7

Russia's Policies to Settle the Conflict over Transnistria

Throughout 1991 the separatist opposition in the PMR led to armed clashes with Moldovan groups, and in spring 1992 the confrontation escalated into a short, but violent, civil war, which was mainly fought in and around the Bender and Dubossary areas. The intensive period of the war lasted from March to July and killed some seven hundred people on both sides of the conflict. The political aims of the Transnistrian leadership, who remained loyal to the old Soviet structures while the Soviet Union disintegrated instead of supporting the new Federation led by Boris Yeltsin, did not prompt much interest in Moscow. At the same time, Yeltsin chose to retain the remnants of the Soviet 14th Army, which had been stationed in the Moldavian SSR since the end of the Second World War, as part of the armed forces of the Russian Federation. Had the Kremlin chosen to make these troops, which amounted to about 9,600 (50 per cent of which were ethnic Russians) before the dissolution of the Soviet structures, swear an oath to the declared republic (thus following the pattern in Belarus), Transnistria's power basis would have been decisively strengthened in relation to the rest of the country. Because forces led by Chisinau were mainly police and other security forces and the army was developed with meagre resources, such a merging of the Soviet army with the Moldovan army would have supported the hard-line conservatives and probably prompted a civil war that would have been far more devastating than the one that occurred. This did not happen because, following the practice of the late-Soviet decades, Moscow sought to prevent by force the escalation of the conflict in a country that had become culturally and politically divided in the final years of the Soviet Union. Another reason is that this conflict, which is not ethnic in nature even though cultural and historical affiliation does play an important role, more directly reflects the union-level political forces at play during the dissolution of the Soviet Union than do the conflicts of the South Caucasus. More than a year after the ceasefire had been agreed upon in July 1992, the leadership in Tiraspol still supported the anti-Yeltsin opposition in the Moscow-White House (parliament) incidents of October 1993.

The fact that General Alexandr Lebed was sent to Transnistria in June 1992 to replace General Yury Netkachev, the Soviet commander of the remnants of the 14th Army, signalled that Russia was not considering withdrawing its troops from Transnistria in the short term. Lebed brought about a turning point in the war when he allowed the armoured units of the 14th Army to join the Transnistrian defenders of Bender on the historically Bessarabian side of the Dniestr and used this military pressure to force Chisinau to agree to a ceasefire on Moscow's terms.[210] While Russia's military presence added to Russia's leverage in the ceasefire negotiations, it also meant that it supported the de facto split. Lebed's advocacy of the political idea of restoring the 'strong state' in Russia was in harmony with the wishes of the leadership in Tiraspol to be supported by Moscow. Because Lebed initially had the strong support of Minister of Defense Pavel Grachev and his authority also was based on the popular support that he enjoyed throughout Russia, he was able to act relatively independently of the Kremlin as long as he could keep the conflict under control. The focus of the policies in the Kremlin and the foreign ministry was elsewhere, and in the case of Moldova it was on creating a working relationship with the newly independent Republic of Moldova led by Chisinau. This state was expected to join the union treaty, which was negotiated by Russia and Belarus during 1993–4 and signed in 1996. In the light of these expectations Transnistria, which was initially a matter of a state in which people affiliated with Russia and people affiliated with Romania could live together, also became a means to advance Russia's plans about wider regional cooperation.

Already during the period of fighting Russia tried to mobilize the newly established Commonwealth of Independent States (CIS) as a multilateral political frame for settling the conflict. In March 1992 the CIS heads of state met in Kiev and adopted a declaration which stated that the territorial integrity of the Republic of Moldova was the key element of stability in the region. Experts from Eastern Europe (including Romania and Hungary) participated in the attempts to create a wider international engagement for resolving the conflict. A few months later, in July, a ceasefire agreement was brokered by Russia and a three-party peacekeeping force (Russia, Moldova and the separatist region of Transnistria) was set up.[211] The Agreement on the Principles for a Peaceful Settlement of the Armed Conflict in the Dniester Region of the Republic of Moldova was signed in Moscow by presidents Boris Yeltsin and Mircea Snegur on 21 July 1992. Two weeks before this, at a CIS meeting in Moscow on 6 July, a decision had been taken to deploy a CIS peacekeeping force in which Russia, Ukraine, Belarus, Bulgaria and Romania would participate. This would be a preliminary arrangement for peace-keeping, should Moldova request it. Moldova did indeed make such a request, but this particular composition of peacekeeping forces was never deployed because all of these countries bar Russia were, in the end, unwilling to participate in the CIS joint effort. In June 1992, at a time of intense fighting in the Bender area, the Moldovan President Mircea Snegur appealed to the UN Security Council through the organization's Secretary-General. He also appealed to the Conference on Security and Cooperation in Europe (the predecessor of the OSCE) and a number of Western states in order to discuss matters of mediation and the international organization's role in peacekeeping.

However, the modest role that the Western states were prepared to give to Russia – and also Russia's belief that Western states showed only meagre interest in building common European security – made a mockery of any hopes of such wider international cooperation. The ceasefire was set as proposed by Moscow, and it established a borderline in the form of the security zone along the Dniestr River and its 'right embankment', which included the town of Bender. The agreement included three roles for Russia: as participant, mediator and guarantor of the settlement of the conflict and military stability in the region. Before the war in Moldova, Russia had signalled its readiness to adopt international peacekeeping practices, but the war that flared up in spring 1992 resulted in an emphasis on Russia's own policies. International peacekeeping was an idea especially supported by Foreign Minister Andrei Kozyrev during the formative period of the policies in 1993–4 and, later, by Evgenii Primakov (foreign minister from January 1996 to September 1998).[212] In February 1993 the CSCE Mission was established in Chisinau.[213] This was a sign that the Western states intended to make the peacekeeping format more genuinely multinational and to meet the standards of the UN and CSCE, including a clear definition of the terms of the mission.[214] In a sharp contrast to these aims, the bilateral agreement signed by Yeltsin and Snegur on 21 July 1992 gave Russia a central role by stipulating that the security zone on the right embankment of the Dniestr River was to be under the joint control of representatives of 'the three Parties involved in the settlement', i.e. the Russian Federation, the Republic of Moldova and the entity acknowledged as the Transnistria region of Moldova. The agreement further emphasized the role of Transnistria by stipulating that the implementation of the ceasefire agreement would be ensured by the military of the Russian Federation and the two parties directly involved in the conflict. The Russian military contingent was introduced to the conflict in the form of six battalions the following month.[215] In 2013, the Joint Peacekeeping Forces (also translated as 'Collective Peace Keeping Forces', which thereby invokes images of the intended CIS frame) included 400–450 personnel from the Russian Federation, 350–400 from the Republic of Moldova and 490–500 from the PMR. Additionally, ten military observers from Ukraine were included in the mission from 1998 onwards.[216]

Although the peacekeeping units have operated at checkpoints in three different sectors within the security zone, Russia and the PMR work together closely, which allows Tiraspol to maintain an upper hand in its military power in relation to Chisinau's forces.[217] About 50 per cent of the peacekeepers in the Russian sector are permanent residents of Transnistria. In addition to the troops operating within the peacekeeping format, the Russian presence in Transnistria includes units that are remnants of the Soviet 14th Army. In 1995 these units (now reorganized and downsized) were renamed the Operational Group of Russian Forces in Transnistria (abbreviated as OGRV in Russian).[218] By 1998–9, the manpower of the Russian troops (i.e. its peacekeeping forces and the OGRV) was decreased to fewer than 3,000 men (down from 9,600 during the last years of the Soviet Union), and by 2014 the total number had been further reduced to 1,500. These troops are located in Tiraspol, Bender, Dubossary and Colbasna, and the peacekeepers and the ordinary military both operate under the command of the Moscow Military District. In April 2012 Dmitry Rogozin, newly appointed as Russia's presidential envoy to Transnistria, announced that the military equipment in the region would be modernized by 2020 as part of the overall modernization of Russia's military. During his visit to Tiraspol on 16 April 2012, a new operational group within the military was established. This military reorganization was announced at a time when the EU had opened negotiations on the Deep and Comprehensive Free Trade Area (DCFTA) with Moldova and the United States was developing its missile-defence system in Poland and Romania, and it destroyed any hopes in Chisinau that the military equipment and ammunition depot in Transnistria could come to be regarded as mainly environmental problems left by the Soviet past in the near future.[219]

Although the conflict has remained politically deadlocked, lethal casualties have been rare and largely accidental since the end of armed encounters in July 1992.[220] Tensions rise each time when elections, voting and referenda take place, especially on the Transnistrian side, but attacks are generally verbal in nature. There have been 'school wars' over language issues, 'railroad wars' that cause economic blockages, rows over the unilateral opening of border crossing points and a contest over winning citizens by handing out Russian as well as Romanian passports. The lack of open violence and, in fact, of any large-scale mutual hostility between the populations on either side of the Dniestr has prompted some to say that this conflict should be far easier to resolve than many other 'post-Soviet' conflicts. However, the lack of violence does not obliterate the conflict, although it does tell us that there appears to be no need to resort to such means in the present situation. The different political interests reflect a cultural as well as historical difference between the two Moldovan parties in the conflict, and this difference is sustained by the procedural rule of these parties' 'equal participation' in the process of political settlement in the '5+2' format of negotiations.

Conflict settlement and instruments of vertical power

The '5+2' negotiations for a political settlement (officially titled 'the Permanent Conference for Political Questions in the Framework of the Negotiating Process on the Transdniestrian Settlement') have dragged on since 1993 between Chisinau and Tiraspol as the main parties, and Russia (since 1992), the OSCE (starting from early 1993) and Ukraine (since 1998) as mediators. In 2005 the United States and the European Union formally joined the negotiations as observers. When the liberal coalition gained political power in Moldova in autumn 2009, expectations grew among Moldova's pro-European political forces that the United States and the EU would participate more actively in the process of reintegration in the format of the '5+2' negotiations and would demand to upgrade their status from observers to mediators. Russia's response to these pressures was to repeatedly reconfirm the existing international negotiating format in which Transnistria participates as an equal with the Republic of Moldova and where the EU and the United States remain observers.

In these negotiations practical issues have been discussed in eleven different working groups, but no political breakthrough has been in sight.[221] With long-lasting, recent stalemates – one from February 2006 until late autumn 2011, and another from April 2014 until summer 2016[222] – these negotiations have turned out to be a sign of maintaining contact with the other party which has made it possible to make advances on a number of practical issues but which has not brought any progress on an agreement on a political settlement. Advances have been made in terms of agreeing on issues of logistics and traffic, the conditions for Transnistrian business on the 'right bank', disputes over language in the schools on the 'left bank', the recognition of university degrees and the facilitation of the freedom of movement from Transnistria. While Transnistrian authorities have welcomed the idea that small, concrete measures about improving logistical infrastructure and economic cooperation is a relevant way to proceed in the politically deadlocked settlement process,[223] this has resulted in using such opportunities to improve technical infrastructure in the separatist region without making advances on the political issues. Meanwhile the conflict has become more and more entrenched through the de facto separation of authority. With their negative attitudes the parties have been able to prevent international initiatives such as the 'Merkel–Medvedev dialogue' (2010–12) from increasing the political will to strive for a settlement of the conflict.[224] Paradoxically, the entrenched nature of the conflict has made it possible for the OSCE to facilitate cooperation between the parties in the 'confidence-building' format, thereby allowing the meetings to continue informally even during the hiatus of 2006–11. Similarly, when the negotiations once again were suspended in spring 2014 due to political tensions caused by the war in Ukraine, it was possible to resume them quickly and achieve progress within the confidence-building format despite the ongoing tensions.[225]

Russia has consistently argued that the 'parties themselves', i.e. Chisinau and Tiraspol, must be the main negotiators and that the parties 'must be regarded as equal participants in the process'.[226] It emphasizes that this follows from the ceasefire agreement, according to which the implementation of the agreement has to be ensured by the military of the Russian Federation and the two parties that are directly involved in the conflict. Chisinau, by contrast, is concerned that the procedural aspect of negotiating with Tiraspol as an equal could pave the way for a substantive settlement that is in opposition to its interests. Chisinau's liberal policymakers, in particular, have emphasized the importance of the bilateral structure that is reflected by the signatories of the ceasefire agreement (presidents Yeltsin and Snegur). On this basis the conflict becomes a dispute between Russia and the West instead of an internal Moldovan conflict, and Russia can be seen more as a participant in the conflict than as the 'guarantor of peace', which is the role it assigns to itself. Such an interpretation uses for its own advantage the formal features of the agreement which in 1992 were a consequence of Yeltsin's preference to develop relations with Chisinau and not to support Smirnov as the leader of Transnistria.

Because 'equal participation' has considerable normative appeal – the principle is a symbol of democratic ways as opposed to imposition from above and the suppression of the weaker party's voice – it is easy to use as an abstract principle that remains open to political instrumentalization. This principle helps to veil the power vertical that exists between Moscow and Tiraspol in these negotiations and, as a consequence, offers an instrument for Russia's vertical power in this process. Based on its equal participation in the negotiations, the PMR can voice its own conditions on any settlement scheme and, like also the Republic of Moldova, it can block and redirect negotiations by acting as a 'gatekeeper' for initiatives. The representatives of the PMR have announced that a unified state requires a referendum in Transnistria and that the requirement of the PMR, in case a unification plan should emerge, is that pre-term elections must be organized in both the PMR and the Republic of

Moldova under the observation of the 'guarantor-states' and international organizations.[227] Such conditions support the PMR's basic point of departure in the negotiations: the 'normalization' of relations, which leaders in the PMR like to consider as the conceptual frame introduced in the 'Primakov Memorandum' of 8 May 1997, which is titled a 'Memorandum on the Bases for the Normalization of Relations between the Republic of Moldova and Transnistria'.[228] While this memorandum did not specify a particular path for the resolution of the conflict, in diplomatic practices 'normalization' connotes relations between two separate domains of sovereignty. It is thus an approach directly opposed to Chisinau's policy of 'reintegration'.

From Russia's perspective the participation of Transnistria with a voice on par with the Republic of Moldova makes it possible to indirectly steer developments in the settlement process. It also makes it possible to bypass problematic issues in the negotiations and to concentrate on the more general level of diplomatic communication. For example, when negotiations resumed in summer 2016 with the active support of Russia, for whom such continuity was important in the light of the upcoming presidential elections in both the Republic of Moldova and the PMR (in October and December, 2016, respectively), it was left to the PMR to question the legitimacy of Ukraine as a mediator. The PMR did so by referring to the measures relating to the establishment of border control on the Ukraine–Moldova border as a 'full economic blockade' of Transnistria.[229] While the 'blockade' remains a deep and tangible problem for Transnistria, from Russia's point of view the demonstration of the overall impact of the conflict in Ukraine upon the '5+2' negotiations is a way of reminding Western states of the risks of an escalation of the conflict and the necessity of having Russia as a participant in European security frameworks.

'Equal participation' as Russia's point of departure in the negotiations also provides legitimacy to the trilateral meetings (the so-called '2+1' meetings) which Russia regularly convenes with the two conflict parties, including during the almost six-year-long hiatus (2005–11) in the '5+2' negotiations. From Russia's point of view, the three-party meetings reconfirm the structure laid out in the trilateral peacekeeping format agreed upon in the ceasefire agreement of 1992, and they serve to extend management of the conflict from the military domain to its political settlement. When Russia is criticized for not notifying the other parties in the '5+2' negotiating format about the trilateral meetings, the Russian response has been that its conduct does not differ from that of the EU: Russia is not notified about meetings between the EU's representatives and Moldovan decision makers. Such a comparison is not accepted within the EU, but the point here is not the detailed comparison. Instead, Moscow's response is to claim that Russia has the legitimate right to develop its own ways of communication, just as the EU has established its ways of communicating with the Eastern Partnership countries by appointing Special Representatives for individual countries. The impasse of such communications raises the question, How the two approaches of, on the one hand, Russia and, on the other, the Western states have come to differ so much as to exclude any logical basis for dialogue between the two?

Contested legitimacy: The mutually different approaches of Russia and the West

In 1993, when the negotiations for a political settlement started between Chisinau and Tiraspol as 'the parties' and Russia and the CSCE (OSCE since January 1995) as 'mediators', the newly opened CSCE mission in Chisinau prepared a report on the conflict over Transnistria (report no. 13, November 1993). This report suggested setting up a constitutionally guaranteed 'special region' of Transnistria, which would have its own regional executive, elective assembly and court.[230] The report also suggested Moldova's demilitarization, arguing that building up an army made little sense because Moldova would not be able to build a credible defence against its neighbours. Moldova accepted this point, kept its army at a modest level for domestic tasks only and inscribed neutrality into its constitution. In the Constitution adopted on 29 July 1994, article 11 deals with the 'Republic of Moldova as a Neutral State'. It states that (1) 'the Republic of Moldova proclaims her permanent neutrality' and that (2) 'the Republic of Moldova will not admit the stationing of any foreign military troops on its territory'.[231] However, while Moldova was not prepared to commit itself to neutrality without a demilitarization that meant the full withdrawal of Russian military forces from Transnistria, it by then had become obvious that Moldova and Russia could not agree on this issue. In order to facilitate a compromise Chisinau's decision makers concluded that the way to proceed would be along the lines that President Mircea Snegur had sought in June 1992, that is, to replace the Russian peacekeeping contingent in Transnistria with a multinational unit under the auspices of either the UN or the OSCE. The idea was to separate the presumably 'easier' question of the peacekeeping format from the politically weightier question of the continued presence of the remnants of Russia's 14th Army in Transnistria. Because Moldova preferred to avoid open conflict with Russia, decision makers in Chisinau welcomed the approach of the Western international community appropriating the conflict as its own and treating it as a principled issue over the post–Cold War order in Europe.

The CSCE 1994 summit in Budapest concluded that Russia's regular troops had to be withdrawn 'timely, orderly and completely'. The summit also concluded that Russia's military withdrawal and the search for a political settlement in the conflict over Transnistria should take place as 'two parallel processes which will not hamper each other'.²³² This was a diplomatic compromise between Russia's stance, according to which demilitarization is a part of a 'comprehensive political settlement'²³³ and must be approached as a result of the process, and the Western position that supported Moldova in considering demilitarization as a principled condition of the country's neutrality and, hence, as a condition embedded in the initiation of the process. At the OSCE Summit of November 1999 in Istanbul, the Western states led by the United States forced the issue of Russia's complete withdrawal from Moldova (and also from Georgia) to be made a condition for signing the Adapted Treaty on Conventional Armed Forces in Europe (CFE). Russia made a political commitment to withdraw troops and to remove or demolish, by the end of 2002, the military materiel stored in Transnistria.²³⁴ The condition of the US-led West was repeated in the frame of the High-level Conference of the Conventional Forces in Europe Treaty. Following these developments the Western states reiterated the Istanbul requirements of 1999 ('Istanbul commitments' with reference to Russia) and made the ratification of the Adapted CFE dependent on the removal of all Russian troops from Moldova. The OSCE Ministerial meeting in 2002 gave Russia a one-year extension to complete this withdrawal process. During 2000–3 Russia withdrew 141 self-propelled artillery and other armoured vehicles by rail and, within Transnistria, destroyed 108 T-64 tanks and 139 other items of military equipment mentioned in the CFE treaty. Additionally, 51 armoured vehicles of the type not limited by the CFE treaty were destroyed and 22,000 tons of ammunition were withdrawn. The OSCE mission, which had been given the task of monitoring the process, reported these facts and counted that altogether 48 trains had been loaded with ammunition and materiel. By summer 2003, about 35 per cent of the storage armaments in Transnistria were removed. The political sign was positive, notwithstanding the fact that a large part of the materiel was outdated.

However, the process was discontinued after March 2004, and about 20,000 tons of ammunition, some military equipment and 1,500 military troops (including both ordinary and peacekeeping personnel) were left in Transnistria. March 2004 was the month in which the three Baltic States, Romania, Bulgaria, Slovakia and Slovenia formally became members of NATO.²³⁵ Russia's attitude had already changed some years earlier, when it became evident that these countries' NATO membership would be realized while they simultaneously remained outside the obligations of the CFE treaty. Russia, which has direct borders with all three Baltic States, would be left without legal guarantees about armaments in the proximity of its borders in Europe. When the 'Kozak plan' for the settlement of the conflict was prepared in 2003, it was already a sign of Russia's decision to act alone. It had become obvious in Moscow that the idea of offering the 'Istanbul commitments' as a cooperative effort in exchange for building European security with Russia's participation, with the CFE as the first accomplishment, had failed to produce results. This was one more episode in the chain of developments that underlined just how naive the last Soviet president, Mikhail Gorbachev, had been when he, in connection with the discussions on the unification of Germany, had trusted the vision that NATO could take a course which was open enough for even Russia to eventually become a part of.[236] The promise about NATO's transformation, in accordance with its summer 1990 summit in London, had been the political context in which the Soviet Union, already then on the verge of breaking up, had agreed to the CFE treaty at the end of 1990 – a treaty then celebrated as a landmark that would end armed confrontation in Europe. Against this background March 2004 was a symbolic date for a drastically changed military reality, and by then the political context had also come to entail new uncertainty. The 'Rose Revolution' occurred in Georgia in mid-November 2003 – during a time when Russia was negotiating the Kozak plan in Chisinau – and the future of Ukraine looked uncertain as the country prepared for a change of power after the departure of ailing president Leonid Kutchma.

Once the 'Istanbul requirements' became linked to the resolution of the conflict in Moldova, Western states found themselves unable to discuss any solution for Transnistria that could be interpreted as legitimizing the stationing of Russian troops in the region. This position also applied to the long transition period, which was one of Russia's preconditions for a political settlement. As a result of the linkage to the CFE, the sentiment in Moscow was that Russia, after it had shown flexibility and realized a large part of the withdrawal, had been diplomatically entrapped and was being forced to retreat from Europe militarily and, as a consequence, to give up its leverage to influence developments in the region. In December 2007 Moscow responded by announcing a moratorium on its implementation of the adapted CFE treaty. Wishing to avoid any further deterioration of relations with Russia, Germany and France, together with the United States, gave their support to an approach which, instead of demanding an outright replacement of the Russian peacekeeping troops in Transnistria, would incorporate them into an international peace force under the mandate of the OSCE and set up an OSCE civilian mission to supervise the military peacekeepers. This suggestion for a compromise did not meet Russia's requirements about its 'active' role in any future peacekeeping arrangement. For the same reason, the attempt to establish a civilian mission under an international mandate to oversee Russia's peacekeepers failed to work in Abkhazia at that time. The question about the peacekeeping format languished, and references to Russia's commitment to the 'Istanbul requirements' continued to refer to more than only Transnistria: they symbolized the principled position of the West that Russia's military must leave the territory of independent states that had formerly been part of the Soviet Union.

In Chisinau, the change of government in September 2009 strengthened the position that 'demilitarization must come first', that is, prior to negotiating a political settlement, and that it means the full removal of the Russian military and all ammunition from Transnistria. After the Russia–Georgia war in August 2008 Western opinion had become increasingly supportive of the principled position that arguments must be made with reference to legal norms. Already in 2005 Moldova had stipulated a domestic law (Law No. 173, 22 July 2005) which referred to the Istanbul requirements of 1999 and considered demilitarization in terms of a Russian withdrawal from Transnistria. The law was inspired by the key points of a series of studies and proposals prepared in the trilateral meetings between Moldovan, Romanian and Ukrainian experts and policymakers in the political atmosphere created by the event of the 'Orange Revolution' in Ukraine. The key terms of the new liberal wave were demilitarization, democratization and decriminalization of Transnistria. In the same way as the requirement for demilitarization had been made a precondition for the process of settlement, the argument that Transnistria must have democratic institutions before it can be reintegrated with Moldova offers a political means to block undesirable directions in the settlement process. Anxieties about undesired developments arose especially during the two to three years when German Chancellor Angela Merkel and Russian President Dmitry Medvedev, based on the Meseberg Memorandum of June 2010 outside the '5+2' format (the 'Merkel–Medvedev dialogue'), attempted to create a breakthrough in the settlement process with an eye to developing EU–Russia relations in the field of European security.[237]

The discussion above shows that Moldova and the Western international community, on the one hand, and Russia, on the other hand, have mutually opposed views on the timing of the settlement process and its sequencing in relation to the envisioned final goal. Russia considers the transformation of the peacekeeping format that was established in 1992 into a civilian 'peace-guaranteeing' mission to be a component of the final settlement and argues that the withdrawal of Russia's military must come as the result of this process, whereas Moldova prefers a clear commitment to withdrawal and demands credible signs thereof as a prerequisite for the entire process. The conditionality embedded in Russia's approach is articulated, for example, in the joint declaration of Russia, Moldova and the PMR on 18 March 2009. This declaration (which was signed by President Voronin for Moldova) emphasizes the stabilizing role of the existing peacekeeping operation in the region and advises its transformation into a 'peace-guaranteeing' (*mirogarantiinyi*, a notion closer to peace enforcement than traditional peacekeeping) operation 'under the aegis of the OSCE following a Transdniestrian settlement'.[238] Russia has consistently emphasized that the peacekeeping operation is the most important element of stabilization in 'the security zone of conflict that has been guaranteeing peace on the banks of the Dniester for almost two decades'.[239] From Russia's perspective it would be ideal if the military control of the conflict, in which it pursues a dominant position, would be internationally legitimized and in this way connected to the political settlement process. Because the issue of balancing Russia's role in the peacekeeping format with the participation of Western states has been the main focus of international critical opinion, rather less attention has been given to the profoundly different approaches of Russia and the Western states. The argument that the peacekeeping operation is flawed because one party (Russia) is too dominant and keeps its ordinary military units in the conflict area all too hastily mobilizes international opinion for one-sided support of Moldova. Such support has been provided in particular by parliamentary bodies within the OSCE, the Council of Europe and the EU. In July 2010 the OSCE Parliamentary Assembly supported the 'transformation' of the military peacekeeping units into a multinational civilian mission under the auspices of the OSCE.[240] After an incident at a border checkpoint in the security zone was fatal to a local civilian in January 2012, Germany and Ukraine (under the presidency of Viktor Yanukovich) announced their support of transforming the peacekeeping unit into a civilian one.[241] An agreement about a civilian arrangement would render irrelevant the maintenance of Russia's regular military in the conflict region. However, Russia's approach is to see this not as the way to start but to end the process of settling the conflict. In this thinking frame it makes little difference whether or not the peacekeeping format is discussed separately from the withdrawal issue. In Chisinau their separation served the task of mobilizing the international community, with the explicit backing of the United States, to normatively apply pressure on Russia.[242] While the approach of the Western international community became a principled political position detached from the possibility of dialogue with Russia, Russia lost its diplomatic credibility as it tried to square the circle through its incremental approach. This approach enabled it both to send positive signs and to refrain from taking the final step that the Western states expected as the fulfilment of its 'commitments'. The next chapter will examine this approach more closely.

The political conditionality of Russia's policies

The European Union has consistently emphasized that it backs Moldova's 'fundamental principles of sovereignty and territorial integrity' (Statement of the High Representative on 17 May 2010). The emphasis on 'fundamental principles' allows Moldova to argue that it has the right to exercise control over its territory as a sovereign state, and this emphasis reveals that such principles exist independently of considerations about their application in specific contexts. Russia has also announced its support of a peaceful solution 'based upon the observance of sovereignty and territorial integrity' of Moldova, as stated in a joint statement of presidents Dmitry Medvedev and Viktor Yanukovich on 17 May 2010 (the same date as the aforementioned EU statement). Like the Western states, it has reaffirmed that it respects these principles, and that it has done so ever since the heads of states of the CIS countries adopted a declaration in Kiev in March 1992 – at the time when the conflict was flaring up – which stated that the territorial integrity of the Republic of Moldova was the key element for stability in the entire region. Moldova's sovereignty and territorial integrity have also appeared repeatedly in the communications of the Russian foreign ministry as well as the State Duma. However, these principles are not defined *a priori* but in relation to concepts and legal instruments that are also central in Russian policies. In comparison with the Western approach, in which the politically instrumental uses of the principles are rather more concealed and must be unfolded through interpretation, Russia's approach is more overtly related to its own interests.

To illustrate this difference, we can consider the example of the Russian foreign ministry, when it speaks of 'the principle of Moldova's territorial integrity as enshrined in the basic political treaty of 2001'.[243] The reference to the Treaty of Friendship and Cooperation suggests that the primary relation of importance for interpreting the principles of territorial integrity and sovereignty in the case of Moldova is Moldova's bilateral, treaty-based relationship with Russia. In its Treaty of Friendship and Cooperation with the Republic of Moldova, which was concluded in November 2001 and extended for another ten years in 2011, Russia commits itself to 'the process of political settlement of the Transnistrian problem, in which the Russian Federation acts as a co-mediator and guarantor'. The preamble of this treaty states that the process of settlement is 'based on respect for sovereignty and territorial integrity of the Republic of Moldova'.[244] The reaffirmation of these principles with reference to the bilateral intergovernmental agreement does not simply lie in the words that are used, namely that 'territorial integrity' is an attribute that describes Moldova. Instead, the words are an act to state Russia's commitment to the respect for international law in the settlement process, and that this is to be done in no abstract sense but, instead, with reference to the legally valid treaties that pertain between the two countries. Moreover, Moldova's territorial integrity is stated in the treaty's preamble, which mentions the parties' commitment to the process of a political settlement. In other words, the meaning attributed to Moldova's sovereignty and territorial integrity is contingent upon the process of settlement and interpreted in relation to the other concepts specified in the policy texts. Although we could argue from a more general point of view that the meaning of any word lies in its practical implications and emerges through such textual relations, the specific feature of Russian practices is the designation of its text context in the policy texts.[245] This habitual feature can be understood against the background of Russia's long tradition of building its own discourse of legitimacy based on international legal norms. Unlike Western states the USSR could not simply refer to the norms established within the Western international community but, in order to defend its own normative boundaries, it had to explain how exactly it related to these norms.[246] The same practice continues in issues such as frozen conflicts, where Russia's policies are in conflict with the Western position.

While Chisinau's policymakers and experts are aware that Russia emphasizes its bilateral treaty relations, they prefer to consider the bilateral Treaty of Friendship and Cooperation as a totality in which all parts weigh equally. Therefore they emphasize that the legal commitment made by the Russian State Duma in its ratification of the Treaty means that the respect of sovereignty and territorial integrity has been recognized in Moscow as the principled starting point and, for this reason, should instruct all action. Chisinau's approach has been to distinguish between the negotiations as a temporary situation and the status of the country in the principled sense of international law: Unlike the unconstitutional formation of 'left-bank' Moldova (Transnistria), Moldova is emphasized to be a subject of international law, whose sovereignty and territorial integrity must be the principled point of departure in the negotiations. The remark that Russian decision makers should respect the decisions of their own parliament is a variation of the argument, repeatedly made in the West, that Russia must show 'deeds in accordance with its words'. A gap between words and deeds is perceived to exist when Russia supports the organization of elections in Transnistria, or when it treats the representatives of Transnistria on a par with state representatives, and so on. Such 'breaches' of the sovereignty of the Republic of Moldova occur daily because the PMR cannot function as a polity without Moscow's support.

In the West's criticism of Russian policy, the argument about the discrepancy of 'words and deeds' is common and represents continuity in relation to Western criticism of Soviet-era uses of ideology. The interpretation that considers words as mainly a rhetorical 'smokescreen' to veil 'real' interests and action obstructs, rather than opens up, communication, and it reflects conflict over the issues that are discussed. Words are detached from the speaker's context and framed in a way immediately understandable to the interlocutor. The philosophy of interpretation speaks of a prejudice that is incapable of releasing the reflective interplay of first-order (the original speaker's context) and second-order (the interlocutor's own context and life-experience) references.[247] For the purposes of the present discussion it suffices to note that Western policy discourse tends to interpret Russian diplomatic communications outside of their own context, whereas Russia's approach is to relate principles to other concepts and legal instruments in the policy texts and, in this way, to articulate its practical meaning in the context of its interests.

The conditionality built into Russia's approach to recognizing Moldova's sovereignty means that its horizontal international relations (i.e. the relations between states) intertwine with policies of verticality. Although Russia has repeatedly mentioned its recognition of the sovereignty and territorial integrity of the Republic of Moldova, it has also indicated that this does not mean the 'unitary and indivisible state' inscribed in Moldova's Constitution (Article 1) of 1994.[248] Instead, it is on the basis of the respect for the principle of neutrality enshrined in this Constitution that Russia is prepared to 'support the negotiation of a long-term mutually acceptable political solution which will provide a guaranteed special status for Transnistria within the Moldovan State'.[249] In May, 2012, when the Russian Ministry of Foreign Affairs celebrated the 15th anniversary of the 'Memorandum on the Bases for the Normalization of Relations between the Republic of Moldova and Transnistria' – the 'Primakov Memorandum' from 1997 – a press release called to mind that this memorandum had provided ways with which to solve the Transnistrian problem 'on the basis of respect for sovereignty, territorial integrity and neutral status' of the Republic of Moldova. Thus, the meaning of Moldova's sovereignty and territorial integrity as underlying action which Russia is prepared to take in its policies is announced to emerge in relation to Moldova's neutral status, i.e. in relation to the realization of the policy proclaimed in the Moldovan Constitution in 1994. At the same time this meaning is conditional and dependent on formulating an acceptable 'special status' for Transnistria, and setting up a federal structure of the state would require changing the Constitution.[250]

These principles are points of departure for Russia's negotiations and appear in different contexts in slightly different formulations. The words used at the meeting between foreign ministers Sergey Lavrov and his Ukrainian counterpart Konstantin Grishenko in Nizny Novgorod in February 2012 are 'efficient political settlement within the framework of the Republic of Moldova's territorial integrity and with the observance of securely guaranteed special legal status for Transnistria'.[251] The meaning of the 'special status' of Transnistria, which has been the preliminary consensus of all international negotiations over the conflict ever since CSCE (OSCE) Report no. 13 proposed it in 1993, is specified by Russia with reference to a political entity which would be allowed to have international relations of its own in all fields except security and whenever such relations do not require the form of an international legal personality. The federative or a confederative model has explicitly been part of Russia's agenda since 2003 and appeared under various, less specific formulations since the mid-1990s.

This discussion illustrates how words are the semantic surface of communication and that it is the different contexts – inter-textual relations, institutional practices and political conditions of application – through which the meaning of these words can be identified. In Russian practice, the non-abstract, relational character of the basic principles and concepts means that they are a part of a performative speech act which articulates the conditional character of Russia's policy instead of merely describing its content.[252] This mode of the proposals is semantically articulated in the statements which speak of a 'comprehensive' political solution and specific measures 'in the context of a political settlement'. These are code words for an entire package of conditions and implications. This package includes Moldova's neutrality, a special status for Transnistria within a federative frame of the state and a set of international guarantees that include the maintenance of Russia's regular military units in Transnistria until the settlement is secured. The political conclusion that the horizontal structure of formal interstate relations cannot assure the continuation of the settlement arrangements required by Russia is reflected in the proposals that the military units should remain on the ground in Transnistria for several decades (i.e. for an undefined period of time). In these interrelations of diplomatic communications, the principled conceptual points of departure about Moldova's sovereignty and territorial integrity are elements of architecture but do not yet determine the design of the house that is to be built. Similarly, the joint declaration of Russia, Moldova and Transnistria of 18 March 2009 states that the parties support putting the current operation to guarantee the peace under the aegis of the OSCE 'following a Transdniestrian settlement'. The context that is yet to be built makes any agreement provisional in nature. While the Western states have demanded the fulfilment of initial conditions (i.e. the withdrawal of troops and military equipment), the Russian approach is to first require setting out the political frame of the settlement. Foreign Minister Sergey Lavrov argues that the 'questions of trust, demilitarization and peacemaking are derivatives of a political accord'.[253] A 'political accord' about the structure of elements is expected to be in place first before an agreement on individual items and binding commitments can follow. This also means that an initial 'no' to any specific point is not final but, instead, a sign of further conditions.[254]

The political performative about the conditionality of policy is the mode of the proposals and a modality of conduct in the negotiations. It was not possible to build this kind of conditionality in the negotiations at the time when Gorbachev agreed to the unification of Germany and a new, post-Cold War security framework for Europe was envisioned, but the need to build policies from this point of departure seems to be the lesson that Putin learned during his first five years in the Kremlin. A proposal 'in the context' of something else is an 'only if' which indicates a gap of trust. This situation invokes the testing of trust in the sense of mutually conditional relationships, which logically are beyond the scope of formal interstate relations. In Moscow's relations with Chisinau this means that sovereignty and territorial integrity, with reference to the Transnistrian problem, are real possibilities once they are seen in relation to the elements of the design through which Russia can sufficiently realize its interests. In addition to stating the obvious – that the two countries have diplomatic relations and that Russia continues to recognize the Republic of Moldova as a sovereign state with signs of its own statehood – the emphasis on sovereignty conveys a promise that is conditional. The next chapter will discuss the basic elements of the process and the specific content of Russia's approach to settling the conflict in Transnistria.

Russia's design for settlement: Guarantees for Moldova's neutrality

A bilateral treaty signed on 21 October 1994 by the Moldovan and Russian prime ministers, Andrei Sangheli and Viktor Chernomyrdin,[255] included the point of departure which Russia had been negotiating ever since the ceasefire was achieved in summer 1992: the practical steps of withdrawing the Russian troops – within three years of the agreement coming into force – would be synchronized with the political settlement of the Transnistrian conflict. Moldova subsequently contested the interpretation that such synchronization means a direct conditionality, i.e. that Russia's military withdrawal would be dependent on reaching a political settlement on the status of Transnistria.[256] Such an accommodation of interests was never acceptable to Chisinau, irrespective of whether the government and the president were communist or liberal. However, the Russia–Moldova treaty of 1994 failed because President Yeltsin decided that this treaty, which was prepared as an executive-level agreement, needs the ratification of the State Duma; and this in turn became impossible after the 1995 elections, which were won by nationalist-minded conservative parties. By contrast, the Parliament in Moldova ratified it soon after it had been signed. The agreement reached in the treaty was considered to be the best option available, although there also was considerable frustration over Russia's inaction in relation to military withdrawal.[257]

The 'Primakov Memorandum' – 'Memorandum on the Bases for the Normalization of Relations between the Republic of Moldova and Transnistria' – was signed in 1997 by Moldova's President Petru Lucinschi and the Tiraspol leader Igor Smirnov, with the mediation of Russia, Ukraine and the OSCE CiO, Denmark's Foreign Minister N.H. Petersen. This memorandum set up an equation that was just as impossible to solve as the conflict itself: it put Tiraspol on a par with Chisinau in the negotiations and, at the same time, introduced the concept of the 'common state' (*obshchee gosudarstvo*) as the basis upon which a solution should be negotiated. No agreement could be reached on the interpretation and legal meaning of this concept, which in Primakov's opinion would more flexibly leave space for federal and confederal arrangements than the concept of a 'unified state', which also appeared in the negotiations, would be able to do.[258] In the Russian language 'unified state' (*edinoe gosudarstvo*) has strong connotations of unity (*edinstvo*). The negotiations fell apart, and the discussions carried out between the parties over the next decades failed to advance in terms of agreeing on a basis for outlining a division of competences between the Republic of Moldova and the entity acknowledged only through the initials of its self-declared statehood – the PMR. Between September 2001 and May 2002 Chisinau completely withdrew from the negotiations following the tightened customs regulations introduced by President Voronin, which had changed the permissive course that had obtained since 1996.[259] While in 1996 there was optimism about the further progress of the talks, by 2001, when Voronin came to power, relations had deteriorated and plunged even farther with the adversarial personal relations between the two leaders. In July 2002, a document (the 'Kiev document', presented in Kiev on 3–4 July 2002) proposed by Moscow with the support of the two other mediators, Ukraine and the OSCE, made the federalization of Moldova the key point for a solution. The document outlined the divided and shared competences, federal institutions and international guarantees in a way that insulated Tiraspol from Chisinau's federal powers and gave Russia a predominant role as the guarantor of security. In Chisinau, right-wing and pro-Romania political forces opposed this concept because they considered it to be a 'Trojan horse' for Moscow's continued influence over Moldova. In Tiraspol, too, there was strong opposition to this concept as it was considered to infringe upon the rights that the PMR had gained as a political entity of its own.

The 'Kozak Memorandum', which Putin's aide in the Kremlin, Deputy Head of the Presidential Administration Dmitry Kozak, worked out in Moldova and released in November 2003, built on the Kiev document and included several draft documents before its finalization. It tried to solve the disagreement about the conceptual point of departure by using two different terms: 'united state' (*ob"edinennoe gosudarstvo*) when the reference is territorial (i.e. the Republic of Moldova) and 'unified state' (*edinoe gosudarstvo*) when the reference is to the general attributes that would make the 'unified' state, i.e. features such as being an independent, democratic state with federal principles. Initially the Kozak plan (Memorandum on Basic Principles of State Structure of the United State, 23 November 2003)[260] seemed to present a major breakthrough. In Chisinau, President Voronin was dissatisfied with the failure of the Kiev initiative of summer 2002 and, already in February 2003, he proposed – with Smirnov's later approval – to set up a Joint Constitutional Commission in order to draft a new constitution for a federal Moldova that united the 'right' and 'left' banks of the Dniestr. Consequently, Voronin and Smirnov both were ready to accept the Kozak plan in November 2003. The OSCE was also working for a breakthrough in the settlement, and a new momentum of optimism over a possible solution had developed. However, Voronin decided to reject the plan shortly before President Putin was to fly to Chisinau to sign it due to domestic and Western opposition. Although Voronin was attracted to Moscow's promises of compelling the Transnistrian separatists to the reunification of the country, he withdrew from the process because Moldovans who opposed the plan had gathered at the airport to hinder Putin's landing by forming a human carpet. Their dramatic resistance was encouraged by the example of Georgia's 'Rose Revolution', which was unfolding simultaneously. During those critical hours, Voronin received phone calls from Western leaders, reportedly from the Council of Europe secretary-general Walter Schwimmer and EU High Representative Javier Solana. According to William Hill, Solana's message was that signing the Kozak plan would sink Moldova's prospects for European integration.[261]

The Kozak plan envisaged the foundations on which the country was to be unified within the borders of the Moldovan Soviet Socialist Republic as they had been on 1 January 1990. Its statement that Moldova would be a neutral demilitarized state (item 3.5) confirmed that the preservation of constitutional neutrality was the basic precondition for settling the Transnistrian conflict in the frame of Moldova's sovereignty. More than a decade later, in December 2012, Foreign Minister Lavrov emphasized that if Moldova were to drop the neutral position, this would mean 'radical changes in all coordinates' of the issue.[262] The Kozak plan proposed that the armed forces would be organized in territorial bases until full demilitarization was achieved; this would therefore leave their command by federal organs largely nominal. The period of transition was initially agreed to be about twenty years, during which the Russian troops – peacekeepers and parts of the former 14th Army – would remain in Transnistria; the exact length of time was left to be specified later in the negotiation process. The Kozak plan also proposed that the state structure of Moldova would be transformed with the goal of creating a federal state and to this end presented a draft outline of the competences of the federation, as well as the joint competences and competences of the subjects of the federation – subjects which were yet to be determined by a new constitution. The PMR was given the status of a 'state entity within the federation', whereas the autonomous territorial formation of Gagauzia is mentioned as a 'subject of the federation'. The combined power of these two entities – Transnistria with nine and Gagauzia with four representatives – would equal Moldova's thirteen representatives in the upper house of the federal decision-making body, whereas the lower house would be elected without such quota system. The three subjects of the federation would maintain their own state agencies of the legislative, executive and judicial branches of government. Transnistria would have its own constitution, whereas Gagauzia would be entitled to its own 'fundamental law', i.e. to the kind of status it has had since 1994. Both subjects of the federation would have their own legislation, state property, independent budget and tax system, and also their own state symbols. Moreover, neither their constitutional-legal status nor their borders could be changed without their consent. By stating that a subject could leave the federation with a majority of votes from its registered voters 'in case a decision is taken to unite the federation with another state', or should the federation experience a 'full loss of sovereignty',[263] the plan was prepared for the possibility that the 1920 merger with Romania might reoccur in some form. Should such a situation arise, the territorial organization of the army units ('till complete demilitarization of the Federation', item 3.5) would prevent the country-wide deployment of troops and, consequently, the use of the army in the unification process. Thus, the federal state structure would guarantee the upholding of neutrality as the bedrock of foreign and security policy. Transnistria's 'special status' would enable it to develop its own cultural and economic relations, which would necessitate the use of the Russian language. While the state language of the federation would be Moldovan, Russian would be an official language throughout the entire territory of the state. Other official languages could be established in the constitutions of the federation's subjects (such as Ukrainian in Transnistria and the Gagauz language in Gagauzia).

Contrary to the prevalent practice within the OSCE, according to which no single member state should contribute more than 50 per cent of the peacekeeping forces, the Kozak Memorandum (item 18) stated that, based on a bilateral treaty to be signed by Moldova and Russia, Russia would provide 'stabilization peacekeeping forces' of up to 2,000 men ('without heavy military equipment and weapons') on the territory of the federal state during a transition period until full demilitarization. The two other mediators (the OSCE and Ukraine) and the EU could join the bilaterally initiated treaty arrangement under conditions that would be agreed upon by the original signatories. In this way, Russia reserved for itself the leading role in the 'peace-guaranteeing' (*mirogarantiinyi*) operation. In addition, the Kozak plan included the provision (item 17) that the signed agreement would be enacted with one side only should the other side fail to implement it. Thus, if Russia's lead role failed to be realized, Russia would be able to refer to the provision that the three mediators must guarantee the enactment of the memorandum and, in fact, continue with one party (Transnistria) alone. The territorial organization of the army ensures that this alternative exists during the long transition period that was to last from 2003 until the 2020s or until full demilitarization. The possibility of the final secession of Transnistria was thus included in the memorandum, and this was not without implications for Gagauzia, although the question about this region was not as weighty during the first decade of the twenty-first century.

In summary, the Kozak plan outlined a settlement design with a structure of 'guarantees'. The continued *military presence*, together with a *weak federative structure* or a confederation justified by the existence of a significant Russian-speaking population, would be the guarantees by means of which Russia could pursue the implementation of its basic policy goals: to keep the territory neutral, and to secure the ethnically and administratively independent position of the Russian-speaking population. Beyond this, *international guarantees* would be realized through ratified treaties of the federation and 'generally accepted principles of international law'. The memorandum does not elaborate on this point, because obviously this would have been a matter for international negotiations in the '5+2' format and, most crucially, would have to be achieved in relations with NATO members. The Kozak plan shows why Russia's continued military presence in Transnistria, with its long and vague transition period that is the major source of Chisinau's dissatisfaction, is so important to Russia: It is the main guarantee for achieving the political goal of securing Moldova's neutrality as well as the position of the Russian-speaking population. Because the last-mentioned goal has considerable importance for domestic discussions within Russia, it increases the legitimacy of the policies that include maintaining an external military presence: in Russia this makes the borders of Transnistria into 'ours'; in other words, the borders of military, political and cultural influence are not merely instrumental and symbolic representations of the security of Russia but, instead, they are about Russia. Because this internal connection is by no means unambiguous it is actively endorsed by Transnistrian leaders. I will return to this issue further below; but first the next chapter will discuss the developments that followed the Kozak plan.

8

After the Kozak Plan

In 1994, when the point of departure about the 'synchronization' of interests was put on paper signed by the Russian and Moldovan prime ministers, the elements of the political solution were not yet clear but expected to emerge in the negotiations. They were not pinned down until the Kozak plan, and they were then fixed according to the following political equation: The less trust there is that the neutral line of security policy will be maintained, the stronger the pressure for a weak central government. A federal state with a weak central government allows Russia to influence Moldova's development from the inside and, in this way, not only to look after the Russian and Russian-speaking population but also to ensure Moldova's line of neutrality. It was primarily the proposal of a federal structure that aroused opposition in 'right-bank' Moldova. Critics pointed out that the plan was about a confederation, which put the Republic of Moldova on a par with its two 'federative subjects'. The plan gave Transnistria not only the formal possibility to leave the federation in case Moldova joins another country (i.e. Romania) but also enabled it, together with Gagauzia, to block any decisive action by the federal government in a two-chamber parliament. The many shared competences between the federal government in Chisinau and the federal subjects prompted criticism that the realization of this plan would too easily paralyze the state.

Russia's unilateral move in preparing the Kozak plan frustrated the OSCE Mission in Chisinau, which, at the same time, was preparing the mediators' document for the settlement plan.[264] It was not until January 2004 that Russia officially presented the Kozak plan to the OSCE and Ukraine (the two other mediators), and a modified version of this plan was then worked out as the joint plan. However, there was no possibility to revive political momentum. Already during 2003 a counter-proposal to Russia's 'Kozak plan' had been prepared by non-governmental Moldovan experts gathered around Chisinau's Institute for Public Policy. The proposal, which was publicized in 2004, had three key concepts: democratization, demilitarization and decriminalization (the '3-D Strategy'). Instead of a federal state structure it emphasized the need to adopt policies of democratization and decriminalization before reintegration could take place in Transnistria as well as in the country at large. After Victor Yushchenko replaced Leonid Kutchma in January 2005, the cooperation between Ukraine, Moldova and Romania took centre stage in the settlement process. As a consequence of this, a series of plans emerged with the aim of shifting the weight of negotiations towards Moldova and Romania and dealing with Transnistria in the context of the specific issue of democratization.[265]

A scheme presented by Ukraine at the summit of GUAM (an organization formed by Georgia, Ukraine, Azerbaijan and Moldova) in Chisinau in April 2005 was later developed into what was called the 'Yushchenko plan'. This plan built on Ukraine's cooperation with Moldova and Romania and proposed the democratization of Transnistria as the point of departure for its reintegration with Moldova. The plan was complemented by a number of more detailed plans and proposals by the Moldovan government and parliament. The problem with the many proposals prepared in the wake of the 'Orange Revolution' was that the focus on democratization alone proved to be too superficial. Ambitious ideas about an international, civilian provisional administration that would implement a post-conflict recovery plan had little chance of winning the support of Russia and the PMR; and the suggestion to exclude Tiraspol as a party in the negotiations and to increase the weight of the Western states by adding Romania (which from 2007 onwards would have participated as an EU member state) and the United States threatened to break up the negotiating format. During 2006 a Trilateral Policy Paper by Ukraine, Romania and Moldova continued the work which had been started in the political environment of the 'Orange Revolution'. It repeated the request of the OSCE's Istanbul commitments from 1999 and the connection made with the CFE: A complete and prompt withdrawal of Russian troops and munitions from the PMR was demanded. This requirement, together with the quest for democratization, has remained the key element of Western initiatives, which in the region have had Romania's consistent backing. From the perspective of Russia, the requirement about military withdrawal abolishes the one element that Russia considers as the military guarantee for the realization of the plan. The request for democratization, in turn, makes proposals attractive for Western countries and, at the same time, offers a possibility to block negotiations when they go in an undesirable direction. As a result of these developments, the approaches of Russia and the pro-Western political forces in Moldova grew farther apart, while the PMR was prepared to negotiate at the most a loose federation.

In June 2008, Voronin approached Moscow and offered to settle the Transnistrian conflict on the basis of Moldova's withdrawal from GUAM and to give up aspirations of joining NATO. Moscow for its part eased the requirements of the Kozak plan by agreeing that Transnistria would have only 20 per cent of the seats in the Moldovan parliament. Nonetheless it did not give up the principle that Transnistria would have the right to secession in case Moldova's status as an independent state were to change.[266] These negotiations were interrupted by the war that broke out between Russia and Georgia in August. A change of political power in Chisinau followed, and the liberal government put new emphasis on the firm requirement for Russia's withdrawal. In April 2010 Acting President Mihai Ghimpu again called to mind that the unconditional withdrawal of Russian troops and the removal of Russian ammunition from Transnistria, to be followed by 'demilitarization and democratization', were the necessary prerequisites for any viable solution to the conflict.[267] Centre-right opinion in Chisinau soon rejected the idea of a federal state altogether. Under the presidency of Dmitry Medvedev, Russia convened the tripartite meetings in Moscow in August 2008 and in March 2009 to reconfirm, in a joint statement, that the synchronization of a comprehensive settlement with Russia's military withdrawal remained the point of departure in the negotiations. However, the consent reached with Moldova had not advanced from the situation of the bilateral treaty of 1994. Russia's position was to wait while the basic political and military elements of the assurances of the policies that it required were steadily built into its settlement scheme.

Under the presidency of Viktor Yanukovich (February 2010–February 2014), Russia regained Ukraine's support for its policies. Yanukovich and his Party of the Regions provided Ukraine's non-aligned position – the policy adopted upon independence – with a legal basis by introducing a bill that excludes membership in any military alliance.[268] Transnistria was opened to Ukrainian goods and transit, and Ukraine's social, educational and cultural relations with Transnistria were given a political boost. A few weeks before the initiation of the so-called Merkel–Medvedev dialogue, which aimed to develop EU–Russia cooperation in European security and conflict management and specifically focused on Transnistria, the presidents of Russia and Ukraine restated the basic conditions of the Kozak plan for negotiating a settlement. According to their joint statement on 17 May 2010, their point of departure, as 'mediators and Countries-Guarantors',[269] is the need to resolve the Transnistrian problem through equal dialogue aimed at determining the 'special, reliably guaranteed status of Transnistria', which is based on 'the observance of sovereignty and territorial integrity of Moldova', its constitutional neutrality and the 'formation of common legal, economic and defense space'.[270] The two-entities approach is also implicated in the term 'unified space' (*edinoe prostranstvo*, also translated 'common space'), which invokes the adjustable idea of the 'common state' proposed by Russia in the negotiation processes in accordance with the Primakov Memorandum (1997) and the Odessa Agreement (1998).[271] The latter of these documents regulates military activity in the security zone and, hence, solidifies the military guarantees in the political process.

The decision by the Russian foreign ministry to celebrate the 15th anniversary of the Primakov Memorandum with an announcement (on 15 May 2012) retroactively made the Memorandum into a landmark of Russian policy. At a point of time when the Medvedev–Merkel dialogue had failed to bring any substantive results, it was celebrated as a symbolic sign of the long-term consistency and continuity of Russia's policies. It was emphasized that the fifteen-year-old memorandum entailed 'specified objectives for the settlement' and that in it 'the basis of equality defined the logic of agreement of [the] special status of Transnistria as a part of the Republic of Moldova' and enabled Transnistria to establish its own international relations. While the Kozak plan of 2003 envisioned Transnistria as a 'state entity within the Federation' (Article 3.8), the foreign ministry in May 2012 denoted 'the region [Transnistria] as state and territorial formation' entitled to its own international relations in the domains of economy, science and cultural relations in accordance with a 'federative constitutional model of comprehensive settlement of [the] Transnistria conflict'.[272] The message, with its many ambiguous concepts, is once again one of a federalist state model with weak central authorities, i.e. close to a confederation. The policy experts in Chisinau who in collaboration with German experts had studied federal models of the state in the frame of Chancellor Angela Merkel's diplomatic efforts did not reject the concept out of hand; instead, they called to mind that a federal state 'does not mean three armies, two coins, two customs systems and two border guards'.[273] The autonomy which Chisinau was prepared to consider for Transnistria was modelled on the status that had been granted to Gagauzia in 1994.[274] The right of the Gagauz people to secede has been recognized by Chisinau's government only for the case that would anyway make such a choice self-evident: the break-up of Moldova itself.

In 2013, ten years after the Kozak plan, its key elements re-emerged in the concept paper proposed by the Socialist Party of Moldova. Whereas the Kozak plan aimed at an international treaty, the 2013 plan (called 'the Dodon plan', after Igor Dodon, the chairperson of the Socialist Party) emerged in the domestic political process as a program crafted by an opposition party. Russia's support of it is evident on the basis of the clearly articulated support given to the plan by prominent figures such as Sergei Naryshkin, Speaker of the State Duma (2011–16) and former head of the

Presidential Administration (2008–11), and Sergey Mironov, leader of the political party Just Russia (also known as Fair Russia) and former Chairman of the Federation Council (2001–10).[275] Just like the Kozak Memorandum before it, the Dodon plan proposed a neutral demilitarized state in which the armed forces would be territorially organized (seemingly under the command of federal organs) until full demilitarization was achieved. On the federal level, the armed forces would have a nominal function because their tasks would be limited to action against 'external aggression', whereas matters of internal security and order would be organized within the constituent entities: the Republic of Moldova, the Autonomous Territorial Entity of Gagauzia and Transnistria (Transnistria's status is not defined with specific terms in the plan).

The Dodon plan is a scheme to federalize the country, and its proponents claim that it will 'save the country from disintegration'. The status outlined for the constituent entities of the federation entails more than a government and a legislature (which are in accordance with the present status of Gagauzia based on the law from 1994): Each entity would have its own constitution and economic autonomy ascertained through its own state property, budget and tax system, and foreign economic relations would be regulated through only relatively general federal-level principles. The right to leave the federation is not mentioned but it is obvious in such a structure. The plan includes other states (first and foremost Russia) in the federalization process by proposing that the borders between the three constituent entities will be determined by means of local referenda in the border regions, and that these referenda are to be organized by the OSCE and the 'guarantor-states'.[276] While federalization is the main point in the plan, it relaxes certain other elements in relation to the Kozak plan. Unlike the Kozak plan it does not require formal changes in the status of the Russian language as a language of 'inter-ethnic communication'.[277] Additionally, it offers the possibility of negotiating Russia's shouldering of Transnistria's energy debt by proposing that the financial obligations, which were accrued before the federation came into existence, would be covered by the budgets of the respective entities. The Dodon plan also proposes a practice that Moldova did in fact resume in March 2016: to elect the president by popular vote, as had been the case before the Constitution was amended in 2000 to shift this responsibility to the parliament. These modifications and political concessions in relation to the Kozak plan have little chance of making the proposal acceptable to those who already were opposed to the Kozak plan, and the external pressures which Moldova encounters between Russia and the West can only reinforce these internal political and cultural lines of division.

A changed game and uncertain guarantees

The question of NATO membership has been present in Moldovan politics since Mihai Ghimpu (Liberal Party) proposed a referendum on it in the election campaign that brought the liberal coalition to power in 2009. During the four years of the liberal government, which was mainly led by Vladimir Filat (Liberal Democratic Party), Moldova's European path steered it closer to the United States and NATO, and it also created pressures to modify the traditional notion of neutrality. The description of Moldova's policy as a policy which, on the basis of the Constitution, is neutral but which simultaneously develops cooperation with NATO on the basis of Moldova's status as a 'non-bloc' (*vneblokovoe*, i.e. 'beyond the blocs') state suggests a direction towards military non-alignment.[278] This can be a rather formal notion during peacetime and does not require strict neutrality during wartime. This serves the needs of membership in the EU, which also entails close cooperation with NATO. In Moscow's view the inscription of neutrality in the Constitution is not a sufficient guarantee for policy continuity. Much uncertainty prevails in the situation where Romanism is a cultural force that propels Moldova closer to not only the EU but also NATO, and a large number of people remain undecided over the desirability of cooperation with NATO.[279] Because a sovereign country makes its own decisions in the formal sense, vertical means of influence become more important – Russia's support of the Dodon plan is an example of this. In contrast to the Kozak plan, which was meant to become a bilateral treaty (following the model that Yeltsin had introduced in 1992 and in 1994, with the ceasefire and withdrawal treaty, respectively), the Dodon plan is a sign of Russia's increased emphasis on the means of influence through Moldova's domestic politics.

At the same time the changes in Moldova's external security environment challenge the entire approach taken by Russia during the 1990s to control and settle the conflict over Transnistria. In the immediate aftermath of the dissolution of the Soviet Union, Transnistria did not have much geopolitical significance for Russia but was mainly a concern over Russians living outside Russia. As Russian nationalist sentiments grew in the new federation, the small strip of land nourished concerns about the need to construct a sense of common belonging by means of compatriot policies.[280] Unlike South Ossetia and Abkhazia, Transnistria is not situated along crucial energy-transit routes – instead, it is the territory controlled by the Republic of Moldova which has significance for the transit of Russian gas, although this significance has markedly decreased since the 1990s. When the United States and NATO started to strengthen their military presence in formerly socialist Eastern Europe from the early 2000s onward, it gradually became less attractive for Russia to offer to withdraw from Transnistria in exchange for political cooperation on issues concerning European security. At the turn of the millennium the United States started to use a former Soviet base near the city of Constanta on Romania's Black Sea coast, and plans were devised in Washington to make countries in Eastern Europe operative parts of the United States and NATO ballistic missile defence system. After its opening in 2015 (after a similar construction plan was withdrawn from the Czech Republic), the US base for naval support in Deveselu in southern Romania was furnished with SM-3 interceptor missiles and radar equipment. Based on a Presence Agreement signed in 2005, Romania's Black Sea coast has become the location of one of the largest US military bases in Europe.[281] Especially the ballistic missile defence system, which has installations in Poland and in Romania, is considered in Russia to shatter its strategic balance with NATO and, hence, undermine the possibilities for cooperation between the major powers on common European security, which had been the policy pursued by Moscow during the 1990s. Russia must 'think twice before taking any swift steps relating to Transnistria', one of Moldova's pro-Russian newspapers emphasized in May 2011, before going on to state: 'Those who wish to "swap" the unrecognized republic once again step on a rake.'[282] In other words, if Russia's decision makers are foolish enough to step on the 'rake' (which metaphorically lies hidden in the grass) – that is, to once again trust the good intentions of the West – the 'rake' will again strike them on the forehead. The point that can easily mobilize support in Moscow is that Transnistria provides an outpost that should be used to counter the 'encirclement', which in Russia is part of the sense of the experience of vulnerable borders that was generated by the traumatic experiences of major wars and, most recently, the Second World War.

Russia's annexation of Crimea in March 2014 accelerated geopolitical tension in the region, and a new escalation in terms of armaments occurred when the United States transferred its nuclear weapons from Turkey to Romania (to Deveselu in the first phase) after the failed coup of August 2016 in Turkey. Romania's transformed geopolitical role has intensified its cooperation with Moldova and brought Moldova closer to NATO in the frame of the bilateral cooperation between the two countries. Together with the United States, Romania is Moldova's 'strategic partner' in the efforts to restructure its military to meet NATO standards.[283] Interoperability and capacity-building were boosted in September 2014 when Moldova was invited to participate in NATO's Defence and Related Security Capacity Building (DCB) Initiative.[284] One year later, the plan was introduced to open a NATO liaison office in Chisinau (where a NATO Information and Documentation Centre had been functioning since September 2006), and arrangements also were made to set up a joint Romanian–Moldovan peacekeeping battalion with headquarters in Iasi, Romania, near the Moldovan border. When Igor Dodon in 2017 assumed the tasks of president, he immediately opposed the government on several issues; among them were the opening of a NATO liaison office, the participation of Moldovan troops in a multinational exercise under the aegis of NATO in Romania and the status of Romania and the United States as Moldova's main defence partners. Although the position of the president entails little actual power in Moldova, such action has significance in view of the next parliamentary elections, and it is through the increase of the votes for his party that Dodon (or any incumbent president) can increase the possibilities of having his (her) powers strengthened through the legislative process.

During the preceding decade, the rapid changes in the security environment had started to fuel quite loaded communication. In early 2010 Igor Smirnov, the leader of Transnistria until the year 2012, had announced that the PMR was ready to welcome Russian Iskander missiles on its soil.[285] The political context of this statement was the verbal threat made by President Dmitry Medvedev in June 2009 when he spoke of deploying these missiles in Kaliningrad, should the United States proceed with its plans to install radar bases and missile interceptors on the territories of its new allies in Eastern Europe.[286] In the years that followed, joint US-Moldovan exercises conducted in Moldova raised concerns in Tiraspol and spurred domestic protest in Moldova.[287] Tiraspol's protest in April 2016 against what it considered a violation of its airspace by a Romanian reconnaissance aircraft, which allegedly was tasked with the aerial mapping of Transnistria, signalled a new escalation of tensions. The use of the airspace over Transnistria raises Moscow's concern because of the extensive US military presence in Romania and the fact that Romania has modernized its army with US-made equipment, including fifth-generation F-22 Raptor fighter jets. Romania's use of Moldovan airspace sends both a political and military signal: in the case of hostility, Russia would be unable to open a corridor from the Black Sea through Ukrainian territory (see Map 2, page 84) without risking a confrontation with the Romanian air force (and, consequently, with NATO in case of further escalation). The change of government in Ukraine in February 2014 and the increased US and NATO equipment in Romania have made Russia's reluctance to leave Transnistria a firmly held position. Smirnov's message apparently confirmed the earlier warning that Russia was prepared to consider strong military responses to the extension of NATO military infrastructure in Eastern Europe. The mode of communication which leaves it to the PMR to make suggestions while Russia remains silent sends a message to the West without being a direct threat.[288]

In regard to Tiraspol's relations with Moscow, Smirnov's move was an offer of political loyalty in terms of a mutually conditional relationship in which politicians in person become 'guarantors' of a policy orientation that secures Moscow's interests. In return these politicians gain economic and political support from Moscow to strengthen their own bases of power. Such relationships may have considerable flexibility as long as political situations do not become critical. Igor Smirnov did not support Yeltsin; yet he was able to rule Transnistria for more than two decades because he represented the PMR's uncompromising determination to join Russia (initially to remain part of the Soviet Union) and he was able to sufficiently deliver what Russia expected in terms of security policy and economic integration. Simultaneously he was able to increase the political space of his own action by acquiring control of Transnistria's economy. In the elections of December 2011 Moscow's preferred candidate was Anatolii Kaminskii, the Speaker of the PMR's Supreme Soviet; yet it was Evgenii Shevchuk who was elected instead. Like in the case of Smirnov, Russia's policy was not to press for an outcome but, instead, to oversee that this outcome would sufficiently realize Russia's security political and economic interests in the region. When Shevchuk's term neared its end in 2016, speculations emerged that he was not Moscow's preferred candidate for the next term. In June 2016, a poll conducted by the Russian Public Opinion Research Center (VTsIOM) was claimed to show that Vadim Krasnoselskii, the Speaker of the PMR's Supreme Soviet, was the most popular candidate (at 24 per cent) and that 86 per cent of Transnistrians felt that joining Russia represented the most suitable future for the region.[289] In December 2016 Krasnoselskii was elected president with 62.3 per cent of the votes (Shevchuk received less than 28 per cent). In the previous September, ten years after the referendum of 2006, Shevchuk issued a presidential decree on the implementation of the outcome of the referendum to join Russia and ordered that the legislation in the PMR was to be harmonized with federal law in Russia.[290] Krasnoselskii's presidency confirms the power of the *Obnovlenie* ('Renovation', 'Renewal') Party, which holds the majority in the Supreme Soviet. Because this party is supported by the Sheriff company, which controls a large part of Transnistria's economy, his presidency also unites the political and economic power structures in the de facto state. The new president is expected to guarantee a close and loyal relationship with Moscow during a process which could include both slow, incremental integration and drastic political turns, and which is likely to be economically painful for the population. The way has been paved in Transnistria for Moscow's decision to attach Transnistria to the Russian Federation – if and when such decision could be justified as an immediate response to the actions of the United States and NATO or the EU.

9

Prepared for Either Way: Strengthening Vertical Ties and Social Integration

Since the Kozak plan, the overarching logic of Russia's policies has been that the precondition of a demilitarized Moldova is a neutral Moldova, and that the main constitutional guarantee of neutrality is a federal Moldova which enables the separation of Transnistria in the case that its neutral status is threatened. However, in order to be prepared for the situation that this reasoning cannot be realized, preparations were also made for the conditions for the other 'variant' of the settlement. This, in itself, did not yet force Moscow to make a decision on which variant to pursue. Although strengthening economic ties and harmonizing the PMR's legislation with the federal law in Russia prepare the way for a final separation and generate the ability to make quick decisions, they also facilitate the option – up to a point where the frustrations in Transnistria would be politically too costly in Russia – that clearly remains Russia's preference: a weak federation or a confederation in Moldova. As long as the situation remains unresolved, it is important from Russia's perspective that the 'special, reliably guaranteed status of Transnistria' remains a sufficiently open term: a potentiality of meaning which can be specified towards a weaker or a stronger central government in Chisinau.

In this situation the political, economic and social structures that tie Transnistria to Russia have been developed quite consistently and in response to Moldova's approach to the EU, and the cultural affiliation that provides the justification for such integration has retained its central place in public discussions, especially in Transnistria. Already before the change of government in Moldova, President Medvedev had promised Igor Smirnov that Transnistrians with a Russian passport would be protected by Russia, and Smirnov had publicly acknowledged this promise. By 2012, more than 160,000 inhabitants of Moldova (120,000 of whom lived in Transnistria) were reported to own a Russian passport. As a result of the increasing numbers of Russian citizens in Transnistria, about two-thirds (65 per cent) of all property in Transnistria is in Russian hands. In May 2011 Igor Smirnov announced that Transnistria would equalize service tariffs in the natural-gas sector in conformity with Russian rates, and that the implementation of the new policy would be guided by the Krasnodar Territory (*Krasnodarskii krai*) of Russia. Starting in 2012, a new tariffs policy was adopted with the aim of gradually narrowing the gap between the high price that Transnistria is supposed to pay for Russian gas, and the low rate ultimately paid by Transnistrian consumers. As a result of this policy, the price of gas increased for households, and similar policies were adopted for electricity and water. Smirnov emphasized that Transnistria must have 'a target program' to start operating in terms of the tariff arrangements in the Russian Federation, and officials in Tiraspol emphasized that even with increased prices the regional tariffs on utility services remain two to five times lower than in Chisinau-led Moldova.[291] The main reason for this is the accumulating debt to Gazprom. In addition, Russia's annual direct economic support to Transnistria is US$20–30 million. Transit infrastructure projects, energy subsidies, education and the social sector (pension subsidies and humanitarian aid to pensioners, children and adolescents) are the main fields of assistance. During his visit to Tiraspol in October 2012 the Russian foreign ministry's special envoy Sergei Gubarev suggested that Transnistria may have access to the Customs Union, which was established between Russia, Kazakhstan and Belarus in 2010 (and was succeeded by the Eurasian Economic Union from January 2015).[292] Russia's assistance to Transnistria in the framework of humanitarian cooperation, a sum which exceeds US$100 million for the three-year period 2013–15, has been directed towards supporting this goal through the 'autonomous non-profit organization Eurasian Integration'.[293] All this support, including humanitarian support, becomes a mechanism of vertical power whenever it is relatively permanent and serves the purpose of affiliating the population with the Russian state and society rather than the Republic of Moldova.

In March 2012 the Kremlin made an appointment that confirmed Tiraspol's direct connection with Moscow. The appointment of Dmitry Rogozin, who had served as the deputy prime minister in charge of the defence industry since December 2011 and who had earlier been Russia's ambassador to NATO, as the President's special representative for Transnistria signalled Russia's tougher position on Moldova's reunification. At the same time as Russia's ambassador in Chisinau is a sign of the 'horizontal' relations between states,[294] the appointment of a presidential envoy for Transnistria is, in substance, a formal sign of a power vertical that exists between Moscow and Tiraspol. Similarly to the decision taken the same spring in Moscow to open a consulate in Tiraspol in spite of Chisinau's protests,[295] it sends the message that the region is controlled from the Kremlin in spite of its internationally recognized status as a region within another state. In comparison with the equivalent appointments in Abkhazia and South Ossetia, the appointment of Rogozin, a well-known nationalist voice in Russian politics, was a statement that reconfirmed Russia's strong role – its 'exclusive right', in Rogozin's own words – to maintain peace and security in conflict regions that were once part of the Soviet Union.[296] Soon after his appointment Rogozin restated Russia's conditions for the resolution of the conflict. He reinforced the requirement that Transnistria must be an equal party to the negotiations and, moreover, argued that it must be a party with 'equal rights' (*ravnopravnyi*). He also brought up the next step, which is to be the 'normalization' of the Moldova–Transnistria economic relations. (His position as the Russian chairman of the Russia–Moldova Inter-Governmental Economic Commission gave him credibility to speak on this issue.) Rogozin not only repeated the well-known points of departure of Russia's policies but also angered decision makers in Chisinau by instructing them not to undermine the existing peacekeeping arrangement, not to join any 'bloc of countries' and not to join Romania.[297] From Moscow's point of view, Rogozin's appointment was a way of stating that Russia had 'had enough' and to paralyze serious negotiations: Chisinau's negotiators now had no other choice but to conclude that to negotiate in earnest had become impossible. However, Rogozin's voice – although his voice is not just that of a single individual voice but, instead, represents an institution and articulates opinions which are very real in Russian decision-making circles – is not the same as the Kremlin's. Instead, his appointment was a political statement that more hard-line policies could take centre stage should Chisinau and the Western states fail to reconsider their political course. In August 2017, the Moldovan government decided to declare Rogozin as persona non grata. The foreign ministry's explanation that Rogozin's public comments did not correspond to the character of relations that Moldova prefers to build with Russia tried to minimize the conflict with Moscow. Yet, such complaint about the style of diplomacy was not heard in Moscow, because Rogozin's appointment already in itself was a restatement of the conflict, i.e. a manifestation of Moscow's unwillingness to have its relations with Moldova confined by the rules of horizontal international relations.

Rogozin's appointment came after the joint initiative together with Germany had failed to bring the federalization issue back into the negotiations. By spring 2012 it had become obvious that Russia faced more serious setbacks than the failure to launch a new form of European security cooperation with Germany based on the Meseberg Memorandum of June 2010. The US plan to construct a missile defence system in Eastern Europe was being realized with only nominal cooperation with Russia, and the diplomatic process to discuss the proposal made by President Medvedev for a European Security Treaty (EST), which included the Corfu Process and its aftermath to evaluate the chances of this proposal, was empty of substance. The EST proposal promoted Russia's long-standing goals, but the means were changed from the more flexible 'concert' idea (meaning an agreement among major states)[298] to the elaboration of legal instruments.[299] By stipulating that no state or international organization could have the exclusive right to regulate peace and security in the Euro-Atlantic area ('from Vancouver to Vladivostok'), the treaty would give Russia a voice on any issues it considered as a threat to its national security.[300] Of particular importance from the point of view of Russia's policies on Moldova was the attempt to restore neutrality as a crucial part of European security.

Concomitantly the conflict in Moldova has clearly demonstrated that, in Moscow's view, neutrality in proximity to Russia's geographic borders entails more than its legal definition, which, however, is the only way that Moldova is prepared to proceed. In Chisinau, the repetition of the statement that Moldova's Law of July 2005 (Law No. 173) considers Transnistria to be a part of the Republic of Moldova, and that this is in accordance with its Constitution and internationally recognized borders of Moldova, supports the categorical requirement for Russia's military withdrawal. Moscow, however, is interested in clear guarantees in terms of constitutional, legal and political structures which ensure the continuity of a neutral policy. From its point of view, the knot in Transnistria can be untied only by attaining legal guarantees that the United States and NATO would be prepared to show restraint in their military presence in Moldova and Eastern Europe. Consequently, relations between Moscow and Chisinau only returned to revolve around preliminary consensus – the starting point that enables the negotiations – when Foreign Minister Sergey Lavrov met the Moldovan Foreign Minister Andrei Galbur in April 2016 and supported the resumption of the '5+2' negotiations. This was designed to allow the parties to focus on complex issues, including 'defining the final status of Transdniestria as part of the united, indivisible and neutral Moldova'.[301]

The statement of the OSCE Ministerial Council in December 2017 reiterated the organization's aim to attain a similarly 'comprehensive' settlement of the Transnistrian conflict, 'based on the sovereignty and territorial integrity of the Republic of Moldova within its internationally recognized borders with a special status for Transdniestria that fully guarantees the human, political, economic and social rights of its population'.[302] However, this starting point of negotiations is continuously challenged by the approach in which the Transnistrian conflict is primarily considered as a principled issue over the post–Cold War order in Europe. A resolution adopted by the UN General Assembly in June 2018 upon the initiative of the Republic of Moldova, Georgia, Ukraine, Romania, Estonia, Latvia, Lithuania and Canada puts pressure on the OSCE to expedite the implementation of Russia's commitment to withdraw from Transnistria 'as agreed' at its summit held in Istanbul in 1999, and it urges Russia 'to complete, unconditionally and without further delay, the orderly withdrawal of the Operational Group of Russian Forces and its armaments from the territory of the Republic of Moldova'.[303] The decision here to include an item on the 'complete withdrawal of foreign military forces from the territory of the Republic of Moldova' in the General Assembly's provisional agenda for its next session in 2018–9[304] is not only an attempt to keep the Transnistrian conflict at the centre of international attention but also to ensure closer cooperation between Moldova, Georgia and Ukraine in the broader context of NATO. By strengthening their common political front vis-à-vis Russia, it is more likely to aggravate the geopolitical conflict between Russia and the West inside Moldova than to facilitate the resolution of the conflict over Transnistria.

The legitimization problem: The capability to protect as a quality of power

Until the recognition of the independence of Kosovo was put on the political agenda in the West, Moscow had very little reason – and possessed very few normative means in relation to the international community of states – to discuss the policy alternative of recognizing Transnistria's independence. In March 2008 (a few weeks after Kosovo had declared independence) discussions in the State Duma emphasized that the recognition of Kosovo's independence had become a new factor in the resolution of conflicts in Abkhazia, South-Ossetia and Transnistria. One representative remarked that the recognition of Transnistria's independence was the only option that remained for Russia if Moldova and Transnistria did not reach an agreement. Other representatives argued that this would be premature because the conditions are not yet there. A hasty recognition would shatter the CIS and lead to disruptive conflict. A reasonable intermediate solution which would stabilize the situation for the next decade or so and focus on economic cooperation was argued to be the best option.[305] Although these discussions may remain separate from the Kremlin's final decision, they serve to prepare the political ground for potential policy options. In March 2008, they signalled that the recognition of Transnistria's independence does exist as a future option and that such a decision would depend on the circumstances created by the policies of other states.

The leadership in the PMR has used the geopolitical momentum created by events in Kosovo to gain support for its own case. In August 2010, Vladimir Yastrebchak, the foreign minister of the PMR, emphasized that the statement made by the International Court of Justice on 22 July 2010 to confirm that Kosovo's unilateral declaration of independence contradicted neither international law nor the resolutions of the UN Security Council 'will have major importance for the negotiations on Transnistria'.[306] Simultaneously Igor Smirnov continued to emphasize Transnistria's unity with Russia and to argue in favour of the 'Slavic roots' of the population. These arguments found a positive response in the State Duma, which, according to Transnistrian media in April 2010, promised 'to back Transnistria' with reference to it being 'an inseparable part' of 'our Slavic unity'.[307] However, the Slavic connection alone is a politically controversial argument for supporting Russia's policies, which build on the idea of both Russia and Moldova being multinational states. Upon his return from Moscow in May 2011, Smirnov was able to announce that 'Russia will not betray Transnistria' and that Russia has declared commitment to the principle of respect for the will of the people.[308] However, this message was not publicly confirmed by either Sergei Naryshkin, head of the presidential administration, or Nikolai Patrushev, Secretary of the Russian Security Council (who also met with Smirnov), but, instead, by Konstantin Kosachev from the State Duma and Boris Gryzlov of the *Edinaia Rossiia* party. 'Russia was always together with Transnistria' and is remaining with Transnistria, and shall never leave it in trouble or to face its problems alone, Kosachev assured in Tiraspol later in the same month.[309] Although Russia has consistently assured its support, such support has been expressed at the parliamentary level of cooperation and in the cooperation between political parties. The Kremlin and the government have been cautious not to make commitments and to ensure that actions concerning Transnistria serve Russia's policies in the wider region. During his visit to Tiraspol in October 2012 – a few weeks before José Mañuel Barroso, the President of the European Commission, was to visit the Moldovan capital city – the Russian foreign ministry's special envoy Sergei Gubarev stated that in the case that 'loss' relating to Moldova's sovereignty or neutrality emerges, Russia's response will be to focus on the question about 'realizing Transnistria's right to self-determination'.[310] The next years demonstrated that neutrality, rather than the issue about the possible change of Moldova's status as an independent state, was the main point which Russia emphasized in the formulation of its policies on the Transnistrian conflict and Moldova's separatist problems.[311] This meant that the focus of its policies was consistently in Chisinau.

While such openness in Russian policies has done little to help Transnistria, the harmonization of the Transnistrian economy with the Russian market and the boosting of political integration through passport policies have aggravated the problem of international legitimacy created by Russia's support of Transnistria. The normative conflict became more polarized when the change of power in Chisinau in autumn 2009 intensified the conflict over the political and cultural identity of people on either side of the Dniestr River and, as a consequence thereof, strengthened the cultural connection of Moldova's Russian speakers with their historical motherland. Political speculation also emerged in the Russian-language media: should 'Bessarabia' ('right-bank' Moldova) join in a union with Romania, then the independence of the Dniester region would soon follow. Chisinau consistently denied such plans and explained that 96 per cent of the population was opposed to the idea of repeating the union of 1920.[312] However, the suspicions were more general in nature and included concerns over the impact of Romanian influence, which revives ideas and images of historical Bessarabia in Moldova and exacerbates the social and political conflict that for historical reasons persists between the Romanist movement and the cultural counterforce that the affiliation to Russia represents to it.

After the riots of 7 April 2009, in which protesters expressed their dissatisfaction with the results of parliamentary elections that were reported to give victory to the Communists, the government of Vladimir Voronin limited Romanian influence by imposing a visa regime on Romania. Simultaneously the Moldovan Constitutional Court ruled that it was constitutional to bar dual citizens from holding state offices. This was against the recommendation of the European Court of Human Rights, which had called upon Moldova to reconsider this provision in its law. Voronin's anti-Romanian policies collapsed after the re-elections in July. By 2010 the number of people in Moldova who held a Romanian passport on the basis of lineage in Bessarabia under Romania's rule (1918–40) had grown to half a million, and in 2018 this number was almost one million.[313] In the Russian and Transnistrian media, claims that Romanian passports are also increasingly held by residents of Transnistria prompted speculation over Romanian ambitions to regain 'Zadnistrovya', the 'side of the Dniester' (as the pre-Soviet term designated this geographical region) that overlaps with the Odessa area. The remarks made by the Romanian President Train Basescu to the effect that parts of those territories received by the former Ukrainian SSR after the Second World War should have been returned to Romania instead created much anxiety amongst that part of the population whose main affiliation is Russia.[314] Alongside the financial flows and the social and educational programs of the EU to support Romania, Moldova and Ukraine, it is these developments that continue to generate suspicions over the political consequences of historical and ethnic tensions in the near future and which become a fertile ground for the implementation of Russia's policies to support 'compatriots' and the local Russian-speaking population.[315]

In May 2009 a group of citizens' organizations and deputies in the *Obnovlenie* Party – the majority party in the Supreme Soviet of the PMR – proposed to introduce the Russian flag alongside the Soviet-style flag of the PMR. This suggestion was believed to confirm the course of action demanded in a referendum in September 2006, in which 96.9 per cent of the population was reported to have voted in favour of the separate existence that Transnistria claimed from Moldova already on 2 September 1990, and to have voiced their support for becoming part of the Russian Federation. The new practice of flying the Russian flag, which was rapidly implemented, was justified by arguing that the Russian flag on Transnistrian soil would reflect Transnistria's centuries-long history together with Russia.[316] Moscow's official response emphasized that such practice was not contrary to the Russian law and could be compared to the practice of flying the EU flag side-by-side with the Moldovan flag in front of the Mayor's office in Chisinau.[317] Simultaneously to the development of Moldova's relations with the EU, an equivalent political symbolism was introduced in Transnistria's relations with Russia. The decision by the PMR in October 2012 to create its own 'Eurasian region *Pridnestrovie*' after having refused to join the 'Euroregion Dniestr' established by Moldova and Ukraine the preceding February is a further example of such imitative policies. Whereas the Euroregion includes one Ukrainian region and seven Moldovan districts, the Eurasian region includes all districts under the control of the PMR – that is, it covers Transnistria and conceptually remains open to partners in Moldova and Ukraine. The political significance of this merely nominal institutional invention is not as absurd as it initially appears to be: it emphasizes that Transnistria's future lies in Russia's Eurasian integration and not in the integration processes connected with the EU. This is one more measure in the incremental integration that is taking place in small, concrete steps as well as through images and political promises – that is, a process through which Russia shows its commitment to support Transnistria yet refrains from making final decisions until the situation is deemed to be practically and politically ripe. This notwithstanding, the gradual and largely inconspicuous integration, which has accelerated since 2011, increases the political and normative pressure inside Russia to make a final decision on this matter.

'Imperial protection' and the legitimacy of rule

Already during the 1990s Transnistria presented a troubling conundrum for Russian rule because, domestically, it questioned how central rule was to respond to the wishes of a people in a distant corner of the former Soviet Union. The question emerges in relation to the domestic tradition of power, according to which the provision of such protection is an incontrovertible part of the legitimacy of rule as well as a sign of the greatness of the state. The ruler's demonstrated capability to protect the people and to directly appeal to, and have appeal for, the people is a historically important element in the legitimacy of rule in Russia. This tradition concurs with the Soviet ideals of social protection (i.e. the welfare of the people) and patriotism but its background lies in the earlier notion of 'imperial protection'. This is derived from the religious idea that the tsar's relation to his people is direct, i.e. that it bypasses and exists independently of the administrative apparatus and political institutions. In spring 2015, sixty-six social organizations in Transnistria decided to appeal directly to President Putin and ask for his protection of the people in Transnistria, who, according to them, found themselves 'blocked' from the sides of both Moldova and Ukraine.[318] Although arguably such action is meant to send a signal about the developments expected to follow should an external threat emerge and, thus, may not have been an initiative undertaken without political coordination, its form and content are firmly tied to centuries-old tradition. The religious notion that the people should appeal directly to the ruler because administrative and political institutions are ever-changing and unreliable in their wordly character is especially applicable to present-day formulations in contexts such as Transnistria, where relations to Moscow are not regulated by the institutions of the modern state. 'Protection' in this sense is strongly symbolic and demonstrates the greatness of Russia. It is a political performative and, as such, logically independent from its consequences in terms of any measurable actual change in the condition of the people who are addressed.[319]

In the modern day, the greatness shown through such protection is often demonstrated through 'humanitarian assistance', which in Russian practice is a far wider concept than is suggested by its Western connotation of universal altruism. Examples of the social protection that is aimed at earning respect for Russia's greatness amongst Transnistria's residents include the support provided for the health and education sectors as well as for the most vulnerable part of the population, in particular minors (maternity care, school meals, etc.) and the elderly.[320] While such support is all the more important because the liberal-utilitarian raison d'être of the state has failed in the eyes of ordinary people in Russia, its significance lies less in the welfare of citizens (in terms of a modern idea of the state) than in the clear demonstration of the traditional greatness of the state. The capability to protect is a quality of power, while the question of administrative form (Should Transnistria be part of the Russian Federation?) is a second-order issue. The specific quality of power, the appeal of which originates from the relation of ruler-to-ruled in the Russian tradition, connects the situation of the people in Transnistria to the question of the legitimacy of authority in Russia: not 'betraying' Transnistria is a symbol of the legitimacy of rule in Moscow. Therefore, the utilitarian argument, which calls to mind that the breakaway polity is an economic burden for Russia that cannot provide much benefit in return, has only little appeal in comparison with the protection which makes Russia great.

This quality of greatness does not refer to the 'great power' that carries the signs of its greatness in its external relations, but instead stems from the historical idea of great power-ness, *derzhavnost'*.[321] The emphasis here on external relations completely bypasses the core meaning of the term which comes from the verb 'to hold' (*derzhat'*): *derzhava* ('historical great power') unifies the power and authority held and the capability of holding it.[322] Legitimacy of rule requires a capability to 'hold' well: to protect and care for the well-being of the people. *Derzhavnost'* does not mean only military might, and although the emphasis of economic revitalization and the improvement of people's lives in the contemporary Russian project of the state gives it a modern meaning, it is not the people as individuals who are in focus here. Instead, it is the state's capability to ensure and protect the population's well-being and, on this basis, its capability to foster a collective sense of pride amongst them.[323] Against the backdrop of this tradition even people in the distant corner of Transnistria cannot be denied the requested physical and social protection because the provision of such protection is part of the legitimacy of rule and of the greatness of Russia. When the Moldovan president Vladimir Voronin indicated in 2008 that Russia could be ready to guarantee the restoration of Moldova's territorial integrity in exchange for its refusal to join NATO, this aroused much anger in the State Duma. It was argued that even if Georgia and Moldova should be 'lost' for Russia, it was 'shameful' and 'inappropriate' to use the rights of the population in Transnistria as a bargaining chip.[324] To speak of 'rights' is a contemporary type of discourse but its appeal lies in invoking the strong state which is capable of protecting its citizens. The moral obligation towards the people and, in terms of the historical idea of the greatness of the state, the impossibility of disregarding any specific part of the country form the dilemma encountered by Russian statehood in the contemporary world. This is a dilemma because in this present case the borders of the country are wider than the linear state borders, and also because Russian nationalism and ideas of Slavic unity create tensions within Russia's project as a multinational state.

The multifarious nature of Russia's connection to the population in Moldova reflects its long and multilayered historical presence in this country. The segment of the population which enjoys a special, privileged relationship with Moscow is not as easy to define as is the case, for example, in Estonia and Latvia, where Russia has consistently defended the rights of the Russian-speaking population to work and obtain education in their own language. Twice as many ethnic Russians live on the 'right bank' of the Dniestr River than in Transnistria (the 'left bank'), although their proportion of the population in 'right-bank' Moldova is lower – just over 10 per cent of the total population of 3.5 million – than it is in Transnistria, where they amount to one-third of the total population of 550,000 people. At first glance, Russia's idea of the Moldovan state does not fundamentally seem to contradict the argument made by Victor Osipov, Moldova's Deputy Prime Minister, in spring 2010: 'Moldovans, Ukrainians, Russians and other ethnicities on both sides [of the Dniestr River] – mostly Orthodox Christians, united through deep historical roots, kinship, mixed marriages, common culture and traditions – are compatible and capable of living together in the same state in peace and understanding.'[325] However, instead of the multicultural state with 'minority rights', the frame of interpretation is the 'Moldavist' culture, which is sharply opposed to the influence of Romanism and argues to offer a basis for the cultural identity of not only the people in Transnistria but all ethnic groups in Moldova. Opposition to the influence of Romanism is the firm dividing line of Russia's deep borders in Moldova and lays the basis for its policy alternatives which allow for both the reunification and the final separation of Transnistria from the Republic of Moldova. In the first of these alternatives, deep borders are created through the comprehensive package of settlement which would give Moscow the means of overseeing the implementation of neutrality in Moldova. The second alternative draws the border along the Dniestr River's right bank, where it has been since the ceasefire agreement of 1992. Although Moscow concentrates its efforts on the first alternative, the second alternative is also kept open. Developments in Ukraine can abruptly change the course of policies in Moldova and lead to situations in which Russia argues that Romanism is a security threat for the multinational character of Moldova, which the Russian military presence is designed to defend. The probability of Transnistria's final separation is increased if Chisinau's policies prompt Moscow to conclude that Romanism is becoming the kind of politically mobilizing force in Moldova that it was during the final years of the Soviet Union and that Moldova also has its own equivalent of 'a Saakashvili' i.e. a leader who would prompt speculation about crossing the Dniester and seeking alignment with NATO.[326] Such interpretations can be provoked by an occurrence of violent incidents at the de facto border and lead to a military confrontation that would accelerate Transnistria's process of final separation from Moldova and push it to join Russia. This part of the book concludes with a discussion of Gagauzia, which is a further example that supports the argument that it is the first alternative, rather than these other kinds of developments, which is the priority of Russia's policies.

10

Gagauzia and the Quest for Guarantees of Autonomy by Regional Powers

While Transnistria is an issue in Russia because it appeals to notions about protecting the people whose language and culture are Russian, the question about the obligation to protect Gagauzia exists in a wider multinational frame. In March 2013, Mihail Formuzal, the Bashkan (Governor) of the 'autonomous territorial formation' of Gagauzia (Gagauz-Yeri) in Moldova, made a proposal that aimed to increase the region's autonomy by lending support to the idea of Moldova's federal structure. If Gagauzia were part of a federal Moldova, the autonomy that it presently enjoys in its internal affairs on the basis of a Moldovan law in force since 1994 would be extended and provide it with a position to influence Moldova's foreign and security policy. In his speech at Istanbul's Aydin University, the bashkan envisioned a model for Gagauzia's cultural and political existence that would be very similar to the Soviet autonomous regions which were established in connection with titular nations within the Soviet Socialist Republics and which were protected by the central power in Moscow. He argued that 'the main strategic goal of all small nations' is to counteract processes in which 'each year, dozens of nationalities and ethnic groups disappear, and with them languages, culture, traditions and customs are dying'. The strategic task that he outlined for the small nations includes 'a peaceful dialogue with the titular nation or constructive partnerships with the guarantor-countries', which the bashkan describes as 'the major powers, which provide assistance and support to small nations'.[327] Gagauz-Yeri has a population of 150,000 (2017), 83 per cent of which are ethnic Gagauz and 93 per cent Orthodox Christians.[328] The Gagauz declared themselves an autonomous republic in August 1990, after the Moldovan (Romanian) language was accepted as an official language in August 1989 and suspicions were raised that Moldova might join Romania.[329] During 1992–3, when the power structures were in upheaval, Gagauz paramilitary forces clashed with Moldovan authorities and were supported by the passive presence of Russia's army (the numbers of which remain unclear). The conflict did not develop into an armed encounter but, politically, Comrat (the Gagauz administrative centre) worked together with Tiraspol to promote the idea of Moldova as a confederation of three states. In February 1994 Comrat agreed to drop the idea of confederation and to settle on a degree of autonomy envisaged by a law on the special legal status of Gagauz-Yeri. Based on this law the Gagauz are today recognized as more than only a national minority and an ethnic population, which was their status during the Soviet period. [330] Nowadays, the status of the region is formally close to a federal arrangement within a non-federal state. The recognition of 'the self-determination of the Gagauz people' has rather wide implications for internal administration and external cooperation in economic and cultural affairs.[331] It does not, however, include the right to separation, and the only 'constitutional guarantee' that the Gagauz have for their autonomous status is their right to apply to the Constitutional Court of Moldova with enquiries over the constitutionality of Chisinau's acts. Moldova's politicized judicial system increases the weaknesses in this guarantee and, less than a decade after the adoption of the special law in 1994, the Gagauz started to express their dissatisfaction with Moldovan authorities' interference in the region's affairs, especially in the elections of the bashkan through universal suffrage.

Just like all of Moldova, Gagauzia was subject to Russification policies during the rule of tsarist Russia and, especially, during Soviet rule in the late 1950s. However, although nationalist sentiments were suppressed until the final years of the Soviet Union, the Soviet state was a protective superstructure for the Gagauz in much the same way as the Russian Empire had been. Their anti-Romanian sentiments were greatly strengthened under Romanian rule (1920–40 and 1941–4) when they were repressed because of their historical loyalty to Russia. Like Transnistria, Gagauzia almost unanimously voted to maintain the Soviet Union in the referendum organized by Gorbachev in March 1991, and most of them supported the coup in Moscow five months later in August. When Moldova was preparing for its declaration of independence in August 1991, the Gagauz were divided on this issue and, in order to keep their future in their own hands, ultimately declared their own, independent Gagauz Soviet Socialist Republic. Today, their striped flag is a modified version of the Russian tricolour with the addition of three stars, and the region is a stronghold of pro-Russian political parties.[332] The three stars in the flag symbolize Gagauzia's three different cultures and languages. In addition to the Moldovan (Romanian) language, which is Moldova's national tongue, Gagauzia has two further official languages, Gagauz and Russian, the latter of which is their main language of communication with the wider world.[333]

These symbolic practices are signs of the lasting significance of the history of Russia's imperial protection for the Gagauz today. A central element in the old Russian tradition is the conception that the ruler has the moral obligation (in front of God) to recognize and respect the specific character of the Russian people (*narod*); and by extension of the same logic, the ruler (although, in this case, based on the grace at his or her discretion) was also expected to respect the specificity of the *non*-Russian peoples, especially if they adopted the Russian Orthodox religion in exchange for Moscow's protection. Consequently the Gagauz, while their existence under the protection of an Orthodox ruler is a constitutive part of the history and identity of their community, are able without problems to identify themselves as a small nation among the Turkic peoples. In the modern world, the divine connection in the tsar's rulership (which derives from Moscow's framing as the 'Third Rome') is no longer a metaphor which can be used, and legitimacy of action must be sought in front of the 'people', i.e. in the moral obligation to protect them. The bashkan's initiative did not specify the names of the 'guarantor-states' but presented its argument without any specific political context. By speaking of 'guarantor-countries' who are 'powers', the historical idea of the great power is actualized in it in the present-day frame of the protection of an ethnic group's cultural rights and the autonomy required for its survival as a distinct group. In the context of Moldova it is clear that his proposal appeals to Russia's role as 'guarantor-state' (which is the term used by Russia about its role in the Transnistrian conflict). Because the Gagauz are ethnically relatively homogenous, their case is very different from that of the Transnistrians. However, historically as well as today they offer a piece in the ethnic mosaic that weakens another regional power – Romania and Romanian cultural influence – and diminishes the political authority of the Western states in Moldova. It is also significant that the proposal was presented in Turkey, a major power amongst Turkic peoples and a country that is historically important in Moldova and, today, vital for its economy. Turkey has supported the autonomy of Gagauzia, although it has aptly avoided politicizing the issue.[334] The idea of such collaborative protection is intriguing also from the perspective of the settlement that Russia pursues in the conflict over Nagorno-Karabakh, where Russia and Turkey are the two background powers in the wider region in a far clearer way than in Gagauzia.

By contrast to Moldova's conflict regions, in Nagorno-Karabakh (where no peacekeeping forces could be established) the risk of violent confrontations and their escalation remains continuously very real – as was shown so clearly by the eruption of violence and the need for a new ceasefire in April 2016. The examination in Part Three of this book tries to identify the course charted by Russia's settlement policies in the Nagorno-Karabakh conflict between Armenia and Azerbaijan. Border is the thematic dimension that dominates this conflict, because Nagorno-Karabakh has little any other significance to Russia than being a part of its extensive policy arrangements in the region. It cannot be overlooked that the State Duma Declaration on the policy of the Russian Federation on Abkhazia, South Ossetia and Transnistria of 21 March 2008[335] does not mention independence as a goal for Nagorno-Karabakh, although it mentions it in the three other cases. However, as will be seen in the following chapters, this does not mean that Russian policies totally exclude the possibility of Karabakh's independence.

Part Three

Nagorno-Karabakh: Leverage for Controlling Russia's Deep Border Arrangements with Armenia and Azerbaijan

11

The Failed Policies of the Past and the Complexity of the Contemporary Conflict

The conflicts in Transnistria and Nagorno-Karabakh differ from each other in respect to the resolution processes. The Concept of the Foreign Policy of the Russian Federation approved by President Putin in November 2016 (Article 58) emphasizes that 'Russia strongly advocates a political and diplomatic settlement of conflicts in the post-Soviet space', and that it, specifically, 'works within the existing multilateral negotiating mechanism to find an inclusive solution to the Transnistrian issue, respecting the sovereignty, territorial integrity and neutral status of the Republic of Moldova in determining the special status of Transnistria',[336] and

> to settle the Nagorno-Karabakh conflict by working together with the other States that are co-chairs in the Minsk Group of the Organization for Security and Cooperation in Europe (OSCE) and basing on principles set forth in joint statements by the presidents of Russia, United States of America and the French Republic in 2009–13.[337]

In Moldova, Russia typically pursues its policies on its own, whereas in Nagorno-Karabakh the international frame of cooperation (the OSCE Minsk Group) has more significance for Russia, partly because this conflict lacks a peacekeeping arrangement. Moreover, Nagorno-Karabakh has no ethnic Russian or predominantly Russian-speaking population, and Russia has no economic or major geostrategic interests in the area which, as a de facto state, claims a territory of 11,458 square kilometres (the area within the 1991 Soviet administrative lines is 4,400 sq. km) and has a population of just over 100,000 (official figures from recent years give numbers around 140,000). Instead, the region's significance for Russia is indirect and lies in Russian attempts to maintain and develop relations between the two adversarial countries in the conflict, Armenia and Azerbaijan, and to pursue its economic and geopolitical interests in the wider region of the Caucasus and Northwest Asia from Turkey to the Himalayas. Russia's repeated emphasis of the importance of maintaining 'peace and stability' in the region[338] amounts to general goals and is an encoded expression of Russia's specific interests and aims in the region.

Russia's interest in preventing destabilization in 'Transcaucasia' – as Russia's Foreign Policy Concept from February 2013 still denoted the region[339] – has a long history in policies of tsarist Russia and the Soviet Union, which have always sought to douse conflicts that have repeatedly flared in the region in order to prevent them from spreading into neighbouring regions. In *The Black Garden*[340] (2003) Thomas de Waal cites Luigi Villari, a British journalist and writer, who witnessed the conclusion of a violent encounter between Armenians and Azeri ('Tartars') in the town of Shusha (Shushi for the Armenians) in Nagorno-Karabakh in 1905: 'a peace conference was held at the Russian church ... Tartars and Armenians publicly embraced each other and swore eternal friendship – until the next time... The Russian troops 'seem to have done nothing at all while the fighting was going on, but the military band performed to celebrate the conciliation.'[341] In 1905, the Russian Empire had been weakened by the Russo–Japanese war and the growing pressure to modernize and democratize its autocratic rule. By the late 1980s, the conflict, which had remained simmering beneath the surface of Soviet rule and had been aggravated after Nagorno-Karabakh was declared an autonomous *oblast'* of Azerbaijan in 1923, started to unfold with Armenia's demands to end the division of the 'Armenian homeland' and to attach Nagorno-Karabakh to the Armenian SSR. When the conflict flared up in 1988 a large majority of Karabakh's population (more than 90 per cent, according to some estimates) were ethnic Armenians.

Earlier, in 1918, both Armenia and Azerbaijan had declared independence and made territorial claims on Nagorno-Karabakh. This rivalry was ended with the Red Army's conquest of the region in 1920, and it was held in abeyance until the late-Soviet period. A new source of frustration was the Soviet Constitution of 1977, which stipulated that in the Soviet republics the language of the titular nation was to become the official language throughout the republic. In Nagorno-Karabakh this meant increased Azeri dominance over local authority structures, especially in the domains of education and internal security. When the conflict escalated into serious communal violence in the summer of 1991, Soviet president Mikhail Gorbachev was reported to have been not only uninformed about the scope of the violence but also indifferent to the conflict parties' arguments. The Kremlin was preoccupied with too many other pressing matters to spare much concern for Karabakh, and the main goal was to cap the conflict and prevent any spillover. 'What meaning does that have?' Gorbachev is reported to have asked when Armenian leaders pointed out to him that his information was one-sided and stemmed only from the Azeri side.[342]

Inter-communal violence had erupted in 1987, and the Karabakh Armenians proceeded to actively appeal to Moscow; they also sent a petition on the administrative relocation of Nagorno-Karabakh (as they had already done in 1945, 1965 and 1977). In February 1988 the local-government *Sovet* (Council) of the Nagorno-Karabakh Autonomous *Oblast'* (NKAO) of Azerbaijan made a request to the Azerbaijani and Armenian SSRs to transfer the NKAO from Azerbaijan to Armenia. After pogroms occurred in late February against the Armenians in Sumgait (near Baku),[343] in June the Armenian Supreme Soviet voted to accept this transfer, while the Azerbaijani Supreme Soviet reaffirmed that Nagorno-Karabakh was part of Azerbaijani territory. In July, the Presidium of the Supreme Soviet in Moscow resolved that the region was to remain part of Azerbaijan, and the Politburo sent its own representative, Arkady Volsky, to Karabakh. When in September Azerbaijani troops took the town of Shusha and Armenian troops took Stepanakert, Moscow introduced special rule over Karabakh, and by January 1989 Nagorno-Karabakh had been put under the control of the special administrative committee led by Volsky. This arrangement was ineffective and the committee was dissolved in November, just before the Armenian Supreme Soviet and the Karabakh Armenians' National Council declared unification. The conflict had already started to have a serious economic impact months before this when Azerbaijan imposed a rail blockade on land-locked Armenia and the NKAO, and the events had resulted in labour strikes in Armenia.

Moscow failed to react to the signs of escalating violence and intervened only when the pogroms of late February 1988 in Sumgait threatened to further exacerbate the tense situation – and gave it a reason to intervene also because of the increasing sense of independent decision making in Baku. While Azerbaijani officials were not active in preventing the violence, Moscow implemented a curfew and sent troops of the Ministry of the Interior (MVD); soon after, they added a local state of martial law and brought in the military with armoured vehicles. After the Sumgait events, Gorbachev reconfirmed his policy of refusing to change the borders of the union republics. The Kremlin argued that the Soviet Union had at least nineteen potential territorial conflicts and that it would be unwise to set a precedent by making concessions in any one of them. Instead, a futile attempt was made to defuse the conflict by providing financial aid to improve Karabakh's economy.

Violence against Armenians in the Baku area flared up again in the 'Black January' of 1990, when the events became even more clearly intertwined with the rise of the Azeri nationalist movement against Soviet rule. This time the Kremlin's military intervention was more serious and resulted in the deaths of 93–130 civilians in Baku. Additionally, 20–30 Soviet military personnel died, many of them due to friendly fire. Like previously, the Kremlin's response was to prevent information about the violence from spreading in order to prevent any spillover into other regions. When the Kremlin made a decision to interfere militarily to end the violence in January 1990, a state of emergency was, at first, not declared in the Azerbaijani capital but rather in the other areas and regions, including Karabakh. Moscow's approach was to douse the conflict by referring to 'criminals' and 'hooligans,' as well as by initiating criminal investigations and sending into the conflict areas 'People's Groups' meant to represent 'Soviet values' so as to counter the demonstrators. These values – friendship, mutual assistance and the equality of all Soviet subjects – failed to appeal to the Karabakh Armenians, who were frustrated about the situation in which all public infrastructure, including internal security structures and education, was under Azeri control, and where their ability to communicate with Armenia, at that time more affluent than Azerbaijan, was limited.

In spring 1991 command structures within the Soviet army had become confused, and Azerbaijan was able to use the air-defence facilities of the Soviet 4th Army stationed in Azerbaijan against the Karabakh forces, which initially had no air defence. Due to the circumstance that it neighboured on Turkey, Soviet Azerbaijan was far more heavily armed than Armenia. In March 1991, Azerbaijan, which the Kremlin clearly backed in the face of Karabakh separatism, supported the maintenance of the Soviet Union in the referendum introduced by Gorbachev. Armenia, whose parliament had passed a resolution on sovereignty in August 1990, refused to participate in the referendum. By this time the advocates for Armenian independence were developing relations with the new Russia that was emerging under the leadership of Boris Yeltsin. When the coup of August 1991 failed in Moscow, it was too late for Azerbaijan to withdraw its support for those who aimed at the restoration of Soviet rule. After the attempted coup in Moscow, the conflict over Karabakh escalated into a war, which reached its peak in May 1992 but lasted until the ceasefire of May 1994.

Accompanied by Nursultan Nazarbayev, Boris Yeltsin visited Nagorno-Karabakh in September 1991 and negotiated a peace plan, which was signed in Zheleznovodsk in the same month.[344] Peace was brokered but then broken in November when an Azerbaijani helicopter carrying the country's political establishment as well as Russian and Kazakhstani participants in the peace process was shot down, presumably by an Armenian faction. Azerbaijan immediately abolished Nagorno-Karabakh's autonomous status by a vote of its National Council on 26 November. The Karabakh Armenians responded by reconfirming the declaration of an independent Nagorno-Karabakh

Republic, which had already been declared earlier on 2 September, with a referendum on 10 December – a referendum in which the Azeri population did not participate. In January 1992, when the Soviet Union no longer existed, Nagorno-Karabakh's parliament confirmed its independence through yet another declaration – the third in only six months.

Nagorno-Karabakh's announcement of its secession from Azerbaijan on 2 September 1991 came three days after Azerbaijan's declaration of independence on 30 August 1991. Armenia declared independence three weeks later, on 23 September. In the process of the dissolution of Soviet power, the Karabakh conflict was transformed from a bilateral territorial dispute into a vastly more complex question which also came to entail the question of national self-determination and the demand for independence. Already in spring 1988, the Karabakh Armenians had mooted independence yet received a clear rejection based on the Kremlin's policy of intact borders between the union republics. Article 72 of the Soviet Constitution of 1977 gave the union republics – but not the autonomous regions – a formal right to secede from the Union, and article 78 stipulated that changing the territory of a union republic required the consent of this republic; this gave Azerbaijan formal legal justification and laid the basis for its policy even after the authority of the Soviet Constitution crumbled in Moscow's August 1991 coup.

The Belovezh Accords of December 1991, which recognized only the former Soviet republics (SSRs) as new sovereign states, were a continuation of Soviet-era principles and, thus, not a frame within which the Karabakh Armenians' request for the recognition of the independence of a Soviet autonomous region could be accommodated. Although Yeltsin entered into complex negotiations over the position of national subjects within the Russian Federation, the principle of only recognizing those borders which had existed between the former Soviet republics for the newly independent republics was retained and unquestioned until the issue of Kosovo's independence became a dispute with the West in 2007 and the Russia–Georgia war took place in 2008. However, the reality of Russian policies was more multilayered already during the 1990s, as was evident in the support that was provided to the separatists by supporting Armenia militarily. Nonetheless the continuity embedded in the Belovezh Accords gave Azerbaijan the privilege of being able to present itself as upholding the basic norms of the international community. Nagorno-Karabakh, just like Transnistria in relation to Moldova and Abkhazia and South Ossetia in relation to Georgia, was able to argue that it had separated from the Soviet titular nation-country before this entity became independent, i.e. that it was never a part of *post*-Soviet Azerbaijan; despite this, its argument remained in contradiction with the premise of continuity which is not only embedded in the Belovezh Accords but also reflected in a number of normative international contexts, such as the Helsinki Final Act (1975) of the establishment of the CSCE.

According to Azerbaijani President Ilham Aliyev, the Helsinki Final Act means that the principle of the 'self-determination of peoples should be provided within the territorial integrity of countries'.[345] Although a different interpretation was not possible in the mid-1970s when the CSCE was established, we must keep in mind that the Helsinki document was a diplomatic compromise on a set of principles which both East and West could agree on during the late Cold War period. In this context the meaning of these principles was recognized as being dependent on how a segment in the document was read in relation to its other segments. In the UN General Assembly, and also in the Non-Aligned Movement after Azerbaijan became a member (in 2012), Azerbaijan has been able to mobilize international opinion from especially formerly colonized states for the support of the principles stating the inviolability of state borders. After the referendum in the Crimea on March 16, 2014, President Ilham Aliyev underlined that the territorial integrity of states cannot be changed without their consent and that Crimea and Sevastopol remain inalienable parts of Ukraine.[346] Armenia on the other hand accords primacy to national self-determination and, in this context, mentions the principle of territorial integrity. The difference which follows from the different words and the differing hierarchy of concepts is crucial and opens up two entirely different contexts for argumentation: one in relation to the Soviet origins of the multinational state, and the other advocating independence on ethno-national grounds.

Two Different Patterns for Building Statehood

Azerbaijan, which borders on Iran and is culturally connected with Turkey, has historically been a frontier territory for Russia and today constitutes an important bridge in the transport network of the Caspian Sea region. Landlocked Armenia, for its part, has long played a geopolitical role as a buffer between Turkey and Azerbaijan. During the tsarist era and the early Soviet decades, the Armenians were among the ethnic groups held to be most loyal to central (Russian) power, and they were utilized as a balancing force vis-à-vis the 'Turks' – a notion which includes the Azeri population. Especially in the military and in the Communist Party Armenians held a superior position in relation to the Azeri, who were Muslim and traditionally suspected of collaborating with Turkey and the Azeri population in Persia (Iran). During the first years of the Soviet Union (1922-3) the Soviet government established the Nagorno-Karabakh Autonomous Oblast' (NKAO) within Azerbaijan as part of its policies to gain control of the South Caucasus.[347] Massive population exchanges between tsarist Russia and the Ottoman Empire had made the Armenians a 'diaspora nation' in Russia, and the NKAO with its predominantly ethnic Armenian population further strengthened this identity. The position of the Armenians was unique in the Soviet Union because they were endowed with both a republic and an autonomous region within another union republic. In Nagorno-Karabakh the authority structures, which were in Azeri hands, fuelled the interplay of socio-economic conflict and historical animosities. In late-Soviet and post-Soviet Armenia the Armenian Movement, which has its background in the Karabakh Committee,[348] became an articulate expression of a strong, ethnically based national identity. Thus, the Karabakh cause was not only about Karabakh but also about Armenian national identity and independence. The intensity with which this cause was pursued was much strengthened by the memory of the Armenian people's centuries-long oppression and suffering under Turkish rule, of which the Azeri 'Tartars' (who were also called 'Caucasus Turks') were considered an extension.[349]

Azerbaijani identity, by contrast, is multi-ethnic and emphasizes territorial integrity as a constituent principle of statehood. The traditional habitual affiliation of the population is strongly local and regional. The delicate task of maintaining the unity of the multi-ethnic country is reflected in the Azerbaijani Constitution, which seeks to provide the ethnically heterogeneous state with an ideational frame by emphasizing – paradoxically, when we consider the rather authoritarian rule that pertains – the rights and the duties of the individual, and by adopting 'people's self-determination' as an approach to local governance and regional autonomy. It follows that giving up Karabakh would risk triggering the internal disintegration of ethnically heterogeneous Azerbaijan. While the Azerbaijani state structurally resembles the Soviet and Russian ideal of a multinational state, Armenian ethno-nationalism, by contrast, has more in common with the ethno-nationalist movements that in Russia contributed to the dissolution of the Soviet Union. However, it also must be noted that the movement among Armenians to change the status of Nagorno-Karabakh by emphasizing national self-determination did not start out with any substantive anti-Communist or even anti-Soviet elements.[350] This feature was brought in only later, after the fall of the Soviet Union, when Western states made Nagorno-Karabakh into a symbol of a small people's struggle for independence from the repressive regional structures which were perceived as a legacy of Soviet rule.

The conflict is extremely tense because Nagorno-Karabakh has iconic significance for the recently established statehood of both Armenia and Azerbaijan. In other words, 'losing out' in this conflict would cripple the entire idea of either of the new states to have emerged from the dissolution of the Soviet Union in the early 1990s.[351] The making of concessions to the other party easily constitutes political suicide in both countries' domestic politics. In 1998, four years after the ceasefire came into force on 12 May 1994, the first president of the Republic of Armenia, Levon Ter-Petrosian, was forced to resign due to strong domestic opposition to the concessions he was ready to make in order to end the conflict. During the next two decades (1998–2018) the Armenian leadership was *in persona* tied to the issue of Nagorno-Karabakh, which means that this issue became tightly bound to the identity and statehood of independent Armenia. Ter-Petrosian was succeeded by Robert Kocharyan, who had been the first president of the self-declared Nagorno-Karabakh Republic (NKR, the Republic of Artsakh since 2018).[352] Serzh Sargsyan, who became president in 2008, was Armenia's minister of defence during the Karabakh war, which erupted in autumn 1991 and lasted until the ceasefire in May 1994.[353] When in April 2018 Sargsyan resigned from his short-lived position as prime minister (which had been made the centre of power through a constitutional reform undertaken in 2015), the personal tie that had made it possible for Yerevan to speak on behalf of Karabakh was unravelled. At the same time the reorganization of political power in spring 2018 through a 'Velvet Revolution', which brought the opposition leader Nikol Pashinian to power as prime minister, demonstrated that the Karabakh issue is firmly a part of Armenian identity and statehood, and that therefore the country's security policy remains unaffected even by radical changes in domestic politics.[354]

In Azerbaijan the goal of regaining Karabakh and its surrounding regions under Armenian control is closely tied to the public legitimacy of rule. Now in their second generation, the number of refugees from Karabakh, Armenia and the seven regions that Armenia holds in its military control next to Karabakh has grown from 200,000–250,000 during the early 1990s to 750,000–990,000 people.[355] In compliance with Article 78 of the Soviet Constitution of 1977, which stipulated that the territory of a union republic may not be altered without its consent, the Azerbaijani Constitution demands that any change of the state borders requires a referendum.[356] In spite of the firmness of its principled point of departure, Baku's communication with Yerevan's political elites was still possible in the decade following the ceasefire due to the habitual links of the Soviet period. Heydar Aliyev, who had risen to power in 1969 when he became the first secretary of the Azerbaijani Communist party, represented the old Soviet elite. He had resigned from the Soviet Politburo in October 1987 due to a combination of ideological disagreements and political rivalries but made his political comeback four years later, first as the speaker of his native Nakhchivan autonomous republic and then, in June 1993, as the speaker of the Azerbaijani parliament. Thereafter he became president of the country, which at that time was on the verge of disintegration due to the Karabakh conflict and the war with Armenia. While in Armenia Heydar Aliyev was considered as a leader with whom contact for negotiation was possible, his son Ilham, who became president in 2003, soon gained the reputation of being a young president who exacerbated the conflict with rhetoric and conduct that was meant to toughen his image in his own country. Simultaneously it was Armenia that had gained a militarily dominant position by the time of the ceasefire. Although the ceasefire of May 1994 was continuously breached by incidents across the Line of Contact, it was not until the four-day war of April 2016 that Azerbaijani military forces took back a tiny part of the territory. The significance of this event was political rather than military in that it served to remind the international community of the existence of the still-unresolved conflict and to show the continued determination by Azerbaijan, which had by now evolved into an energy-rich state, to gain back the territories. From Russia's point of view, tightening the knot from both sides – that is, reaffirming the link with Nagorno-Karabakh by supporting Armenia, while at the same time threatening Azerbaijan with the possibility of losing Karabakh and the surrounding areas under Armenian control – is instrumental in its relations with both countries: with Armenia, where military deterrence is ultimately dependent on a functioning alliance with Russia; and with Azerbaijan, which, with its newly found wealth, is increasingly independent from Russia in its foreign and security policies. In both countries, Nagorno-Karabakh is the issue which enables Russia to secure its deep borders by cleaving deeply into their societies. However, the success of such policies requires complex balancing policies towards both Armenia and Azerbaijan, and in a dynamically changing regional environment this cannot mean merely the maintenance of the status quo in Karabakh.

12

Russia's Settlement Policies in Karabakh: The Centrality of Diplomatic Efforts

For fifteen years following the ceasefire of May 1994, Russian intervention in the Karabakh conflict was limited to attempts to prevent its escalation and the normative principles of the policies were guided by the Belovezh Accords that represented continuity based on the norms advocated by the Soviet Union for the security of its borders during the late Cold War period. More flexible policies appeared after 2008, which was the year that Western states recognized the independence of Kosovo and Russia recognized the independence of Abkhazia and South Ossetia. In September 2010 the chairman of the State Duma Committee for CIS Affairs and Compatriot Relations Konstantin Zatulin provoked Azerbaijan by stating in the Armenian press that 'it will not be possible to deprive Nagorno Karabakh of its independence. This must be recognized'.[357] His argument remained on the margin of opinions in Russia and, for instance Alexei Ostrovsky, member of the State Duma Committee on International Affairs and representative for the Liberal Democratic Party of Russia, by contrast reiterated Russia's official line of policy by calling to mind that 'the whole world, including the Russian Federation, supports the territorial integrity of Azerbaijan'. However, the public articulation of a different opinion was a sign of new uncertainty over the future direction of Russian policies.

In Russian society the 'demonstrated will of the people' has mobilized far less support for Karabakh's cause than it has for the separatist regions of both Georgia and Moldova. The reason for this lies in the geographic, cultural and political distance of this conflict from Russian society, i.e. the lack of a direct and apparent Russian connection. The people of Karabakh are connected to Armenia instead, in terms of both ethnicity and protection. The residents of Nagorno-Karabakh are generally not holders of Russian but Armenian passports. In the economic sense the major 'Russian' features there are the investments made by rich Russian Armenians, often in their native districts. Because there is neither a significant compatriot connection nor a direct 'special relationship' based on a historical relationship of protection, the domestic Russian discussion is relatively insignificant outside the

Armenian and Azeri diaspora. Thus, in Russia the Karabakh issue has iconic, 'existential' significance within these communities, whereas the significance for Moscow's policies is symbolic and relates to Russia's capabilities to act as a power in the wider region. Against this background the range of the discussion in the State Duma, in particular, reveals the 'policy variants' which are considered beneath the surface of a repeated emphasis on 'peace and stability'. This tells us about the variants which may or may not be used later on, depending on the circumstances created by the policies of other states. While the threat of recognizing Nagorno-Karabakh's independence previously served mainly as a warning designed to restrain Azerbaijan from major military action in the conflict, Kosovo's independence and Russia's subsequent recognition of the independence of Georgia's separatist regions relaxed the normative conditions which previously obtained in Russia's relations with the international normative community. In this way, the possibility of recognizing the independence of Nagorno-Karabakh became far more instrumental for Russian policies than had previously been the case. Consequently, the entire structure of relations through which Russia tries to control this conflict became potentially more agile in its policymaking.

The conflict has a structure which has made it possible to keep it relatively stable. Should Azerbaijan strive to restore its sovereignty over Nagorno-Karabakh by military force it could not reckon on winning a new war, in spite of its well-equipped army. Even in the case that a potential war could be kept in a local theatre, it would be a long battle in the trenches and, moreover, defeat would be immediately political in nature: Russia could be prepared to consider Nagorno-Karabakh's independence or leave the matter to Armenia. This possibility is rendered likely due to the military confidence which Russia's military presence creates in Armenia as well as the uncertainties over how the obligations of collective security in the frame of the Collective Security Treaty Organization (CSTO), where Armenia is a member state, would come into effect in case of such a crisis. Azerbaijan's resort to a full-scale conventional war is a hypothetical scenario, and the purpose of the political and military threat is to prevent the emergence of conditions and circumstances that would be conducive to war. Such conditions include Azerbaijan's close cooperation with NATO and tying its Caspian Sea energy resources more closely to Western networks so as to facilitate this political direction. Consequently, the development of economic and political cooperation with Azerbaijan is an essential part of the mechanism through which Moscow seeks to keep the conflict in Karabakh in balance between Armenia and Azerbaijan. However, because this cooperation also serves a number of other important goals, both economic and geopolitical, Karabakh is a regulatory piece in a much more comprehensive strategy designed to increase Russia's presence in the region by developing regional and interregional networks of cooperation.

Russia's immediate goal is to prevent violence from erupting in a conflict that lacks a peacekeeping arrangement and could place Russia in a difficult situation in regard to its military alliance relationship with Armenia – a development which would seriously and unexpectedly limit the political space that Russia needs in order to be able to pursue its more comprehensive interests in the wider region. Russia's long-term leverage over Armenia is the military relationship which enables Armenia to guarantee security for Nagorno-Karabakh. However, the more tightly Russia aligns itself with Armenia and provides it with aid, the more its relations with Azerbaijan will deteriorate, and this situation, in turn, increases Armenia's political space of manoeuvre. Should violence escalate beyond the areas adjacent or close to the Line of Contact (unlike in April 2016, when it remained so), Russia may not be able to prevent further escalation without deploying its military forces – which would thereby generate pressure for the other co-chairs and OSCE members to bring in their peace enforcement units and possibly even establish their own military presence in the volatile situation that would ensue. If the conflict escalates and Russia chose not to interfere, it would lose credibility in terms of its bilateral as well as collective security arrangements in the region (CSTO). For all these reasons Russia's first and immediate goal is to prevent any escalation whatsoever of violence in the Karabakh conflict.

In Russia's deep border arrangements with the two opposing countries in the Karabakh conflict, it is the military alliance with Armenia that is a basically stable element; Azerbaijan remains the less controllable element and hence requires Russia to set up political restraints with military and economic incentives. In the early 1990s Azerbaijan was economically disadvantaged in comparison with Armenia, but its oil and natural gas resources as well as its fortuitous location as a transit country for energy from Central Asia to Europe have abruptly changed the situation. Azerbaijan's defence budget has more than doubled in the new millennium and is now double Armenia's entire state budget. Its new geo-economic heft has geopolitical implications in the 'strategic alliance' that is being constructed between this country and Georgia and Turkey as energy transit countries to European markets. Pipelines also bring an increased desire for the military capacity to protect them, and major Western investments are unlikely to be made without ensuring military support to the region. In the light of these developments, the unresolved status of Nagorno-Karabakh provides Russia with political leverage to influence the choices made in Baku. However, there are serious issues which reduce the credibility that Russia would actually use the heaviest political weapon it has against Azerbaijan, i.e. permitting

Nagorno-Karabakh to become independent: such a measure would not only push Azerbaijan towards the West but also destabilize Russia's relations with Armenia. Consequently, the best path is diplomatic in character and consists of trying to hold both states in a mutually balanced relationship with Russia.

Russia's mediating role

In connection with the meeting of the Collective Security Treaty Organization (CSTO) in September 2008, Russian Foreign Minister Sergey Lavrov emphasized that no parallel exists between the situation in South Ossetia and Abkhazia, on the one hand, and the Nagorno-Karabakh settlement process on the other hand. At a press conference Lavrov argued that Georgia systematically undermined negotiation formats and the settlement mechanism as well as seeking to change arrangements in the security zones which had been set up in the early 1990s, but 'nothing of the kind occurs around [the] Nagorno-Karabakh settlement'.[358] Later that autumn the declaration signed by Russian president Dmitry Medvedev and his Azerbaijani and Armenian counterparts Ilham Aliyev and Serzh Sargsyan in Moscow on 2 November was celebrated as a diplomatic success. It was the first document jointly signed by Armenia and Azerbaijan since the ceasefire agreement of May 1994 (and, in fact, the first document ever to be signed jointly at the presidential level), and in it the parties reaffirmed their commitment to resolve the dispute through political means and based on the norms and principles of international law. Armenia and Azerbaijan also bound themselves to ongoing international mediation in the frame of the eleven-country OSCE Minsk Group by agreeing that a peaceful resolution should be accompanied by 'judicially binding international guarantees in all aspects and stages of settlement'. Russia took merit for reconfirming the diplomatic track of resolution and emphasized that 'new possibilities have opened up' with the signing of the declaration by the presidents of both Armenia and Azerbaijan.[359]

Serving as a co-chair (together with France and the United States) in the Minsk Group, Russia has given itself the task of ensuring that the dialogue between the two states continues at the highest level of trilateral meetings. However, the Moscow Declaration of November 2008 was not any new defining moment in the process of the efforts to solve the conflict. New optimism had already gathered momentum due to a series of meetings between Azerbaijani and Armenian foreign ministers who, since 2004, had been ordered to yield an accord in terms of the basic principles of resolution (a list of principles developed from what were initially named the Madrid

Principles). These expectations failed to materialize, and Russia's repeated statements suggesting that it was because of the success of its own efforts that the resolution of the conflict had taken a diplomatic path had more to do with the continuity of relative stability than with the prospect of a new breakthrough.[360] Because the Moscow Declaration did nothing to change the nature of a military confrontation held in abeyance through conventional deterrence, in effect this made the parties agree on maintaining the existing military and political situation of the peace process. At the same time, however, Russia's confirmation of the unchanged situation in itself was a signal of something new: more than ever before, Russia was determined to use its weight in the process for raising the stakes for a potential resumption of hostilities by either of the two countries.[361] By making itself the indispensable third party to sign the documents agreed upon the three-party meetings, Russia has ensured that it can retain the resolution process under its own control.

Simultaneously a clear priority for Russia is that the Minsk Group, which has provided the negotiation frame in connection with the OSCE since 1992,[362] prevails as the frame of the negotiations vis-à-vis other initiatives such as the committees established in June 2005, and again in January 2011, within the Parliamentary Assembly of the Council of Europe (PACE). This is a forum which would increase the voice of the EU member states and Turkey in the process.[363] Since the stalemate in the negotiations of a solution based on the Madrid principles, the Minsk Group has concentrated on sector-specific issues in a confidence-building frame. The three-party meetings convened by Russia have a different frame because they are closely interlinked with Russia's bilateral relations with Armenia and Azerbaijan (and normally precede the Kremlin's meetings with both countries individually). This structure of diplomatic interaction enables Russia to regulate the inputs to the conflict resolution process by also negotiating, in an indirect linkage connection, the whole range of bilateral relations with the two countries, including steps to develop relations between Azerbaijani and Armenian civil societies. Nagorno-Karabakh, which Azerbaijan refuses to see as a participant in any of these mediation efforts, prevails as the formal reason for convening these meetings and provides Russia with political leverage to control the military stability of the region and to influence the region's economic and political development through its diplomatic efforts. Russia did not embark upon this specific path of diplomacy – in which the trilateral meetings, in its view, are legitimate within the multilateral Minsk format – by being politically far-sighted and determined from the beginning. It did so because circumstances were such that other options could not be realized.

The conflict on the international agenda and the failed peacekeeping plan

The Conference on Security and Cooperation in Europe (CSCE) made the Karabakh conflict part of its agenda in January 1992, when Armenia and Azerbaijan became member states. In April and May observer teams were sent to both countries for the preparation of an observation force which would facilitate the implementation of a peace agreement. The Minsk Group was established in March and a fact-finding mission was dispatched to Nagorno-Karabakh. The co-chairs of the Minsk Group (Russia, France and the United States)[364] were established at the Budapest summit in December 1994, and the following March the Permanent Representative of the OSCE to the conflict region received a mandate which included monitoring the implementation of the ceasefire. However, it was not until after the CSCE was transformed into the Organization for Security and Cooperation in Europe (OSCE) in December 1995 that Nagorno-Karabakh was firmly included on the agenda of the organization. Because the political stalemate in the conflict could not be resolved after the ceasefire was established in May 1994, the OSCE was unable to do much more than monitor the ceasefire on the 175-kilometre-long Line of Contact between Azerbaijani and Armenian forces. In August and September 1993, a ceasefire had been negotiated by the mediating Russian mission headed by Vladimir Kazimirov from Russia's foreign ministry. Although this ceasefire did not hold, it was prolonged until early November. When a new ceasefire agreement was finally signed in May 1994, Armenia had occupied an area which by various estimates covered 14–16 percent (20 percent according to Azerbaijani sources) of Azerbaijan's officially recognized territory. The territory taken between May 1992 and November 1993 became its 'security zone' for 'defensible borders' around Nagorno-Karabakh.[365]

In the peace negotiations that ensued Armenia's point of departure was the non-use of force, which, after the ceasefire, helped to maintain the new status quo. Heydar Aliyev, who had been called upon to assume the presidency after the country had plunged into a political crisis – President Abulfaz Elchibey had fled to Nakhchivan in late June 1993 and the military commander Suret Husseinov was poised to take power – had no choice but to agree to President Yeltsin's demand to reject any military solution to the conflict.[366] Over the course of only six months Azerbaijan had lost five districts and was on the verge of internal dissolution and civil war. The violence, which had escalated between 1988 and spring 1994, had claimed the lives of more than 35,000 people, left 50,000 wounded and created 1.1–1.4 million refugees.[367] The large numbers added to domestic conflict in both countries and especially in Azerbaijan, at that time the poorest country in the South Caucasus and whose economy had been wrecked by the war and subsequent political disarray.

In Moscow the historical background of Russia's active presence in the South Caucasus since the mid-nineteenth century was believed to make it natural for Russia to have a dominant role in any peacekeeping operation planned for Karabakh. The military dimension of the Karabakh conflict was handled by Minister of Defense Pavel Grachev, whose plan was to have Russia monitor the ceasefire and to place 1,800 Russian military troops in the Kelbajar district, which had been part of the Azerbaijani SSR and where the Karabakh Armenians and the military of the Armenian Republic had gained control of during March–April 1993. The rationale of this plan was to let the Armenians control Kelbajar in order to restore a balance that would be kept under Russia's control and, consequently, provide it with leverage in negotiating the settlement of the conflict and the future of the wider region. Before the winter of 1992, Azerbaijani forces, who were able to use the Soviet-era military infrastructure and capabilities on Azerbaijani territory,[368] had gained military dominance and also threatened to retake Lachin, Armenia's main corridor to Karabakh. Armenia's conquest of Kelbajar, a wide area in the military rear of Lachin, in April 1993 then started to turn the military situation to Armenia's advantage. This shift took place with Russia's silent approval and also put international political pressure on Armenia.

The takeover of Kelbajar prompted a resolution by the UN Security Council to demand an 'immediate withdrawal of all occupying forces from the Kelbadjar district and other recently occupied areas of Azerbaijan' (Resolution 822 on 30 April 1993),[369] and Armenia had no choice but to accept a new peace plan. This plan, which was sponsored by both Russia and the United States as well as by Turkey, demanded the withdrawal of troops in exchange for security guarantees for Nagorno-Karabakh. With Armenia facing international condemnation and Azerbaijan militarily weakened and wrecked politically, Russia was now in a position to provide security guarantees with its peacekeeping mission. However, the circumstances were dynamic and soon turned aside the Russian plan: Yerevan managed to defer it by leaving its acceptance to Stepanakert. These two 'Armenian sides' were able to play for time because Azerbaijan had fallen into the aforementioned political crisis. The crisis in Baku was solved through a compromise when Heydar Aliyev, whom Moscow considered to be one of the few political figures who could prevent Azerbaijan from breaking up, became president and nominated Suret Husseinov as the prime minister.

Russia's peacekeeping mission was planned with the idea that it could be set up in the framework of the Commonwealth of Independent States (CIS).

The CIS frame would provide it with international legitimacy and limit the rival activities expected from Ankara and Tehran. A protocol (the 'Bishkek Protocol') was signed in connection with the organization's parliamentary cooperation on 5 May 1994, that is, only days before the ceasefire agreement was signed in the period of May 9–13. This protocol appealed for the conflict parties to 'come to common senses' and supported an initiative (made in the name of the chair of the CIS Inter-Parliamentary Assembly) to establish a CIS peacekeeping force in Nagorno-Karabakh.[370] By this time it had become clear that Western states were reluctant to approve an arrangement which would acknowledge the post-Soviet regions as lying in Russia's 'sphere of interest'. Consequently, a few weeks before the Bishkek Protocol was signed the Russian foreign and defence ministries issued a joint statement that announced that, as a matter of principle, no UN or CSCE mandate was needed if the operation was a *sine qua non* (necessary condition) of avoiding war and came upon request of the parties and with their consent and in agreement with the UN Charter and other norms of international law.[371]

The ceasefire agreement was signed by the three parties (in Nagorno-Karabakh the commander-in-chief Samvel Babayan, in Armenia defence minister Serzh Sargsyan and in Azerbaijan defence minister Mamedrafi Mamedov) and came into effect on 12 May 1994.[372] The agreement was presented by Russia and bore the signatures of the foreign and defence ministers, A. Kozyrev and P. Grachev, and that of V.N. Kazimirov, the Russian president's representative and head of the Russian mediating mission in Nagorno-Karabakh. A few weeks earlier, on 16 April, Azerbaijan and the other CIS member states had accepted the aforementioned protocol decision that provided Russia's peacekeeping initiative with a CIS mandate and requested the UN and the CSCE to support Russia's initiative.[373] However, Grachev's plan to establish Russian peacekeepers as a wedge between the conflict parties in Kelbajar would have created military conditions unfavourable to Azerbaijan: a Russian presence in the region would prevent any future Azerbaijani attempts to regain any of the areas around Nagorno-Karabakh. Although formally agreeing to the Russian initiative in the CIS frame, Azerbaijan ultimately obstructed it by attaching a principled condition for the positioning of Russian peacekeeping forces in Kelbajar: Armenia would have to withdraw from all territories outside Karabakh, without preconditions. This was a non-starter because the very reason for Armenia's costly battles during 1991–3 had been to gain defensible borders for Nagorno-Karabakh. None of the territories were negotiable, although Yerevan was prepared to accept some degree of withdrawal in exchange for security guarantees for Nagorno-Karabakh, and although it also was in the position to pressure the leaders of Karabakh to move in the direction of a solution that it supported.

In Baku the question of Russia's peacekeeping role was linked to the issue of the withdrawal of Russian military forces from Azerbaijani territory, which was demanded in compliance with a decision made by the Azerbaijani parliament in late 1991. During the Soviet period Azerbaijan had stationed the Soviet 4th Army with its motor rifle divisions and air defence brigades, including missile brigades.[374] Russia's withdrawal was almost complete in 1993, but there remained one important issue: despite agreeing to the withdrawal, Russia demanded for its border troops to be allowed to remain on Armenia's border with Iran, of which two-thirds was Azerbaijani territory controlled by Armenian military forces (see Map 3 on this page). In terms of Russia's military doctrine of early 1994, the Iranian border – together with the border with Turkey, which Russia could control through its alliance relationship with Armenia – was defined as Russia's strategic border.[375] Azerbaijan did not concede to Russia's demand, but while it demanded the full withdrawal of Russian troops, it did acquiesce to Russia's maintenance of some infrastructural sites such as the early-warning radar station in Gabala, which had been monitoring the Caucasus, the Middle East and South Asia since 1985 (the Gabala station was finally returned to Azerbaijan at the end of 2012). However, it was not willing to accept Russian troops back onto its territory, especially if this meant peacekeepers in those regions occupied by Armenia, and Azerbaijan obstructed such plans by formulating demands that no Armenian leader could ever accept.

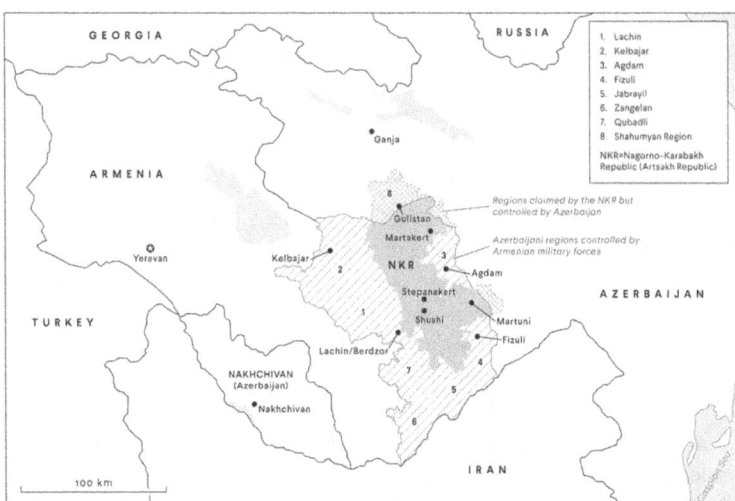

Map 3 Nagorno-Karabakh in regional context (illustration by Ilkka Janatuinen; used with permission).

The political deadlock in the conflict foiled attempts in the CSCE/OSCE to achieve progress on the issue of peacekeeping. In December 1994 the CSCE declared its will to 'provide, with an appropriate resolution from the United Nations Security Council' a multinational peacekeeping force for the Karabakh conflict.[376] After re-establishing its organization in 1995, the OSCE prepared its concept for such peacekeeping operation, which was meant to be its first such operation. According to the organization's founding principles, an OSCE mission could be only supplementary to a political agreement. A formal condition was for it to follow the agreement and formula requested by the parties themselves. The ceasefire agreement had not been followed by this type of political agreement, and the Russian proposal, which could be seen as a first step towards its negotiation, was trapped within the conflict. At the same time the Western states were reluctant to participate in an operation under conditions proposed by Russia, and Armenia was opposed to Turkey's participation. Additionally, Azerbaijan was prepared to accept a mission that lasted for months, while the Armenian side supported a long-term mission that would last up to a decade. The question of an OSCE mission ended up in a political stalemate that was a direct reflection of the conflict, and subsequent attempts to outline mission plans with more impartial participants remained futile. Since 1995, the monitoring mission has been realized as a regular patrol by the representative of the OSCE's chairperson-in-office with five assistants along the Line of Contact, which is just over one kilometre in breadth and separates the 20,000 troops on one side from the same number of troops on the other side.

Because the ceasefire established in May 1994 meant a loss of territory for Azerbaijan, its action concentrated on diplomatic efforts to mobilize the UN in defence of the principles of sovereignty and territorial integrity. Such political mobilization was not difficult with the support of formerly colonized 'Third World' countries in the UN General Assembly. However, of more importance were the Security Council resolutions which required Armenia to withdraw from the areas adjacent to Karabakh. Although Resolution 822 (30 April 1993) called for the withdrawal of 'all occupying forces from the Kelbadjar district and other recently occupied areas of Azerbaijan', it did not refer to Armenia as an 'aggressor' – which would have invoked the articles on collective security in the UN Charter (Chapter VII).[377] Instead, it called for both parties to end hostilities and respect the CSCE Minsk negotiating format. Consequently, both Armenia and Azerbaijan were willing to accept the text which had been approved unanimously in the Council. This resolution, like also Resolution 853 of 29 July 1993,[378] when the main part of Agdam had been taken by the Armenian side in the conflict, reconfirmed that the issue should be handled in the already existing frame of international negotiations.

The diplomatic pressure which the global international community exerts on Armenia with Russia's consent has made Armenia increasingly dependent on Russia. When Turkey broke off diplomatic relations in 1993 and closed its border with landlocked Armenia as a response to the capture of Lachin and Kelbajar, Georgia, which in the years following the ceasefire still hosted Russian military bases, was left as Armenia's main pathway to the outside world. Militarily and now also economically dependent on Russia following the closure of Turkey's border, Armenia has little choice but to abide with Russia's mediation efforts and the international initiatives supported by Russia. However, the failure to achieve more in the context of the OSCE was problematic for Russia, too. With the collapse of the Grachev plan to place Russian peacekeepers in Kelbajar, Russia lost the kind of internationally recognized legitimacy for a military foothold which it claimed to have in South Ossetia and in Abkhazia prior to its recognition of their independence, and which it still claims to have in Transnistria as the 'guarantor-state' of security in the conflict. Consequently, diplomatic mediation through the tri-party meetings and the development of bilateral relations with both countries became the centre of Russian action.

Stalemate in the process of conflict resolution

During the almost quarter-century since the ceasefire was negotiated, the main achievement of the OSCE Minsk Group has been to keep the resolution process alive by maintaining contact points and confidence-building cooperation. Simultaneously the alternation of high expectations and disappointment in the question of finally resolving the conflict has contributed to frustrations over the work in the OSCE frame. Especially the government of the de facto Artsakh Republic, which has been excluded from the Minsk Group since 1998, has criticized the mediatory efforts for concentrating on technical questions while neglecting to establish a political format. The first opportunity for a compromise emerged in September 1997, when Heydar Aliyev accepted Armenia's 'staged withdrawal' as a point of departure and a preliminary consensus was reached based on the postponement of the most difficult questions, including the control of Lachin, which since May 1992 had functioned as a corridor between Armenia and Karabakh, to a later stage. At that time, the Artsakh president Arkady Ghukasian was prepared to discuss an arrangement in which Karabakh would remain formally a part of Azerbaijan while its local administration would be in the hands of the majority population, i.e. Armenians. However, although Armenia's President Levon Ter-Petrosian was concerned about the international reputation of his country after the takeover of the Azerbaijani provinces and prepared to adopt a path towards compromises, this window of opportunity soon closed because large parts of Armenian society were opposed to the plan, and because the Karabakh leadership was not unanimous in its support of such new steps. Ter-Petrosian, who had been active in the Karabakh Committee and therefore had been imprisoned by Moscow from December 1988 until May 1989, was forced to resign. The Armenian side ensured its unity in the Karabakh issue by electing Robert Kocharian, who had served as the chairman of the state defence committee and as the prime minister of Nagorno-Karabakh during the war of 1992–4 and became the Artsakh Republic's president in December 1994, as the president of Armenia in March 1998.[379]

After the heavy losses suffered by both sides in the war, it was easy for the political elites in both Yerevan and Baku to mobilize public opinion against making 'concessions'. While the Armenian side became more unified, Azerbaijan hardened its own position. As a result, the 'common state' approach, which was drafted within the Minsk Group in late 1998 and envisaged a loose federation between Azerbaijan and Nagorno-Karabakh, never made it onto the table for serious consideration. Armenia showed readiness to accept the 'common state' as a basis of negotiations that would also, in some format, include Russia's military guarantees for Karabakh, but Azerbaijan declined: the concept was seen to infringe upon its sovereignty and de facto to deprive it of a part of its territory; moreover, it would legitimize the status quo which Armenia had brought into being through military force. Therefore, in the last years of Yeltsin's presidency Azerbaijan rejected the approach which the Russian foreign ministry at that time was also negotiating with Moldova (the federal arrangements based on the so-called Primakov Memorandum of 1997), and which Moldova's Communist president rejected six years later when a specified agreement finally made it onto the table. Like Moldova in its law of 2005, Azerbaijan has cemented its principled point of departure with jurisdictional measures by stipulating in its Constitution (1995, Article 3, II) that a nation-wide referendum was to be included in procedures designed to resolve questions related to the change of state borders.

In February 2001 the yet-uncoordinated peace plans of the OSCE mediators were prematurely publicized in both capitals, apparently because the leaders in both countries wanted to use domestic criticism to thwart these plans. Then, between April and July the US State Department, led by Secretary of State Colin Powell, sought a new breakthrough in the negotiations arranged in the frame of the Minsk Group in Key West, Florida. During this round of talks Heydar Aliyev, whose main concern was to consolidate the Azerbaijani state and to establish controllable borders, showed readiness for a compromise by not rejecting a 'common house' concept that intended for both states to share competences over Nagorno-Karabakh. This was a form of a power-sharing agreement that retained the region's administrative subordination to Baku but simultaneously allowed its economic and cultural integration with Armenia. A similar approach with transparent borders was brought up in Moscow at that time as a possible model for Georgia's separatist regions, and in the case of Nagorno-Karabakh it was even more natural that a solution would have to be sought in the direction of some kind of common-state approach. In Key West a corridor was negotiated that was to lead through Armenia to Azerbaijan's exclave (the Nakhchivan Autonomous Republic) as a compensation for leaving the Lachin corridor at least partly under Armenia's control. Such a compromise would have left Azerbaijan more territorially united than it could hope for after a prolonged conflict. Nonetheless this scheme, in which the disputed areas would have been made into nodes of linkage between the conflict parties, failed to gain support in either Baku or Yerevan. From Armenia's point of view, credible international guarantees for the status and security of Karabakh were a minimum condition to preclude domestic opposition to the maintenance of even a thin link of subordination of Karabakh to Baku, and these issues remained on the sidelines of the agenda. The negotiations in Key West failed despite the willingness of both presidents, Heydar Aliyev and Robert Kocharian, to personally participate in the negotiations that were supported by the three co-chairs as well as Turkey; the agreement prepared in Key West lacked support in both Baku and Yerevan, and in both capitals it was simply ignored. The breakthrough that the United States had expected to create in the amenable surroundings of Key West turned into an example of how consensus that comes about in a context detached from a conflict's political processes is only ever superficial and does little to contribute even minimally to creating more flexible attitudes in the conflict.

Russia, now under the presidency of Boris Yeltsin's successor Vladimir Putin, reiterated its position, as explained by Viacheslav Trubnikov, First Deputy Foreign Minister and head of Russia's delegation: 'The keys to the solution of the conflict are in the hands of Azerbaijan and Armenia.' Russia emphasized that the 'keys' in the Key West round of negotiations were not to be found in the West, and Russia was 'not going to use any kind of arm-twisting tactics'.[380] When Ilham Aliyev succeeded his father as president in October 2003 and, in January, 2004, declared that Azerbaijan would never accept either the independence of Nagorno-Karabakh or its integration with Armenia, the political deadlock intensified further. The presidents of both countries continued to meet and to signal the possibility of a compromise, which would then evaporate again and lose their substance in the next round of talks. International proposals sought to construct a way to the resolution of the conflict by leaving aside the complex political disagreements during initial stages and, instead, suggested practical measures to solve issues that obstructed normal life in the region (such as ending the economic blockade of Armenia in exchange for some degree of withdrawal); yet none of these proposals succeeded.

After Key West, new momentum in international expectations for a breakthrough did not appear until a series of meetings between the foreign ministers of Azerbaijan and Armenia in Prague in 2004 (the so-called Prague process). The outcome of the Minsk Group proposals, known as the 'Madrid principles' and (in their further elaboration) as the 'basic principles', was officially presented to Armenia and Azerbaijan at the OSCE summit in Madrid in late November 2007. These elements of a 'comprehensive peace agreement' had been previously elaborated in the reports of the International Crisis Group.[381] The basic idea was that the final status of Karabakh would be decided by a popular vote in the last stages of the process, while all other 'confidence measures', including the renunciation of the use of force and withdrawal of the Armenian and Karabakh forces from the surrounding territories, would construct the path towards it. Although no breakthrough was achieved in the settlement of the conflict, the process which started in 2004 facilitated the identification of the most difficult issues at hand. These included the question of corridors and security buffer zones in the Lachin and Kelbajar districts, the form and timing of the vote on Nagorno-Karabakh's final status, and the arrangements and timing for the return of internally displaced persons.[382]

From Armenia's perspective, the most problematic issue is the uncertainty over the ultimate status of Nagorno-Karabakh, which connects with the question of who would be permitted to participate in the referendum. Withdrawal from the districts bordering on Nagorno-Karabakh before a decision has been made on the future status of the unrecognized republic vis-à-vis the central Azerbaijani administration would mean a security risk relating to the borders as well as giving up the leverage for future bargaining acquired through the war. Azerbaijan, on the other hand, argues that the internally displaced persons must be allowed to return before a vote about the region's status can take place, and that this temporal order in the stages of the settlement is demanded by the internationally accepted norms of human rights. An additional requirement by Baku is that both countries must be able to use the Lachin road, which is Armenia's main military route to Karabakh. While such arrangements over the uses of the territory take into account Armenia's requirement that it must be guaranteed a land border with Nagorno-Karabakh, and hence are elements in a possible compromise, the details of the return of the Azeri population and the vote by which Nagorno-Karabakh's final status would be decided remain major sources of disagreement. Azerbaijan does not accept that the status, which would be decided during the last stage of the settlement, would be determined in a referendum which would then become binding through its international recognition (which is Armenia's approach to the referendum). Instead, Azerbaijan supports an advisory vote and argues that the decision which it accepts as binding must be its own. This position is in line with the provision of its Constitution of 1995, which calls for a nation-wide referendum on the acceptability of any status proposed for Karabakh that would change Azerbaijani state borders. The threat of a popular veto leaves Baku with the possibility to make void in one stroke the results of a long, incremental process, including the investments of the international community in an interim administration. A possible compromise would seem to lie in arranging a binding referendum after Azeri resettlement in Karabakh. This option is burdened with practical difficulties related to timing, the large and already ambiguous number of Karabakh refugees in Azerbaijan, and not least the principled opposition in Azerbaijan that follows from its emphasis on its sovereignty and territorial integrity.

Since the drafting of the 'basic principles' in 2007, both parties have hardened their position. In Armenia, the opinion has strengthened that Karabakh must be either independent or a part of Armenia. Supported by Armenia, Nagorno-Karabakh expects that the many decades of its de facto existence will finally compel the international community to recognize its legitimacy and that this situation will become a fait accompli for Azerbaijan and its supporters. Azerbaijan, in turn, argues for the importance of the legal frame of its position by counting on the normative support that its position receives in the form of statements and declarations in a variety of international forums – the UN Security Council, OSCE decisions, resolutions of the Organization of Islamic Cooperation, the European Parliament, the Council of Europe, the Non-Aligned Movement and NATO.[383] This normative struggle is strengthened by the practices of international organizations, including the EU and NATO, which through this discourse also seek to ensure cooperation in the field of energy and to reduce the dependency of Central and Eastern European states on Russian energy supplies.

Both parties to the conflict try to consolidate their position by demonstrating that their line of action is supported by practices that already prevail, and the conflict becomes more and more institutionalized once it is incorporated into law and doctrine in both Armenia and Azerbaijan. Moreover, the territorial conflict has escalated into an international, normative war due to the demand by Azerbaijan to recognize the Khojaly massacre of February 25–26 1992 as a genocide.[384] The Azerbaijani demand, supported by Turkey, can be seen as a counterclaim in response to Armenia's long-standing demand that Turkey recognize the Armenian genocide by the Ottoman Empire in 1915–16. The recognition of the Khojaly massacre as 'genocide' by the parliaments or parliamentary committees of several countries, including the Czech Republic, is interpreted in Azerbaijan as support for its position in the conflict.[385]

The Karabakh conflict is a manifestation of not only a continuous buildup of political confrontation but also of preparedness for war. However, although the level of armaments has spiralled upwards,[386] and even if casualties are reported on the frontline every year and the situation erupted into a four-day war in April 2016,[387] the escalation of the violence into a full-scale war has been avoided. One reason for the maintenance of this relative, fragile stability is the memory of a war that was extremely costly in more ways than one for all parties; another is the heavy buildup of arms on both sides, which has served to establish a deterrent with conventional arms. The third reason is that the Minsk Group, despite its very meagre advance towards an actual resolution, has provided a frame to maintain the conflict under external control because it has been able to rely on the support of the UN Security Council and neither of the parties in the conflict can afford to ignore the significance of international support for their respective cause. After the four-day war in April 2016, in which Azerbaijan took back less than two square kilometres of land and which killed approximately one hundred people on both sides (figures given by both Armenia and Azerbaijan are higher), the co-chairing countries consolidated the role of the OSCE mission by setting up an OSCE investigative mechanism on the violent incidents that had breached the ceasefire.[388] From Russia's perspective, the Minsk Group enables it to act as a mediator and provides the kind of wider international frame and legitimacy which it has consistently sought in all frozen conflicts by making appeals to both the OSCE and the UN. The next chapter examines the complex political equation in which the means employed in Russia's relations with the two countries in conflict, Armenia and Azerbaijan, are mutually very different.

13

The Delicate Equation: Russia's Policy Arrangements with Armenia and Azerbaijan

The negotiations to reach a political agreement were launched in Moscow in late August 1994, three months after the ceasefire agreement was agreed in May. Initially, Nagorno-Karabakh, whose commander-in-chief had signed the ceasefire agreement together with the Armenian and Azerbaijani defence ministers, was a participant in the negotiations. The document adopted at the CSCE Budapest Summit in December 1994 acknowledged Nagorno-Karabakh as a conflict party, and having this separate entity participate in the negotiations was in line with Russian policy as outlined in the communiqué of 23 September 1991. This document summarized the talks held in Zheleznovodsk, Russia, on the initiative of Boris Yeltsin and Nursultan Nazarbayev, i.e. the presidents of the Russian Soviet Federative Socialist Republic (at that time one of the fifteen constituent republics of the USSR) and Kazakhstan. However, Azerbaijan objected to a procedure that, in its view, risked legitimating 'another Armenian state' while failing to represent the internally displaced Azeri population in the peace process. Nagorno-Karabakh, for its part, claimed a seat in the negotiations by refusing to prioritize the principle of the continuity of Soviet borders in the Belovezh Accords and by emphasizing that Nagorno-Karabakh, as a state entity, had been born simultaneously with the post-Soviet Republic of Azerbaijan.

The procedural issues over representation have continued to hamper the negotiations, and it was not until 1999 – one year after Stepanakert had been formally excluded from the negotiations – that the presidents of the two countries could meet with each other in the frame of the Minsk Group. In the years following the ceasefire international opinion tilted towards supporting Azerbaijan, which on the basis of international law and its fundamental principle of the territorial integrity of states was largely perceived as the 'victim state' in the conflict. When France, as one of the Minsk Group's co-chairs and the host of a large Armenian diaspora, distanced itself from its traditional support for Armenia and adopted a policy that argued for listening to the Azerbaijani population which had previously been living in Nagorno-Karabakh, Russia settled for an approach that saw the main axis of parties in the resolution process as lying between two independent states, Armenia and Azerbaijan. In contrast to the case of Transnistria, Russia has chosen to accommodate the Azerbaijani position that Nagorno-Karabakh cannot be a party directly involved in the negotiations. This issue has generated discord with Armenia, where the National Assembly has announced that by excluding Stepanakert from the negotiations only 'an illusion of a negotiating process is created'.[389] Russia however has repeatedly emphasized its readiness to support an option which would suit the parties in the conflict, and to act as a 'guarantor of the settlement' in the event that a compromise accord is achieved.[390] The position which emphasizes that the final choice of a settlement formula lies with the Azerbaijanis and Armenians and that 'the imposition on the conflict parties of any recipes from outside' is not acceptable creates an illusion of openness and support of the sovereign decision making of the two states. Simultaneously, it justifies objections to Western influence in the region. According to Russia, 'a solution is going to be viable' only when it 'will help preserve the historically established geopolitical balance of forces in the region and [will] not lead to its becoming an arena of international political and military rivalry'.[391]

The delicate equation of Russia's policies in the region is easily disrupted by interventions from other major and regional powers. Should conflict arise Russia would come to the assistance of Armenia, which is its military ally and a historically trustworthy ethnic community; this would destroy relations with Azerbaijan, which in turn is strategically important because of its energy resources and which has become economically, socially, culturally and also politically closely affiliated with another regional power since the collapse of the Soviet Union – Turkey. However, if the relationship of military alliance with Armenia is not credible, Russia has no leverage over Azerbaijan's security and foreign policies. While the crux of Russia's policies lies in balancing its relations with both Armenia and Azerbaijan, such a balancing act – maintaining stability in the region and preventing a flaring of violence – requires flexibility in all of its lesser elements, including the entire Karabakh issue and the question of its representation in the peace process. Because Karabakh has existential, identity-constitutive significance for the state projects of both Armenia and Azerbaijan, it represents Russia's ultimate leverage in its efforts to develop ties of cooperation with both countries. It follows that the uncertainty over Karabakh's undefined status in the settlement process and over Russia's actions in case of flaring violence or even war is an essential part of this leverage. In other words, if the framework of the settlement were to be predefined, Russia would as a consequence lose the space for action that is necessary for its approach of accommodating both of the adversarial countries while steering developments throughout the wider region.

The years that have followed the events of August 2008 have seen an intensification of Russia's trilateral diplomacy with Armenia and Azerbaijan, and by 2013 more than ten tri-party meetings had been held on the initiative of the Kremlin. After the four-day war in April 2016 these meetings, which normally take place at least once a year on the presidential level, were intensified again with three meetings before the end of that year. Although Russia's immediate goal is to maintain the resolution process in the two formats brought together through its policies – the Minsk Group format and Russia's tri-party meetings – this is more for the purpose of maintaining positive relations with both Armenia and Azerbaijan than to achieve any major breakthrough in the specific issue of Karabakh, which Russia argues should take place mainly in the Minsk format anyway. Nevertheless this attitude must not be confused with an interest to maintain the status quo in the conflict. Instead, Russia's interest in the stability of the region is about delicately steering a path of compromises without shattering the security arrangements and foreign and security policy orientations which keep both Yerevan and Baku in a close relationship with Moscow. This, again, enables Russia to pursue its strategic goals in the wider region and to develop its economic and political cooperation with Turkey and Iran. In the light of these intertwined goals, it makes much sense that Russia claims diplomatic credit for its efforts at mediation even if progress towards an actual settlement of the conflict remains meagre.

These policies also make it rational to emphasize that the 'basic principles' worked out since the OSCE Madrid Summit of late November 2007 prepare the way for finding a political solution to the Karabakh conflict. The 'basic principles' outline the conditions and confidence-building measures towards a final settlement and a comprehensive peace agreement and leave the most difficult question, i.e. the specific status of Nagorno-Karabakh, to be determined in the final stages of the process. Together with the other Minsk Group co-chairs, Russia has advocated a compromise in which Armenia would give back some of the territory adjacent to Karabakh while being allowed to keep a small number of crucial corridors. In particular, Russia has argued in favour of an approach in which Armenia's return of some of the areas in exchange for ending the economic blockade imposed on it would be a way of opening up a path for mutual compromises. At the same time Russia must take into account the degree to which Azerbaijan stresses the importance of the issue of the internally displaced persons' right to return to their former places of residence. While all these are necessary elements of a compromise, the problems lie in the details – which Russia prefers to leave to the conflict parties themselves. This, in turn, means that the process easily becomes entangled in ever new disputes even when a major breakthrough seems to be imminent.

In the main conflict issue, i.e. the question over the final legal and internationally guaranteed status of Nagorno-Karabakh, Russia's approach, like in the case of Transnistria, focuses on the idea of a 'common state'. The recipe for 'stability and peace' is based on what Russia refers to as the Minsk Group's three fundamental principles: the territorial integrity of states, nations' right to self-determination and the non-use of force. Although the mediation efforts of the Minsk Group are not possible without abiding by the non-use of force, emphasis on this principle arguably also contributes to the persistence of the current situation. However, it is crucial to note that in its attempt to pursue balanced policies towards both Azerbaijan and Armenia, Russia seeks to keep tensions in balance by speaking about territorial integrity and nations' right to self-determination without defining a mutual hierarchy or prioritizing either of these principles over the other.[392] This approach has become Russia's main thrust in the second decade of the new millennium, and it not only gives the negotiations the kind of flexibility which is required to maintain the participation of both Armenia and Azerbaijan; it also signals that Russia keeps its policies open and that it could prioritize one or the other of these principles should a critical situation arise.

The procedural point of departure in regard to these two principles is not a new invention and has a specific historical background in Soviet practices: as discussed above, Karabakh was an example of an administrative structure in which a nation was provided with a special status within a state (the Soviet republic) and where an authority external to both of them (the central power in Moscow) made itself a guarantor of the peace. However, when this notion of building a vertical structure of control is brought into the context of horizontal international relations, the two principles, which in the Soviet frame could be authoritatively adjusted vis-à-vis one another, become mutually incompatible normative points of departure. Because the circumstances of prioritizing one or the other principle require careful consideration, it is practical to maintain a considerable degree of openness in the common-state concept that would unite Karabakh with Azerbaijan and convert Karabakh into a 'common house' for the two states of Armenia and Azerbaijan. In this way the principles can be weighed against each other in the context of a comprehensive political settlement that is not only about Karabakh but also about the bottlenecks and preferences of Russia's policies in the wider region.

The Karabakh conflict also demonstrates how problematic it is within the horizontal system of states for Russia to establish its military control between the conflict parties in the form of its peacekeeping. In all the other conflicts discussed in this book, Russia has succeeded in establishing such military support elements in its efforts to bring about a 'comprehensive political settlement' to conflicts. Achieving the same in Karabakh would mean establishing a demilitarized zone between Armenia and Azerbaijan, probably in Lachin and Kelbajar (see Map 3 on page 157), as well as the participation of the Russian military as leaders in a peacekeeping operation. In the light of the Minsk Group proposals (the 'basic principles') the question of Russia's participation in a possible peacekeeping operation is part of the agenda dealing with international security guarantees. Thus, the idea of the Grachev plan is not dead at present even despite the lower significance today of a large number of troops – hence, not the full contingent of 1,800 troops envisioned by the Russian Ministry of Defense in 1994 – due to the fact that Russia has built up its alliance relationship with Armenia bilaterally as well as through the CSTO. An international mandate to provide legitimacy to a possible peacekeeping operation in the frame of the Minsk Group is important from Russia's point of view for reasons of general foreign policy as well as for the specific reason of maintaining the Minsk Group, which provides Russia's mediatory efforts with international legitimacy, as the central format of negotiations. However, the obstacles to Russia's peacekeeping lie not only in the attitudes of the Western states and Azerbaijan, but also in Armenia's reluctance to allow Russia to become too involved in Karabakh in spite of the importance of its military alliance with Russia.

Consolidating the relationship with Armenia: Legal and political mechanisms

Armenia declared independence on 23 September 1991, after the Soviet Union had de facto collapsed with the August coup. Although the Karabakh conflict had weighed upon relations with Moscow since the late 1980s, no anti-Russian movement comparable to the movements in Georgia and the countries of Eastern Europe emerged in Armenia. A bilateral treaty signed in March 1995 ascertained that the Russian 102nd military base would continue to function on the basis of the former Soviet army units, and in 2010 this agreement was prolonged until 2044.[393] In August 1997, a Russian–Armenian Treaty on Friendship, Cooperation and Mutual Assistance (FCMA) was signed for a period of twenty-five years (and is to be automatically renewed for a ten-year period unless cancelled). This bilateral political framework consolidates Armenia's military cooperation with Russia in the regional geopolitical context. In addition to the bilateral treaty of 1995, cooperation over the Russian military base was already agreed upon in connection with the multilateral collective security cooperation signed in the Treaty of

Tashkent in May 1992. When the CSTO started to develop as an organization of collective security a decade later (in 2002), Armenia as one of its founding members in 1992 was already its cornerstone in the South Caucasus. Both Georgia and Azerbaijan had discontinued membership upon the renewal of the agreement in 1999.

The CSTO prohibits its members from joining other military alliances, denounces the use of force between member states and interprets a military aggression against one member as constituting aggression against all members. The FCMA treaty lays the basis for the bilateral integration of the Russian and Armenian military forces and commits the two countries to 'refrain from participating in any actions or measures, as well as alliances and blocs directed against the sovereignty, independence and territorial integrity' of the other party (Article 7). Based on the FCMA treaty, Armenia and Russia undertake to 'jointly take all available steps' to eliminate any 'threat to the peace, breaches of peace and counter acts of aggression against them by any State or group of nations' and to give each other military and other types of assistance (Article 3).[394] The signatory states agree to 'immediately consult with each other every time, according to one of them, there is the threat of armed attack' (Article 2).[395] While they agree to cooperate closely with each other 'in protecting the sovereignty, territorial integrity and security' of both countries (Article 2), it is obvious that Russia's protection of Armenia is of a different order than Armenia's protection of Russia. For Armenia its alliance relationship with Russia provides the security guarantee against a major military attack from Azerbaijan. Armenia in turn protects Russia by providing an extended zone of defence towards its traditional regional rivals Turkey and Iran, and by providing a front in regard to the influence wielded by the United States and NATO in the region through Georgia.

In comparison with the collective security arrangements within the CSTO, the bilateral FCMA treaty significantly lowers the threshold for joint military action when 'a threat to the safety of a party' is perceived. Although the treaty speaks of cooperation between two 'national armies' as its principled point of departure, increasing the cooperation for joint defence does not formally call for a mutual and shared recognition of the deterioration of the security environment. Moreover, the treaty not only prevents the parties from joining another alliance or 'bloc' but also prevents them from allowing actions to take place on their respective territories which could be interpreted as directed against the independence and territorial integrity of the other signatory state (Article 7).[396] The unspecified consultation mechanism leaves much room for flexibility and fuses the line that separates military from political consultations. Because of the continuous nature of the threat posed by Azerbaijan to Armenia, the consultations are in essence constantly present in the relations between Yerevan and Moscow, and the need to conduct them can be requested whenever one or the other of the parties desires to do so. From Armenia's point of view, the treaty-based consultation mechanism leaves much leeway to Moscow's interpretations, yet it also provides it with special access to Moscow.

The physical infrastructure of Russia's military presence in Armenia includes the military bases (the 102nd base at Gyumri and an airbase at the Erebuni airport near Yerevan) and installations and, in addition, the joint protection of Armenia's borders with Turkey and Iran.[397] Military cooperation comes in a wide range of forms and includes joint and reciprocal use of facilities, the sharing of technology and its joint production. Armenia's military doctrine (Chapter V, 23) states that 'strategic partnership' with Russia is its first priority of action and means establishing 'permanently acting combined forces', such as the joint formation of troops. The 'active and practical participation in the programs of the Collective Security Treaty Organization' is mentioned as the second main dimension of military cooperation. The main areas of development are the joint Russian–Armenian military force (a contingent set up in 2000) and the development of joint air defence in the multilateral context of the CSTO.

In the Karabakh conflict the alliance relationship compensates – and in fact overcompensates – Armenia for the arrangement which Azerbaijan obstructed in 1994 when it refused Russia's dominant role in peacekeeping. The Russian military in Armenia consists of regular military personnel instead of troops with a peacekeeping mandate, and they are not located in the 'occupied'/'liberated' territory surrounding Karabakh. The main body of the 4,000–5,000 troops (the numbers vary due to regional mobility) are stationed at the base near Gyumri in the proximity of the border with Turkey. Yet the practical consequence of the bilateral alliance relationship, which is further consolidated by the commitment to collective security within the CSTO, is that it effectively deters Azerbaijan from initiating military action that seeks to cut off Nagorno-Karabakh from Armenia. The additional treaty arrangements, signed as addenda in 2010 to the earlier treaty of 1995 in order to extend Russia's lease of the military base until 2044, also expanded the territorial scope of Russia's responsibilities in protecting Armenia. The previous, Soviet-era focus on threats arising from Turkey and Iran was expanded to cover the entire territory of Armenia as an area of joint protection, and specific mention was made of threats from Azerbaijan and Georgia. In this way Russia prepared for the possibility that the territory of especially Georgia could become NATO's military outreach area and that its direct military presence consequently would be required also at this border.

Russia's responsibilities in relation to the protection of particularly Nagorno-Karabakh remain unspecified and leave it with room to consider its line of action under the specific circumstances of this conflict. However, although the 2010 extension of the scope of Russia's responsibility, in its formal sense, covers only the internationally recognized borders of Armenia, it is hardly possible that the Azerbaijani–Armenian border, of which Karabakh and the areas under Armenia's control constitute a main part, would remain intact. In Armenia, the extension of Russia's defence responsibilities in the country in 2010 has strengthened the interpretation that the bilateral agreements between the two countries are Russia's security guarantees in regard to Armenia in the Karabakh conflict, too. From Russia's point of view, this undefined, 'grey' area of action provides it with leverage to maintain its military presence at Armenia's borders. Simultaneously such openness towards Azerbaijan and Turkey, in particular, is needed to reduce the military confrontation on the borders and to be able to develop logistics and energy networks for wider regional and inter-regional economic cooperation and integration.

While Armenia's security policy is firmly based on its military alliance relationship with Russia, it remains keen to develop economic relations with the United States and other Western countries through enterprises and a civil society deeply connected with the Armenian diaspora. Yerevan's relationship with the Armenian diaspora in the West was re-established when Gorbachev, after a massive earthquake struck Armenia on 7 December 1988, decided to open this Soviet Republic for humanitarian aid. Assistance started to flow in from especially the United States, where the Armenian diaspora is especially large and influential, and where the US Senate a few months earlier had called on the Soviet government to 'respect the legitimate aspirations of the Armenian people' in view of the petition for Karabakh's independence.[398] The connectedness to the Armenian diaspora that is widespread in both Russia and Western states made it natural that from its very beginning in the early 1990s Armenian foreign policy was actively oriented towards the West and the flexibility between Russia and the West – which Foreign Minister Vartan Oskanian later termed 'complementarist' policy[399] – was also reflected in Armenia's international cooperation, including its security cooperation. A few years later, when Armenia took control of the areas surrounding Karabakh and Azerbaijan agreed on the exploitation of Caspian Sea oil reserves with Western companies, the US policies were brought to support Azerbaijan's territorial integrity. Since the 9/11 events in 2001 it has strengthened military cooperation with both countries with an emphasis on counter-terrorist action.

Consequently, the third and fourth directions of cooperation mentioned in Armenian military doctrine are the bilateral cooperation with the

United States (with an emphasis on military reform, development of the interoperability of units and Armenia's participation in international peacekeeping) and the cooperation with NATO and its member states in the frame of the Euro-Atlantic Partnership Council, respectively. Armenia's cooperation with NATO developed with its participation in the Partnership for Peace program (since 1998) and the implementation of the Individual Partnership Action Plan (IPAP) focused on military reform (since December 2005).[400] Its participation, under the auspices of NATO, in the operations in Kosovo and Afghanistan signalled that the country positions itself in the Western international community. Armenia's aspirations to intensify its cooperation with the European Union (EU) was given a legal frame when the Partnership and Cooperation Agreement (PCA) was signed in 1996 (entering into force three years later in 1999) and Armenia's place in the Union's European Neighbourhood Policy (ENP, launched in 2004) was concretized through the Eastern Partnership policies initiated in May 2009. In July 2013 Armenia finalized its negotiations for the political Association Agreement including the Deep and Comprehensive Free Trade Agreement (DCFTA), but after President Serzh Sargsyan returned from Moscow a few weeks later in early September it revoked this by announcing that Armenia would join the Customs Union of Russia, Belarus and Kazakhstan (which was transformed into the Eurasian Economic Union in January 2015).[401] As a consequence of this, the attempt was wrecked to deepen cooperation with Europe – a strategy supported by 70 per cent of the population – and in this way to pursue 'complementarist' policies to counterbalance the influence of Russia in the region without compromising Armenia's own security interests and goals in the Karabakh conflict.

Armenia's heavy economic dependency on Russian loans, its almost complete dependency on Russian energy, as well as Russia's four-billion-dollar arms supplies to Azerbaijan were among the issues that provoked this abrupt turn.[402] Additionally, the political weight of the Karabakh conflict cannot be ignored: Armenia's ability to choose otherwise was decisively narrowed down when Azerbaijan showed itself reluctant to pursue the European path as suggested by the EU and increased its cooperation with Russia in the military and other domains.[403] In Moscow Armenia's initial willingness to sign the Association Agreement including the DCFTA (although Yerevan had refrained from asking about the prospects for membership)[404] had prompted a readiness to revaluate Russia's reduced energy prices for Armenia, its investments in Armenia and the access of Armenians to Russia's labour market, and also to reconsider its cooperation in terms of security. In Yerevan, a severe economic crisis combined with a deep political crisis relating to the very real possibility of eventually losing

Karabakh was considered a far greater evil than was the wave of political protests and the failure to improve the state's economic condition brought about by the decision to join the Eurasian integration process.

Armenia's connectedness with Russia and the West and its cornered position in the region

Armenia's military doctrine from 2013 states that Armenia is 'a guarantor and supporter of security for the population of the Nagorno Karabakh Republic and the course of development it has chosen'.[405] This role was confirmed already in the National Security Strategy of 2007[406] – at a point of time when new momentum emerged in the resolution process in the form of the Prague process and the Madrid principles. Armenia's credibility in playing the role of guarantor, however, depends entirely on its alliance relationship with Russia. In other words, Armenia's close connectedness with Russia's security interests in the region could be loosened only if Armenia chose to give up Karabakh – which would immediately destroy the legitimacy of the government in Yerevan and stir up Armenian society with revitalized notions of an Armenian nationhood motivated by more than a century-long experience of victimization by the 'Turks' (the Ottoman Empire and the Azeris).[407] The importance of Karabakh was demonstrated already in 1918, before the nascent Soviet Union gained control of the region, when both Armenia and Azerbaijan in their short independence staked their claims to this land in which mountains offered protection and the fertile soil in the valleys provided the means for livelihoods.

Although the Artsakh Republic to this day has considerable potential for self-sufficiency in terms of basic commodities (including energy in the form of hydropower), its development as a modern political community and as a de facto state is entirely dependent on its integral connectivity to Armenia. The Armenian economy itself heavily depends on the contributions of the worldwide diaspora. The investment from Russia, Armenia's primary source of foreign trade and investment, has been 50–60 per cent of total foreign investment in independent Armenia and is focused mainly on energy, metal industry, railways, telecommunications and banking.[408] The magnitude of the economic flow from the United States, which is Armenia's second-largest trading partner, is illustrated by the fact that Armenia comes after only Israel in receiving assistance. The frame of the assistance from these two states differs greatly, however. While assistance from Russia is based on a close relationship at the state level (which was strengthened in the aftermath of the war in the 1990s because of Armenia's dependency on Russian loans), assistance from the United States comes mainly in the form of private donations and investments, with an emphasis on small and medium-size business integrated into business networks within the United States. Unlike Russia the United States also allocates small sums through its state budget to specifically support Nagorno-Karabakh.[409] However, despite the considerable lobbying power of the Armenian diaspora in the United States, American interest in supporting Armenia in the Karabakh conflict weighs little in comparison with the interest for Azerbaijan's oil and gas.

In Armenia's relations with Russia the FCMA treaty not only outlines the conditions of an alliance relationship in the field of military security but is also a framework treaty for a wide range of cooperation in the domains of economy, energy, communications, education, health, academia and science. The security-structured relationship generates multilevel interaction between Armenian and Russian society and includes not only top-level political decision-making and security structures but also government branches, parliamentarians, business communities and public organizations. The Armenian diaspora in Russia supports economic and social development in both Armenia and Karabakh, but their contribution is far more visible in Karabakh because of the smaller geographic area in which it is concentrated – usually the home towns and villages of the donors. Such activity is sustained by strong sentiments in Russia about Armenian national survival. The Union of Armenians in Russia sets as its goal the 'promot[ion of] an environment conducive to the spiritual and physical preservation and development of the Armenian ethnos'.[410] It reports that ever since 'the formation of an independent Artsakh statehood', the Union's members have committed themselves to be 'directly involved in the process of settlement and development of the home country'.[411] The commitment to both Armenia and Karabakh in a unifying ideational frame – which is deeply influenced by the undercurrents of Russian geopolitical thinking – is demonstrated by the habit of always mentioning the two entities in one breath when discussing support and investment in the region. In Armenia and Nagorno-Karabakh the experience that makes people feel connected to Armenians outside the region serves to sustain the notion of Armenians as a 'diaspora nation', whose historical homeland lies in Armenia and of which Karabakh is considered a part. The strength of the diaspora connection with not only Russia but also Western countries, and especially the United States, in part explains why 70 per cent of the population was in favour of strengthening the relationship with the European Union when President Sargsyan decided instead to support Eurasian integration in September 2013.

From the perspective of increasing Armenia's interaction with Europe, the closed border with Turkey remains a major obstacle. This problem was exacerbated when transit through Georgia, which relays all of Armenia's gas and a large part of its petroleum from Russia, also became problematic following the war between Russia and Georgia in 2008.[412] Moreover, Georgia has announced that it would stay neutral should the conflict between Armenia and Azerbaijan escalate – that is, it would close its borders for Russia's transit of troops and materiel. In such a situation northwestern Iran could serve as an alternative route, at least in terms of economic transactions. This geographic area is as yet an unknown part of the regional security problem around Karabakh. Its future development does not so much depend on the neighbourhood relations between Armenia and Iran – which are already comparatively stable – as it does on the question of how Russia prioritizes either Armenia or Azerbaijan in its plans to strengthen its own economic cooperation with Iran.

In the bilateral relations between Iran and Armenia, Iran's Armenian population, which is traditionally well integrated in Iranian business and society, provides a connection that maintains the habitual interaction across the border. From the point of view of Iran's foreign and security policies, this neighbourhood is important because of growing tensions in its relationship with Azerbaijan. Iran has a Turkic-speaking minority consisting of the diverse ethnic groups that are called 'Azeri' – 25 million, in comparison with Azerbaijan's own population of 9.2 million – most of whom live in areas adjacent to the northern border. Consequently, Nagorno-Karabakh's affiliation with Armenia forms a zone between Azerbaijan and this population, which could become an issue for conflict between Iran and Azerbaijan in the future. Because it is not in Iran's interest to see Azerbaijan's influence grow in the region, and also not to see the Western international community significantly contribute to the resolution of the conflict, it quietly lends what help it can to Karabakh and develops relations with Armenia. Through the border with Iran, both Armenia and Nagorno-Karabakh have been able to obtain inexpensive 'grey trade' petroleum and other transportable commodities to ease the dire economic situation caused by the closed borders with Turkey and, of course, Azerbaijan. In 2008, an Iranian–Armenian gas pipeline was launched, and further pipelines for oil are under construction.

Against the geopolitical background where the interests of Russia and Iran mutually complement each other in the region, it has not been difficult for Armenia to promote the construction of a railway that connects it with Tehran. However, despite discussing this plan for several years, it has yet to be implemented because of Russia's reluctance to bear the main responsibility for its financing and its subsequent decision to go ahead with a competing and geopolitically more appealing project. In July 2016, Russian Railways (RZD) signed an agreement with Tehran and Baku to open a north–south rail line from Russia to India through the territories of Iran and Azerbaijan. The priority given by Russia to this project and the 'trilateral format of cooperation' which is being developed upon Iran's initiative between Iran, Russia and Azerbaijan and connects with transport networks in Turkey and Georgia[413] brought a major disappointment to the Armenians, who had hoped that the politically costly agreement of September 2013 to join the Customs Union would be compensated through Russia's economic support. Although the railway from Yerevan to Tehran remains part of Russia's plans to construct a transport and logistics network in the CIS space and, in this way, to strengthen the Eurasian Economic Union,[414] such a long-term perspective is not sufficient to alleviate frustration in Armenia. Its railways are controlled by the Russian Railways company, and its prospects to benefit from an alternative project – the East–West railway corridor planned to connect China with Europe – are obstructed by the conflict with Azerbaijan.[415] From Russia's perspective, all plans in Moscow to expand the logistics and energy networks in the wider region make it vital to keep the Nagorno-Karabakh issue stable while maintaining the promise of prospects for moving forward in the resolution of the conflict. This chapter can be concluded with the argument that Russia's relationship with Armenia is firmly structured by means of the security guarantee through which Armenia can guarantee security for Nagorno-Karabakh. Although the question of whether Russia thus also guarantees security for Nagorno-Karabakh is more complicated, and although its answer depends on the circumstances of specific crisis situations which may emerge, this structure of relations encloses both Armenia and Nagorno-Karabakh within Russia's deep borders. Even if Russia is militarily present in Karabakh through the support it provides to Armenia, the military alliance between Russia and Armenia not only bars Azerbaijan from entering Karabakh but also fends off the military presence of other states. The next chapter will show that Russia's relationship with Azerbaijan remains far more open and unpredictable.

Negotiating the relationship with Azerbaijan: Legal and political mechanisms

Azerbaijan declared independence on 18 October, a few weeks later than Armenia declared its own, and after the leadership's initial support of the August 1991 coup in Moscow. With the settlement of the situation following the ceasefire of May 1994 and with the work of the Minsk Group on track, Russia also negotiated a comprehensive friendship treaty with Azerbaijan. The treaty was signed in early July 1997, one month ahead of the signing of the FCMA treaty with Armenia.[416] In the Russian–Azerbaijani Treaty of Friendship, Cooperation and Mutual Security (FCMS), the parties 'condemn separatism in all its forms' (Article 5) and commit themselves to 'not recognize the forcible change of internationally recognized borders of states' (Article 3).[417] Because Russia's assistance to Nagorno-Karabakh, with the exception of only modest 'humanitarian' cooperation, takes place through Armenia, the strict denouncement of separatism is of little practical significance. Similarly, the commitment not to recognize borders changed by force is in harmony with the formal aspects of Russia's mediatory role. Despite the fact that the treaty encourages mutual consultations, it is merely the importance of communication between the signatory states which is emphasized because of the lack in this treaty of the kind of mechanism regarding the initialization of such consultations which exists in the treaty with Armenia. What Russia specifically gained through the treaty is the stipulation according to which:

> Each High Contracting Party undertakes not to participate in any actions or activities of military, economic and financial issues, including through third countries, directed against the other High Contracting Party, and not allow its territory to be used for aggression or other violent acts against the other High Contracting Party. (Article 6)

Simultaneously the treaty recognizes the right of the signatory countries to determine and implement their own measures aimed at protecting their respective 'sovereignty, territorial integrity, inviolability of borders and defense' (Article 7). While it emphasizes mutual cooperation, it leaves all concrete forms of cooperation to a subsequent agreement. From Russia's point of view, the treaty presents an obstacle should Azerbaijan, like Georgia, decide to pursue membership in NATO. Russia expects Azerbaijan to follow a security policy which confirms and guarantees Azerbaijan's commitments in Article 6, and what it can offer in return is its political and military control relationship with Armenia.

While Azerbaijan's policies confirm a security policy orientation that keeps it militarily non-aligned, it refrains from any constraints on its sovereignty in the form of the guarantees that Russia prefers to set in place in post-Soviet frozen conflicts. Unlike Moldova, Azerbaijan has not inscribed in its Constitution any provisions on neutrality, military non-alignment or the rejection of foreign troops and military installations on its territory. Azerbaijan's national security concept, which was prepared in 2004 and finally signed by the president in 2007, is further specified through a military doctrine completed in 2011. This doctrine states that the 'continuing occupation' of Azerbaijani territories by Armenia is the most important military threat to the national security of Azerbaijan. In it Azerbaijan reserves for itself the rights of a sovereign state, in principle, to make its own decisions:

> Azerbaijani Republic does not allow placing of foreign military bases within its territory, except [in] the cases stipulated in the international treaties which it supports. However, in case of fundamental changes in military-political conditions, Azerbaijani Republic has a right to place foreign military bases within its territory or temporarily to allow foreign military participation in other form.[418]

Foreign bases can be allowed on the basis of international agreements to which Azerbaijan is or *will be* party; and, should 'fundamental changes in the military and political situation' occur, Azerbaijan may grant *temporary* permission for a foreign military presence, including the temporary stationing of foreign military bases on its territory. Azerbaijan's Law on Armed Forces (amended in 2005) injects flexibility into international cooperation by stipulating that the armed forces can be ordered to engage in activities outside their scope of competence through the decision of the National Assembly upon proposal by the president (Article 2).[419] The possibility reserved for itself by Azerbaijan to deviate from its policy of military non-alignment is contingent on profound changes in the security environment and, therefore, designed to diminish the room for manoeuvre which Russia has in the Karabakh issue.

Azerbaijan participated in the CSTO between 1993 and 1999. Becoming a member of the CSTO went hand-in-hand with the withdrawal of Russian (former Soviet) military troops and installations from Azerbaijani territory, which Russia tried in vain to combine with Baku's permission to allow Russian border troops to return to the Iranian border. When Russia left the Gabala radar station upon expiry of the permission to utilize this Soviet-time facility at the end of 2012, Azerbaijan announced that it was at last completely free from external military presence.[420] From the point of view of Western states the interest to connect Azerbaijan's oil and gas fields with pipeline networks to Europe, and to have Azerbaijan serve as a transit country for energy from Turkmenistan as well as for the military materiel to Afghanistan after September 2001, made it far-sighted to develop military cooperation designed to assist the country in modernizing its army.[421] Azerbaijan joined

NATO's Partnership for Peace in May 1994 and continued its cooperation with the organization's partnership mechanisms (PP, PARP and IPAP). A Strategic Defense Review (SDR), which in the frame of NATO cooperation provides for conducting reforms in the armed forces, was initiated in 2009 and extended until 2015. Azerbaijan chose to adopt a moderate pace and emphasized that the technical nature of its cooperation remained detached from Western political values.[422] Its interest in NATO relates to the need to modernize its armed forces as well as the political need to facilitate access to Western markets and to engage more actively with NATO in the resolution of the Nagorno-Karabakh conflict. However, while Azerbaijan has developed cooperation with NATO without making membership part of its agenda, NATO has chosen to stay in the background in this conflict and supports its political resolution in the frame of the OSCE.

Azerbaijan has also demonstrated the independence of its position in its participation in the EU's Eastern Partnership programs. At the Vilnius summit at the end of November 2013, it signed a visa facilitation agreement with the EU but abstained from joining the political Association Agreement with the DCFTA. Energy-rich Azerbaijan needs assistance rather less than its neighbours in the South Caucasus do. Prioritizing the visa facilitation agreement signals that Azerbaijan aims to develop economic relations with the EU without political conditions, and this was especially the case at the time (in 2012) when the Association Agreement affected 40 per cent of its foreign trade; at the same time the Union's member states provided 36.5 per cent of Azerbaijan's foreign investment outside the energy sector. From the perspective of the European Union the motivation for cooperation with Azerbaijan is likewise not limited to the European Neighbourhood policies. Connecting Azerbaijan's oil and gas reserves with pipeline networks in Europe serves the purpose of building political relations and a strategic partnership, and this makes it possible to bypass the energy routes controlled by Russia and dramatically reduce the dependency of Central and Eastern Europe on Russian energy.[423] The Southern Energy Corridor, the Trans-Adriatic Pipeline (TAP) and the Azerbaijan–Georgia–Romania Interconnector (AGRI) are the project highlights in Azerbaijan's relations with the EU.

Azerbaijan has adopted the practice of confirming its policy of military non-alignment in political declarations. In this way, it seeks to maintain its independent line of action while also responding to the pressures that arise from Russia. In 2007 it signed the Tehran Declaration of the Caspian Sea littoral states, according to which the parties 'will not allow other countries to use their territories for acts of aggression or other military operations against any of the parties' (Article 15).[424] In 2011 Azerbaijan became a member of the Non-Aligned Movement. In its emphasis of cooperation based on concrete benefits, mutual respect and non-interference in internal affairs, Azerbaijan argues that it continues the principles worked out in East–West relations during the final years of the Cold War and does not consider international relations merely as an extrapolation of Western political values. Thus, when Azerbaijan joined the Non-Aligned Movement it argued that the movement, together with the UN, represents the 'international community'.[425] The Non-Aligned Movement became Azerbaijan's main forum for accumulating diplomatic support for its position in the Karabakh conflict when the support it had initially enjoyed in the UN General Assembly began to dissipate.[426] Baku frequently reports the multilateral declarations – which as a rule are diplomatic compromises and tend to support the status quo rather than any one party – as support for its position and policies in the Karabakh conflict.[427] In order to prevent one-sided interpretations, Armenia has found it necessary to participate in the Non-Aligned Movement by acquiring the status of an observer. Since 2014 Azerbaijan has received political support from the Cooperation Council of the Turkic-Speaking States (the 'Turkic Council').[428] Because this brings into focus the cultural lines of division in the conflict it is a controversial diplomatic gain in the wider international community and, in fact, reveals Azerbaijan's aspiration to strengthen its state identity with more culturally oriented international relations.

With very little cost and commitment, Azerbaijan's membership in the Non-Aligned Movement conveys the message that NATO membership is not on the agenda; 'NATO members cannot be members of the Non-Aligned Movement,' President Ilham Aliyev confirms.[429] The treaty-based assurances which Azerbaijan has given to Russia about the continuity of its security policy leave much space for military cooperation which, it can be argued, is not to be 'directed against' Russia. Such openness in their mutual relationship makes it comprehensible why the political discourse between the two countries places so much emphasis on 'the principles of good-neighborliness, friendship and mutual trust'. In a joint declaration made in Baku in January 2001, Russia and Azerbaijan raised their mutual cooperation to a 'new, higher level of strategic partnership', which includes long-term military and military-technical cooperation and also emphasizes the need to cooperate on issues concerning the Caspian Sea. This declaration also contained a statement that later, in November 2008, was taken up and agreed upon by both Azerbaijan and Armenia and which was celebrated as a victory for Russian diplomacy: the parties committed themselves to a political solution to the Nagorno-Karabakh conflict, based on UN Security Council resolutions and decisions of the OSCE.

This advancement in Russia's trilateral diplomacy was preceded by yet another political declaration of friendship and strategic partnership. In July

2008 Russia and Azerbaijan confirmed the role of the Minsk Group and Russia's central role in it, and repeated their commitment to the promotion of a peaceful settlement to the Nagorno-Karabakh conflict while also declaring to continue to work together for the eradication of the activities of 'organizations, groups and individuals against the state sovereignty and territorial integrity of each other' on their territories.[430] In other words, Russia made a political commitment not to allow, *on its own territory*, activity advocating Karabakh's independence. In the context of political friendship intentions declared at high political levels matter most. This is part of an institutional discourse which regulates the mutual relationship in both countries and sets up political boundaries for mutually acceptable action. The declaratory policies leave much space for political flexibility in concrete cases and, consequently, offer a means to observe and 'test' political friendship and trust. From the perspective of Azerbaijan, the bilateral relationship with Russia offers economic favours and nourishes a sense of independence from the West, while at the same time preventing Russia's policies from skewing the weight of favours towards Armenia and acknowledging Karabakh as a functioning state entity.

Russia's limited ability to control Azerbaijan's geopolitical affiliation

The FCMA and FCMS treaties, both concluded in summer 1997 yet quite different in content, increase Russia's capability to manage the conflict by bringing the two adversaries into close cooperation with Russia. Cooperation with Armenia is an established alliance relationship, whereas with Azerbaijan there exists no integrated control mechanism and constant political reconfirmation is required for it to function. The open, negotiable and sanction-free character of this relationship is reflected in the diplomatic communications and documents which are typical of a 'win-win' bargain: some items derive from Russia's interests, and others from Azerbaijan's. This also means that the mutual agreement suggested in the political rhetoric about friendship, mutual trust and strategic partnership does not readily correspond to the actual strategic areas of military-technological and energy cooperation. Friendship is not a description but a request, and the speech of trust appears only when trust is at risk.

It is therefore not surprising that domestic discussion in Azerbaijan differs greatly from the discourse in bilateral relations at high levels of decision making. While not directly at war, Azerbaijan is seen to be 'in the situation of war' with Armenia, a state with which the Russian Federation is militarily allied. Iran in the south is accused of breaching Azerbaijan's territory and air space across the border and, hence, only Turkey and Georgia are left as Azerbaijan's 'potential and natural allies'.[431] After the Russia–Georgia war of 2008, Azerbaijan persuaded Turkey (its neighbour along a 15-kilometre stretch of the border in Nakhchivan) to conclude a bilateral Treaty on Strategic Partnership and Mutual Assistance. This treaty provides for cooperation in defence and military technology and stipulates that either party will assist the other with all available means in the event of an armed attack of aggression by a third state or group of states.[432] The significance of this bilateral commitment, which was signed in 2010, is chiefly political and adds stakes to the need for Russia to control Armenia's actions.

In addition to policies that directly deal with the Karabakh conflict, Russia's political means to control Azerbaijan's geopolitical affiliation include the provision of armaments and favourable economic relations, especially in the energy trade. During the Karabakh war (1992–4) the Tashkent Treaty on Collective Security, which was set up in May 1992 as the frame for redistributing the military resources left behind by the Soviet Union outside Russia and later developed into the CSTO, provided normative justification for Moscow's policies to give armed support to both sides in order to maintain the balance between them. Azerbaijan left the CSTO in 1999 but Russia continued this policy, which benefited its industry and kept both Armenia and Azerbaijan within its sphere of military technology. Using a favourable pricing system, it provided the same weapons and weapons systems to both parties in the conflict, including tactical missiles and anti-missile systems. Such an approach has accelerated the arms race in the region and established a precarious conventional deterrence between the two states in the conflict. This requires Russia to employ well-coordinated management skills, including the divulgement of only selective information about arms deals and deliveries.

The arms trade related to the Karabakh conflict was in Russia's hands until Azerbaijan started military trade with Israel in the 2010s. Israel buys almost one-third of the oil extracted annually in Azerbaijan and in return sells advanced military technology to Baku. This trade started with drone technology and was followed by a more comprehensive arms deal worth US$1.6 billion in 2012. From the perspective of Azerbaijan (which in its diplomatic relations supports Palestine), the armaments bought from Israel offer an alternative to its dependency on Russia. Moreover, it provides a way to streamline its military equipment with the United States which is free of the more burdensome program-context of NATO partnership. In response Armenia announced after the four-day war of April 2016 that the weapons acquired by it on the basis of an agreement with Russia in 2013 included ballistic missiles with a range of 400 kilometers.[433] With a defence budget that is nine to ten times higher than Armenia's (amounting to US$4.8 billion in 2015, in comparison with Armenia's under-US$500 million budget), Azerbaijan is determined not to give up its overwhelming dominance in the arms race.[434] Before the year 2016 ended, it had acquired an Iron Dome air-defence and anti-missile system from Israel.[435] Armenia, for its part, compensates for this imbalance by relying on Russia's military presence.

In energy relations, Azerbaijan demonstrated its intent not to remain dependent on Russia when it concluded agreements with Western companies about the exploitation of its gas fields in 1994, immediately after the ceasefire agreement. Within a decade it had a gas surplus for export in addition to satisfying its domestic demand. The oil pipeline from Baku to Ceyhan (Turkey) via Tbilisi (Georgia) started to operate in 2006 and was complemented the following year by the South Caucasus Pipeline (SCP, Baku–Tbilisi–Erzurum) for gas. During these years Russia's Gazprom had more than doubled its gas price (from US$110 to US$235 per 1000 bcm) for both Azerbaijan and Georgia, whereas the prices paid by Armenia, which continued to expand its alliance relationship with Russia, remained unchanged. In 2007 Azerbaijan agreed to supply gas to Georgia and, after the war in August 2008, its state oil company SOCAR acquired the majority of Georgia's gas distribution networks and, just like Russia previously, started to provide Georgia with subsidized gas.[436] Russia lost the political leverage provided by its subsidized energy prices in Georgia, and SOCAR became a competitor of Gazprom in the regional market and soon also beyond it.

The state of Azerbaijan could claim ownership of up to only 25 per cent of the pipelines built during the first decade of the new millennium; then, in 2015, Azerbaijan started to construct the Trans-Anatolia Pipeline (TANAP), of which the state-owned company SOCAR controls 58 per cent. This new pipeline will enable the South Caucasus Gas Pipeline from Azerbaijan's Shah Deniz gas fields to Georgia to connect with a pipeline that runs through Turkey – from its border with Georgia to its border with Greece – and connects further with the Trans-Adriatic Pipeline (TAP, through the territories of Greece, Albania and Italy). This transmission network will make it possible to bring Azerbaijani gas to Europe without using the pipelines controlled by Russia. While Azerbaijan has been able to take markets away from Russian companies – which are not equally welcome in the EU's member states – it has also toned down any conflict and emphasized that 'co-existence' is possible especially in the markets of Turkey and the Balkans.[437] Gazprom is among its largest customers (taking third place in 2013), and the diplomatic attempt to avoid conflict in all fields of bilateral relations is shared in Baku and in Moscow. Consequently, Baku prefers to keep a low profile in pipeline projects such as the Trans-Caspian pipeline and the Turkish Stream across the Black Sea, in both of which Russia has much geopolitical interest. As illustrated by SOCAR's entry to the European market via Greece in June 2013, Azerbaijan emphasizes that its decisions are made on commercial grounds. The decision in June 2013 meant that it withdrew its direct support from the Nabucco pipeline project, which had become a symbol of providing an alternative to Russian energy. Azerbaijan has similarly demonstrated its independence by staying outside the CIS agreement of 2010 on energy transit.[438] On issues of regional economic integration within the CIS, it tries to steer away from conflict by explaining that its policies are guided by the 'principle of expediency': 'When we see that integration will bring us additional economic benefit, we, of course, participate actively. But if we see that it will either bring us nothing or may actually take us back, we have a rather reserved attitude.'[439] Simultaneously, Azerbaijan actively supports humanitarian (non-state-level yet state-guided) cooperation in the CIS frame, which provides it with a way to strengthen its standing in the region.[440] It is also an active participant in GUAM (a cooperative body that brings together Georgia, Ukraine and Moldova and was established to oppose the influence of the CIS) and other regional bodies.

Russia is the largest importing country to Azerbaijan and dominates its electricity supply market, whereas export to the Russian market is important not only for Azerbaijan's oil and gas but also for its agricultural products. Russian gas deliveries to Azerbaijan ceased in 2007, and already ten years earlier SOCAR had started to provide gas to Russia's southern parts and especially the North Caucasus when the Baku–Novorossiysk line (based on an agreement between Russia and Azerbaijan in 1996) began to operate. In Azerbaijan, the level of prices constitutes Russia's main asset. It has been able to keep oil and gas producers satisfied with the price it pays for its imports, which also reduces the incentive in Azerbaijan to turn to European buyers. In Europe, Russia has been able to offer discounts to consumers in countries where Russian gas continues to dominate the market (in Bulgaria, Romania and Moldova) and, consequently, threatens to render competing large pipeline projects, including Azerbaijan's, commercially unviable. The competition over network construction is likely to intensify when Azerbaijan, whose own resources are limited, begins to make use of its position as a transit country for gas going from Kazakhstan and Turkmenistan to Europe.

In Azerbaijan, just like in other post-Soviet countries, Russia strives to promote cultural relations and, in particular, the standing of the Russian language. An international humanitarian forum has been established as a joint initiative at the top-most level and is now an annual event. Azerbaijan's direct border with Russia, which runs through politically volatile Dagestan, keeps Russia interested in maintaining the border and pacifying its adjacent areas. The fact that the Baku–Novorossiysk pipeline, which was opened in 1997 for gas deliveries to Russia through Chechnya and closed only two years later because of the war in the region, has been rebuilt through Dagestan and has been in operation there since 2013 increases the importance of this issue. On its side of the border in Dagestan, Russia supports Azerbaijani minority languages, among them the language of the Avar people. The Avar are the largest group in Dagestan – about 850,000 people – and compose about 30 per cent of its population. Russia's support for the maintenance of indigenous cultural identities in Dagestan realizes its general, federal-level policies and is also meant to strengthen pro-Russia attitudes in Dagestan as well as among the Avar people on the Azerbaijani side of the border.

In comparison with Armenia, where relations to Russia are structured through the state and its strategic sectors (both military and economic), Azerbaijan's ties to Russia are mainly at the level of the population. This relates to the conflation of the border through the transboundary communities mentioned above and, in addition, to the exceptionally large number of Azerbaijani migrant workers in Russia: up to one-quarter of Azerbaijan's population of nine million works in Russia. Within Russia the Azeri people are part of the Turkic cultural sphere and hence regarded as a very different group than the Armenians, who are traditionally well integrated in Russia's business and political elites. From Russia's perspective, attempts to complicate access to Russia's labour market is a controversial means of pressure because it also undermines the efforts to maintain positive attitudes about Russia, and its negative implications are especially obvious in Azerbaijan, where much of the Westernized elite is attitudinally opposed to Russia. To conclude, Russia ultimately does not have much leverage at its disposal that can actually be used in regard to Baku; it is only Karabakh, as long as Azerbaijan holds onto it, that can be effectively used as a means of political pressure.

It follows that Nagorno-Karabakh's pursuit of independence has little value *per se* for Russia. The conflict remains in gridlock because Karabakh has strong iconic significance for the security and identity of both Armenia and Azerbaijan: in both countries, security and identity crumble if they are seriously threatened with the loss of Karabakh. While Russia's security and identity, if not altogether disintegrated, can be at least seriously crippled by instability in the North Caucasus, the value of Karabakh is only instrumental (symbolic in the sense of immediate political expediency) for Russia's deep borders in the 'Transcaucasus' (South Caucasus). Militarily speaking, Russia is only indirectly present militarily in Karabakh – through its alliance relationship with Armenia – and the actual use of this military strength in a major encounter would risk upsetting the delicate military and political stability which Russia is trying to maintain, and in which relations with Azerbaijan are the most uncertain and fragile element.

14

Nagorno-Karabakh and Its Precarious Relative Stability

For more than a quarter of a century the self-declared Nagorno-Karabakh Republic (NKR), which in 2018 changed its name to the Republic of Artsakh, has survived as a political entity that functions with its own state institutions and symbols. The residents have local identity certificates that are also valid in Armenia and, as a rule, an Armenian passport. The local currency, the Artsakh dram, is a symbol of independence yet not widely used in Karabakh, and its value is pegged to the Armenian dram. The economic survival of the Karabakh state is dependent on the budget support provided by Armenia in the form of governmental credits and the flow of assistance from the global diaspora and especially the large Armenian populations in the United States, Russia and France. The private donations from the diaspora are Karabakh's most important capital inflow. Since 1998, the Hayastan All-Armenian Fund[441] has raised US$236 million for projects in Armenia and the Nagorno-Karabakh Republic combined – far more than EU programs' assistance to Armenia. These funds are used mainly to develop the educational and health systems and to improve communal and agricultural development as well as roads and other infrastructure. They provide the Karabakh state with limited economic independence, which makes its case very different from Transnistria, Abkhazia and South Ossetia, which are all entirely dependent on Russia. Yet, the economy of the Artsakh Republic remains seriously crippled due to a lack of sustainability arising from the unsuitability of donations as the basis for a state's budget.

Similarly, the maintenance of its military defence, which Nagorno-Karabakh has built up since the ceasefire in 1994 and which for a population of little more than 100,000 is impressive in its sheer number of anti-tank weapons and artillery, is dependent on Armenia's support, which itself is militarily dependent on Russia. The link to Russia would have been more direct if Russia's then-minister of defence Pavel Grachev had been able to establish Russian peacekeepers in Kelbajar between Armenian territory, Nagorno-Karabakh and Azerbaijan as planned in 1994. Because Nagorno-Karabakh's survival in the struggle for independence from Azerbaijan is militarily guaranteed through Armenia's relationship of military alliance with Russia rather than Russia's own immediate presence in Nagorno-Karabakh, Russia's role in this conflict takes shape mainly in the formal frame of international relations. In other words, the conflict over Karabakh is controlled through the deep border arrangements which are interstate relations with Armenia and Azerbaijan. The specific vertical relations – the practices through which Russia has direct presence and influence in Karabakh – take shape in this formal frame and, consequently, remain modest so far.

As in the military field of cooperation, Russia's economic assistance and contacts with Nagorno-Karabakh are also routed through Armenia. The complexities related to Russia's direct economic presence in Karabakh are illustrated by the conditions under which Russian finance institutions operate. In relation to Armenia, they encounter justified attempts by the Armenian Central Bank to maintain through different regulations and requirements of reciprocal practices the country's financial system based on the dram vis-à-vis the much larger Russian market system, in which many Armenian and Karabakh residents place more trust than their own country's system.[442] At the same time those Russian institutions that operate in Karabakh face sanctions on the Azerbaijani market. The result of these cross-pressures is that the question of having the branch of a bank in Karabakh loses out when Russian businesses negotiate access to Azerbaijani markets, while Armenia's countermeasures to make life more complicated for those institutions which yield to pressure from Baku further increase the practical difficulties experienced by Karabakh's population.[443] The conflict contributes to keeping Russian economic interests out of Karabakh and reproduces the historical image of this region as an imperial 'outback' in relation to Baku and Yerevan, where all new activity with settlers was concentrated even two hundred years earlier.[444]

The most significant form of Russia's economic presence in Karabakh comes through the private donations of Russian Armenians, the results of which are visible in many communal-level infrastructure projects. Although these donations tell much about the presence of the Russian business elite in Karabakh and Armenia, in Russia this interaction remains within an ethnic Armenian frame and therefore separate from the rest of Russian society. Additionally, a limited space for Russia's humanitarian cooperation in Karabakh exists through unofficial business and education channels.[445] Because Karabakh lacks any significant Russian connection and is supported by Russia through Armenia, it – unlike notably Transnistria – has not been internationally labelled as a 'proxy' political entity for Russia.[446] This term also does not describe its relations with Armenia because there is no 'third party' to whom it could represent Armenia's interests. Instead, Karabakh lacks a voice and remains hostage to the conflict over its own status.

Karabakh's need to stay in close connection with Armenia in order to survive politically has been increased by the fact that it has not been permitted to participate in the Minsk Group's negotiations since 1998. The election of Robert Kocharian as the president of Armenia in March of that year enabled Stepanakert and Yerevan to combine their political forces for joint policies on the conflict. But even if Nagorno-Karabakh's voice was merged with Armenia's in this way, Armenia cannot – without grossly violating international law – take this direction of policy to its logical conclusion and unify Nagorno-Karabakh with its territory. This would be considered as an 'annexation' and provoke historical analogies which Armenia would be unable to bear diplomatically, not least because of the economic consequences that could be expected to follow in the form of increased sanctions and decreased flows of capital from abroad. Consequently, any project to merge with Armenia must be preceded by independence. In early autumn 2010 Armenia started legal preparations for recognizing the independence of the Artsakh Republic. Simultaneously, Foreign Minister Edward Nalbandian argued that as long as there is hope for the peaceful resolution of the Karabakh conflict, there is no need for additional actions. And, further: 'We have not recognized Nagorno Karabakh yet and without doing so we cannot recognize, for example, Kosovo, which has the right to independence but not more than Karabakh, or all other newly formed states, which are recognized by some countries, but not by the international community.'[447] For as long as Nagorno-Karabakh's independence has no support in either the West or in Russia, Armenia is unable to do more than use its readiness to recognize Artsakh's independence as a political threat.

Before the end of 2010 Armenian diplomats and decision makers had in several international connections reiterated the position stated by Nalbandian and emphasized the need to continue the international negotiations.[448] In the domestic context of discussions this activity underlined that if Armenia in fact was to use this political weapon, its credibility would depend on Russia's backing. However, Russia is not prepared to provide this type of backing as long as Azerbaijan maintains its militarily non-aligned position and friendly relations with Russia. The sensitivity of the relationship between Moscow and Baku is demonstrated by the disruptions which Moscow's statements easily cause in Baku. For example, the comment made by Sergei Naryshkin, Chairperson of the State Duma, in February 2013 to the effect that an early resolution of the Nagorno-Karabakh conflict cannot be expected immediately required an explanation for Azerbaijan by Leonid Slutsky, Chairperson of the Duma Committee for CIS Affairs and Compatriot Relations. Azerbaijan's diplomatic protests about opinions voiced in Russia's state-supported media similarly reveal the extent of pressures in Baku.[449] The more Azerbaijan glides away from the policies of neutrality that Russia prefers for it to follow, the more Russia prepares to think about adopting another way and arouses further suspicions in Baku. When on his first day in office in early May 2018 Armenia's Prime Minister Nikol Pashinian, whom the 'Velvet Revolution' brought to power in spring 2018, emphasized that the interests of the Republic of Artsakh and its people are best protected by the authorities of Artsakh and that, consequently, Artsakh must have back the seat which it lost in the Minsk Group's negotiations twenty years ago,[450] this was a sign of not only his government's firm support of the pursuit for independence in Karabakh but also a relaxation of the tie between Yerevan and Stepanakert and, correspondingly, an increase of Russia's space for manoeuvre to prepare alternative lines of action. The next chapter discusses the circumstances which can contribute to a situation in which the recognition of the independence of Karabakh could also come to suit Russia's interests.

The threat of escalation from within

Russia has not updated its military alliance relationship with Armenia to support it in violent events despite the fact that the combined numbers of casualties occurring annually in frontline encounters since the ceasefire of May 1994 (including in the four-day war of April 2016) vastly surpass the casualties that prompted Russia's intervention in South Ossetia in August 2008. Unlike in Tskhinvali these soldiers were neither Russians nor even residents of the region holding Russian passports. Russia had neither the domestic support for an intervention nor the means to internationally legitimize such action. While the military intervention in August 2008 was a *political* 'last resort' (relating to the internal and external security of Russia's borders rather than the 'last resort' to save lives, as Russia argued), such a course of action is a much fainter possibility in Karabakh and utterly undesirable from Russia's perspective: it would jeopardize relations with either Azerbaijan or Armenia – most likely with both – and dissolve the whole system of controlling the conflict which Russia has erected in connection with the deep border arrangements, the key elements of which are the relationship of military alliance with Armenia and the political partnership with Azerbaijan.

Simultaneously, Russia's Foreign Minister Sergey Lavrov emphasized in September 2008 that no parallel exists between Nagorno-Karabakh, on the one hand, and South Ossetia and Abkhazia on the other hand (see Part One, pp. 30-4 in this book),[451] and this may be interpreted as an indirect warning that Russia's intervention is a real possibility in the case of a change in the conditions and an escalation in violence. The discussion around Baku's response to the decision by the NKR to start the reconstruction of Stepanakert airport in 2009 (which was built in 1974 but shut after war erupted in 1992) gives some indication of the flexibility over the threshold for intervention. Azerbaijan has announced that the air space in the conflict zone is closed and that it considers any military or civilian flight that takes place without its permission as a violation of the airspace under its sovereignty. With its anti-aircraft missile system purchased from Russia, Azerbaijan is capable of controlling the skies over Nagorno-Karabakh.[452] In January 2013, it adopted a decree which allows its military to shoot down any airplane that does not heed orders to land in Azerbaijan. These measures prompted the CSTO's Secretary General Nikolai Bordyuzha to appeal to Baku: 'I see Azerbaijan as a civilized country that adheres to universal norms. I very much doubt that in our time the leadership of a country can take such a step and command the deliberate destruction of civilian planes, and I have no serious attitude to this kind of information.'[453] His words are a reminder of the normative strings of the international community which Russia imposes upon Azerbaijan through the Minsk Group, and the position taken by the speaker confirms that the collective security of the CSTO is the ultimate basis of the conventional deterrence which has been built on the Armenian side of the conflict. What is more, they also indicate that this state of affairs is closely connected with Karabakh, as the issue of the airfield tellingly reveals.

The Secretary of Armenia's National Security Council, Arthur Baghdasaryan, continued the discussion with stronger words: 'The Republic of Armenia is a sovereign state, which is one of the most active members of the Collective Security Treaty Organization [...]; every occurrence of attack on a civilian aircraft is reprehensible for the CSTO.'[454] By carrying out its threats, Azerbaijan's actions would not be interpreted as the defence of its own sovereignty but, instead, as a violation of the rules of an international community that prohibits attacks on civilian aircraft – any such act would be 'state terrorism'. In November 2014, one day after Azerbaijan had shot down an NKR military helicopter near the Line of Contact and declared the airspace over the NKR a no-fly zone, Armenia's president Serzh Sargsyan not only tested these normative boundaries but also emphatically stretched them by arriving by military helicopter at the newly rebuilt airport in Stepanakert after attending military exercises in eastern Armenia.[455] While Azerbaijan had increased the stakes in the proximity of the Line of Contact, it did not attempt to shoot down the helicopter which, given its sensitive political cargo, would surely have opened a new phase in the war.

The response of the Secretary General of the CSTO to Baku's threats shows that Russia desired to put an end to speculations and uncertainty. However, the fact that the strongest words relating to the CSTO – 'every occurrence of attack on a civilian aircraft is reprehensible' – were uttered by Armenia enabled Russia not to manoeuvre itself into a corner on this issue. Although political guns were brought to bear by directly bringing in the CSTO, Russia avoids aggravating Baku and also, as a rule, avoids indicating any direct military involvement on behalf of the CSTO in order to avoid situations where it may encounter the disagreement of other CSTO members. In an open conflict the CSTO would ideally appear as a supporting and legitimating framework for Russian–Armenian action and do so in the name of defending the norms of the international community (such as the prohibition on attacking civilian aircraft). The lack of more concrete support has little practical significance in the organization's working structure, in which the bilateral, treaty-based alliance agreements between Russia and the other member states are decisive for action. In Armenia not only the Erebuni airport, which is used for mainly military purposes, but also the Zvartnots international airport is under joint Russian–Armenian control, and a refusal to extend this cooperation to the Stepanakert airport in the case of a real threat from Baku would be tantamount to giving up Russia's role of guarantor in the conflict. However, to speak of other than 'civilian' aircraft would be to argue outside the domain of unquestionable international norms and to become implicated as a participant in the specific conflict over Karabakh.

Because the reconstruction of the Stepanakert airport allowed it now to host even heavy transport aircraft, it has logistical significance from Russia's point of view as well. This airport will be practical should international peacekeepers, including Russia's troops, be stationed in the conflict region. Were Azerbaijan to militarily attack this airport, such action would not only push Russia to support Armenia but also undermine Baku's international relations and the support it has gained for its position in the conflict, and it could also disturb the stability which Azerbaijan needs for its energy trade with Europe. The question over flight rights illustrates the normative battle in the Karabakh conflict: Armenia puts the principle of refraining from the use of force first, whereas Azerbaijan's point of departure is the principle of territorial integrity and the respect for what it claims are internationally recognized borders. In this case Armenia – to the extent that it focuses on the severity of the crime of attacking civilian aircraft – is able to garner the support of specific rules of the international community, whereas Azerbaijan's emphasis on sovereignty appears to repeat an abstract principle that is so often politically instrumentalized in international conflicts. The fact that

Armenia also violated a normative line with its military flight served only to create a 'grey', undefined area in the practices of the conflict. Azerbaijan was not prepared to risk a war from which it would have been very difficult for Russia to stay away; instead, it took its political revenge a few months later in the four-day war of April 2016.

Instability triggered by developments in the wider region

Tensions and confrontations in the wider region can also impact Karabakh and draw it into a larger conflict formation. Assuming that the control structure which exists in the frame of the Minsk Group and Russia's role within it remain essentially unchanged, a potentially destabilizing element is presented by Azerbaijan's complex relations with Iran and the conflict-triggering effects of Iran's problematic relations with both Turkey and the United States. At the time of independence in 1991, Azerbaijan's relations with Iran were normal. Alongside Turkey and the United States, Iran was among the first states with which Azerbaijan first established diplomatic relations.[456] After the Soviet borders collapsed, the loss of Karabakh and the surrounding districts diminished the territory of independent Azerbaijan by at least 14 per cent, and with its multiple ethnic groups the country is vulnerable to activity from the outside that seeks to cleave the unity of its state structures. It follows that the large number of the Turkic-speaking, 'Azeri' population in Iran (numbering 25 million) is a potential source of insurgent activity, although it remains unlikely that this population, scattered as it is across northern Iran, could unite to pursue a common political goal.

On Azerbaijan's side of the border the Persian-speaking Talysh, an ethnic group which is roughly equivalent to Karabakh in terms of population (112,000 in 2009), is already used by Armenia to weaken from within the Azerbaijani state's legitimacy as a multinational entity. In spring 2013 Armenia set up a Talysh-language radio station near Azerbaijan's border on land that Azerbaijan calls 'the occupied zone'. The Talysh were the nominal basis of the Mughan Soviet Republic, which in spring 1919 existed for a few months in present-day southeastern Azerbaijan and was used to fortify Bolshevik power against the government in Baku. In 1993 they declared a national republic of their own, an action which at the time was at least tacitly welcomed by Russian officials, who wished to weaken anti-Russian (including pro-Soviet) elements in Baku.[457] The contemporary Armenian activity is risky because internal political instability may prompt a military reaction from Baku, just as it did before Heydar Aliyev became president in autumn 1993, and such pressures would immediately affect Nagorno-Karabakh and increase the likelihood of an escalation in the conflict.

The recurrence of political instability in Azerbaijan would also increase tensions over Nakhchivan, Azerbaijan's exclave Autonomous Republic, which has a 179-kilometre-long border with Iran and which enables Azerbaijan to control the area lying between Armenia and Iran.[458] The exclave also contains a 15-kilometre strip of border which connects Azerbaijan with Turkey. Before Moscow took the decision to establish the Azerbaijani SSR in July 1921, the population in Nakhchivan was roughly 40 per cent Armenian. Over the course of the Soviet Union's lifetime, Baku's measures effectively emptied Nakhchivan of its Armenian population and, in 1979 when the Armenian population had sunk to under 1.5 per cent, the region was transformed into the Nakhchivan Autonomous Republic within the Azerbaijani SSR. Because the population basis had been completely altered, any attempts by Armenia during the Karabakh war to take over Nakhchivan – which, to the regret of many in Armenia, never happened – would have been far more difficult to justify to the international community than was the case in Karabakh. Developments during the Soviet era made Nakhchivan into an integral part of Azerbaijan. In hindsight, it would have been a significant advantage for Russia if this region, which borders on two of Russia's strategic borders (Iran and Turkey), would have been within reach of its troops stationed in Armenia. The geopolitical importance of Nakhchivan has increased since the conflict with Georgia has resulted in the principled blockage of the transit of Russian troops and equipment through the territory controlled by Georgia and led Russia to consider alternative routes across the Caspian Sea and northern Iran.

Azerbaijan's policymakers are well aware of the sensitive role that Azerbaijan plays in Russia's security arrangements in the South Caucasus. If Azerbaijan were to actively seek NATO membership, Moscow would interpret this as a breach of the treaty commitments towards Russia and argue that this change in the circumstances leaves Russia free to reconsider its policies on Karabakh. Although it is unlikely that Baku would be willing to abandon its emphasis of independence towards NATO, developments in Iran, Turkey and the Middle East may trigger a larger role for the United States and NATO in the region. Were Azerbaijan to open Nakhchivan as an outpost for the Western allies, its possibilities to regain the territories lost to Armenia would immediately shrink. However, the greatest risk lies perhaps in events that Baku, Moscow and the Western allies are unable to control. Should a major catastrophe hit northern Iran, possibly in the form of a military attack or a natural disaster, the pressure from the flow of a displaced population to the north could significantly burden Armenia and cause the collapse of the Nagorno-Karabakh Republic. Armenia fears that in such a situation Azerbaijan would be prompted to try to retake Karabakh, and it is an equally realistic possibility that an unsettled situation could induce Armenia to try to gain control of new areas as a 'preemptive' measure.

The words of Nikolai Bordyuzha, Secretary General of the CSTO, requesting Baku to behave in a 'civilized' manner in the issue of the Stepanakert airport also gain more significance in the wider regional context. From the point of view of Russia and the CSTO, this region is not like Osh in southern Kyrgyzstan's segment of the Ferghana Valley in Central Asia, where in June 2010 the organization refrained from intervening militarily in a conflict involving two of its member states (Kyrgyzstan and Uzbekistan) and where the strategic border lies farther to the south, between Tajikistan and Afghanistan. By contrast the Armenia–Azerbaijan conflict is in the immediate proximity of the border with Iran and, through the territory of Azerbaijan, with Turkey and therefore with NATO. A crisis that threatens to escalate, and especially a crisis in the proximity of the border to Iran, would be reason enough to station Russian military outside the Republic of Armenia, in the regions around Nagorno-Karabakh controlled by Armenia. This would become an opportunity to stay in the conflict area and to argue for the transformation of these troops into peacekeepers with an international mandate. Based on its relationship of military alliance Russia can claim a mandate in Armenia and, with reference to a crisis situation, it may also argue for its extension over Nagorno-Karabakh.

The four-day war of April 2016 generated political space for a new attempt by Russia to create a basis for negotiating a compromise that would use the 'Kazan formula' developed during the mediation efforts of President Medvedev in 2011. This idea proposed to lift the economic blockade against Armenia in exchange for the return of the territories of the seven districts around Nagorno-Karabakh, and that these territories would be demilitarized, peacekeeping units deployed in these areas and an agreement about the non-use of force would be signed.[459] With such an arrangement, Russia would establish itself as a military wedge between the conflict parties to ensure the resumption of economic cooperation across the borders and to ensure that the large infrastructure projects, which involve Iran and Turkey, would not be obstructed by the tensions relating to Karabakh. However, Russia prefers not to adopt any major measures based merely on its alliance relationship with Armenia – unless its relationship with Azerbaijan showed signs of crumbling. This did not happen in the four-day war of April 2016, in which Azerbaijan 'punished' Armenia and reminded the international community that it remained firm in its refusal to accept the situation which seems to be making the separation of Karabakh into a fait accompli for Baku. On the contrary, after this flaring of violence Russia intensified its efforts to make Azerbaijan (which has borders with Russia, Iran and also Turkey) into the geopolitical link for its transit infrastructure projects in the wider region. However, Russia's way of freezing the conflict and limiting its negative impacts on the development of economic cooperation in the region are challenged by both Azerbaijan's long-lasting opposition to accepting Russian peacekeepers in the disputed areas and Armenia's reluctance to see Russia control areas which it considers to have won through a costly war. As a consequence of this, the delicate political balance and conventional deterrence of military forces established by the two states in their mutual relations continue to be the main way for keeping the conflict frozen in stalemate. From Russia's perspective, this includes too much uncertainty, and therefore outbursts like the four-day war offer the opportunity for new breakthroughs.

15

Moscow's Main Thrust and Its Alternative

After the four-day war in April 2016, Armenia emphasized that it would accept nothing less than the recognition of Nagorno-Karabakh's independence as a trade-off for negotiating its withdrawal from the districts adjacent to Karabakh. For its part Azerbaijan has indicated that it is prepared to consider a compromise which gives Karabakh the status of an autonomous republic (akin to Nakhchivan) – provided that an agreement can be reached on other issues in the settlement.[460] This, basically, is in line with the settlement policies also supported by Russia. However, in the solution that Russia proposes for Transnistria, the political guarantees of sufficient autonomy include a right of separation under specified conditions. For Baku, like also for Chisinau, this is unacceptable because it is seen as a channel that invites external interference and as a possibility to split the country from within even after a peace settlement is reached.

In the settlement process in Moldova, Russia has clearly expressed its preferences; in the Karabakh conflict however, where its interests as well as the format for an international settlement are different, it has remained relatively silent about the political model for a settlement outside the Minsk negotiations. In the entire process Russia's focus has been on issues relating to confidence-building and the international guarantees which can be provided for the status of Karabakh with Russia's contribution. In addition to the military guarantees – peacekeeping arrangements and the conflict parties' agreement to the principle of the non-use of force – other types of guarantees that third states can give to the Armenian and Azeri populations are also under consideration. In this connection the possibility that Russia could act as a guarantor for maintaining the cultural identity (an agreed form of administrative autonomy) of the Armenians in Karabakh – along the lines suggested by the bashkan (governor) of Gagauzia in spring 2013 in the case of Moldova – has considerable relevance. From Russia's perspective, such a task is in harmony with the 'protector's' role it has traditionally assumed in relation to many smaller ethnic populations, including the Gagauz and the Ossetians. In the Karabakh conflict such an arrangement could involve Turkey as a co-guarantor (to represent the Azeri population) and, consequently, integrate Ankara's bilateral security guarantee for Azerbaijan (the treaty of

2010) into a more comprehensive frame of international guarantees. From Moscow's perspective, bringing in Turkey and succeeding to negotiate for itself the role of guarantor would constitute a considerable diplomatic victory in its trilateral negotiations with Armenia and Azerbaijan. However, the kind of guaranteeing arrangement sketched out by the Gagauz bashkan for the Gagauz Yeri can become an actual element in the negotiations on Karabakh only in case these negotiations should advance far enough to include, at the very least, the conditions for the refugees' return to Karabakh on the agenda. Such advancements have not come about for a number of reasons, and from Russia's perspective this situation has made it possible to uphold an openness and flexibility of policies which can keep both Armenia and Azerbaijan committed to the settlement process. It also enables Russia to keep both countries in close cooperation with itself and to control the obstructing effect which the conflict has on its plans to develop trade and logistics infrastructure in the wider region.

While Russia's relationship with Armenia is firmly structured as a military alliance, its relationship with Azerbaijan is based on political and economic cooperation and entails an openness which keeps this element in Russia's deep border arrangements in the South Caucasus uncertain. From Russia's perspective the crucial issue in this relationship is about security, i.e. about Russia's traditional preference to see close neighbours who are not allies pursue neutral policies. Were Azerbaijan's security policy to take the path adopted by Georgia, this would entirely change the situation in Karabakh. From Russia's perspective, Karabakh would no longer merely represent the knot that ties together the tensions in the South Caucasus and is symbolic for Russia's success or failure in its role as mediator and 'guarantor of the peace'. Instead, Karabakh would become the core area of Russia's deep borders in the South Caucasus, militarily and geopolitically – to be defended against NATO's further expansion in the proximity of its traditional strategic borders with Iran and Turkey. Azerbaijan's turn towards aspiring to gain membership in NATO could not take place without profound changes in its society. This vision of the future presumes that the meaning of the Karabakh conflict in Azerbaijan can be transformed in such a way as to exclude the trauma of loss and victimization from being a part of the national identity sustained by the state. Although this is not the reality today, the situation is liable to change under new leadership and once the sentiments of new generations become established. If Azerbaijan ceases to play a part in the regional security arrangements erected by Russia, including rejecting its role in constituting a geopolitical link with Turkey and Iran, Russia's alliance relationship with Armenia would probably also shatter because there would no longer be a region-wide knot of interests to sustain it.[461] Because Armenia would be able to leave behind the conflict that has permeated its society and state structures, it could finally yield to long-time internal pressure to relax its security ties with Russia and the CSTO. Consequentially, the focus of Russia's policies would be redirected to only a small area (i.e. Nagorno-Karabakh), and the direct vertical relationship, which so far is only modest in that it consists of humanitarian cooperation, would likely be strengthened.

From the perspective of Nagorno-Karabakh, a drastic increase in its strategic importance for Russia would significantly increase its prospects for independence. Although Moscow has consistently kept the question of such a prospect on the margins of its main policies, it is an alternative that is kept open and even groomed as a possibility. In summer 2013 Russia activated its humanitarian relations (i.e. non-governmental relations developed and controlled by the state) with the NKR. In connection with a visit by a journalists' delegation to Karabakh in August, Denis Dvornikov, a member of the Civic Chamber (Russia's official civil society organization), mentioned to Karen Mirzoyan, the foreign minister of the NKR, that 'according to his observations' in Armenia there was concern over the possibility of establishing direct relations between Russia and Nagorno-Karabakh, including the recognition of its independence. Mirzoyan's reply, according to media reports, was that it was the first time he had heard of such concerns in Yerevan but that such a development was welcomed in Nagorno-Karabakh.[462] Irrespective of how much this was a 'trial ball', it shows that Moscow is prepared to strengthen its initially weak direct relations with Karabakh even if this, under present conditions, means mainly humanitarian cooperation.

In Karabakh itself independence first became a desirable goal for largely tactical reasons, as a way to escape from the conflict between post-Soviet Armenia and Azerbaijan. In the present era it can serve similarly temporary purposes in the sense that independence, even if unacceptable to a large number of states who have supported the notion of Azerbaijan's intact borders, still remains more acceptable than does formal unification with Armenia, which would entail accepting the use of military force to gain territory (although the question as to whether legal borders were breached is disputed by the Armenian side). However, for a number of reasons full independence would have little viability from a long-term perspective: Armenia and Nagorno-Karabakh are united through Armenian ethnic, cultural and historical identity; they have fought together in a war which has come at vast cost to both of them; and Karabakh's economy has been sustained in close connection with the Armenian economy and has few chances to develop in isolation from it. Thus, if the variant of policies in which Azerbaijan turns to the West and no longer plays a part in the regional security arrangements erected by Russia is followed, the recognition of independence would likely be the first step and rapidly followed by the formalized structure of an associated state which would have some features of a federation. Ensuring the stability of such a structure would be a politically challenging and administratively delicate task. The rifts between Stepanakert and Yerevan, which more peaceful times would be likely to bring to the surface, would offer possibilities to a large number of external actors, Russia among them, to intervene and legitimize action with reference to a desire to support the smaller party in its pursuit of greater self-determination. In such changed circumstances friction between Yerevan and Stepanakert can induce Moscow to support Karabakh's attempts to secure for itself a position that may not have much political tailwind in Yerevan, and it may also induce Moscow to increase Karabakh's military strength through favourable arms deals and training in advanced military technology. Such a vertical structure would be likely to remain subtle as it would reflect the development of Yerevan's relations with both Moscow and Stepanakert. From the perspective of Stepanakert, it would offer leverage to ensure a degree of independence to which it already is accustomed – including the control over its military, which for more than a quarter of a century has been an important part of Karabakh society. Because these developments become possible if Azerbaijan gives up the delicate role it plays in Russia's security arrangements in the region, it is also Azerbaijan which mainly holds the keys to keeping Russia's interest in the region focused on strengthening horizontal (rather than vertical) international relations.

Conclusion: Russia's Deep Border Practices in Its Post-Soviet Borderlands

The *pragma* of Russian power in the frozen conflicts

The past twenty-five years have shown that there are profound problems in encounters with Russia, and that these problems persist regardless of the efforts in the West to pressurize Russia to 'behave like a normal state'. The present book has sought to unravel some of the reasons for this 'hard reality'[463] with Russia, and it has done so with the normative thrust that the ramifications of inadequate understanding are unfortunate because reciprocal acts of military responses prompt policies in Moscow which ostensibly appear to confirm Western suspicions that Russia's main interest lies in territorial expansion. This study has argued that the vertical characteristic of Russia's power – of Russia as a power – reveals itself in the light of the idea of the system of states in which the states are equal in their capacity to control affairs within their linearly defined borders and in which these borders therefore conventionally mark state sovereignty. The examination in the preceding chapters has emphasized that the vertical connections which are part of Russia's post-Soviet borders are not just a 'Soviet' practice but part of Russia's historical constitution as a state. Inspired by the idea that history is alive in the habitual practices of language, this book has argued that the vertically integrated domain of the sovereign (*gosudarstvo*) in which relations of protection are legitimized by the modern forms of the *derzhava* is the qualitative dimension of Russia's power as we know it in its performed practices. These characteristics become manifest in a variety of ways: in the 'domestic' status which specific groups of people outside Russia's formal state borders have in the context of the institutions of the Russian state; the institutional arrangements which connect the de facto state to the development of economic infrastructure in Russia's regions and the mutually conditional political trusting relationships which enable the implementation of such vertical structures in the political process. These are some examples of the factual relations and the habitual practices in which the vertical character of Russia's power becomes manifest.

Besides the qualitative ('existential') experience and the factual relations of the various conflicts, the study in this book has focused on the discourse, the policies and the institutions that communicate this experience and seek to justify the action to which it is related. The argument that concludes the examinations of the preceding chapters is that the range of policy arrangements – from the preparation of territorial annexation and the creation of quasi-states to a neutral position which entails a multifaceted system of guarantees, and which also includes relationships of military alliance with asymmetric base arrangements, combined with the political conditionality of mutual benefits and favours – is all variations of policies by means of which Russia tries to solve its post-Soviet border security dilemma. They are arrangements of practices to solve the problem of how the wider border regions beyond the linear state borders can best be secured – in other words, how they can be kept politically stable in their relations with Russia – in the post-Soviet situation where direct military presence cannot be the solution without the receiving state's consent and where there are transboundary groups who expect (or are receptive to) Russia's support. It is for this reason that they are termed 'deep border arrangements' in this book. The argument that has bound together the study of the various conflicts is that Russia's action in these conflicts must be seen in this broader connection, for without such a perspective it remains impossible for us to understand how, and why, a 'freeze' takes place in both open warfare and the resolution of the conflicts.

Russia's deep border practices can be summarized in the following figure (Figure 2) on the *pragma* (pattern-ness) of Russia's action in the

Figure 2 The *pragma* of Russia's Deep Borders.

frozen conflicts. This figure shows how the analysis and interpretation, which has been instructed by the three thematic dimensions discussed in the Introduction to this book (Figure 1, page 16), have produced a 'key' to understanding Russia's bordering practices beyond its formal state borders.

The figure presents a scheme of practices (an analytical construct) abstracted from the performed practices and events discussed in the present book. It argues about a recurrence of action which is not merely empirical but, instead, an abstraction of the basic elements which appear in their distinct ways in the different conflicts and, consequently, which make a pattern that (in its variation) can be anticipated as shaping Russia's policies also in the future. Although each of the three themes highlights one of the three dimensions of experience, all three dimensions are always included in the interpretation of these practices and events. For example, Russia's subsidies to the pensions in Transnistria (an instance of factual relations) can be examined with a focus on the power that it entails as a habitual ('imperial') practice and the agreement (formal and informal) that it represents in the relations between Tiraspol and Moscow. Such practices also make deep borders. While this book provides a key to their further study, its focus is not on such relations in the local context of the conflicts but rather on Russia's policies of resolving these conflicts.

The pattern that can be identified in the different conflicts refers to action that, rather than following a pre-existing rule or a predefined strategy, takes place 'as a rule' and, in the variation of a pattern, shows a way of being patterned. The study of the conflicts in Georgia, Moldova and Nagorno-Karabakh presented above has shown that Russia's priority in settling these conflicts is to ensure the neutral policy of the respective countries of conflict by means of different types of guarantees, and by maintaining a country's openness to economic cooperation with Russia and the multilateral economic organization under its leadership (policy variant 'A'). Simultaneously, rival external influences make these countries more and more cleaved and, while Russia continues to pursue policy variant 'A', it also prepares for variant 'B' by adopting policies which bring the people in the separatist regions closer to Russia. The pattern appears in different ways in the different conflicts. Neither of the two alternatives ('A' or 'B') was clearly present in the early stages of the efforts to solve this conflict in Georgia, whereas in Moldova policy variant 'A' (with different interpretations of neutrality) was the point of departure adopted already in the 1990s for the resolution of the conflict. Similarly, the two policy variants take a distinct form in the regional context of the Nagorno-Karabakh conflict: the 'A' variant involves both Azerbaijan's neutral policy and Armenia's close alliance relationship with Russia, and the 'B' variant involves Russia in a far more complex way than it does in Georgia and in Moldova. Because the 'pattern-ness' which can be abstracted from the policies and action in the different conflicts is a qualitative dimension of existence, it is a substantive idea about Russia's *interest* beyond what we can know based on its verbalized policies. This is not an assumption about a pre-given inner substance but an idea demonstrated in its practical implications, that is, the arrangement of practices to solve Russia's post-Soviet border security dilemma. Although patterns can break down and change, the conclusions of the examination in the preceding chapters suggest that when Russia is viewed through the window provided by the themes of the present book, it shows considerable continuity in its policies and action.

This understanding of Russia as a power is different from the approaches of the writers who have developed the realist school of international relations, including Martin Wight who has elaborately discussed the concept of a power in the light of historical examples. Wight defines a power based on its capacity to draw from resources and events from geographic areas outside its own linearly bounded territory and, consequently, evaluates the quality of being a power in terms of the external appearance of this accumulated capacity.[464] This approach turns one's attention to examining Russia's position in a hierarchy of powers rather than offers insight for making sense of the practices through which Russia builds security around its own borders. The specific power-character that can be abstracted from Russia's actions to control the outcomes of the frozen conflicts discussed in this book does not emphasize definable capacity but, instead, focuses on the specific, vertical characteristic of power. The insight that can be gained from the study of Russia's tradition of power is that while it can provide legitimacy to the extension of Russia's power beyond its formal state borders, it does so in specific cases and, consequently, requires that such action be justified in corresponding terms. In fact, if Russia tried to expand its territory by relying on repressive, military means, it would not only increase its confrontation with the international community but also act in a way which does not find resonance with its own tradition and, from inside Russia, looks like adventurism led by idealist projections of the Soviet past onto the future. Even at a time when many Russians feel indifferent about politics, exceptional action must still be in harmony with features that the majority of Russia's citizens can recognize as being those that make the country 'their own'. If it fails to do so, it also fails to sustain the basis of legitimacy which authoritarian rule in Russia traditionally enjoys in popular sentiment. In the case of the annexation of Crimea, the strong Russian connection gave the controversial act a basis in reality that is both factual and meaningful in terms of the tradition because it demonstrated Russia's imperial concern for the people, as well as the power of the sovereign as the ultimate centre of decision making (as discussed above in the context of the tradition of the *gosudar'*) to correct the violation of norms and interests which the donation of the Crimea to the Ukrainian SSR in 1954 was considered to be in hindsight. Additionally, it should be noted that although Russia can demonstrate its power by ignoring the rules of the international community, such action cannot be more than 'the exception that confirms the rule', i.e. its persistent goal to remain a prominent member in the international community.

In addition to bringing together the results of the examinations in the preceding chapters, the aim in these concluding chapters of the book is to deepen the discussion of the character of the power that is part of Russia's historical tradition and manifest in its contemporary practices. The following chapters first make concluding reflections on the border-making practices in the four frozen conflicts and sum up the significance that each of the conflicts has for Russia's deep borders, as well as the mechanisms of power which maintain it. Second, they address the issue of how the connections developed by Russia with the societies of the four conflict regions manifest a historical tradition that has been considerably strengthened through institutional developments in Russia and, on this basis, become an important part of its contemporary project of the state. In this context, the future prospect of the intricate Russian connections in the conflict regions is also touched upon. Third, they bring into focus the neutral policy which is an important part of Russia's policy variant 'A'. The discussion of this policy is relevant to this book because the examination of the conflicts in the preceding chapters shows that the disappearance of the ideological conflict has not diminished the value of neutral policies from Moscow's point of view and that these policies continue to be important for reasons that relate to the security of its borders and its economic access to markets. Finally, the book concludes by turning to the conflict in Ukraine and reflecting on the basic lessons that can be learnt from these other conflicts, despite the differences that pertain in terms of geopolitical environment and longevity.

Four conflicts and three different borders

Since autumn 2008, the arrangements concerning the fourth military base in South Ossetia and the seventh military base in Abkhazia, where the combined number of Russian troops is about 7,000,[465] have set up Russia's extended military borders. Based on bilateral treaties signed in April 2009, Russia has formal control of the borders of these two entities towards Georgia. Moreover, its Treaty on Alliance and Integration with South Ossetia (2015), which abolished border checkpoints between the two parties, signals plans to merge this region with Russia in a more formal manner.

The Russian troops which control the borders claimed on territory that the international community recognizes as Georgian are visible signs of Russia's extended borderline, and they also have wider symbolic significance: They demonstrate Russia's capability to acquire military outposts outside its own state borders in spite of international resistance and offer it possibilities for reaching out, territorially and functionally. In South Ossetia, Russia's fourth military base has confirmed the role of this geographic area as a military outpost from which Russia's missiles can reach any location in Georgia, and South Ossetia's geographic position in the middle of Georgia's North also makes it a bridgehead for a possible military corridor to Armenia. Abkhazia also serves the purposes of Russia's military outreach, not only in regard to the possibility of a renewed bilateral conflict with Georgia but also to a wider regional confrontation where control over the Black Sea is at stake. By using the Bombora aerodrome in Gudauta, Russia's fighter-inceptors (such as Su-27) can reach Georgia's naval port of Poti in just seven minutes, and they can reach north-eastern Turkey in twenty minutes. After August 2008 Abkhazia provided Russia with the ability to reduce the risks that existed in relation to its primary naval base near Sevastopol which, at that time, was on lease from Ukraine until 2042; and Abkhazia also enabled Russia to patrol the Black Sea coast from Georgia all the way to Turkey. Even today, after Russia's annexation of the Crimean Peninsula in March 2014, a modernized port in Ochamchira in Abkhazia can be used to provide an additional supply base for Russia's fleet, and it also offers a handy location for special operations in case a political or a military crisis emerges in the Crimea. Although contemporary technology has diminished the strategic importance which Abkhazia had during the Cold War,[466] its location on the Black Sea broadens Russia's aerial and naval access to this area where the United States and NATO also are increasing their military presence.

The instrumental role which Abkhazia in particular plays for Russia's military ambition in the wider region must not lead us to adopt one-sided interpretations about Russia's conflict with Georgia, as if the issue were a 'zero-sum' contest over the control of territory in a geopolitical contest with NATO. Similarly superficial, 'realist' assumptions can result in thinking that the war in Tskhinvali in August 2008 was merely a pretext for gaining control of Abkhazia. Such interpretations leave aside the significance which the border with Georgia has in both cases for Russia's internal security and political unity. In particular Abkhazia, which borders the Krasnodar Territory (*krai*) and the Republic of Karachay-Cherkessia in the North Caucasus, is important for controlling the ongoing separatist and Islamist insurgency inside the Russian Federation. The *Krasnodarskii* region in the immediate proximity of the North Caucasus includes (in its northwestern corner) Sochi, a major hub for economic activity which helps to tie Abkhazia to the logistical networks and regional development of Russia's southern regions. Such integration serves the purpose of making Abkhazia not only a 'buffer zone' against the United States and NATO in the region but also a barrier against the militant insurgency which Russia has sought to subdue in the North Caucasus yet has been unable to prevent from re-emerging in areas that lie beyond its state borders.[467] Consequently, the two political entities not only represent extended border zones *for* Russia but they also *are* Russia's border in the sense that they as such consolidate or weaken Russia's internal unity and strength as well as its long-term survival as a state. In other words, they have iconic, and not merely symbolic, significance for Russia.

In Transnistria Russian military servicemen guard the border between the region and the Republic of Moldova, in this case as part of the implementation of the peacekeeping arrangement agreed in 1992. In contrast to the irrefutable iconic significance of Crimea and the more diffuse, yet uncompromising sentiment about the need to support rebellious regions in eastern Ukraine, Moldova in the south-western corner of Ukraine is a symbol of Russia's persistent efforts to be a participant in European affairs – primarily through Moldova's guaranteed neutrality or, should this not become the case, by securing its own outpost (Transnistria) in south-eastern Europe. Such importance had yet to be attached to the Russian bastion into which General Alexander Lebed, who served as the Commander-in-Chief of the 14th Guardian Army over a period of two years starting in June 1992, made Transnistria in his endeavour to restore Russia's great power status. Lebed's service in Transnistria had signalled that Russia would keep its army units in this region to avoid the risk that the conflict would escalate and serve to extend Romania's political influence in the region. Later, when the first decade of the second millennium was coming to an end, Moscow's concern over Moldova's 'Romanization' appeared in a new form: by joining the EU, Moldova would also share Romania's security policy and be drawn towards NATO; or, frustrated by decades of waiting for its European future to materialize, Moldova would start to speed up its path to Europe by cooperating closely with NATO through its bilateral relationship with Romania. From Moscow's perspective, Moldova's internal cleavage over the issue of NATO membership and Transnistria's affiliation with Moscow are the two main assets that could prevent such a course from coming about. Neither the first nor the second of these factors carries significance in connection with Russia's state borders. Instead, they symbolize Russia's participation in European security and, more generally, its strong interest in not being excluded from European affairs. Consequently, on issues of economic cooperation Russia's policy has not initially been to try to prevent Moldova, which has very little economic significance for Russia's economic exchange, from approaching the European Union, even with an eye to eventual membership – as long as the EU as an organization does not create supranational structures that exclude cooperation with Russia. Simultaneously the focus of Russian policies has been to make Chisinau step up its participation in the frame of the agreement on creating a free-trade area within the CIS (CISFTA) and to honour the treaty's commitment to developing the frame of the cooperation.[468] Since the preparatory phase of the EU's Eastern Partnership in 2009, and even years after Moldova signed the Association Agreement in 2014, Russia has striven to create a trilateral agreement which would adjust Moldova's economic integration with its trade agreements with Russia and within the CIS and, in this way, connect Russia to the EU's arrangements with the Eastern Partnership countries. Thus, Moldova's path towards the EU – and Russia's attitude of accommodating it – has been an element in the more comprehensive approach that would make Russia a partner in European affairs, most importantly in security cooperation (along the lines of President Medvedev's proposal for a European Security Treaty (EST)) but also in terms of economic cooperation.

Russia's action in the military field – its decision to keep its Operational Group of ordinary forces in Transnistria, with numbers of troops (including its peacekeepers) ranging from 1,500 to 1,900 – has ascertained the military backing enjoyed by the PMR in negotiating Moldova's future. However, the tensions that have mounted in recent years over the events in Ukraine and the existence of US bases in especially Romania are changing this environment: the recent modernization of Russia's armaments in Transnistria militarily compensates for the failure to establish cooperation on the issues of missile defence and the EST. Because the geographically tightened position in which Transnistria found itself following the change of government in Kiev in February 2014 does not allow Russia to transfer significant amounts of military equipment, in a possible military crisis it will be crucial to control a small stretch of land (less than 100 kilometres) which allows the opening of a corridor through the territory of Ukraine from the Black Sea along the Dniestr River. Without it, and should Transnistria remain isolated in the region, the left bank of the Dniestr will serve Russia mainly as a military foothold to be held in reserve for possible use, depending on future developments. Because Transnistria is a strip of land on Ukraine's south-western border, Ukraine's opportunities to cooperate with the United States will either accelerate or slow down the processes of making Transnistria into Russia's military outpost and exclave. If the war in eastern Ukraine continues to jeopardize the prospects of Russia's political and economic affiliation with Ukraine, Transnistria is likely to become an ever more persistent symbol of Russia's determination to maintain its political presence in Europe through military means – and to do so even in the case that the question of Transnistria's final separation remains undecided. Yet, should the tide turn in Europe towards more cooperative security and the prospect of establishing non-exclusive structures of economic cooperation, Transnistria would be in a good position to serve the function of being an economic and cultural bridge between Russia and the EU.

In comparison with the other conflict regions, Nagorno-Karabakh bears least iconic significance for Russia itself. Losing the possibility of control over Nagorno-Karabakh in no direct way threatens Russia's internal unity and security. Rather, Nagorno-Karabakh is a symbolic sign of Russian power and presence in the South Caucasus, where Russia also encounters two of its historical rivals, Turkey and Iran. The main threat to the precarious balance through which Russia seeks to control this conflict, which involves not only the originally disputed area (Nagorno-Karabakh within the borders of the Azerbaijani SSR) but also the districts around it, lies in any form of instability that would involve Turkey or Iran. These two states are too large and complex to be part of the system of arrangements that in Russian policies tie together Armenia and Azerbaijan in the region. In this specific context, the rapid growth of Azerbaijan's military capacity – to which Russia's sale of arms contributes – maintains Armenia's interest to actively make itself part of Russia's deep border and thereby gain security guarantees from this major ally; Russia in turn tries to maintain its leverage on both Armenia and Azerbaijan by avoiding specification of its own thresholds of participation in a possible military escalation of the conflict. If Russia loses its ability to control developments in Nagorno-Karabakh, it also loses its leverage to control outcomes of security policy in Armenia and in Azerbaijan, and consequently also risks losing the entire region. In comparison to the quite clearly defined zonal areas of the deep borders which currently exist in Georgia, as well as in the two policy variants (reunification and Transnistria's final separation) which are possible in Moldova, the deep borders around the Karabakh conflict are a rather more complex arrangement with the two conflict states and lack clear boundaries. Geopolitically, the South Caucasus connects the Black Sea with the Caspian Sea as well as with Russia's Eurasian frontiers, which are not only economic but also military in the sense of multilateral cooperation within the CSTO. This underlines the importance of Nagorno-Karabakh as a symbolic representation of Russia's capability to control policy outcomes in the South Caucasus and to maintain military outposts south of Georgia. Because this book argues that we cannot satisfactorily understand Russia's policies in the frozen conflicts without understanding the dimension of Russia that can be seen through the window provided by these conflicts, the next chapter brings into focus the contemporary practices of power which reflect Russia's historical tradition and undermine the rules of the horizontal organization of states in the geographic area of the former Soviet Union. It begins with a focus on the institutional developments which reactualize the imperial tradition of protection by giving directions to the policies which connect Russia to society in the former Soviet republics and their separatist regions and, in this way, provide domestic legitimacy to Russia's efforts to strengthen deep borders.

Grounds for Russia's vertical power: Connectedness within the 'Russian world' and beyond

As described earlier in this book, South Ossetia's and Abkhazia's transformation into states was preceded by Russia's flexible passport policies, which increased the number of Russian citizens in these two regions.[469] However, such policies were not a mark of any major change, because most people in these regions had retained their Soviet passports and Russia initially allowed residents of the former Soviet Union who had not acquired citizenship in the new independent states to apply for Russian citizenship. This tendency was strengthened as the conflict in Georgia's separatist regions severed. The people who were disappointed in the Georgian government's capability to protect them chose to apply for a passport in Russia instead of renewing it in Georgia.[470] The circumstances were different in Transnistria, where the residents were able to apply not only for a Russian but also for a Ukrainian and a Moldovan passport (the same individuals often had all three).[471] Russia's passport policies in Transnistria developed simultaneously with Western policies in the region, and they are also a reaction to the tightened customs regulations and border control adopted by the Republic of Moldova and Ukraine. In Moldova as a whole, passport policies continue to be a part of the historical contest between Russian and Romanian influence. In 2018, almost one million out of a population of 3.5 million in 'right bank' Moldova had a Romanian passport.[472] The number of the people who have a Russian passport is not available but a rough estimate of the total in Moldova (including Transnistria, where this number is approximately 160,000)[473] is less than half a million. In Nagorno-Karabakh, where most residents have Armenian passports, the Russian passport does not create similar dividing lines amongst the population.[474]

The question of the groups of people to whom the state should extend its protection became acute in Russian policies after the dissolution of the Soviet

Union, when there was an outflow of the Russian as well as non-Russian population from the newly independent states and an entirely new and uncertain situation was created for the 25–30 million Russians who remained in those countries.[475] Russia attempted to control the situation by flexible policies which included drawing the former subjects of the Soviet Union into bilateral agreements.[476] Shortly after the war with Georgia, in September 2008, the adjustable approach which Russia adopted in the early 1990s was given a new emphasis through the establishment of a federal agency to deal with diaspora issues and humanitarian cooperation, with a focus on the area of the CIS. The Federal Agency for the Commonwealth of Independent States, Compatriots Living Abroad and International Humanitarian Cooperation (commonly known in its abbreviation *Rossotrudnichestvo*) was set up to function under the jurisdiction of the Ministry of Foreign Affairs.[477] It serves to strengthen the domestic legitimacy of a broad variety of transboundary connections by giving them a status in the governmental context. The agency's target groups range from people considered to be 'compatriots' (*sootechestvenniki*) to students and the kinds of vulnerable groups (e.g. minors, victims of natural disasters) who normally can be justified as the recipients of 'humanitarian' assistance. The statuses which relate to entire groups of people in the context of Russia's state institutions and enable them to gain social benefits in exchange for strengthening their connection with Russian society are visible signs of vertical power. Their functions range from the integration of the residents of other countries into Russian society as citizens to granting privileges offered in the frame of compatriot policies and humanitarian support. The Russian passport provides ordinary citizens' advantages, such as educational opportunities for those who have sufficient financial resources, as well as specific advantages such as the exemption of male passport holders performing military service in Transnistria from the obligation to do full military service in Russia. While these policies increase the mobility of people to Russia, they do not help much the migrant workers in Russia. Amongst these people, only the highly educated with special professional skills have a chance of getting a Russian passport, whereas the large numbers of people who work illegally in Russia – more than 200,000 of them from Moldova – can become subject to deportation and a ban on re-entry.[478]

During the same period of time when the federal agency known as *Rossotrudnichestvo* was established, new institutional developments were introduced to provide the promotion of Russian culture in other countries with fresh impetus. In 2007 the government-funded 'Russian World' (*Russkii Mir*) foundation was established by presidential decree and endowed with the mission to promote Russian language and cultural heritage not only in the post-Soviet states but as a 'global project'. The foundation not only seeks to advance Russian artistic culture and higher education but also represents a concentrated effort to create contact on ethnic and cultural bases and, in this way, to develop the 'Russian world' outside Russia's borders. The foundation is one of the frames in which the Moscow Patriarchate is actively working to make Orthodox Christianity the prime basis for modern Russian culture. In May 2007, speaking on the occasion of re-establishing canonical ties between the Russian Orthodox Church and the Russian Orthodox Church Outside of Russia (ROCOR, established after the Bolsheviks had taken power in 1917), President Putin emphasized that 'The restoration of a unified church is an important provision for uniting the entire "Russian world", which has always been based on Orthodox faith'.[479] With support from the Patriarch in Moscow, the *Russkii Mir* foundation seeks to establish contact with post-Soviet countries not only within the old Orthodox fold, such as Moldova, Ukraine and Belarus, but also with those that have independent Christian churches which consider themselves to be the heirs of ancient Christianity (Armenia, Georgia) as well as with Muslim countries (Azerbaijan and the post-Soviet states of Central Asia).[480]

Using religion to rule and unite the people is an integral part of the old, officially articulated 'idea of Russia', which Tsar Nicholas I, who reigned from 1825 to 1855, tried to construct for the purposes of the country's identity and government and which the regimes of Yeltsin and Putin have used for similarly political purposes.[481] Whereas Yeltsin's attempt in 1996 to give the Russian idea focused on rule, religion and the people modern content through political initiative was futile from the outset, Putin has managed to use religion to consolidate the idea of Russian culture as the frame with which to unite Russia's partners in Eurasian integration through a common spiritual bond. The establishment of the *Rossotrudnichestvo* in 2008 is a political act which generates institutional policies of protection – instances of the modern art of holding the power of the *derzhava* – with a wide range of activities.[482] The endemic[483] Russian connection, which was authoritatively claimed through the establishment of this federal government agency, intertwines the protection of a group of people with the protection of Russian culture, language and religion and, through the vehicle of common history, extends this argumentation to relate to populations other than those that are ethnically Russian or Slavic. Under the influence of Russia's 'neo-Eurasianist' geopolitical thought, the argument about the need to protect rapidly became an argument about nothing less than the very existence of a Russian 'civilization'. In his annual address to the Federal Assembly in December 2012, President Putin referred to this idea through which the 'Russian world' could be presented with an ideational foundation:

'For centuries, Russia developed as a multi-ethnic nation (from the very beginning), a civilisation-state bonded by the Russian people, Russian language and Russian culture native for all of us, uniting us and preventing us from dissolving in this diverse world.'[484] A few years later 'neo-Eurasianist' thinking which argued that culture and geography give Russia a special position in world politics – and which, consequently, easily served political purposes within the nationalist wing of politics, including the Communist Party – waned as a background discourse in Moscow's policymaking circles. The rhetoric about the need to protect the 'Russian world', which often was outdatedly Romanticist and as a consequence politically counterproductive, became more muted.[485] However, the emphasis of the need to support Russian culture in other countries and to establish connection with local Russian-speaking populations remained as the central building-block of policies.[486] In his address of 2015 Putin emphasized that 'Russia's strength lies in the free development of all its peoples, its diversity, the harmony of cultures, languages and traditions, mutual respect for and dialogue between all faiths, including Christians, Muslims, Judaists and Buddhists', and in his address of 2016 the central focus to tie all of this together was 'patriotic political values'.[487] Common history and patriotic values became the continuous focus for filling the ideational void which had been left by the dissolution of the Soviet Union. Putin regularly pays tribute to the strength of the unity that the people, regardless of their ethnic diversity, demonstrated during the quintessential moment of this unity, that is, the Second World War. Addressing the Federal Assembly in 2012, he stated:

> To the rest of the planet, regardless of our ethnicity, we have been and continue to be one people. I recall one of my meetings with veterans. There were representatives of several ethnicities: Tatars, Ukrainians, Georgians, and ethnic Russians of course. One of the veterans, who was not an ethnic Russian, said, 'As far as the entire world is concerned, we are one people [*odin narod*], we are Russians [*my russkie*].' That was true during the war, and it has always been true.[488]

The argument that common history has produced a Russian identity uniting a multitude of ethnicities serves to recast historical tradition in the modern frame of the multinational state. In imperial Russia the outward-oriented pan-Slavic movement had intertwined the old conception of a God-endowed Orthodox mission with the geopolitical concerns that emerged during the latter half of the nineteenth century, thereby calling for non-Russian peoples to accept the Russian privilege to act as a dominant power among 'a family where all had the same Fatherland, same faith, same language, the same memories and legends'.[489] In the anti-religious context of the Soviet state, this historical tradition supported the legitimization of Russia's ideological leadership. When the Soviet state collapsed and the ideology of progress – which reflected the ideals of European Enlightenment rather than Russian history – was turned aside, the political sensitivities, which the claims about Russia's cultural eminence raised in the other CIS member states, were managed by putting a strong emphasis on common history and the sacrifices jointly made for the defence of the fatherland. Amongst the sensitive political identities in Russia mentioned by Putin in the speech quoted above are the Tatars, the most northerly Muslim people in the world. Their pursuit of autonomy in Crimea had variably, and especially in the years following Ukraine's 2004 'Orange Revolution', received support from Russian society. Inside Russia the Tatars not only represent a subjugated historical minority (the Crimean Tatars), but their homeland – Tatarstan – is also a contemporary example of the historical features which make Russia into a negotiated political entity in which the 'internal' and the 'external' relations are not always mutually very different. The next section continues the discussion of the contemporary manifestations of Russia's tradition of power. It touches briefly upon Tatarstan because this is an example which, in essence, reveals the specific historical character and composition of Russia as a power and, thus, illuminates the historical context of policies in which the internal/external dichotomy – that is, the idea of sovereignty as the legal sphere of competence with linearly defined territorial borders – remains an alien concept.

The past in the present: Habitual practices of power

In the early 1990s the Republic of Tatarstan refused to participate in the Federal Treaty (concluded in March 1992) and, in addition to a set of bilateral agreements (*soglashenii*) with the Russian Federation, in February 1994 signed a treaty (*dogovor*)[490] on the Demarcation of Objects of Jurisdiction and the Mutual Delegation of Powers Between the Bodies of State Power of the Russian Federation and the Republic of Tatarstan. In international relations it demanded a degree of autonomy which would make it a subject of international law and give it a seat in the UN. This idea was not surprising in the 1990s against the background that Belarus and Ukraine had a seat in the UN during the Soviet decades on the basis that they were among the constitutive states of the Soviet Union. Tatarstan's independent action encouraged other strong regions, such as Bashkortostan, to negotiate privileges in the Federal Treaty, and by the end of 1998 President Yeltsin had signed 47 bilateral treaties with the subjects of an increasingly asymmetric federation. Consequently, the federation developed towards a confederation in which subjects could selectively apply (in other words, nullify) federal law. However, the high political authority assigned to these treaties, which were signed at the highest executive level, i.e. between the heads of state, could also be regarded as their main substantive weakness: because the treaties lacked ratification by legislative bodies, it was possible to argue that their status was low in the legal hierarchy. As a result of this President Putin was quickly able to erase the significance of these treaties through a series of policies he undertook during the first years of his presidency in the 2000s to restore central control in the name of 'the dictatorship of law'.[491] Tatarstan's aspiration, as expressed in its 1992 Constitution, to be 'associated with the Russian Federation' and to be able to emphasize its own 'sovereignty' was made void by the constitutional authority of the President of the Russian Federation to suspend executive acts he considered to contradict federal legislation, the international commitments of the federation or 'the rights and freedoms of man and citizen'.[492]

Yet, the flexibility embedded in the executive axis works in two directions: even if relations with the Kremlin in Moscow have priority in Kazan (the capital of Tatarstan), the nature of these relations as a highly personalized political process allows them to be kept apart from the idea of the nation invoked in Tatarstan's Constitution. As Jeffrey Kahn's reference to Bashkortostani expert opinion on the rulings of the federal Constitutional Court which in June 2000 renounced the idea of 'treaty-constitutional' federalism also suggests, in Russia the duality of political process and law makes political reality ambiguous: the political process and consequently the agreements of the heads of the regions with the Moscow Kremlin are considered more important 'than the law itself',[493] and the selfsame situation makes it possible for the subjects of the federation to hold on to a notion of subjectivity provided by the *idea* of law (the frame of identity provided by their own Constitutions) and to keep cultivating a distinct identity within the 'family' of nations in the Russian Federation. These features are part of an 'Asian' idea of integration and opposed to the idea of self-limitation based on law.[494]

Tatarstan's bilateral negotiations with the central power of the state of which it is a part within a federal structure, and its relative autonomy in internal matters (beyond the sphere of the central power's interests), are a contemporary illustration of the historical modality of power which underlies the Russian idea of the state – *gosudarstvo*, which literally means the sphere or circle of the sovereign, *gosudar'*. The historical logic of rule based on collaborative associative relations between the Moscow Kremlin and regional and local leaders helps to make sense of the contemporary interplay of central control and the many and diverse 'islands' of relative autonomy which exist not only in geographic and economic terms (in the form of regions and state-owned companies) but which also pertain to political power.[495] It helps in our understanding of why regional leaders are allowed independent action, within certain limits – a fact which may be pointed out abruptly with measures that are indirect as well as direct and harsh. Although there is no novelty in arguing that in Russia the geographic scope and ethnic diversity of the country have left little possibility to organize administration as a tightly functioning system, it is worth remembering that the same feature has generated specific mechanisms of vertical control – a strong secret service, privileged political parties and political elite networks. There is also a deeply rooted cultural reason as to why even today relationships based on the exchange of loyalty for protection influence political life in the background of the modern state: specifically, this is the traditional idea that subordination to the rule of the *gosudar'* leaves the people free to concentrate on leading a 'higher life in peace', which traditionally meant practicing the Russian Orthodox religion and cultivating the soil of the land. The attitude amongst the majority of the population is that it is desirable to remain free from the sphere of politics, which is conceived as the struggle for power (whereas the local, community-level affairs are traditionally an altogether different thing); and this has contributed to the oft-mentioned resilience of the population to the flux of changes. It has also meant that the Russian autocracy has not been able to thoroughly reorganize society in a totalitarian manner – even in its culturally anti-Russian Soviet forms this was never consistently achieved, although the terror that during the years before and after the Second World War manifested the arbitrariness of Stalin's power was close to it.[496]

Because the subject of the discussion is a modality of power that belongs to the *political process* of negotiating the regions' relations with the central power (Moscow), it is pointless to argue just how limited the autonomy of a region 'in fact' is – such a question derives from a different, constitutional perspective typically dominant in Western discussions of Russia and federalism. The historical modality of state power which functions through mutually conditional relationships helps us to decipher why Russia's relations with the former Soviet subjects beyond its formal state borders hinge on the acceptance of Russia's predominant position; it also shows how this position, which does not mean imposing a whole system of rules of governing and organization over populations within the sovereign's sphere, is different from the Western (including Soviet) notion of domination. Consequently, by emphasizing the plural ('multipolar') nature of the international community and the need for Russia to act as 'a firm barrier against the dictating of alien rules and values from outside',[497] the role through which Russia seeks to make its own legitimacy discourse in this community is not merely instrumental in its contest with Western states but is rooted in a historical tradition which maintains a difference between the sphere of the sovereign's (the autocrat's) interests and the everyday concerns of the people. Hence, although Russia's practices are a form of repressive power, in the traditional sense of 'man's control over the minds and actions of other men',[498] the logic of territorial expansion is not a (neo-)imperial subordination of one society to the rules of another society's organization. Rather than in the control over territory, power is manifested in the collaborative relationships of political association; and it is for the same reason that borders are more complex than linear lines, and the establishment of 'buffer zones' does not predict further territorial expansion.

While the Russian term for 'the state', *gosudarstvo*, provides a clue for understanding the specific historical characteristic of the state as a power, the more archaic notion of *derzhava* helps in grasping another important dimension of the historical idea of the state, namely the idea of the might of the great power, in the sense of the art of holding (*derzhat'*) power (i.e. authority).[499] Because of the need to present the argument for protecting the Russian language and culture in the former Soviet republics within the frame of the modern state's conventions in order to appeal to the international community, the starting point must be the idea that it is the state's obligation to protect its residents and that the different groups, with their different ethnic titles and languages, must be granted rights that enable them to survive as a community. Russia's criticism of the situation in states that formerly were part of the Soviet Union (most notably in Estonia and Latvia)[500] has followed this format but lacks credibility because Russia itself is subject to similar criticism from Western states. This is not the first time that Russia's use of Western perspectives for the purpose of demonstrating 'double standards' in Western policies leaves in the dark the tradition which sustains its own policies in a domestic context and produces confusing communications in international connections. Russia's policy think tanks have been eager to pick up concepts from Western discussion and, among other things, to emphasize the politically instrumental 'soft power' which the transboundary Russian connection can provide for foreign policy purposes. The argumentation that the ability to influence former Soviet states lies in the spheres of language and culture and that a shared past can be reactivated with an eye towards political purposes emerged already during the early years of the Russian Federation, that is, at a time when official discourse was not yet under pressure to adjust to nationalist sentiments;[501] within a few years policy circles in Moscow already began to speak of a specifically Russian form of 'soft power'.[502]

Nevertheless, while the notion of 'soft power' operating with the 'attraction to shared values and the justness and duty of contributing to the achievement of those values'[503] resonates well with understandings in the United States of that country's pre-eminence in the implementation of liberal values, it can only scratch the surface of the situation that pertains in conflicted post-Soviet cultural spaces. The idea that Russia can use 'soft power' by being attractive in terms of values for people who, in fact, through the representations of Russia are drawn to a language and culture with which they are already familiar – mainly in the institutional contexts of the state, but perhaps also in their habitual world – tells us very little about Russian speakers' wish to make their troubled home sites (which is especially the case for separatist regions) part of something bigger, in other words part of Russia. Rather than wanting 'more Russia' due to a feeling of attraction, many people are attached to Russia because they prefer to see their future in ways which enable them to make sense of their past, and they do not wish to be faced with the insecurity that derives from the threat of being deprived of those cultural resources which provide them with social access and which are often the only means they have for making their livelihoods better. The Russian kind of 'soft power' is thus closely related to the vertical power through which Russia can strengthen its connection with the societies of former Soviet republics. Although the structural economic dependency on Russia in these countries is not vertical power as such, it can be used for the purposes of such power. The ban on re-entry, which Moscow has repeatedly declared for Moldova's illegal migrant workers in Russia, is an example where such a declaration is followed by the information, in this case released some time later by Moldovan politicians, that Russia has decided to grant amnesty to these people.[504] Whereas Moldovan politicians are able to gain credit for having contributed to a change in policy in Moscow, Moscow is able to strengthen its cultural and moral connection to the people to whom it shows 'benevolence' and 'grace' in the manner that is part of the Russian tradition of authoritarian rule. Such mechanisms of political power can be used in all spheres of major structural economic dependency to produce immediate impacts upon the lives of large sections of the population and they, as a consequence, can affect political development in the country. Such impact is not the power of 'attraction' that lies in 'soft power', and its mechanisms also cannot be discovered as long as Russia's presence is classified as subjugation, dominance or occupation. In this context the next section now examines the threads – historical, economic and cultural – which form the close connection to Russia in the different conflicts at hand and which lay the basis for attempts to legitimize policies that consolidate the respective separatist political entity's vertical relation to Russia.

The threads of the Russian connection as the future unfolds

South Ossetia's connectedness to Russia was made clearly visible by the flow of tens of thousands of people across the mountains to North Ossetia in August 2008.[505] Although the present-day population in South Ossetia is reported to be 70,000–80,000, many sources estimate it to be only half of this number due to the outflow of the population, which for economic reasons has continued to North Ossetia-Alania (where the population count is 713,000) and other parts of the Russian Federation (where the total number of Ossetians is about 1 million). For the South Ossetians, North Ossetia is the 'ethnic home' to which they are drawn – it is far larger than their own region in all respects. Since 2013, the unification of South Ossetia with North Ossetia-Alania within the Russian Federation has been on the agenda of political parties in South Ossetia.[506] Even if this path is not smooth in South Ossetia's domestic political process and Russia's reluctance to make a move which is politically costly in the international community with little benefit in return, South Ossetia's total dependence on Russia leaves no alternatives in the foreseeable future. With an economy that is 90 per cent dependent on subsidies from Russia and a political status that remains unrecognized by even Russia's closest allies, it cannot become a party of the Eurasian economic cooperation. In the economic sense, South Ossetia is increasingly a satellite of North Ossetia-Alania, and it is mainly the military sector – Russia's military presence – that experiences growth in a region (without, however, developing its economy) whose only local source of income lies in its dilapidated agriculture. While the mountain range had made it convenient for early Soviet decision makers to leave South Ossetia attached to the Georgian side of an administrative line in order to constrain nationalist tendencies in Georgia, the war in 2008 disconnected this piece in the Soviet nationalities' puzzle from the territory of Georgia and set it on the path to becoming a de facto part of Russia and awaiting formal annexation at a point in time that is politically appropriate.

Russia's military action in Abkhazia in 2008 similarly meant that Soviet national policy had come to an end in Georgia. However, in this case there is no administrative entity on the Russian side of the border which would connect this part of Georgia to Russia. Merging with Russia would be difficult due to its history of semi-independence within Georgia and the South Caucasian mix of its population which makes territory, rather than ethnicity, the relevant focus of building a common Abkhaz identity. The tie to Russia is not similarly historically specific as it is in South Ossetia; instead, this tie reflects Abkhazia's historical role as a small entity which has relied for its security on one of the various vying regional powers and, since the establishment of the Soviet Union, continuously on Russia. In the current situation Abkhazia's non-recognized international status creates a favourable context for policies which promote the fusion of the local population and the Russian population in Abkhazia. The number of the Russian population (presently 10–11 per cent of the 216,000 inhabitants of Abkhazia) is slowly increasing and becoming merged with the Abkhaz population as investments from Russia increase, and as more and more people in Abkhazia – the local residents and the Russian settlers alike – have the passport of both Russia and Abkhazia. Even if ethnic Abkhaz constitute one half of the population and in the other half both Armenians and Georgian-related Mingrelians and Svans outnumber ethnic Russians, these local ethnic titles do not give residents any meaningful political or economic rights in relation to the Russian residents, who also have citizenship in Abkhazia.[507] Abkhazia's Constitution (which dates from the year 1994 and consequently emphasizes the continuity that relates to Abkhazia's separate existence from Georgia) makes Abkhazian the official language but recognizes both Abkhazian and Russian as 'the language of the government, public and other institutions'.[508]

Abkhazia needs external investment to modernize its tourist industry and fruit production and to diversify an economy that is dependent on seasons; and while it remains internationally isolated, its only prospect is investment from Russia, which subsidizes 60–70 per cent of its budget. In Moscow the extension of business to Abkhazia is supported by the inclusion of Abkhazia in regional development projects intended to modernize Russia's southern regions and to improve the logistical infrastructure in the Krasnodar Territory (*krai*). However, this process lacks vigour because Abkhazia's economic structure is similar to structures throughout the wider region and it has few alternatives to remaining in a peripheral position in relation to the economic hub of the Sochi area. The deteriorated economy creates a conducive environment for the establishment of business relations which, together with the political conditions that treat the Russian language and ethnic label on a par with the Abkhaz language and local labels, are the main ways by which Abkhazia is being made into Russia's de facto region, even if its formal frame is that of an independent state. Additionally, although the bond of religion is not strongly present in everyday life, Abkhazia is connected to Moscow by the Orthodox Christian religion, which 60–75 per cent of the Abkhaz population confess.[509] Much like the state which remains outside of the Western international community, the Orthodox Church in Abkhazia remains outside the Eastern Orthodox ecclesiastical hierarchy in which Abkhazia (with the support of the Moscow Patriarchate) continues to be recognized as a canonical territory of the Georgian Orthodox Church.[510] Consequently, the Russian Orthodox Church, which positions itself outside political conflicts, is the main direction from which the Orthodox Church in Abkhazia can receive support.[511]

In Transnistria, the Russian connection is exceptionally strong because of two factors: the population, one third of which (180,000 people) are Russian by language and family origin while another third are Ukrainian and, in this case, culturally affiliated to Russia (the remainder are Moldovan); and the existence of this stretch of land under Russian rule in its various forms ever since 1792 (except for the period from August 1941 to January 1944). Transnistria is Russia's historical frontier in Eastern and Central Europe in the face of Romanian cultural and political influence, which it has encountered in different connections – during the Ottoman and Austrian empires, during the rise of Romanian nationalism and Nazi Germany, and, more recently, through the presence of NATO and the US military as well as the political influence of the EU in the region. For this reason, Moscow approaches the entire area of Transnistria as a cultural sphere which, with its multinational population, is part of Russia. Hence it is also not surprising that the annexation of Crimea in March 2014 raised hopes among Transnistria's Russian-speaking population about the region's formal merger with Russia and that Moscow, which prefers to keep the situation open, would be left with little choice but to try to reassure the territory of its protection of the population through various forms of economic and social support.

Although the official culture sustained by the PMR gives the 'left bank' a distinctly 'Russian' flavour, the absolute number of ethnic Russians is larger on the 'right bank', i.e. the Republic of Moldova. However, in this case the number of Russian speakers – approximately 350,000 people – represent only 10 per cent of the total population. Moreover, these people live scattered throughout the country, mostly in urban areas, and instead of invoking notions of a shared history (which in contrast to Transnistria is not continuous) Russia's protection focuses on citizens' political rights to a native language and culture in the frame of a multinational state. As a consequence, and in contrast to Transnistria, which is a sphere of its own separated by a physical line, the entire 'right-bank' of Moldova is an area of contestation over cultural space and the content of a homogenizing 'national' culture – over religious organization and language policies, access to media and other public spaces. On the 'right bank', the Moldovan Orthodox Church organized under the Moscow Patriarchate is the religious affiliation of more than 80 per cent of the population and therefore presented as a major cultural force in the efforts to maintain the country (i.e. the 'right' and 'left bank' combined) in terms of its spiritual unity. Its institutional backing from Moscow and the relatively significant role which religion and tradition play in largely agricultural (though secular) 'right-bank' Moldova are the two main reasons for its strength.⁵¹² Yet its position as the dominant ecclesial institution has been shattered by the re-establishment under the Romanian Orthodox Church of the Metropolis of Bessarabia (created in 1918 and reactivated in 1992) to which 10–13 per cent of the population belong.⁵¹³ This spiritual split will be reinforced by the decision, in October 2018, by the Ecumenical Patriarchate of Constantinople (with its See in Istanbul) to revoke the decision from 1686 to include the Orthodox Church in Ukraine within the canonical territory of the Moscow Patriarchate. The pronouncement of 2018 began a process of granting the Ukrainian Orthodox Church autocephaly (self-governance), which has defined the position of the Romanian Orthodox Church since the late nineteenth century.⁵¹⁴

Religion has become an arena of open contestation in recent decades, whereas language issues have for a long time been sensitive indicators of political tensions. Educational policies and cultural programs are instrumental in the political struggle in which Moldova is being drawn either to Romania (as a 'kinship state') or to Russia (through its historical affiliation). Although Transnistria's public image is that of a political community in which Ukrainians, Russians and Moldovans 'can all live and work together', only the Russian language is consistently promoted. Formally the PMR allows teaching in Romanian, but only a few schools are permitted to use the Latin alphabet, and school boycotts and closures occur frequently. Similarly, although 'right-bank' Moldova presents itself as a multicultural society, language is used to make a social and political distinction between the Romanian and Russian speakers. Moldovan (Romanian) is the national language, while Russian has the lesser status of a language for inter-ethnic communication.⁵¹⁵ The contest between the Romanian and Russian cultural spheres is manifest in the media, too. Studies of the 'right-bank' media report that people have little trust in the media's reliability and that the ownership of media companies has not been made transparent. Especially private broadcasting channels are owned by circles close to politicians and oligarchs.⁵¹⁶ In contrast to the 'right bank', where the media space is congested with numerous outlets, the media on the 'left bank' operates in a more unified, government-controlled space. The local supply of broadcasters is less numerous and restrained by political control, while at the same time aerial devices and satellites provide access to Moldovan as well as Russian broadcasting. This situation is similar in Abkhazia and South Ossetia, where broadcasting space is contested between Georgia and Russia while reporting that deals with the region's own affairs is closely monitored and kept under political control.

Unlike in the cases of the other frozen conflicts, Russia's relationship with the people in Karabakh has started developing in recent years. It lacks the historical and habitual basis which makes this connection endemic in

South Ossetia, and which also makes it possible to tie the population more closely to Russia in Transnistria and in Abkhazia. Nagorno-Karabakh, as it has emerged from the current conflict, is firmly seen as ethnically akin to Armenia and part of the same culture. This culture is strongly unified through its history and, traditionally, it has been influenced by Russian culture only to a small degree.[517] This situation is clearly manifest in issues related to the Church and religion. Since 2009 it has only been the Armenian Apostolic Orthodox Church that is allowed to hold services in the Nagorno-Karabakh Republic. Because the territory is a diocese of the Armenian Church, the Moscow Patriarchate cannot approach it directly. Russia in turn has activated its direct, humanitarian relations with Nagorno-Karabakh, and included in this activity has been the establishment of a direct, if modest, presence of the Russian Orthodox Church, in the form of a place of worship to run the affairs of Karabakh's two or three hundred Russians (the total population in Karabakh is around 100,000).[518] From Yerevan's point of view Stepanakert's direct relations with Moscow are ambiguous, even if relations are indirect through the means provided by the church and Russia's official civil society and other agents of humanitarian relations: while they may be taken as a sign of Russia's willingness to commit itself to Karabakh's defence, they also relax the connectivity of civilian life between Karabakh and Armenia by offering interaction with Russia as a way to overcome the region's isolated position. Increased exchange and interaction with the population enable Russia to increase its presence in Karabakh and circumvent the dilemma which would arise should it decide to militarily intervene in Karabakh in case of a crisis. If Russian citizens in Karabakh can be counted in their several hundreds, it increases the credibility of the argument that a possible military intervention is necessary so as to defend Russian citizens and *not* to support Armenia against Azerbaijan. Moscow would be enabled to continue the line of policies which reproduce the historical role it has assumed in this conflict – namely to keep it under its control. However, although strengthening the connection to the population in Karabakh provides Moscow with ways to justify involvement in this conflict, being prepared for unexpected situations and a possible military crisis must not be confused with Russia's goals in the conflict. A more detailed interpretation emerges when we explore how the tradition of the practices of extending the sovereign's domain (for which the term *gosudarstvo* provides the key to understanding) lives on in those contemporary practices which are termed Russia's deep border arrangements in this book. The next chapter argues that Russia's approach to neutrality is an integral part of these practices.

The arrangement of guarantees on neutrality and its alternatives

The examination above shows that the war in August 2008, which resulted in the line of policy that this book terms the 'B' variant, was a sign of the failure of the 'A' variant of policy. In other words, the recognition of the independence of South Ossetia and Abkhazia emerged as Moscow's solution to Russia's post-Soviet security dilemma after it became obvious in early 2007 that Georgia would not accept the non-aligned position (i.e. a legal commitment not to accept a third country's military forces on its territory) which Russia expected it to adopt in exchange for Russia's full military withdrawal from Georgia by the end of that year. In relations with Georgia, neutrality was brought seriously to the table of negotiations too late, because Russia clung to its attempts to commit Georgia to security cooperation in the CIS frame. Simultaneously in Western security discourse the argument was strengthened that because the ideological confrontation had ended, the term 'neutrality' was obsolete, and it was replaced with 'military non-alignment'. A new ideological approach emerged with a principles-minded emphasis on liberal values; and the militarily non-aligned states were drawn into a form of cooperation with NATO that stopped just short of formal membership. From Moscow's perspective, the question of the boundaries of acceptable cooperation with NATO in the proximity of its borders became difficult to articulate beyond the obvious signs of military alignment (i.e. formal membership and stationing of foreign military forces in a country's territory), and its relations with the United States and NATO in the Eastern Europe and its adjacent areas turned into a political contest replete with reciprocal military threats. It is also easy to see that the exclusivity, which the EU has introduced in the form of the free-trade area agreement that constitutes the substantive core in the political association agreement with selected Eastern Partnership countries (Georgia, Moldova and Ukraine), is perceived in Russia as an attempt to obstruct the transcendence of bloc politics and non-exclusivity of economic relations which are important to it. As the EU policy tightens the strings of economic relations in favour of the Union, it also shatters security policy: when the countries participating in the EU's Eastern Partnership lose the ability to develop economic relations with Russia *on par* with the EU, they also lose the immediate utility of implementing the neutral policy which, in Moscow's view, opens the possibility for developing a whole range of relations by first setting in place security policy.

Moldova could not avoid becoming part of this confrontation, and an important domestic reason was disappointment with neutrality: although it had incorporated neutrality in its Constitution (1994), this did not lead to the withdrawal of Russia's military from Transnistria. Yet, Russia's decades-long attempt to build relations with Moldova (and likewise with Azerbaijan) demonstrates that a guaranteed neutral position – which, as a minimum, means a policy which does not seek membership in a military alliance and a country's refusal to accept permanent structures of foreign military on its territory – is Russia's prime objective in situations where its bases and other signs of military presence are inacceptable to the country in question. Simultaneously, Russia's approach of tying up several issues into a 'comprehensive political settlement' (the words 'comprehensive political solution' are also used) has hampered the possibility to present a credible idea of neutrality. Consequently, Moldova did not set a positive example which could have ameliorated anti-Russian sentiments in Georgia. Unlike Moldova, Azerbaijan has been able to turn the political and military importance which its neutral policy has for Russia to its own political advantage. Its way to implement neutrality is a unilateral commitment within a policy concept, reinforced with its membership in the Non-Aligned Movement. Due to its energy trade with the West and its position as a logistical hub, Azerbaijan is not crucially dependent on economic relations with Russia and therefore able to establish a reciprocal system of relations with mutual leverages and benefits. Simultaneously Karabakh remains Moscow's ultimate leverage towards Baku and, like also in the case of Moldova, neutrality is an initial condition for Russia's preparedness to settle the conflict in a way which excludes the disputed region's total secession. In Moldova, where the government has strongly emphasized its European path, this conditionality has been clearly articulated by Russia, whereas in Russia's relations with Azerbaijan this is more implicit in the structure of the relationship which entails a promise of political and economic gains for Azerbaijan. Consequently, from Russia's point of view denouncing neutrality would change the whole set of coordinates within which a solution to the separatist conflict can be sought in the frame of these countries' territorial unity. For this reason, NATO's presence in Chisinau, even if it is only in the form of a liaison office, also represents the development of closer cooperation between NATO and the government in Chisinau: it is a sign of a tendency and a trend.[519]

Neutral security policy in the post-Soviet area is formulated in a large number of ways. In Central Asia, energy-rich Turkmenistan has incorporated its neutral position in its Constitution (1992) and by bringing it to the attention of the UN has also sought to make international acceptance the guarantee for this policy. Uzbekistan, without mentioning the term, has committed itself to this policy in its law on foreign policy (2012), which states that Uzbekistan is not involved in military-political blocs and does not allow the deployment of foreign military bases and facilities on its territory.[520] For these countries, neutrality is a way to maintain functioning economic relations with Russia while distancing themselves from military cooperation. It is a way to engage in relations with all countries and organizations while signalling to Russia that the country in question does not intend to join another military bloc and permit the use of its territory in ways that could threaten Russia's security, and that the condition for the continuity of this policy is that Russia also respects such an approach.[521] The content of a neutral policy ranges from Turkmenistan's strict interpretation (its refusal to accept any troops or equipment on its territory, even temporarily for logistical purposes) to the kind of flexibility that gives Azerbaijan leverage in its relations with Russia and which, in Uzbekistan, enables a country to adopt an independent line of policy. Russia's bilateral approach to neutrality is demonstrated by its clear preference to have the condition of not accepting the troops or equipment of third parties stated in treaties of friendship and cooperation which establish the bases of its relations with close neighbours. The content of neutrality is not derived from a universal, context-independent concept or model and, hence, is very different from the concept of neutrality in Western discourse – i.e. the neutrality that applies to wartime and entails strict rules about impartiality (classical neutrality) and the concept of permanent neutrality based on a centuries-long historical path and legal, normally constitutional and sometimes international, treaty-based instruments. The neutrality which Russia historically favours in its immediate neighbourhood is referred to in Western doctrinaire discussions as 'political neutrality', which casts doubt on the entire notion: it lacks a foundation in traditional international law and is mainly a policy that emphasizes peacetime activity in favour of peace and stability between Russia and the West.

Similar to this politically pragmatic approach adopted in the post-Soviet situation, neutrality in the geopolitical sphere which was vital to the Soviet Union was also based on an individualized relationship; and this because it was part of the centuries-long historical tradition of building state power through bilateral relationships rather than generalizable relations (which again was the Soviet, more doctrinal dimension and in its ideological dualism left meagre space for 'traditional' neutrality).[522] Finnish–Soviet relations during the Cold War illustrate the tensions related to neutrality policy in such an individualized relationship. Finland claimed a neutral position for itself but was militarily aligned with the Soviet Union through a treaty of Friendship, Cooperation and Mutual Assistance (FCMA), even if the military cooperation based on this treaty – which Finland was obliged to conclude as a losing party in the Second World War – was not operative during times of peace.[523] Sweden, Finland's neighbour to the west, pursued a more classical form of neutrality built on the idea of a strictly neutral position during times of war. In relation to this concept, Finland's neutral policy sought to square the metaphorical circle: neutrality and alignment needed to be considered as mutually *complementary* policies (in situations of peace and war, respectively) rather than opposed concepts. Based on the FCMA treaty, Finland would have been an operative part of Russia's forward defence in case a military crisis occurred in the region. Such a possibility put a heavy strain on Finnish policies, but Finland also benefitted greatly from its trade with the Soviet Union.[524]

The kind of neutrality that is part of Russia's bilateral 'special' relationship does not need to be defined by international legal guarantees *in order for it to exist*, even if legal measures, and especially the constitutional guarantees of the state concerned, are important in order to confirm the policy and provide it with continuity. Neutral policy is part of the security arrangements which seek to ensure stability in the region – in other words, unchanging geopolitical conditions – and, consequently, security in the proximity of its borders. Thus, Georgia's announcement after the war in 2008 that it would close its borders for the Russian – and, in principle, for any foreign – military in case a crisis emerged in the South Caucasus (for example in Nagorno-Karabakh) invokes the idea of classical wartime neutrality and in its implications for Russia is the direct opposite of the concept of neutrality that Russia promotes.[525] Because the continuity of the neutral policy that Russia promotes is dependent on the political forces and agents who make the decisions, it calls for a whole range of relations to sustain it – economic deals, political conditionality of 'trusting relationships' between policymakers and the strengthening of the social bonds between Russia and the people in another country. Developing these ties is a continuous process, and even if a relationship has formal treaty-frames, it is the vertical tie that ensures continuity. In cases where chaos and violent conflict reign and endanger the functioning of such ties having military troops on the ground (in the capacity of regular units or peacekeepers) becomes a means for Russia to ensure that it can present its starting points in the negotiations to settle the conflict.

The initial setting: Military presence in order to create negotiating space

Retaining its Soviet-time military capacity in Georgia at a time when this country lacked military equipment of its own provided Russia with leverage in negotiating Georgia's reunification in the way that tied this process to Russia's aims of establishing security cooperation within the CIS structures. The way in which the Gudauta base in Abkhazia was kept in reserve and brought back into operation is an example of the same practice under the changed circumstances of later developments, when it became increasingly clear that Russia was unable to realize its aims in Georgia. Initially the conflict in Moldova was far more peripheral to Moscow's own security interests, but also in this case the maintenance of the Soviet-era military base enabled both Transnistria and Gagauzia to pursue their own distinct paths, and this increased Moscow's political leverage in relation to Chisinau. Because the situation in all these cases was complex and changing, delaying the withdrawal of troops from the Soviet-era bases kept open a political space for negotiating a 'comprehensive political settlement' with several elements, and it also helped Russia to prepare for the possibility that this might fail.

Russia's use of military force in these conflicts can be described by adopting Thomas Schelling's notion of 'compellence', which refers to military action meant to force, by means of persuasion, the other party to adopt a desired course of action. It means that the threat of using military force serves a political, rather than military, purpose, and that this purpose is to get the other party to do something.[526] However, although this conclusion is logical in the case of all international conflicts where Russia pursues a political settlement while keeping a military component in its policy arsenal, 'compellence' is easily self-defeating and can turn the countries in question away from Russia – as the examples of Georgia and Moldova show. This is because its rationality and effectiveness depends on the credibility of Russia's own flexibility and preparedness to act as expected by the countries that are targeted by such policies, i.e. the trust that they can invest in Russia in believing that it will eventually withdraw its military presence. However, from Russia's perspective such a presence serves multiple purposes in the context of the 'comprehensive political settlement' and, consequently, must be kept in place until the whole package has been negotiated with sufficient guarantees. It is Russia's way to strive to hold politically together a very complex and changing environment. Thus, the more fixed Russia's military presence seems, the more paradoxical it becomes as a 'compellent' policy instrument for political purposes.

Rather than functioning in a conflict's settlement, Russia's military presence is its way of stating by kinetic means that conflict is real (i.e. that it cannot be belittled by means of political rhetoric) and that a settlement must include its active participation. Simultaneously it is a rough instrument with which to negotiate desirable policy outcomes – even subtle military threats can ruin Russia's ability to pursue policy variant 'A', i.e. a country's reunification under certain conditions. In the case of Transnistria, variant 'B' would make this region a formal exclave (like Kaliningrad), and its separatist goals could no longer provide the *political* 'guarantee' of Moldova's neutrality and, consequently, of Russia's deep borders towards Romania. Although this turn of events is indeed conceivable, it is not the line of policy that Russia is willing to pursue in any circumstances other than when it is trying to prevent Western advances into areas which it considers vital to its own security interests. Because the future is uncertain, Russia's requirement that Moldova remains on a path of neutrality goes hand-in-hand with its de facto military alignment with Transnistria; and this duality – odd and thoroughly paradoxical from a Western perspective on the concept of neutrality – continues to serve the conditionality built into the process of the settlement. Although this policy can become counter-productive in bilateral relations and damage the entire settlement process, from Moscow's perspective there is no other alternative but to hold on to it – at least until a settlement emerges of which it can approve.

Russia's relations with Armenia and Azerbaijan also illustrate such a 'tandem' arrangement, but in this case the structural context is entirely different. The expectation of neutrality and military alignment relate to two different countries, and Russia's policies seek to keep them in mutual balance. In Azerbaijan, like in Georgia initially, Russia's expectation is that no military troops and infrastructure, weapons systems or major weapons of third states will be allowed in the territory. Although a bilateral treaty between Russia and Azerbaijan seems to assure this, Azerbaijan has made its own commitment dependent on its assessment of the situation (i.e. on the condition that the security environment will not change) and, in this way, it increases its space for manoeuvre by using its non-alignment as leverage towards Russia.[527] As a consequence, Russia's military cooperation with Armenia becomes an important means of counteraction. From Moscow's point of view the 'guarantee' for Azerbaijan's non-aligned position is provided by Russia's military alignment with Armenia, which, alongside the openness maintained by Moscow in its policies concerning Karabakh, deters Baku from changing its line of policy. In Armenia, joining the Eurasian, rather than the European economic integration process, is expected to increase Russia's political commitment to the defence of Armenia, including Karabakh. The extent to which Armenian expectations are met by Russia's military action remains an open question – and keeping it open is part of Russian policy.

Internal and external guarantees for neutrality

While the military presence, which ranges from major military bases to favourable arms deals, is meant to increase Russia's political weight in the peace process, the elements of the peace settlement provide the internal political and external (international) guarantees for the neutral foreign and security policy in the specific country meant to be reintegrated through that settlement. In contrast to the Constitution's formal and explicit commitment to neutrality, the internal political assurances provided by the integrated structure of the state are indirect and function through the legal and administrative instruments which can ensure the continuity of policy in the future. The multilateral peacekeeping arrangements and the bilateral treaties discussed in this book play a central role in providing external guarantees. In addition, new ideas of cooperation, such as those presented by the Gagauz bashkan in March 2013, tell about Russia's preparedness to include the role of an international protector ('guardian') of the rights of the disputed region's population as a formal part in a controlling role which Russia prefers to establish in cooperation with other states and international organizations.

Although the aim of establishing guarantees for neutral policies is often clearly expressed in Russia's policies, these policies do not include any predefined system of guarantees. This would not, in fact, be practical, due to two major reasons: first, the openness of the resolution process in relation to its final aims; and, second, because the guarantees are not only legal but also political in nature, and interlinked in different ways in Russia's policies in the different conflicts. Although the direction of policies is clearly stated, definitions are avoided until a time when political circumstances are favourable for agreement on a whole set of elements. Consequently, the 'comprehensive political settlement', which builds a conditionality between Russia's military presence (in a direct or indirect form) and the country's commitment to neutrality through the Constitution as well as the state's structure, becomes the complex and unwieldy way through which to steer the process while the various elements remain unfixed. In Georgia, a comprehensive plan for a compromise solution was never clearly on the table, and in Moldova it was not until 2003 that this stage was achieved. After the failure of the Kozak plan, Russia's policies became significantly more indirect in Moldova. The changed circumstances (including the 'colour revolutions' in Georgia and in Ukraine) made Russia retreat from pursuing settlement through an international agreement and, instead, induced it to concentrate on supporting those political forces which in Moldova's domestic process were able to sustain the path for settlement in harmony with Russia's goals. In the Nagorno-Karabakh conflict, the multilateral international frame of the Minsk process serves to support Russia's active role in the resolution and makes it diplomatically feasible for Russia to refrain from articulating its own preferences on the future status of Karabakh, at least until it becomes evident how this status can best serve its goals in the wider region.

Russia's starting point in the question of the disputed regions' status is logical: a flexible federal or confederal structure of the state, which provides a high degree of autonomy in the disputed regions, enables it to exercise the role of an international protector of a population's interests and, in this format, to consolidate the connections which it already may have with this population. The Kozak plan of 2003 outlines the conditions for a loose federal solution which includes the possibility of separation (which is the reason why it can also be called a confederal solution). These conditions relate to the independence of the executive and legislative processes, the use of economic resources and language rights, and the relative independence of the armed forces at the regional level, especially during the transition process. The scheme of a judicial system in which the members of federal-level courts are appointed according to regional quotas tells about Russia's preferences concerning the channels through which complaints about possible violations of rights relating to regional status would be voiced and which also would provide Russia with the possibility to act in their support.[528] The failure of the Kozak plan in 2003 demonstrated the force of the suspicions that a weak federal or confederal structure of the state would increase Moscow's possibilities to influence political affairs within the country and that this would ultimately result in disassembling a country believed to be too small for such a state structure. While the Socialist Party and President Igor Dodon have actively promoted the discussion on a federal state structure, the liberal and pro-EU political forces have been strongly opposed to keeping this issue on the national agenda.

In Georgia, the political prospect of the kind of guarantees which would set conditions on the country's internal structure and external relations was similarly unacceptable. A confederal arrangement, which the Abkhaz Supreme Soviet initially had proposed in June 1992,[529] would have enabled Abkhazia to effectively connect with Russia and limited Tbilisi's ability to introduce unifying policies within Georgia's borders. In Armenia, proposals for a federal-type solution, which would even moderately connect Nagorno-Karabakh to Azerbaijan, provoke major opposition and shatter political stability. This is what occurred in 1998, when Armenia's first president, Levon Ter-Petrosian, resigned from office, and the conflict and war of the decades that followed have only served to reinforce such an unyielding position. Yet, an accommodating federal- or confederal-type of arrangement is the only way to proceed in resolving this conflict, even if little space is provided for this due to, on the one hand, Armenia's strict decision to keep Nagorno-Karabakh connected with itself and, on the other hand, Azerbaijan's consistent refusal to accept any solution that leaves room for the possibility of final separation. In all three cases, a confederal solution is not only about the dispute in question but presents the threat that other ethnically entitled populations could also seek to increase their autonomy in relation to state structures. These populations include the Adjarians in Georgia, the Gagauz and the ethnic Bulgarians[530] and Russians in 'right-bank' Moldova, and the whole mosaic of ethnic groups which in Azerbaijan constitute 9–10 per cent of the population and amongst which the Lezgins and the Talysh have population numbers exceeding the number of Armenians in Karabakh. Like Russia itself, these countries are threatened by a 'parade' of autonomy demands. Even if the geographic scope and political context are too different to allow for direct comparison, this situation arguably undermines Moscow's moral authority to speak for solutions which include the right of separation.

Russia, unlike the Soviet Union, can avoid entering the political minefield brought about by attempts to clearly define the future status of the disputed regions, and it tries to do so because its interest is less about these regions per se than about the countries which make claims to having authority over them. Because Moscow's perception of neutrality is related to Russia's bilateral relationships rather than emphasizes a specific, legally defined concept it also includes the expectation that a country's commitment not to accept foreign military troops or equipment on its territory is combined with a preparedness to treat foreign countries equally in the question of developing economic relations; therefore, and as a consequence of this perception, the countries committed to neutral policies should show a willingness to resist the requirements of Western integration which exclude the development of economic cooperation with third parties – in other words, with Russia. The more excluded Russia's position becomes in this respect due to the European Union's development of economic cooperation with its Eastern Partnership countries, the more important it becomes for Russia to consolidate its own association with these countries through the ethnic groups and regions with which it is historically affiliated. Seemingly isolated issues, such as the question about the guarantees for minority rights and cultural autonomy in Gagauzia, make sense in this broader political context. By making itself an external guarantor of minority rights and cultural autonomy, Russia would make itself a guarantor of Gagauzia's autonomous position within the Republic of Moldova, which again creates an obstacle for plans to give up neutrality (i.e. to join NATO) or to accede to another political entity (Romania, the EU) that, in Moscow's interpretation, would risk the country 'losing its sovereignty' or the political subjectivity that can be recognized by all population groups in the country. Thus, the external guarantees for cultural autonomy (which Russia, in the case of both Gagauzia and Nagorno-Karabakh, might be able to provide in partnership with Turkey) would be interlinked with the internal assurances of neutral foreign and security policies (in Moldova and in Azerbaijan, respectively). Such guarantees – should they gain wider international acceptability, which is unlikely – would consolidate the Russian connection with the population and provide it with legitimacy in the frame of horizontal international relations.

The issue of the rights of ethnic minorities attracts liberal interest and is therefore well suited to lend legitimacy to the international arrangements which Russia seeks to establish in order to gain guarantees of a country's neutral policy. Moreover, it is a treaty element which is not entirely new in terms of the ways in which Moscow has participated in building peace and security in Europe. Issues about minority rights were previously included in the prestigious international arrangements about Austria's neutrality in 1955, i.e. the *Staatsvertrag* which Austria signed together with the Allied occupying Powers (the Soviet Union among them) in exchange for withdrawing their military forces. This treaty stated the conditions for recognizing Austria's sovereign statehood after the Second World War and additionally included provisions about the minority rights of the small Croat and Slovene populations in Austria in order to settle the issue of former Yugoslavia's territorial claims over some of the areas inhabited by these population groups. In Russia the positive experience of having developed stable economic and political relations with neutral Austria after the withdrawal of the occupying Soviet forces keeps alive the memory of the international agreements which clearly demonstrated that the Soviet Union was one of the powers who acted as a guarantor of the post-war order in Europe.[531] In the current situation the guarantor's role is an aspiration which has a different content. Russia's historical connection with the former Soviet republics lays the basis for the argument that the conflicts in these countries require Russia to act as a guarantor of their domestic peace and stability and as a 'guardian' of the rights of their minority populations. The term 'guarantor' relates typically to formal agreements (such as peacekeeping arrangements), whereas the 'guardian's' role is adopted in the context of society. The closer the state's structure is to a weak federation, the more authority this role can gain. Although the legal effects of being such a 'guardian' may be modest as such (and less authoritative than are the verdicts of the institutions of the EU in equivalent cases concerning the protection of the rights of ethnic minorities), they would provide legitimacy to political mobilization on such issues. Thus, the 'guardian's' role is a flexible 'guarantee arrangement' which not only makes it easier for Russia to oversee developments at communal levels, but also increases its space for manoeuvre in preparing alternative lines of action to secure its deep borders.

The discussion in this chapter can be drawn together in the following conclusion: Russia's special, flexible concept of neutrality is an initial condition in its policies to resolve the conflicts discussed in this book, whereas the military presence, which it seeks to establish in one way or another, is the initial setting that keeps the situation stable. This is important from Russia's point of view when the different types of guarantees within the complex arrangement are developed and the right circumstances for the chance of seriously negotiating such guarantees are expected to emerge in the political processes in the conflict regions. The military presence and the political conditionality that ties together different types of guarantees in the comprehensive approach make the arrangement agile in Russia's policymaking. In other words, the specific arrangements can vary considerably in different regional contexts, and it always remains possible for Russia to start emphasizing policy variant 'B' once the prospect for policy variant 'A' is seen to no longer exist. The argument presented in this book will now be concluded by revisiting it in relation to a conflict to which we have until this moment made only passing reference: the recent conflict in eastern Ukraine.

Lessons for preventing the freezing of new conflicts: A focus on Ukraine

As explored earlier in this book, in the conflicts which erupted into warfare in the 1990s equipment from Soviet-era bases was used in the confusion that reigned during the early stages of the conflict; and when the ceasefire agreements were negotiated, the political support that Russia's military presence provided in its multifarious forms became part of the political support structure of the temporary arrangements. By contrast, in Ukraine Russia has used diffuse 'volunteer' troops who do not bear the state's insignia and, hence, in their outer appearance are similar to the kind of front gathered by the Abkhaz rebels to support their cause. This approach strengthens the character of the war as a civil war, i.e. as the type of war that Moldova encountered in Transnistria and only narrowly avoided in Gagauzia. While the backbone of Russia's interventions in both the Crimea and eastern Ukraine consists of regular army units and their heavy weaponry (on the spot and on the other side of the state border, respectively), Russia's cover-up of its participation as a state and the emphasis of the role of volunteer fighters allows it to present the conflicts in Ukraine as a continuation of the processes of the 1990s and, in this way, makes it possible to one-sidedly emphasize their endemic Russian connection.

In Western states, the opaque nature of Russia's military presence has prompted the interpretation of the conflict in Ukraine as a 'gray-zone' conflict that displays 'competitive interactions among and within state and non-state actors that fall between the traditional war and peace duality'.[532] Even if a 'gray-zone' conflict is seen to be ambiguous both in its nature (as it 'pools' several interests) and in respect to the legal frameworks which apply to it, it is seen as a pursuit for gains that are 'normally associated with victory in war'.[533] Consequently, it is assumed that the opponent (Russia) tries to achieve a military victory by not crossing the red lines that lead to overt warfare. The military conflict in the Donbass region in eastern Ukraine certainly has this 'gray' shade, which is closely linked to the terms of 'hybrid warfare' and 'asymmetric conflict'. However, the description of the battlefield must not be mistaken for Russia's ultimate goal in the conflict.

Although the conflict in the Donbass region is very different from the conflicts discussed above, similarities can be found in Russia's policies for settlement. The implementation of the ceasefire agreement (Minsk Agreements I and II)[534] is mired in stalemate because Kiev (supported by the West) has postponed the arrangement of local elections in the disputed areas of the Donetsk and Luhansk regions ('Donbass') until the troops and armed groups from Russia – and with them not only support for the rebels but also important parts of the rebels themselves – leave Ukraine. Russia, for its part, keeps its military support in place and deprives Kiev of its control over the border in order to maintain the negotiating weight of the rebel groups and to push Kiev into negotiating a 'comprehensive political settlement'.[535] This includes local elections and constitutional reform, which together would give the rebellious regions a 'special status' envisioned with a wide degree of self-determination, including in the context of language issues.[536] Much like the emphasis in Chisinau that demilitarization (i.e. the withdrawal of Russia's ordinary military troops from Transnistria, as a sign of respect for Moldova's territorial integrity) must be a basic condition for engaging in serious dialogue with Moscow, Kiev's argument also underlines a principled matter in relations between states: the negotiation of reintegration cannot be started as long as foreign (Russian) armed formations (including mercenaries and illegal groups) remain present in the disputed areas.[537] Russia refuses to regard the conflict in the frame of such rules and, instead, brings forward its nature as a domestic conflict in which the people on the Russian side of the formal border have the right to support their family and friends. Kiev's argument that the conflict is in the first place international is a means to call to mind the Budapest Memorandum of 1994, in which the leaders of the United States, the United Kingdom and Russia provided security assurances to Ukraine (and to Belarus and Kazakhstan) in return for giving up nuclear weapons.[538] If Russia were to recognize the conflict in terms of horizontal relations between states, it would break the crucial line that, in fact, enables its participation and, among other things, warrants its guarantor's role in any future settlement.

By leaving the conflict in deadlock Russia pursues its policy variant 'A' (although it, as always, does not leave variant 'B' unconsidered). The goal is a neutral, reintegrated Ukraine (without Crimea), which in its Constitution and state structure contains guarantees about maintaining the Russian connection of the population.[539] Consequently, it makes sense that Konstantin Kosachev and other politicians in Moscow speak about Moscow's preference for a 'strong' Ukraine, although its military support to the rebels and economic policies are working in the opposite direction. In a similar way, Moscow's preference for Georgia was initially a strong Georgian state which would remain affiliated to Russia. Because the primary goal is 'A', Russia's policies are focused on cornering the Ukrainian state by diplomatic and economic means. 'If you want to give Ukraine such a gift, why don't you pay for it?' was Putin's message to Western states in Europe already in summer 2006, when Russia refused to subsidize natural gas for Ukraine during the presidency of Victor Yushchenko and justified its abruptly changed approach by referring to the rationale of the market price from its taxpayers' point of view.[540] One decade on, Russia continues to reduce its economic dependence on Ukraine, including Russian dependence on transiting gas to Europe through this country. Sergey Karaganov's argument from June 2016, which summarizes a then-recent memorandum prepared by a group of members of Russia's Council on Defense and Foreign Policy, is an example of the long-term vision in Moscow: 'The Ukraine and other similar crises should in the long term be addressed on the basis of agreed permanent neutrality and merger in new formats of cooperation and security. In the first place, Eurasian.'[541]

Unlike Kiev, Moscow can afford to wait, just like it has done in Moldova. Its military presence at the border keeps the situation frozen until it can be assured of a 'comprehensive political settlement'. In a sharp difference to the Crimean Peninsula, the Donbass area has little political significance: it is mainly a border region where the transboundary connections of the people who live there matter.[542] Like in the case of Transnistria, Moscow cannot leave the Donbass region unattended for reasons that relate to the legitimacy of its own power and Russia's internal coherence. Yet, policy variant 'B' would leave Russia in a difficult situation internationally without noteworthy compensation, and domestically it would not be easy for Russia to assume responsibility for dismembering a country that is an integral part of its entire sense of history and culture.[543] By contrast, variant 'A' recognizes Russia's key role in European security and makes it a participant in Ukraine's affairs through the legal and political guarantee mechanisms of the state's structure. A federal state structure is expected to bring neutrality to the national agenda and make it the basis of its foreign and security policy.[544] Because all this is at stake, Moscow struggles to keep the final decisions open and not let tensions with Kiev prematurely push it towards policy variant 'B'.

Although the events in Ukraine have increased the attraction of a neutral line of policies in other former Soviet republics who wish to escape from being part of similar geopolitical rivalries, in Kiev the course is set in the opposite direction. In December 2014, *Verkhovna Rada* (the Ukrainian parliament) abolished the legal basis which since 2010 had existed for a foreign policy that excludes membership in military-political alliances. In the same month President Poroshenko announced the initiation of reforms to meet the criteria of NATO membership as well as his intention to organize a referendum on the willingness of the population to see the country become a member of NATO.[545] A few months later, in June 2015, *Verkhovna Rada* adopted a law which allowed the armed forces of foreign states to be invited to support international operations in the country. This provided a legal basis for extensive bilateral military cooperation with the member states of NATO, which above all meant the United States. In the NATO frame of cooperation, which had been built with political back-and-forth movements since 1991, Ukraine's integration into 'the Euro-Atlantic security space' concentrated on capability development and capacity building. After spring 2014 this cooperation was significantly intensified and the NATO–Ukraine Commission became the main forum for expressing political support for Ukraine. During the next years, Poroshenko repeatedly announced his readiness to initiate the referendum and argued that the public opinion in the country, which shows a trajectory of rapid growth amongst NATO's supporters, must be heeded.[546] If such political momentum could develop and meet with renewed support in Western states (which had waned even before the presidency of Donald Trump began in late January 2017), it cannot be excluded that an event of violence, which could be framed as a threatening humanitarian catastrophe that would also endanger the lives of Russian citizens, could prompt an intervention similar to that of Tskhinvali in August 2008 – and this time the contest would be even more clearly over who manages to lure whom in order for the normative conditions for open warfare to be claimed to exist. The clashes between Russian and Ukrainian vessels in the Kerch Straits off the Crimean coast of the Black Sea in November 2018 were an indication of the possibility of such an escalation.[547] The danger is not that individual incidents accidentally ignite war, but rather that military confrontation escalates because such incidents serve the aims of both parties to establish control over disputed areas both on land and at sea. Whereas Moscow's immediate goal is to build missile defence in the Crimea (at a short distance from Romania, which is the main US base in former Eastern Europe) and to extend its military control over the Azov Sea, Kiev has few alternatives other than to rely on the military assistance of NATO and its member states.

Measures such as the decision by President Poroshenko in November 2018 to introduce emergency rule ('marshal law') in ten Ukrainian regions and, on this basis, to bar the entry of Russian male citizens aged 16–60 into the country cannot close the border between Russia and Ukraine in the rebellious regions but, instead, strengthen the separation of these regions from Ukraine.[548] The Western states can either push the developments towards dividing Ukraine, or they can contribute to making this country a zone of military disengagement and economic cooperation.[549] Although Ukraine is already divided between its eastern and western parts, determining the final line of separation would spell tragedy for millions of people and implant a series of conflicts in the new transboundary relations.[550] From the perspective of European security, the inclusion of Russia into any cooperation promises more stability than would its exclusion. The war in Ukraine has clearly demonstrated that military and political confrontation exists at the heart of Europe and that it cannot be imagined away by emphasizing that such a situation lacks rational basis in the post–Cold War world. The war in Ukraine has also demonstrated that 'neutrality', which was removed from the lexicon of post–Cold War security, persists as an item worthy of serious discussion. In this context it is important to note that the term 'agreed permanent neutrality' (used by Sergey Karaganov in the citation above) can be used as a basis for negotiating a concept of neutrality which would be in harmony with established Western practices and, consequently, would reduce the bilateral emphasis which has kept Russia's approach to neutrality focused on the political assurances of a policy guaranteed by national law and a bilateral treaty with Russia. The combination of words raises a question about the possibility of comprehensive negative security assurances, i.e. refraining from the use of conventional weapons against the neutral state (while the Treaty on Nuclear Non-Proliferation already covers nuclear weapons). The provision of such assurances in treaty-form (in contrast to the Budapest Memorandum of 1994, which has an ambiguous legal status) and with support also from the European Union would be a crucial step towards stabilizing European security and finally integrating Russia into the process of building cooperation based on reciprocal commitment and shared responsibility.

Firmly placing the content of neutrality on the agenda of negotiations would offer a possibility to test Russia's willingness for compromises. The main task would be to develop an internal structure which keeps Ukraine (after the loss of Crimea) together and does not privilege any particular region in its economic relations with external states. In the efforts to resist the divisive influence from the outside, three things are crucial. The first is to adopt social and development policies which respect ethnic diversity but weaken the link between ethnic affiliation and territory for the non-titular (other than Ukrainian) populations. The second is to establish functioning institutional mechanisms on the level of the central administration to deal with Russia's legitimate concerns about non-titular population groups, and to establish such horizontal axis with a reciprocity of issues which cover both countries. The third is democratization, not in the ideological sense but in the sense of rules and procedures that increase the legitimacy of the country-wide political system. Like adult maturity, democratic development can be enhanced by providing a positive example, but it cannot be implanted from the outside. The lesson which Moldova and Ukraine have taught to Western donors is that extensive external funding under political conditions that allow corruption feeds the same system and undermines the legitimacy necessary for a stable security environment and democratic development. Instead of remaining focused on short-sighted geopolitical interests which sustain such adverse developments, the European Union should help in building a widely cooperative trading environment for Ukraine and other Eastern Partnership countries and search for solutions to develop arrangements which can help third markets to adjust to these countries' cooperation with the EU. Together with the effort to make neutrality a meaningful security concept, this would be a concrete step towards correcting the path which has so clearly led to building confrontation in Europe in the early years of the third millennium.

Notes

Introduction

1. Douglas Schoen's *Putin's Master Plan: To Destroy Europe, Divide NATO, and Restore Russian Power and Global Influence* is an example.
2. Examples include Ronald D. Asmus, *A Little War that Shook the World: Georgia, Russia, and the Future of the West* and James J. Coyle, *Russia's Border Wars and Frozen Conflicts*.
3. William Hill, for example, reasons that the persistence of such outdated attitudes is the background to why Russian policy elites permit small entities such as Transnistria to exacerbate situations with their own initiatives. William H. Hill, *Russia, the Near Abroad, and the West: Lessons from the Moldova–Transdniestria Conflict*, p. 181 (pp. 173–81).
4. On conducting a pragmatist way of research in the study of international relations which draws inspiration from C. S. Peirce, see, for example, Helena Rytövuori-Apunen, 'Forget "Post-Positivist" IR! The Legacy of IR Theory as the Locus for a Pragmatist Turn' and 'Abstractive Observation as the Key to the "Primacy of Practice"'.
5. Border-making practices are also ordering ('b/ordering') practices, as Henk van Houtum, Oliver Kramsch and Wolfgang Zierhofer argue in the Prologue of their edited book *B/ordering Space*. These authors' main focus is identity-construction. See also Helena Rytövuori-Apunen, 'The Depth of Borders beyond the State: Analytical, Normative and Epistemic Challenges of Study'.
6. See, for example, Cyril E. Black, 'The Pattern of Russian Objectives' (1962).
7. See Andrey Pertsev, 'Volodin vs. Kiriyenko: The Battle for Influence in Russia's Power Vertical', p. 1.
8. In the context of the concept of Russia's 'regime system', where power is concentrated in the instruments of executive authority and a power network links the formal institutions of the constitutional state to the party-political representative system, 'vertical power' draws attention to the prominent role played by such a power network in Moscow's relations with the subjects of the former Soviet Union and brings into the focus the action and policies through which Russia seeks to influence political outcomes in these countries and, in many cases, also seeks to keep large parts of their populations connected to Russian society. On Russia's 'regime system' see Richard Sakwa, *Russian Politics and Society*, pp. 466–70, and 'Great Powers and Small Wars in the Caucasus', pp. 72–7. The use of informal personal networks to obtain public goals and joint responsibility amongst professional elites is discussed by Alena V. Ledeneva in several of her works

on post-socialist informal practices (see, for example, *How Russia Really Works: The Informal Practices That Shaped Post-Soviet Politics and Business*). The informal practices which (according to Ledeneva) serve to compensate for the defects of the post-socialist system of business and politics, elucidate the duality of formal and informal practices in Russia, and, to a varying extent, arguably 'add fuel' to the relationships of vertical power discussed in the present book.

9   For example, Sergey Markedonov notes that if the South Caucasus had been recognized as an area of Moscow's 'special interests' because of the security problems in the Russian South, anti-Western sentiment in the Kremlin would have diminished. See Sergey Markedonov, 'Unfreezing Conflict in South Ossetia: Regional and International Implications', p. 46.

10 Dov Lynch, *Engaging Eurasia's Separatist States: Unresolved Conflicts and De Facto States*, p. 42.

11 The difference between dispute and conflict is discussed in many books by John W. Burton. See, for example, *Violence Explained: The Sources of Conflict, Violence and Crime and Their Provention*, p. 97.

12 The literal translation of *uregulirovanie* is 'regulation'. The discourse on the settlement of international disputes has developed since the late nineteenth century. After the First World War, it had a significant impact on the drafting of the Covenant of the League of Nations.

13 Matthew Sussex, 'Introduction: Understanding Conflict in the Former USSR', p. 2.

14 See ibid., p. 1, 'The Shape of the Security Order in the Former USSR', pp. 36–42 and 'Conclusions: The Future of Conflict in the Former USSR', pp. 195–209.

15 Susanna Hast argues correctly that the notion of 'sphere of influence' in Western academic and policy discourses refers especially to Russian foreign policy and that it remains outside any critical study despite the fact that this term is extremely common and its uses remain vague and pejorative and, consequently, unfit for analytical purposes (Susanna Hast, *Beyond the Pejorative: Sphere of Influence in International Theory*).

16 Whilst the interactive nature of international relations has been recognized in the systemic theory of this subject of study (Kenneth N. Waltz, *Theory of International Politics*), it is mostly discussed as a feature of theory. The habit to see the other party as the cause of the confrontation and the assumption that the conflict will not end until the other party collapses or changes fundamentally are part of the 'Cold War approach' in international relations, which continues even after the ideological confrontation of the Cold War has ended. See Robert Legvold, *Return to Cold War*.

17 Ideas about ontology of substance are deeply embedded in our Western culture through the discussions of Scholasticism, and the debt of modern science to them is fundamental (see, for example, John D. Caputo, *Heidegger and Aquinas: An Essay on Overcoming Metaphysics*).

Unfortunately, they have been brutally trivialized for modern, anthropocentric usage, of which the rhetorical practices of international relations and world politics are but an example.

18 For example, the publications and reports of the Jamestown Foundation (https://jamestown.org/) are empirically informative but often furnished with such attitudes.
19 See Robert Strausz-Hupé, William R. Kintner, James E. Dougherty and Alvin J. Cottrell, *Protracted Conflict*.
20 Dmitri Trenin, *Post-Imperium: A Eurasian Story*, pp. 6–17.
21 The Belovezh Accords signed by Belarus, Russia and Ukraine on 8 December 1991, in Belavezhskaia Pushcha in Belarus, declared the Soviet Union effectively dissolved and established the Commonwealth of Independent States in its place. These three subjects were the original signatories of the Treaty on the Creation of the Soviet Union on 29 December 1922. (The fourth signatory was the Transcaucasian Socialist Federative Soviet Republic, which ceased to exist in 1936 when Georgia, Armenia and Azerbaijan became members of the Soviet Union in their own right.)
22 *Rubezh* refers to 'border' in the sense of a natural border or a line, whereas the word for border between states is *granitsa*. The prefix *za* means 'outside'.
23 Roger E. Kanet, 'The Return of Imperial Russia', p. 19; Robert Legvold, 'Russian Foreign Policy during Periods of Great State Transformation', p. 120. President Yeltsin made this statement in his speech to members of the Civic Union (ITAR–TASS, 1 March 1993). Foreign Minister Andrei Kozyrev explained Yeltsin's announcement to the international audience by saying that Russia is going to defend its national interests in this region irrespective of international reaction.
24 Thomas Gomart, *Russian Civil-Military Relations: Putin's Legacy*, pp. 11–26.
25 Alexei Gromyko, 'Russia's Conundrum in the Post-Soviet Space', pp. 1–2.
26 Ivan III (*Velikii*, 'the Great', 1440–505) introduced the term *gosudar'* in Russia. Likewise he brought to Russia the Greek and Byzantine terms of the autocrat and the *tsar'*/czar (Caesar). *Gosudar'* (Sovereign) was introduced to denote the end of the Mongol yoke (Nicholas V. Riasanovsky, *A History of Russia*, 103–8). The sovereign ruler in the sense of the autocrat is *samoderzhets*, which word is etymologically related to *derzhava* ('empire', 'realm').
27 Because 'law' is not the original connotation, there is another term for it: *pravovoe gosudarstvo* (corresponding to German *Rechtsstaat*).
28 Unlike most other theorists of the modern state system, who consider states to be 'like units' in the system, Wight is a source of inspiration for a study of the historical character of power that makes the states mutually different. See Martin Wight, *Power Politics*, pp. 23–9.
29 On the European tradition of establishing political loyalties through such exchanges, see Evgeny Roshchin, 'The Concept of Friendship: From Princes to States'.

30 In 1990 – and again in spring 1994, when bilateral treaties with the subjects of the Federation were negotiated – Yeltsin admonished the regions to take as much sovereignty as they could 'hold on to' and 'swallow' (Jeffrey Kahn, *Federalism, Democratization, and the Rule of Law in Russia*, pp. 151–88).
31 Nikolai Petrov emphasizes that the reforms undertaken by President Putin in the early 2000s did not bring any single power-vertical chain of command for controlling the regions because the actions of the federal agencies remained uncoordinated (Nikolai Petrov, 'Who is Running Russia's Regions?'). Sakwa (*Russian Politics and Society*, pp. 255–83) speaks of segmented regionalism, asymmetrical federalism and a power 'triangle' which intensifies bureaucratic conflict. On Putin's policies to consolidate the network of power in terms of key positions and persons (the 'network directorate'), see Olga Kryshtanovskaya and Stephen White, 'The Formation of Russia's Network Directorate'.
32 Dmitri Trenin, 'Russia's Security Interests and Policies in the Caucasus Region', p. 95. The Russian connection weakens the traditional dichotomy between internal and external dimensions of policy. For example, Richard E. Pipes emphasizes that domestic politics and foreign policy are widely separated from each other in the Russian tradition and that the reasons for this relate to the country's large geographic size as well as its tradition as a state. See Richard E. Pipes, 'Domestic Politics and Foreign Affairs', pp. 145–61.
33 Elena Hellberg-Hirn argues that Russia has a history of building 'protective circles' and that the Moscow Kremlin, with its walled area, is a symbol of the first such circle. See Elena Hellberg-Hirn, *Soil and Soul: The Symbolic World of Russianness*, p. 238.
34 Following Charles S. Peirce's pragmaticist interpretation of reality, the three dimensions correspond to the logic of Firstness, Secondness and Thirdness in the trinity of the sign that is *reality as it is experienced*. See, for example, Charles S. Peirce, 'Logic as Semiotic: The Theory of Signs' and 'How to Make Our Ideas Clear'.
35 The opposition in Tajikistan had united different branches of Islamists who had regional political ambitions. As a result of the Peace Accords, moderate Islamists were incorporated in the government system while radical forces went underground and fled across the border to Afghanistan and Pakistan. The present-day ramifications of these events are discussed in Helena Rytövuori-Apunen and Furugzod Usmonov, 'Tajikistan's Unsettled Security: Borderland Dynamics of the Outpost on Russia's Afghan Frontier'.
36 Because the JCC, which is the frame for monitoring by the OSCE, operates through formal consensus, the change of rule in Ukraine in February 2014 has complicated the coordination of action, although this political discord has not brought changes to the peacekeeping arrangement. The main conflict that has emerged because of the war in eastern Ukraine relates to the increased isolation of Transnistria economically and in relation to

communication networks. In July 2015 the Ukrainian Parliament annulled a series of treaties and cooperation arrangements with Russia, including the agreement about the transit rights of Russia's peacekeepers and equipment that had been made in 1995.

37   The voter turnout may have been lower than the reported 83 per cent, because the Crimean Tatars (12 per cent of the population) and an unknown number of the Crimea's ethnic Ukrainians (20 per cent of the population) boycotted the referendum. See, for example, 'Crimea Referendum: Voters "Back Russia Union"', *BBC News*, 16 March 2014. Available at http://www.bbc.com/news/world-europe-26606097 (accessed 24 November 2017). For a concise analysis of the events that led to the referendum, see Shaun Walker, *The Long Hangover: Putin's New Russia and the Ghosts of the Past*, pp. 146–9.

38   President of Russia, 'Address by President of the Russian Federation', 18 March 2014. Available at http://en.kremlin.ru/events/president/news/20603 (accessed 17 December 2018); President of Russia, 'Vladimir Putin's Interview with Radio Europe 1 and TF1 TV channel', 4 June 2014. Available at http://en.kremlin.ru/events/president/news/45832 (accessed 17 December 2018).

39   Pragmatism argues that reality in all its variation is 'dynamic'. By contrast, the signification of an object at any given point of time generates the 'immediate' object and represents a temporary phase in the process of enquiry. According to Charles S. Peirce, reality in its 'dynamic' sense *is reality*, and it can be known only at an ideal 'end of inquiry'. Due to their 'dynamic' nature, the objects of our study can resist our efforts to define and impose meaning on them; therefore, we cannot enquire about reality without genuine doubt. See, for example, Peirce, 'Logic as Semiotic' and 'Chapt. 4 (2nd draft)' (MS 195: Fall 1872) in Charles S. Peirce, *Writings of Charles S. Peirce: A Chronological Edition, Volume 3, 1872–1878*, pp. 32–5. About the importance of this epistemic point of departure in the study of international relations, see Rytövuori-Apunen, 'The Depth of Borders beyond the State'.

40   Coyle, *Russia's Border Wars*, is an example of such quasi-realism. Although it does refer to the empiricist idea of theory (p. 1), it replaces empirical criticism with hasty assumptions ('Putin believes', 'the Kremlin intends') to assert that Russia will 'continue to increase its power regardless of international law' (p. 19). Consequently, international relations theory (realist political theory, nationalism theory) is used as a means to superficially describe events and processes. The argument used in Coyle's book to provide the perspective for discussing the frozen conflicts is that the United States and NATO must forestall and counteract the expansion of Russia's influence globally (see, for example, pp. 111–2, 198, 230, 272–3).

41   Alexander Yanov, 'The Birth of Pan-Slavism' (Parts One and Two), explores the historical and political background of the idea of revanche.

42 Exceptions can be found mainly in the field of political theory, where the ambition is to offer conceptual perspectives rather than to engage in analytical interpretation. Sergei Prozorov, 'Ethos without Nomos: The Russian–Georgian War and the Post-Soviet State of Exception', provides an example.
43 The concentration of research on the 'international system' has a long lineage in the study of international relations. Path-breaking works are J. David Singer's 'The Level-of-Analysis Problem in International Relations', in James N. Rosenau's edited opus *International Politics and Foreign Policy* (New York: Free Press, 1969) and Kenneth N. Waltz's *Man, the State and War: A Theoretical Analysis* (New York: Columbia University Press, 1959). Much of the later discussion in the disciplinary mainstream arises from these works, including Waltz's *Theory of International Politics* and the abundance of research that it has inspired in its further elaboration as well as its constructivist criticism. The works by Alexander Wendt to be mentioned in this connection are 'Anarchy Is What States Make of It: The Social Construction of Power Politics', *International Organization* 46/2 (1992), and *Social Theory of International Politics* (Cambridge: Cambridge University Press, 1999).
44 Vincent Pouliot, *International Security in Practice: The Politics of NATO–Russia Diplomacy*.
45 As early as the CSCE's Budapest summit in December 1994, Yeltsin spoke about NATO enlargement as a reproduction of the divisions of the Cold War and as a threat to European stability. He also argued that it was a threat to Russian democracy because it aroused anti-West sentiments in Russia.
46 Pouliot, *International Security in Practice*, pp. 227–8.
47 See, for example, 'Ion Sturza: Partners Will No Longer Tolerate That in Moldova, Important Decisions Are Taken in Places Other than the State Institutions', *Synthesis and Foreign Policy Debates, APE/FES, Newsletter* 10, November 2015.
48 Charles S. Peirce called this tridimensional interpretation of reality pragmaticism, by which term he emphasized the difference to John Dewey's instrumentalist truth. The tridimensional logic of interpretation is concisely presented in Peirce, 'Logic as Semiotic'.
49 Lena Jonson and Clive Archer (eds), *Peacekeeping and the Role of Russia in Eurasia*.
50 Dov Lynch, *The Conflict in Abkhazia: Dilemmas in Russian 'Peacekeeping' Policy*.
51 Ibid., p. 5.
52 A Statement of Intent signed by the Ministry of Defense of Finland and the US Department of Defense in 2016 mentions 'the strong defense relationship' between Finland and the United States to be 'a pillar of stability in the Baltic Sea region and Northern Europe' ('Statement of Intent between The Department of Defense of the United States of America and

The Ministry of Defense of the Republic of Finland', Helsinki, 7 October 2016. Available at http://www.defmin.fi (accessed 8 November 2017). The development of Finland's bilateral military relationship with the United States follows similar developments in Sweden.

53 In the pragmatist perspective, the possibility of knowing starts with questioning, which is made possible by some initial similarity of a 'new' empirical encounter with our previous experience. This point of departure is closely connected with phenomenology and hermeneutics. See, for example, Paul Ricoeur, *Hermeneutics & the Human Sciences: Essays on Language, Action & Interpretation.*

Chapter 1

54 See Nicholas Kulish and C. J. Chivers, 'Kosovo Is Recognized but Rebuked by Others', *The New York Times*, 19 February 2008. Available at https://www.nytimes.com/2008/02/19/world/europe/19kosovo.html (accessed 13 April 2018).

55 Statement by Vitaly Churkin, Permanent Representative of the Russian Federation to the UN, Security Council Sixty-fourth year, 6066th meeting, 14 January 2009. United Nations S/PV.6066, p. 20. Available at http://www.un.org/en/sc/meetings/ (accessed 12 August 2017).

56 Ministry of Foreign Affairs of the Russian Federation, 'Transcript of Interview of Minister of Foreign Affairs of the Russian Federation Sergey Lavrov with Editor-in-Chief of Ekho Moskvy Radio Station Alexei Venediktov', 14 August 2008 (1194-15-08-2008) and 'Transcript of Speech by Russian Minister of Foreign Affairs Sergey Lavrov at the Foreign Ministry's MGIMO University on the Occasion of the New Academic Year', 1 September 2008. Both available at http://www.mid.ru/en/main_en (both accessed 14 October 2017). See also Sergey Lavrov, 'Face to Face with America: Between Non-Confrontation and Convergence'.

57 Ministry of Foreign Affairs of the Russian Federation, 'Transcript of Remarks and Response to Media Questions by Russian Minister of Foreign Affairs Sergey Lavrov at Joint Press Conference After Meeting with Chairman-in-Office of the OSCE and Minister for Foreign Affairs of Finland Alexander Stubb', 12 August 2008 (1167-12-08-2008). Available at http://www.mid.ru/en/main_en (accessed 14 October 2017).

58 Statement by Vitaly Churkin, Permanent Representative of the Russian Federation to the UN, Security Council Sixty-third year, 5953rd meeting, 10 August 2008. United Nations S/PV.5953, p. 8. Available at http://www.un.org/en/sc/meetings/records/2008 (accessed 10 August 2017).

59 Ministry of Foreign Affairs of the Russian Federation, 'Interview with BBC Television', Sochi, 26 August 2008. Available at http://www.ln.mid.ru/brp_ (accessed 30 September 2008), link no longer working. Transcript of the

interview available at http://www.acronym.org.uk/old/archive/docs/0808/doc09.htm (accessed 14 October 2008).

60 The Independent International Fact-finding Mission on the Conflict in Georgia states that 'genocide' was used misleadingly by Russia: It 'was neither founded in law or substantiated by factual evidence' (Vol. I, p. 22). 'Ethnic cleansing' is reported to have occurred from both sides of the conflict when villages were systematically destructed (ibid.). The report of the mission appointed by the Council of the European Union in late 2008 was published on 30 September 2009.

61 See, for example: Ministry of Foreign Affairs of the Russian Federation, 'Transcript of Remarks and Response to Media Questions by Russian Deputy Minister of Foreign Affairs/State Secretary Grigory Karasin at Press Conference at RIA Novosti News Agency, Moscow, 10 August 2008' (1154-10-08-2008). Available at http://www.mid.ru/en/main_en (accessed 26 November 2017); President of Russia, 'Press Statement following Negotiations with French President Nicolas Sarkozy', 12 August 2008. Available at http://en.kremlin.ru/events/president/transcripts/1072 (accessed 20 November 2017).

62 Vitaly Churkin, Permanent Representative of the Russian Federation to the UN, interview with the Charlie Rose Show (PBS and Bloomberg TV), 12 August 2008. Transcript available at https://charlierose.com/videos/11624 (accessed 22 November 2017).

63 Responsibility to Protect (RtoP) was adopted by the UN member states at the 2005 World Summit and reaffirmed in UN Security Council resolutions in 2006 and 2009 (1674, 1894). According to this principle, states have the responsibility to protect their populations from genocide, war crimes, ethnic cleansing and crimes against humanity. Should they 'manifestly fail', international community should take action through the mechanisms of the UN Charter.

64 Vladimir Baranovsky and Anatoly Mateiko, 'Responsibility to Protect: Russia's Approaches', pp. 49–52; Alex J. Bellamy, *Responsibility to Protect: The Global Effort to End Mass Atrocities*, p. 87. See also 'Transcript of the Interview by the Foreign Minister of Russia S. Lavrov to the Foreign Policy Magazine, published on 29 April 2013', *International Affairs*, 13 May 2013. Available at http://en.interaffairs.ru/ (accessed October 2017).

65 The Russian member in the International Commission on Intervention and State Sovereignty, which published its report *The Responsibility to Protect* in December 2001, was Vladimir Lukin, then Deputy Speaker of the State Duma (Yablako Party) and Russia's ambassador to the United States during 1992–3. Evgenii Primakov, former prime minister and foreign minister, represented Russia on the High-level Panel on Threats, Challenges and Change, which published its report *A More Secure World: Our Shared Responsibility* in 2004.

66 *The Responsibility to Protect: Report of the International Commission on Intervention and State Sovereignty*, pp. 32–7.

67 Russia had introduced about 20,000 troops and 100 tanks into South Ossetia, Abkhazia and other parts of Georgia. Its actions included a naval blockade on the Black Sea and aerial bombings of Gori, Poti and a number of military targets.

68 Vitaly Churkin, Permanent Representative of the Russian Federation to the UN, interview for the Charlie Rose Show (PBS and Bloomberg TV), 12 August 2008. Transcript available at https://charlierose.com/videos/11624 (accessed 22 November 2017).

69 See, for example, Ministry of Foreign Affairs of the Russian Federation, 'Transcript of Remarks and Response to Media Questions by Russian Deputy Minister of Foreign Affairs/State Secretary Grigory Karasin at Press Conference at RIA Novosti News Agency, Moscow, 10 August 2008'. Instead of traditional peacekeeping, 'peace coercion' suggests the militarily heavier version of 'peace enforcement'. The formal concept in the ceasefire agreements for South Ossetia and Abkhazia during 1992–4 was 'peacekeeping'. However, it should be noted that the connotation of the Russian term for peacekeeping, *mirotvorchestvo*, is about creating peace and is hence close to 'peace making'.

70 Ibid.

71 The contributions of Russian experts in the IMEMO Supplement to the SIPRI Yearbook 2009 emphasize that when NATO member states in 1999 justified their military action against Yugoslavia by reference to a humanitarian catastrophe in Kosovo, they could not foresee the consequences. Humanitarian catastrophe, which Russia argued was the situation in South Ossetia in August 2008, is argued to be a wider concept than any references to large-scale violations of human rights can suggest. Nadia Alexandrova-Arbatova emphasizes that 'Humanitarian intervention provides for the use of force for the sake of the rescue of civilians—from genocide, ethnic cleansings, and consequences of civil war, natural catastrophes and cataclysms' and that the UN Security Council has the authority to define such situations requiring external intervention (Alexandrova-Arbatova, 'Framework for a New European Security Architecture', pp. 103–4).

72 The political instrumentalism of 'remedial secession' is discussed in Grace Bolton and Gezim Visoka, 'Recognizing Kosovo's Independence: Remedial Secession or Earned Sovereignty?'

73 Permanent Mission of the Russian Federation to the United Nations, 'Statement by the Ministry of Foreign Affairs of the Russian Federation', 26 August 2008. Available at http://russiaun.ru/en/news/200808265799 (accessed 14 October 2017).

74 Trenin, *Post-Imperium*, pp. 198–9. The population in South Ossetia is 53,000 and in Abkhazia 240,000 people. Of Abkhazia's population 50 per cent are ethnic Abkhaz, 21 per cent are 'Georgian' (mostly Mingrelians or Svans), 20 per cent are Armenians and 11 per cent are Russians. The Abkhaz diaspora in Turkey is about half a million people.

75 Helena Rytövuori-Apunen, 'Disputed Frontiers: Abkhazia in Russia's Sochi 2014 Project', p. 230.
76 Konstantin Kosachev, 'Rezhimy prikhodiat i ukhodiat ... Mif, budto Rossiia oderzhima zhelaniem vernut' Gruziiu v sferu svoego vliianiia'.
77 Ministry of Foreign Affairs of the Russian Federation, 'Statement by the Russian Ministry of Foreign Affairs', 13 August 2008 (1173-13-08-2008). Available at http://www.mid.ru/en/main_en (accessed 20 November 2017).
78 Foreign Minister Sergey Lavrov, cited in 'Moscow Concerned by Georgian Buildup near S. Ossetia, Abkhazia', *RIA Novosti*, 16 January 2009. Available at https://sptnkne.ws/gdcP (accessed 28 November 2017). UNSC Resolution 1244 set Kosovo in international control and authorized international security presence in Kosovo under the unified command of NATO.
79 In an interview in August 2008, Deputy Minister of Foreign Affairs Grigory Karasin argued that this proposal 'merits the most positive response'. See Ministry of Foreign Affairs of the Russian Federation, 'Transcript of Remarks and Response to Media Questions by Russian Deputy Minister of Foreign Affairs/State Secretary Grigory Karasin at Press Conference at RIA Novosti News Agency, Moscow, 10 August 2008'.
80 Ministry of Foreign Affairs of the Russian Federation, 'Interview with CNN, Sochi, 26 August 2008' (Interview of President Dmitry Medvedev), transcript available at www.mid.ru (accessed 23 December 2010) (document no longer accessible). Emphasis added.
81 Dmitry Rogozin, 'Washington's Hypocrisy', *International Herald Tribune*, 18 August 2008. Available at http://www.iht.com/articles/2008/08/18/opinion/edrogozin.php (accessed 23 December 2010) (link no longer working). The 'policy of double standards in international relations' was criticized in a statement of the CSTO summit in September 2008. See Ministry of Foreign Affairs of the Russian Federation, 'Declaration of the Moscow Session of the Collective Security Council of the Collective Security Treaty Organization, Moscow, 5 September 2008', 9 September 2008 (1323-09-09-2008). Available at http://www.mid.ru/en/main_en (accessed 28 November 2017).
82 Embassy of the Russian Federation in Canada, 'Dmitry Medvedev Made a Statement on the Situation in South Ossetia', Press-release, 8 August 2008. Available at http://en.kremlin.ru/events/president/news/1043 (accessed at the embassy's website on 23 December 2010).
83 President Gorbachev's attempts to maintain the union included several legal measures, among them the Act of 3 April 1990, On the Procedures for Resolving Questions Related to the Secession of Union Republics from the USSR. The law stipulated about the referenda and other procedures on the basis of which the subjects could leave the union, but in fact the legal definition of the complex procedures made secession difficult. Foreign Minister Lavrov made these arguments in an interview with the Russian service of the BBC in April 2009. See Steven Eke, 'Lavrov Deplores NATO "Cold War Logic"', *BBC News*, 21 April 2009. Available at http://news.bbc.co.uk/2/hi/europe/8011137.stm (accessed 20 December 2017).

84 Academics too raised their voice to emphasize Russia's privileged historical responsibility. See, for example, 'Independence of the Republic of South Ossetia—a guarantee of safety and reliable future of the Ossetian people', speech by Ruslan Bzarov at the VI Congress of the Ossetian People, Tskhinval, September 2007 [no exact date], Gosudarstvennoe informatsionnoe agenstvo 'Res', Respublika Iuzhnaia Osetiia, 10 September 2008. Available at http://cominf.org/node/1166478243 (accessed 20 December 2017).

85 Two more Pacific-island states, Vanuatu (with reservations) and Tuvalu recognized South Ossetia and Abkhazia in 2011, but later (in 2013 and in 2014, respectively) retracted the recognition upon their conclusion of diplomatic relations with Georgia.

86 Ministry of Foreign Affairs of the Russian Federation, 'Russian Foreign Ministry Comments on the Publication of the Tagliavini Commission Report', 30 September 2009 (1431-30-09-2009). Available at http://www.mid.ru/en/main_en (accessed 9 December 2017).

87 Pavel Felgenhauer, 'Putin Confirms the Invasion of Georgia Was Preplanned'.

88 In early February 2006 President Putin had emphasized that if Kosovo can be granted independence, Abkhazia and South Ossetia cannot be treated differently. 'Russia: Putin Calls For "Universal Principles" to Settle Frozen Conflicts', *RFE/RL*, 1 February 2006. Available at http://www.rferl.org/content/article/1065315.html (accessed 24 November 2017).

89 The argument that language can never be simply manipulative (even if people can be manipulated to utter words – which then are 'empty words', void of meaning) follows from speech act theory, which distinguishes the illocutionary force and the perlocutionary effect from the locutionary meaning of speech. See John L. Austin, *How to Do Things with Words*.

Chapter 2

90 See, for example, Prime Minister Vladimir Putin, remarks at the Meeting of the Government Presidium, 11 August 2008. Available at http://archive.government.ru/eng/docs/1648/ (accessed 26 November 2017); see also Ministry of Foreign Affairs of the Russian Federation, 'Transcript of Remarks and Response to Media Questions by Russian Deputy Minister of Foreign Affairs/State Secretary Grigory Karasin at Press Conference at RIA Novosti News Agency, Moscow, 10 August 2008'.

91 Statement by Ruslan Khasbulatov, Chairman of the Russian Supreme Soviet, 15 June 1992, reported in Ivan Yelistratov and Sergey Chugayev, 'The Russian Parliament May Consider the Question of the Annexation of South Ossetia by Russia', published in *Izvestiia*, 15 June 1992, p. 1. English translation of the Russian original text reprinted from *The Current Digest*

of the Post-Soviet Press (44/24, 15 July 1992, p. 16) in Ana K. Niedermaier (ed.), *Countdown to War in Georgia: Russia's Foreign Policy and Media Coverage of the Conflict in South Ossetia and Abkhazia*, pp. 40–1.
92 James P. Nicol, *Diplomacy in the Former Soviet Republics*, pp. 138–9.
93 George B. Hewitt, 'Abkhazia: A Problem of Identity and Ownership'.
94 The Ossetians have relied on Russia ever since tsarist Russia gained control of the South Caucasus in the 1860s and 1870s, and even earlier Christianity, which they adapted under Byzantine influence in the early Middle Ages, connected them to Russia rather than to any other power influential in the Caucasus region where they once had fled the Mongols.
95 This demonstration took place on 23 November 1989. In 1989, 98,000 people (66.61 per cent Ossetian and 29.44 per cent Georgian) lived in South Ossetia. Additionally, 99,000 Ossetians lived in other parts of Georgia.
96 The date of the decision by the Georgian SSR Supreme Soviet is 11 December 1990.
97 In 1994, North Ossetia added 'Alania', the name of an ancient kingdom in the region, to its name to mark its own historical identity.
98 Based on linguistic features Ossetians are presumed to descend from Persian tribes.
99 North Ossetia-Alania has tense relations with neighbouring Ingushetia, which has made demands on its Prigorodny district as well as the capital Vladikavkaz. A short but violent war, in which Moscow backed the North Ossetians against the Ingush, occurred in autumn 1992 and violent outbursts have continued to take place. The war, which took several hundreds of lethal casualties and pushed up to 60,000 Ingush to flee from North Ossetia, undermined the already weak loyalties towards Russia in the North Caucasus. When the Republic of Chechnya in spring 2013 issued a law by which it demanded territories under the control of its neighbouring Ingushetia, Ingushetia, in turn, pressured Moscow to intervene by threatening to reopen the issue about Prigorodny. See Valery Dzutsati, 'Signs of Balkanization Emerge in the North Caucasus'.
100 The date of these events in Tbilisi was 9 April 1989.
101 See also Catherine Dale, 'The Case of Abkhazia (Georgia)', p. 125.
102 'Shevardnadze Links Russian Troop Presence to Regaining Abkhazia', *Monitor* 1/125 (1 November, The Jamestown Foundation 1995). Available at https://jamestown.org/program/shevardnadze-links-russian-troop-presence-to-regaining-abkhazia/#.Vw0QFo9OJOw (accessed 29 November 2017).
103 Liana Minasyan, 'South Ossetia: "No Compromises with Georgia" – This is the Desire of Alan Chochiyev', published in *Nezavisimaya Gazeta*, 10 April 1992, p. 3. English translation of the Russian original text reprinted from *The Current Digest of the Post-Soviet Press* (44/15, 13 May 1992, p. 21) in Niedermaier (ed.), *Countdown to War in Georgia*, pp. 35–6.

Chochiyev served as the First Vice-Chairman of the Russian Supreme Soviet.
104 Céline Francis, *Conflict Resolution and Status: The Case of Georgia and Abkhazia (1989–2008)* and Lynch, *The Conflict in Abkhazia* provide detailed examinations of these negotiations in relation to Abkhazia.
105 In 1993, the Russian government decreed that while the MD controls ceasefire, the MFA coordinates resolution with the UN and other international organizations.
106 Mikhail Shevelev, 'Epicenter: War Is Coming from the South – The Fate of Peace in Southern Russia Is Being Decided Today in Ossetia', published in *Moskovskiye Novosti*, 21 June 1992, p. 4. English translation of the Russian original text reprinted (in condensed text) from *The Current Digest of the Post-Soviet Press* (44/25, 22 July 1992, pp. 5–6) in Niedermaier (ed.), *Countdown to War in Georgia*, p. 44 (pp. 41–4).
107 On 17 September 1993, the State Duma rejected Defense Minister Pavel Grachev's proposal to deploy two peacekeeping missions in Abkhazia. The previous day had made it evident that the ceasefire had been broken. See Lena Jonson and Clive Archer, 'Russia and Peacekeeping in Eurasia', pp. 16–7.
108 Ibid.; see also Dale, 'The Case of Abkhazia', p. 125.
109 Dale, 'The Case of Abkhazia', p. 128.
110 'Shevardnadze Links Russian Troop Presence to Regaining Abkhazia', *Monitor* 1/125 (1 November 1995). Available at http://www.jamestown.org (accessed 23 November 2017).
111 Francis, *Conflict Resolution and Status*, p. 125.
112 Lynch, *The Conflict in Abkhazia*, pp. 21–2.

Chapter 3

113 Lynch, *The Conflict in Abkhazia*, p. 15.
114 Ibid., p. 30.
115 Francis, *Conflict Resolution and Status*, pp. 121–8.
116 Dale, 'The Case of Abkhazia', p. 131.
117 Lynch, *The Conflict in Abkhazia*, p. 9.
118 In practice, Russia covered the costs for KOPO. Georgia, Ukraine and Uzbekistan were opposed to joint CIS border protection.
119 Lynch, *The Conflict in Abkhazia*, pp. 37–8.
120 Georgia followed suit but relaxed the procedure in 2004; it then became possible to acquire a visa upon arrival in Georgia. Previously, only Turkmenistan had established visa regulations for Russian citizens. In 2000, there were about half a million Georgian migrant workers in Russia.
121 Trenin, *Post-Imperium*, p. 33.
122 Lynch, *The Conflict in Abkhazia*, p. 43.

123 These developments were widely reported in Georgia. See, for example, 'Russian Foreign Ministry's Statement on Putin's Instruction to Boost Ties with Abkhazia and South Ossetia', *Civil Georgia*, 16 April 2008. Available at http://www.civil.ge/eng/article.php?id=17593 (accessed 23 November 2017).
124 *Gumannyi* (human) has the connotation of being civilized in the sense of classical education.
125 See, for example, Mikhail Vignansky, 'A Creeping March – Russia Semirecognizes Abkhazia and South Ossetia'. English translation of the Russian original text published in *Vremya Novostei*, 17 April 2008, reprinted (in condensed text) from *The Current Digest of the Post-Soviet Press* (60/15, 6 May 2008, pp. 7–8) in Niedermaier (ed.), *Countdown to War in Georgia*, pp. 337–40.
126 Ministry of Foreign Affairs of the Russian Federation, 'Article of Russian Minister of Foreign Affairs Sergey Lavrov, "On the Caucasus Crisis and Russia's Ukrainian Policy," published in the Weekly "2000", No. 38, September 19–25, Kyiv', 20 September 2008 (1397-20-09-2008). Available at http://www.mid.ru/en/main_en (accessed 23 November 2017).
127 The present book shares Robert H. Jackson's notion that quasi-states are 'territorial jurisdictions supported from above' rather than 'self-standing structures with domestic foundations' (Robert H. Jackson, *Quasi-States: Sovereignty, International Relations, and the Third World*, p. 5). Jackson argues that many 'Third World' countries exist as states merely in the formal sense of international law whilst their capability to perform the functions of the state is dependent on the material aid provided by the international community. The usage of the term in the present book speaks of an even emptier formality, i.e. the recognition of statehood by only one major state (Russia). However, the present book does not follow Jackson in extending the concept of quasi-state towards an argument of liberal political theory to evaluate the performance of state functions towards the citizens in these political entities.
128 Abkhazia does not allow any other but Russian double citizenship. The situation where about 20,000 residents in Abkhazia's Gali district had received Abkhaz identity documents while keeping their Georgian passports was one reason to the resignation of Aleksandr Ankvab as president in spring–summer 2014. See Olesya Vartanyan, 'The Political Crisis in Abkhazia – Expectations in Tbilisi', *International Alert*, Caucasus Dialogues, blog, 1 September 2016. Available at http://www.internationalalert.org (accessed 6 November 2017).
129 Rytövuori-Apunen, 'Disputed Frontiers', pp. 236–7.
130 'Rossiia vydelit Abkhazii v 2016 godu pochti 8 milliardov rublei', Lenta.ru (ekonomika), 29 December 2015. Available at https://lenta.ru/news/2015/12/29/apsny/ (accessed 21 November 2017).

131 Abkhazia provided gravel and inert materials for the massive construction works in Sochi for the Olympic Games in 2014 (Rytövuori-Apunen, 'Disputed Frontiers', pp. 240–2).
132 The Treaty of Alliance and Integration between Russia and South Ossetia was signed on 18 March 2015.
133 In South Ossetia's presidential elections in November 2011, opposition leader Alla Dzhioeva defeated the pro-Kremlin candidate Anatolii Bibilov in the first-round of voting. The results were annulled by the republic's Supreme Court over alleged vote rigging and Dzhioyeva was banned from running in the second round. In the re-elections in April 2012, the former South Ossetian KGB head Leonid Tibilov was reported to have won over 54 per cent of the vote. In Abkhazia Anvar Ankvab, a former civil servant in the Ministry of the Interior of the Georgian SSR, succeeded the deceased president Sergey Bagapsh in May 2011. Ankvab resigned following a political crisis that in May 2014 erupted with street demonstrations. The election of Raul Khajimba as president in August 2014 signalled a tougher policy towards Georgia: a refusal to negotiate Abkhazia's status and a strict policy of granting only five-year residence permits to the Georgian Abkhaz in the Gali district of Abkhazia.
134 Charles W. Blandy, 'Provocation, Deception, Entrapment: The Russo-Georgian Five Day War', p. 9.
135 Aleksandr Khramchikhin, 'Iuzhnyi okrug: Protivniki na Kavkaze Rossii ne strashny'.
136 'Rossiiskie voennye v Abkhazii pristupili k takticheskim ucheniiam', *RSO News*, News Agency of the Republic of South Ossetia, 9 April 2013. Available at http://rsonews.org/ru/news/20130409/08881.html (accessed 21 November 2017).
137 Although Tochka-U are defined as tactical weapons, it must be emphasized that the distinction between tactical and strategic weapons is dependent on the usage. Moreover, Tochka-U can be installed with biological and chemical warheads.

Chapter 4

138 Lynch, *The Conflict in Abkhazia*, pp. 38–48.
139 Ministry of Foreign Affairs of Pridnestrovian Moldavian Republic, 'Declaration on the Principles of Peaceful and Just Settlement of Georgia–Abkhazia, Georgia–South Ossetia, Azerbaijan–Nagorno Karabakh and Moldova–Pridnestrovie Conflicts', *Tiraspol*, 16 June 2007. Available at http://mfa-pmr.org/en/ (accessed 12 December 2017).
140 The Declaration on the policy of the Russian Federation in relation to Abkhazia, South Ossetia and Transnistria was adopted on 21 March 2008. A news review of this and related events is available at *News from*

Abkhazia, http://www.kapba.de/News-E-March2008.html (accessed 12 December 2017).
141 Stenogramma parlamentskikh slushanii Komiteta po delam SNG i sviaziam s sootechestvennikami na temu: 'O sostoianii uregulirovaniia konfliktov na territorii SNG i obrashcheniiakh k Rossiiskoi Federatsii o priznanii nezavisimosti Respubliki Abkhaziia, Respubliki Iuzhnaia Osetiia i Pridnestrovskoi Moldavskoi Respubliki'. Zdanie Gosudarstvennoi Dumy. Malyi zal. 13 marta 2008 goda. 15 chasov. Predsedatel'stvuet predsedatel' Komiteta po delam SNG i sviaziam s sootechestvennikami A.V. Ostrovskii. (The State Duma Committee for CIS Affairs and Relations with Compatriots, verbatim records of parliamentary hearings, 13 March 2008. Chair A.V. Ostrovskii.) Accessed at http://www.duma.gov.ru, 24 November 2008 (document no longer accessible).
142 During April–May Russia augmented its peacekeeping forces with paratroopers. Additionally, in late May 2008, a battalion of Russian railway troops arrived to Abkhazia with the mission to repair the railway connecting Sukhumi to the port of Ochamchira (Rytövuori-Apunen, *Disputed Frontiers*, 234–6).
143 Ivan Kotlyarov, 'The Logic of South Ossetia Conflict'.
144 Foreign Minister Sergey Lavrov, interview with *Russia Today* (currently *RT*) *TV* by Sophie Shevardnadze, 23 April 2014. Transcript available at https://www.rt.com/shows/sophieco/154364-lavrov-ukraine-standoff-sophieco/ (accessed 11 December 2017).
145 President of Russia, 'Dmitry Medvedev Addressed a Greeting to Delegates and Guests at the Conference of the Association of Georgians in Russia', 3 February 2009. Available at http://en.kremlin.ru/events/president/news/3045 (accessed 20 November 2017). See also Konstantin Kosachev, 'Rezhimy prikhodiat i ukhodiat'.
146 President of Russia, 'Joint Press Conference with Federal Chancellor Angela Merkel', 15 August 2008. Available at http://en.kremlin.ru/events/president/transcripts/1102 (accessed 20 November 2017).
147 Ibid.
148 Fyodor Lukyanov, 'Uncertain World: 5 Years after the 5-Day War, Everyone's Learned Their Lessons'.
149 The military capacity which Georgia used in its war with Russia was bought from former Soviet states, mainly from Ukraine and the Czech Republic. The US direct assistance in equipment was limited to communications technology and expertise.
150 Aleksandr Khramchikhin, 'Iuzhnyi okrug' (transl. by the author).
151 President of Russia, 'Interview with Al-Jazeera Television', *Sochi*, 26 August 2008. Available at http://en.kremlin.ru/events/president/transcripts/1230 (accessed 20 November 2017).
152 Aleksandr Khramchikhin, 'Iuzhnyi okrug' (transl. by the author).

Chapter 5

153 'Tiraspol calls on Moldova to establish Good Neighbor Relations with Transnistria', *Moldova.Org* [September 2010], no date. Available at http://www.moldova.org/en/tiraspol-calls-on-moldova-to-establish-good-neighbor-relations-with-transnistria-212257-eng/ (accessed 24 November 2017).

154 'Transnistrian President's News Conference: Two decades of PMR Existence Were Not in Vain', *Moldova.Org* [September 2010], no date. Available at http://www.moldova.org/en/transnistrian-presidents-news-conference-two-decades-of-pmr-existence-were-not-in-vain-212123-eng/ (accessed 24 November 2017); Ernest Vardanean, 'Elections in Transnistria – are they going to change the situation?' (editorial), *Synthesis and Foreign Policy Debates, APE/FES,* Newsletter 7 July 2016.

155 'Moldovan Parliament Accuses Russian State Duma of Interference in Moldova's Internal Affairs', *Moldova.Org* [October 2006], no date. Available at http://www.moldova.org/en/moldovan-parliament-accuses-russian-state-duma-of-interference-in-moldovas-internal-affairs-19303-eng/ (accessed 24 November 2017). In March 2014, politicians and activists in Transnistria pleaded Russia's State Duma to draft a law that would enable the PMR to join the Russian Federation.

156 Mark Baker, 'Moldova's Missing Millions: Massive Bank Scandal Roils Chisinau', *RFE/RL*, 23 April 2015. Available at https://www.rferl.org/a/moldova-bank-scandal-economy/26973772.html (accessed 21 November 2017). The liberal coalition government led by Valeriu Strelet fell in October 2015 as a result of a no-confidence vote related to the bank scandal. The three banks involved in the disappearance of the sum are Banca Sociala, Unibank and the state-owned Banca de Economii a Moldovei. The corruption charges brought against the government, which led to the revelation of the bank scandal, were prompted by the work of the National Council for judiciary reform. The Council was founded by Acting President Marian Lupu, who served as interim president during 2010–2 after the failure by the parliament to elect the president. Vladimir Plahotniuc, a millionaire businessman who had rapidly ascended through the ranks of the Democratic Party led by Lupu, was included in the administration of the Council. After President Nicolae Timofti in late 2015 refused to approve Plahotniuc for the position of prime minister at the turn of 2015–6, the Democratic Party's choice was the less controversial Pavel Filip, who started as the prime minister in January 2016.

157 In the parliamentary elections in November 2014, the Socialist Party gained 20.51 per cent of the votes and became the largest faction with 25 mandates in the 101-member parliament.

158 The 'Statement by the High Representative/Vice-President Federica Mogherini and Commissioner Johannes Hahn on the amendments to the

electoral legislation in the Republic of Moldova' (Brussels, 21 July 2017) mentions that 'The implementation of these changes will be assessed also in light of the Republic of Moldova's obligations under the Association Agreement'. This statement is available at https://eeas.europa.eu/ headquarters/headquarters-homepage/30221/statement-hrvp-mogherini-and-commissioner-hahn-amendments-electoral-legislation-republic_en (accessed 29 November 2017). The future prospects of the liberal political parties will be considerably diminished by the ethnopolitical electoral territories which the changes in the electoral system establish – and do so not only inside Moldova but also amongst the diaspora population, which is at its largest in Russia (500,000–700,000 people). The electoral system was changed with the votes of the governing Democratic Party and the Socialists (see Vladimir Socor, 'Moldova's New Electoral Law Could Be Fatal to Pro-Western Parties', Parts One and Two).

159 Victor Chirila, 'Moldova: More Focus, Flexibility, and Visibility for the European Neighbourhood Policy', pp. 33–4. In July 2017, Moldova together with Ukraine and Georgia asked the European Parliament to adopt a resolution on their membership prospects (*Synthesis and Foreign Policy Debates, APE/FES, Newsletter* 6 July 2017, p. 1).

160 The commonly used English-language spelling is 'Transnistria', which also is the name of the region in Romanian. It (like also the spelling Trans-Dniestr) means 'beyond the Dniester River'. The Moldovan government refers to the region as Stînga Dniestr lui (Unitățile Administrativ-Teritoriale din Stînga Dniestr lui), which means 'Left Bank of the Dniester ('Administrative-territorial unit(s) of the Left Bank of the Dniester)'. The term used by the authorities in 'Trans-Dniester' (which is a geographic description of the region) is *Pridnestróvskaia Moldávskaia Respública*, Pridnestrovian Moldavian Republic. The short form is Pridnestrovie (Pridnestrov'e), 'by the Dniester River'. The translation of this term from Slavic-language texts is usually 'Transdniestria'. The present book uses 'Transnistria', because this spelling (the Romanian variant) is the most common in Anglo-Saxon practice.

161 'Reintegration' is a term specifically used by Chisinau, whereas Tiraspol's equivalent term is 'unification'. In this book, these terms are used when they are the terms of the agents and actors discussed or relate to their specific approaches. A third term, *reunification*, is used as the most neutral term meant to avoid such political connotations.

162 The EU lacks instruments to oversee that Tiraspol takes steps towards fulfilment of the conditions that bring it closer to a free trade area with the EU. See Stanislav Secrieru, 'Transnistria Zig-zagging towards a DCFTA'. The Action Plan for the visa liberalization agreement was agreed in 2011 and entered into force in September 2014. By summer 2016, about 100,000 of Transnistria's 555,000 residents had utilized the freedom of movement within the Schengen area allowed by this agreement. See 'Iulian Groza: The

current political climate is not favoring an advancement in the relations with the EU', *Synthesis and Foreign Policy Debates, APE/FES, Newsletter* 6, June 2016.
163 'Speech by President Barroso: "European Union and Moldova: a Journey to Share"', Chisinau, 30 November 2012. Available at http://europa.eu/rapid/press-release_SPEECH-12-888_en.htm (accessed 8 December 2017).
164 *Synthesis and Foreign Policy Debates, APE/FES, Newsletter* 5 June 2017, p. 1. In 2017, the share of the EU in Moldova's exports was 63 per cent.
165 The re-elections in July 2009 followed the dissolution of the parliament in mid-June, which was the consequence of the fraud allegations and violent demonstrations related to the elections earlier in April. The re-elections were won by the combined forces of four opposition parties (the Liberal Party, the Liberal Democratic Party, the Democratic Party and the party alliance Our Moldova) by a 5 per cent margin over the ruling Communist Party, which gained 48 mandates in the 101-seat parliament.
166 See Cristian Ghinea and Victor Chirila, 'EU–Moldova negotiations: What is to be discussed, what could be achieved?'
167 'Speech by President Barroso: "European Union and Moldova"', cited above.
168 Ibid.
169 'We are not negotiating with the oligarchs-owned organizations – the Liberal Democratic Party, Democratic Party, Liberal Party and Iurie Leanca bloc. The Party of Socialists does not wish to enter into a coalition with the thieves, gangsters, oligarchs and unionists [i.e. supporters of *Unire*, Moldova's unification with Romania]' (Igor Dodon, quoted in 'Socialists going to demand repeated voting of second round in Chisinau', *Infotag*, 1 July 2015. Available at http://www.infotag.md/politics-en/205722/ (accessed 24 November 2017). See also: 'Socialist MPs Draft Documents on Fulfilling Protesters' Demands', *Infotag*, 5 October 2015. Available at http://www.infotag.md/politics-en/210086/ (accessed 24 November 2017); 'Moldovan Socialists take course for integration into Customs Union', *Infotag*, 29 September 2014. Available at http://www.infotag.md/economics-en/193709/ (accessed 24 November 2017). The bank scandal in 2015 strengthened also the Partidul Nostru ('Our Party'), whose profile centres around its leader Renato Usatii, mayor of the city of Balti, where the electorate consists of mainly Russian speakers.
170 Ministry of Foreign Affairs of the Russian Federation, 'Transcript of Remarks and Response to Media Questions by Russian Minister of Foreign Affairs Sergey Lavrov at Press Conference Following Talks with Republic of Moldova Leaders, Chisinau, 24 February 2009', 25 February 2009 (296-25-02-2009). Available at http://www.mid.ru/en/main_en (accessed 14 October 2017).
171 In December 2014, the estimated number of Moldovan citizens residing abroad was 984,000, 55.9 per cent of them in Russia. See International Organization for Migration, Mission to the Republic of Moldova,

'Extended Migration Profile of the Republic of Moldova 2009–2014' (2017), pp. 20–1, 82. Available at http://www.iom.md (accessed 20 November 2017). Two years earlier the corresponding numbers were 820,222 people and 60.8 per cent (European Training Foundation, 'Migrant Support Measures from an Employment and Skills Perspective (MISMES), The Republic of Moldova' (May 2015), pp. 4, 6. Available at http://www.etf.europa.eu/ (accessed 20 November 2017). In 2013, the number of illegal workers from Moldova in Russia was estimated to be about 190,000. See Kamil Calus, 'Russian Announces New Sanctions Against Moldova', *OSW Analyses*, 2 October 2013. Available at https://www.osw.waw.pl/ (accessed 23 November 2017). The numbers given by Russian sources are around quarter of a million.

172 The Iasi–Ungheni pipeline from Romania to Chisinau financed by the European Union, the European Investment Bank and the European Bank for Reconstruction and Development is Moldova's main alternative to Russian gas. The prospect of reducing the dependence on Russian gas is dependent on the extent to which Romania itself will be able to reduce its gas imports from Russia.

173 In March 2011 Moldova and Russia agreed to divide this debt. A sum of US$300 million was designated as Moldova's responsibility while 2.1 billion remained as Transnistria's responsibility. By 2017 these sums had risen to US$500 million and US$6 billion, respectively. The decisions of the International Commercial Arbitration Court at the Chamber of Commerce of the Russian Federation support Gazprom. The company has not collected the debt.

174 During 2009–16 Moldova had seven different prime ministers. The Alliance for European Integration reformed itself in new elections and continued in the government as a Coalition for Pro-European Governance (May 2013–February 2015).

175 'Moldovan Acting President Satisfied with Recent CIS Summit in Moscow', *Moldova.Org* [May 2010], no date. Available at http://www.moldova.org/en/moldovan-acting-president-satisfied-with-recent-cis-summit-in-moscow-208861-eng/ (accessed 24 November 2017).

176 Aaron M. Hoffman uses sensitivity and vulnerability as the key notions in conceptualizing trust in the study of international relations (Aaron M. Hoffman, 'A Conceptualization of Trust in International Relations'). About the notion of trust in classical sociology, see Guido Möllering, 'The Nature of Trust: From Georg Simmel to a Theory of Expectation, Interpretation and Suspension'.

177 Some forty-six trucks and several rail cars with bottled and bulk wine were reportedly impounded at the *Solntsevo* customs office near Moscow after the controversial decree. Russia's chief sanitary official remarked that Moldovan wine could be used 'to paint fences'. He claimed that between 30 June and 2 July (2010) experts found dangerous substance such as

dibutylphthalate in the wine of three Moldovan producers. Independent Russian sources revealed that neither the Moldovan authorities nor the importers of Moldovan wines had received a laboratory test confirmation of the claim; among these voices was the director of a Russian wine importing company *Iantarnaia Grozd* who confirmed that no analyses for dibutylphthalate had been made. Chemists from the Moldovan Academy of Sciences analysed 180 wine specimens showing that the dibutylphthalate content is several times lower than in the potable water in cities. See 'Moscow Suspends Wine Talks with Moldova', *Radio The Voice of Russia/Sputnik News*, 14 July 2010. Available at https://sputniknews.com/voiceofrussia/2010/07/14/12305595.html (accessed 24 November 2017).

178 Reactions from Russia's Ministry of Foreign Affairs and the State Duma stated that this was an element of 'a pre-planned political campaign spearheaded against Russian–Moldovan partnership' and that the decree was a 'distortion of historical facts'. The State Duma also expressed its concerns that Moldova is becoming a source of 'regional instability' and 'political unpredictability'. Yuri Luzhkov, the mayor of the city of Moscow, admonished the people in Russia to boycott Moldovan goods. Ghimpu replied by making references to the 'will of the Moldovan people' and saying that the fate of the Moldovan nation counts more than 'a few apples and carrots'. See 'Moldovan Leader Defiant in "Soviet Occupation" Row With Russia', *RFE/RL*, 2 July 2010. Available at https://www.rferl.org/a/Moldovan_Leader_Defiant_In_Soviet_Occupation_Row_With_Russia/2089272.html (accessed 24 November 2017).

179 Serafim Urechean, the leader of the party alliance Our Moldova, argued that Ghimpu's policies not only tarnished relations with Russia but also increased the complexities in settling the conflict over Transnistria. Marian Lupu (Democratic Party) likewise emphasized the importance of relations with Russia. The statement of Deputy Prime Minister Victor Osipov upon return from Moscow was that the Russian reaction had been prematurely 'emotional' and that the situation would calm down and not give reasons for further concern in Moldova. See 'Moldovan Official: Russia Won't Act Harshly Over Anti-Soviet Holiday', *RFE/RL*, 7 July 2010. Available at http://www.rferl.org/content/Moldovan_Official_Russia_Wont_Act_Harshly_Over_AntiSoviet_Holiday/2093374.html (accessed 24 November 2017).

180 Since 2009 the Communists, who were the majority party in the parliament, were able to block the election of the president (61 votes in the 101-seat parliament were required). Marian Lupu (Democratic Party) served as the acting president (2010–2), and it was not until spring 2012 when a compromise could be found and Nicolae Timofti was elected as the president. Igor Dodon, who won in the second round of voting in November 2016, is Moldova's first president elected by a popular vote. A referendum to change the Constitution to introduce popular vote had

been organized already twice (in 1999 and in 2010), but the number of participants on both occasions remained too low for the vote to be valid.
181 Interview of Prime Minister Vladimir Filat with *Komsomol'skaia Pravda, Moldova* ('Vladimir Filat: "Ia slishkom uvazhaiu Vladimira Putina i sebia, chtoby dopustit" deshevye piar-triuki'", by Roman Vladimirov) 10 April 2010. Available at https://www.kp.md/daily/24471/630205/ (accessed 6 December 2017).
182 'Moldova's New Government Wants to Cooperate with Russia – Prime Minister', *TASS*, 4 February 2016. Available at http://tass.com/world/854634 (accessed 29 November 2017).
183 The ban in 2014 included fruit only, whereas the bans in 2006 and in 2013 were about wine, fruit and vegetables. Similar claims in 2010 did not bring an actual ban.
184 The customs procedures introduced by Moldova in 2003 required that only the companies registered in Chisinau were allowed in Transnistria. The decision of Moldovan authorities earlier in August 2001 to withdraw customs stamps from the businesses in Transnistria was interpreted in Transnistria as a 'customs blockade' and brought the negotiations on the conflict to a halt for several months. The customs documentation introduced in autumn 2001 continued a dispute from 1996 when the agreement on customs established a Moldovan customs office in Tiraspol (staffed by Transnistrians) and provided for eventual joint Moldovan–Transnistrian customs and border posts to function along the Ukrainian border (Hill, *Russia, the Near Abroad, and the West*, p. 55). The agreement in 1996 enabled Transnistrian business to expand foreign trade but left Chisinau dissatisfied with the implementation of the concept of 'joint' control.
185 The legal basis of EUBAM is a Memorandum of Understanding signed by the European Commission, the government of Moldova and the government of Ukraine in November 2005. The mandate of the EUBAM has been extended in 2007, 2009, 2011 and 2015 (www.eubam.org).
186 Svetlana Gamova, 'Medvedev i Ianukovich otkroiut Pridnestrov'e', *Nezavisimaya Gazeta*, 13 May 2010. Available at http://www.ng.ru/cis/2010-05-13/1_pridnestr.html (accessed 29 November 2017).
187 Joint Statement of Presidents of Ukraine and Russia, Kyiv 17 May 2010. President of Ukraine, available at http://www.president.gov.ua/en/news/17177.html (accessed 20 May 2010) (document no longer available).

Chapter 6

188 The Principality of Moldova was established around 1359 and became the vassal state of the Ottoman Empire in 1504.

189 Bender is situated on the security zone and formally under the control of the Joint Control Commission, which has its headquarters there. It is historically a part of Bessarabia. While the PMR de facto controls Bender, eleven villages on the left bank are under Chisinau's control. Bender is also known as Bendery and Tighina. Bendery is the Russian and Ukrainian form of the name given by the Ottomans. Tighina is the historical name used during Romanian rule.
190 Russia took the territories of Transnistria, Crimea and neighbouring areas in contemporary eastern Ukraine from the Ottoman rulers during the last decades of the eighteenth century. During the same period, in 1775, the northern parts of Moldova were annexed to the Austrian Empire under the name of Bukovyna. Russian power was introduced to the region several decades earlier when the Moldavian ruler Dmitrii Cantemir requested the help of Tsar Peter the Great in a battle against the Turks (1710–1) and a 'union treaty' allegedly was signed on 13 April 1711.
191 Ivan Katchanovski, *Cleft Countries: Regional Political Divisions and Cultures in Post-Soviet Ukraine and Moldova*.
192 'Transdnestr Calls for Union with Russia', *The Moscow Times*, 31 August 2010. Available at https://themoscowtimes.com/news/transdnestr-calls-for-union-with-russia-1043 (accessed 24 November 2017).
193 'Moldova' is the Romanian form of 'Moldavia' in the name of the medieval principality. 'Besarabia' comes from 'Basarab', 'father ruler'.
194 This area remained wholly within Russian rule. The only exception were the decades from the Crimean War (1853–6) to the Berlin Congress (1878), during which time two districts were joined to Moldova under Ottoman rule.
195 The event turned out as a coup. It had developed as an uprising by indigenous peasants and soldiers who had grown tired of fighting for the empire's elites on the fronts of the First World War.
196 The area of the Moldovan ASSR (1924–40) consisted of the left bank of the Dniestr and nine districts in present-day Ukraine. The capital was Balta (which presently belongs to Ukraine) and, since 1931, Tiraspol.
197 The only exception to the long rule of the Cyrillic alphabet in Transnistria is a short period of time during the mid-1930s (Katchanovski, *Cleft Countries*, 140–2).
198 This language, following the older historical term used in Bessarabia, is called 'Moldavian'. 'Moldovan' is the Romanian form.
199 Olga Filippova, 'Dimensions of Transnistrian Identity in Present-day Political Developments'.
200 Nationalist sentiments, as a part of the European influences, had grown primarily in the western parts of Bessarabia during the nineteenth century.
201 Katchanovski, *Cleft Countries*, pp. 152–3.
202 The possible political significance of this connection remains unknown, because the business-level document material from these years has not

Notes 265

been found. Any such material may well have been destroyed during the years of political uncertainty which culminated in the coup attempt in Moscow in 1993.

203 The Gagauz' ancestors had migrated to Bessarabia from the Dobrudja area (located in today's Romania and Bulgaria) during the eighteenth and nineteenth centuries (Katchanovski, *Cleft Countries*, 65–6). It remains unclear if the Gagauz are historically a Christianized Turkic people or linguistically Turkicized Christians who lived in the above-mentioned regions.

204 About the law on the Procedures for Resolving Questions Related to the Secession of Union Republics from the USSR (3 April 1990), see endnote 83 (chapter 1), p. 251.

205 As a sign of this continuity, the flag of the PMR is the same that had represented the Moldavian Soviet Socialist Republic.

206 In Transnistria the vote for the preservation of the Soviet Union was more than 93 per cent. In Gagauzia it was 82 per cent.

207 When communicating the Moldovan aspirations of independence to Moscow, Mircea Snegur is reported to have received the answer: 'Moldova may declare its independence. But there are three independent states in Moldova.' Nurshan A. Guliyev, 'Transnistrian Conflict: The Complicated Problem Which Is Seen Easy-Report', 8 June 2010, *APA* (Baku). Available at http://en.apa.az/ (accessed 13 December 2017).

208 Filippova, 'Dimensions of Transnistrian Identity', pp. 45–8.

209 In October 1990, after the Gagauz had proclaimed their autonomous republic that was meant to be part of the USSR, Moldova's Popular Front gathered up to 30,000 volunteers to be sent to return Gagauzia under Chisinau's central control. The violent confrontation was prevented by the order of Mircea Snegur, at that time Chairman of the Supreme Soviet of the Moldavian SSR, and the concomitant signs that troops from the base in Transnistria were to interfere. In a referendum organized in December 1991 95 per cent of Gagauzia's voters were in favour of independence from Moldova. Based on an agreement negotiated with the government in Chisinau in 1994, Gagauzia (Gagauz-Yeri) was established as an autonomous-territorial unit which has a legal code of its own and is 'an integrant and inalienable part of the Republic of Moldova' (Constitution of the Republic of Moldova, 29 July 1994, Article 111).

Chapter 7

210 Lebed commanded the reorganized 14th army in Transnistria from June 1992 to June 1994, when he resigned from the army to start a political career. Lebed was known as a '*gosudarstvennik*' (a person supporting etatist policies based on the idea of a strong state), which won him the third place

in the Russian presidential elections in 1996. He died in a helicopter crash in 2002 under unclear circumstances.
211 The peacekeeping operation started in the same month, on 29 July 1992.
212 Lynch, *The Conflict in Abkhazia*, p. 9.
213 The OSCE office was opened in April 1993. In 1995 a liaison office was set up in Tiraspol.
214 A decision to establish a special CSCE Mission in Moldova was made by the ministerial summit of the CSCE in Stockholm in December 1992. This summit also called for withdrawal of the Russian troops from Transnistria.
215 The ceasefire agreement of 21 July 1992 is available in English and in Russian at http://mfa-pmr.org/en/ (accessed 12 December 2017). The initial composition of the Russian military contingent included six battalions, a helicopter squadron (Mi-8, 6 units; and Mi-24, 4 units) and a mobile group of the 138th separate regiment of intercommunication Supreme High Command (a total of 3,100 military personnel).
216 An equivalent number of officers with the status of military observers had been included in the units of Russia, Moldova and Transnistria in 1992.
217 In the PMR, military service based on conscription is 18 months. The number of troops in the armed forces is estimated to be 5,000–7,500. In the Republic of Moldova this number is about 6,000 (2013).
218 The Operational Group of Russian Forces in the PMR in 2017 is reportedly 1,200 in number and consists of the 8th Motorized Infantry Brigade and an anti-aircraft missile regiment. One battalion (approx. 400 troops) of the Operational Group are peacekeepers established on the basis of the ceasefire agreement in 1992 (Cristi Vlas, 'Peacekeeping Mission in Transnistria Turns 25, Russia Ambassador: Ending This Mission Would Lead to Another Conflict', *Moldova.Org* [July/August 2017], no date. Available at http://www.moldova.org/en/peacekeeping-mission-transnistria-turns-25-russia-ambassador-ending-mission-lead-another-conflict/ (accessed 24 November 2017).
219 Since the 1990s, the tasks of the Russian troops in Colbasna (on the Ukrainian border) have included guarding the 20,000 tons of largely Soviet-era ammunition and weaponry deposits.
220 A young man was lethally wounded by a peacekeeper in the Russian contingent on 1 January 2012. The victim was a resident of a village on the eastern side of the Dniestr River and refused to stop at the military's command at a road block outside Transnistria's de facto borderline. The military man who fired the deadly shots was a local Transnistrian.
221 Following the model developed by the OSCE on the basis of the inaugural CSCE summit in 1975, the work was divided in three 'baskets': (1) economic and environmental issues; (2) humanitarian and civil society issues, including development of the jurisdictional infrastructure; and (3) conflict settlement and security. In economic issues, revision of the banking sector to implement international rules became a priority.

Other priorities were transportation, telecommunications and education. The technical work was organized in eleven working groups. While the technical cooperation (on fields such as meteorology, environmental issues, telecommunications and transport) established a connection, the political dialogue did not advance. The PMR and Russia together declared that they were not prepared to start negotiations on issues in the conflict resolution and security basket. Chisinau in its turn held to the point that the negotiations concerning the different baskets must be parallel, because it is impossible to advance in the technical issues without a vision of the political goal. (Eugen Carpov, Deputy Prime Minister for Reintegration, presentation (in written) at the Conference 'Increasing the role of Civil Societies in promoting Confidence-Building Measures (CBM) in the areas of "frozen conflicts,"' organized by the Foreign Policy Association of Moldova (APE), Chisinau, 31 October 2012.)

222 In April 2014 negotiations were ceased. The PMR and Russia accused Ukraine and Moldova of holding a blockade against Transnistria.

223 See interview of Nina Shtanski, Foreign Minister of the PMR, with *The Irish Times* ('Thaw in Relations Gives Sense of Hope in Moldovan Conflict', by Daniel McLaughlin), 25 September 2012. Available at https://www.irishtimes.com/ (accessed 25 November 2017). According to Moldovan data from December 2016, 2150 Transnistrian businesses are registered with Chisinau. The trade with the right bank accounts for 40 per cent of the trade exchange, and 65 per cent of the exports are to the EU area ('George Balan: We Need a Roadmap for Development of a Special Legal Status for the Transnistrian Region', *Synthesis and Foreign Policy Debates*, APE/ FES, Newsletter 11, December 2016).

224 Substantive elements of settlement met disagreement from both parties. Among other things, the idea for a compromise that Chisinau would change its law from July 2005 and Tiraspol, in its turn, would abandon the referendum of September 2006 angered both of these parties.

225 Tiraspol explained its withdrawal from the negotiations in spring 2014 by referring to Chisinau's use of 'pressuring tactics'. The Protocol of Intent, which was agreed in the '5+2' negotiations in Berlin in July 2016, agreed about the recognition of Transnistrian license plates for vehicles and the inclusion of the degrees of the Tiraspol State University amongst the foreign degrees recognized (with in casu conditions) in Moldova.

226 Ministry of Foreign Affairs of the Russian Federation, 'Transcript of Remarks and Response to Media Questions by Russian Foreign Minister Sergey Lavrov at Joint Press Conference with Ukrainian Foreign Minister Kostiantyn Hryshchenko after the Russia–Ukraine Interstate Commission International Cooperation Subcommittee Meeting, Odessa, June 4, 2011', 4 June 2011 (841-04-06-2011). Available at http://www.mid.ru/en/main_en (accessed 14 December 2017).

227 See, for example, E. Shevchuk's report (in written) at the conference 'Ways to Solve the Moldovan–Transnistrian conflict – Views from Both Banks of the Dniestr' (Institute of International Relations–Chatham House, London, 24 May 2006) as cited in Anatol Gudim, 'Transnistria: Conflicts and Pragmatism of the Economy'. Available at https://core.ac.uk/download/pdf/11870249.pdf (accessed 29 November 2017).

228 The 'Primakov Memorandum' was signed by the two conflict parties and confirmed by the signatures of the three mediators (Russia, Ukraine, the OSCE) in Moscow on 8 May 1997. It is also called the Moscow Memorandum.

229 'Transdniestria Blames Kiev for Helping Moldova to Blockade Region', *TASS*, 13 July 2016. Available at http://tass.com/world/887916 (accessed 12 December, 2017).

230 In the next year, Gagauzia was granted autonomy on the same basis.

231 Constitution of the Republic of Moldova (1994), Article 11. Available at Presidency of the Republic of Moldova at http://www.presedinte.md/eng/constitution (accessed 14 December 2017).

232 Organization for Security and Cooperation in Europe, CSCE Budapest Document 1994, 'Towards a Genuine Partnership in a New Era', 21 December 1994. Available at https://www.osce.org/ (accessed 30 November 2017).

233 The translation of the term *vseob"emliushchee politicheskoe uregulirovanie* is 'all-inclusive political settlement'. Instead of 'all-inclusive' Russian diplomatic practices use the word 'comprehensive'.

234 Organization for Security and Cooperation in Europe, 'Istanbul Document', 19 November 1999. Available at https://www.osce.org/ (accessed 2 December 2017).

235 Estonia, Latvia, Lithuania, Slovenia, Slovakia, Bulgaria and Romania had been invited to membership talks in the Prague summit in 2002. Earlier in 1999 Poland, Hungary and the Czech Republic had become members. Albania and Croatia joined in April 2009.

236 Pavel Stroilov, 'Revealed: The Kremlin Files Which Prove that NATO Never Betrayed Russia', *The Spectator*, 6 September 2014. Available at http://www.spectator.co.uk/2014/09/russias-nato-myth/ (accessed 29 November 2017).

237 By autumn 2012 it could be concluded that this high-level dialogue was not able to achieve more than to repeat the notion of the 'special status' for Transnistria. Chisinau managed to gain from the 'Merkel–Medvedev dialogue' practical reassurances about its path to the EU, but the suggestion about a federal model for Moldova, to which Germany had wished to give a new boost, was left to the side. Since 2009, the German foreign ministry has convened annual conferences in Bavaria, Germany, on trust- and confidence-building measures between the Republic of Moldova and Transnistria.

238 'Joint Declaration Adopted Following Talks between President of the Russian Federation Dmitry Medvedev, and President of the Republic of Moldova Vladimir Voronin and Head of Transdniestria Igor Smirnov, Barvikha, March 18, 2009', 18 March 2009 (431-18-03-2009). Available at http://www.mid.ru/en/main_en (accessed 29 November 2017).

239 'Working Trip to the Republic of Moldova by Deputy Minister of Foreign Affairs/State Secretary Grigory Karasin', Press release, 21 January 2010. Available at http://www.mid.ru/en/main_en (49-21-01-2010) (accessed 26 November 2017).

240 The OSCE PA Oslo Declaration (6–10 July 2010) 'Invites all participants in the Transnistrian conflict settlement to undertake consultations with a view to transforming the current peacekeeping mechanism into a multinational civilian mission under the international (OSCE) mandate'. The political context of this declaration is the joint statement signed by presidents Medvedev and Yanukovich earlier on 17 May and Prime Minister Filat's response to it, which repeated the demand about Russia's military withdrawal and the transformation of the peacekeeping mission into a civilian mission. See 'While Chisinau Asks Russia to Pull Out Its Troops from Moldova, Tiraspol Demands More', *Moldova.Org* [May 2010], no date. Available at http://www.moldova.org/en/while-chisinau-asks-rusisa-to-pull-out-its-troops-from-moldova-tiraspol-demands-more-209086-eng/ (accessed 24 November 2017).

241 Ukraine has consistently supported the reunification of Transnistria with Moldova. During the presidency of Victor Yushchenko this goal was promoted by developing the cooperation between Ukraine, Moldova and Romania. Although Yanukovich did not continue this policy, his clear priority was a reintegrated Moldova rather than the future of Transnistria (on Ukraine's border) in close connection with Russia.

242 About the central role of the withdrawal issue in the US policies on Moldova, see, for example, Alla Rosca, 'The US Factor in the Transnistrian Conflict's Settlement'.

243 'Working Trip to the Republic of Moldova by Deputy Minister of Foreign Affairs/State Secretary Grigory Karasin', Press release, 21 January 2010. Available at http://www.mid.ru/en/main_en (49-21-01-2010) (accessed 26 November 2017).

244 The dates of signing and ratifying the treaty are 19 November 2001, and 29 April 2002, respectively.

245 In the Western diplomatic practices, the text context is not similarly immediately present in the locutionary act of speaking but must be unfolded through the political context in which the statements have practical implications.

246 Examples from the Soviet times include the discussion of human rights–related issues in terms of abstract principles, detaching them from the context of application which the Soviet Union in its diplomatic

communications sought to establish. For example, in connection with the CSCE 1975 Act the Soviet delegation added specific explanations (in the form of the speeches given on the occasion) to the protocol in order to explain how Moscow intended to apply the principles agreed with the Western states. Osmo Apunen analyses how the Soviet Union, among other things, gave emphasis to political agreement and the positive function of the application of the principles in the 'Helsinki Act' in relations between the signatory states (Osmo Apunen, 'The Principles of Relations between the States of Europe', see esp. p. 44). By contrast to the Western states, which emphasize the letter of the principles (and in this way their freedom to interpret them in a wide range of political contexts), the focus of the Soviet Union was the process that the application of the principles generate.

247 Ricoeur, *Hermeneutics*, passim, esp. p. 141.
248 The Russian translation of 'unitary' is *edinichnyi* (or *unitarnyi*), i.e. the content is slightly different from *edinyi* ('unified'), which also is derived from 'unity' (*edinstvo*).
249 Ministry of Foreign Affairs of the Russian Federation, 'Concerning Transnistrian Conflict Settlement', Press release, 14 June 2011 (872-14-06-2011). Available at http://www.mid.ru/en/main_en (accessed 2 December 2017).
250 Ministry of Foreign Affairs of the Russian Federation, 'Comment of the Information and Press Department of the MFA of Russia in connection with the 15th anniversary since signing Memorandum on the Bases for Normalization of Relations between the Republic of Moldova and Transnistria', 15 May 2012 (975-15-05-2012). Available at http://www.mid.ru/en/main_en (accessed 29 November 2017).
251 'Russia and Ukraine Going to Do All in Their Powers to Help Resolve Transnistrian Conflict', *Infotag*, 16 February 2012. Available at http://www.infotag.md/news-en/593498/ (accessed 25 November 2017). The standard diplomatic position on the points of departure in the conflict settlement can be illustrated by the communiqué which the Ukrainian president Viktor Yanukovich gave, after having met with the OSCE chairman in office, the Kazakh Foreign Minister Kanat Saudabayev. The communiqué states that Ukraine will support the independence, sovereignty and territorial integrity of the Republic of Moldova, while Transnistria will be offered the special status of autonomy. The 'special status' – but now with the specification that it is to have political and economic dimensions – was a few weeks later repeated in the joint statement of 17 May (2010) with Medvedev.
252 The classic text about speech acts is John L. Austin's *How to Do Things with Words*.
253 Ministry of Foreign Affairs of the Russian Federation, 'Transcript of Remarks and Response to Media Questions by Russian Minister of Foreign

Affairs Sergey Lavrov at Press Conference Following Talks with Republic of Moldova Leaders', Chisinau, 24 February 2009. Available at http://www.mid.ru/en/main_en (accessed 15 December 2017).

254 Lionel Ponsard takes note of this feature and considers it as a 'tactic aimed at gradually coercing the interlocutor to alter his position' (quoted in Pouliot, *International Security in Practice*, p. 137).

255 The title of the treaty of October 1994 is 'Agreement on the Legal Status, Terms and Conditions of Withdrawal of Elements of the Armed Forces of the Russian Federation Temporarily Stationed on the Territory of the Republic of Moldova'.

256 Council of Europe, Parliamentary Assembly, 22 May 1995, Doc. 7278 Revised, Report on the application by Moldova for membership of the Council of Europe (part D.b.). Available at http://assembly.coe.int/nw/xml/XRef/X2H-Xref-ViewHTML.asp?FileID=6851 (accessed 13 October 2017). See also Victoria Boian, 'Republic of Moldova's Security Context: Challenges and Future Perspectives', pp. 15–16.

257 Hill, *Russia, the Near Abroad, and the West*, pp. 55–6.

258 Evegenii Primakov, *Mir bez Rossii? K chemu vedet politicheskaia blizorukost'*, pp. 197–8. The concept of 'the common state' within the borders of the Moldavian Soviet Socialist Republic in January 1990 was included in the State Duma Ruling of 19 February 1999 (N 3689-II GD), which became the official starting point for the settlement process that produced the Kozak plan of 2003.

259 Hill, *Russia, the Near Abroad, and the West*, pp. 54–5.

260 The Russian-language version of the Memorandum on Basic Principles of State Structure of the United State (*Memorandum ob osnovnykh printsipakh gosudarstvennogo ustroistva ob"edinennogo gosudarstva*) has been published by Regnum. See 'Memorandum Kozaka: Rossiiskii plan ob"edineniia Moldovy i Pridnestrov'ia', *Regnum*, 23 May 2005. Available at https://regnum.ru/news/458547.html (accessed 15 September 2017). The English-language version (23 November 2003), which has been translated by the OSCE Mission to Moldova, can be found as an appendix in Hill, *Russia, the Near Abroad, and the West*. This last-mentioned version uses the term 'unified state' in the title of the memorandum and with reference to the planned Moldovan state (items 2, 3), whereas the translation in Russia of the Russian-language term in the memorandum – *ob"edinennoe gosudarstvo* – is 'united state'. These two terms are not mutually synonymous in Russian: 'united state' (*ob"edinennoe gosudarstvo*) suggests voluntary association of initially separate (territorial) entities, whereas 'unified state' (*edinoe gosudarstvo*) denotes unity and oneness (*edinstvo*) as a social quality of the state. Arguably the usage of both terms is the result of political compromises. However, the semantic logic of association based on certain unifying structures which ideally represent the unity of the different entities – i.e. the argument that justifies a federal state structure – is lost in the Western translation. (Cf. the translation of *Edinaia Rossiia* as

'United Russia' while the version 'Unified Russia' also appears.) However, it must be noticed that 'unified state' in the English translation of the Kozak plan arguably finds correspondence with the Romanian translation.
261 Hill, *Russia, the Near Abroad, and the West*, p. 152.
262 'Pridnestrov'e v NATO ne poidet, zaiavil Lavrov', *RIA Novosti*, 9 December 2012. Available at http://ria.ru/world/20121209/914035621.html (accessed 29 November 2017).
263 The English-language text as translated by the OSCE Mission to Moldova (see endnote 260) of this item (3.16) in the plan uses slightly different words: 'in the event of a decision about the Federation's *annexation* to another state being taken' and 'on the grounds of the Federation's complete *forfeiture* of its sovereignty' (italics added).

Chapter 8

264 This document, titled 'The Mediators' Document' (no date), is attached to Hill, *Russia, the Near Abroad, and the West* as Appendix A.
265 A summarizing study is *Transnistrian Problem: A View from Ukraine* by the Strategic and Security Studies Group (Kyiv, 2009).
266 Hikmet Hajizadeh, 'Azerbaijan: Regional Integration in an Explosive Region and the Next Ten Years of the South Caucasus'.
267 'Ghimpu: Transnistria Settlement is Impossible without Russian Troop Withdrawal', *Infotag* (*Moldova Azi*), 28 April 2010. Available at http://www.azi.md/en/story/10917 (accessed 25 November 2017).
268 Concomitantly with the confirmation of its security policy which excluded membership in a military alliance ('non-bloc policy'), Ukraine extended the lease for Russia's Black Sea fleet base at Crimea until 2042 and joined the integrated air defence system of the CSTO as a non-member. In exchange for the improved relations with Russia Ukraine gained a thirty per cent discount on Russian gas.
269 Vladimir Socor argues that the Russo–Ukrainian guarantees, which Russia was able to emphasize after Victor Yanukovich became president, are an invention of Evgenii Primakov from the 1990s. See Vladimir Socor, 'Moscow Meeting Fails to Re-Launch 5+2 Negotiations on Transnistria Conflict'.
270 President of Ukraine, 'Joint Statement of Presidents of Ukraine and Russia', Kyiv, 17 May 2010. Available at http://www.president.gov.ua/en/news/17177.html (accessed 20 May 2010, document no longer available). The 'common space' is an official translation. Commentators on the joint statement sometimes use the term 'unified space' instead.
271 'The Moscow Memorandum' ('Memorandum on the Bases for Normalization of Relations between the Republic of Moldova and Transdniestria') of 8 May 1997 is available at http://mfa-pmr.org/en/

(accessed 12 December 2017). The 'Odessa Agreement' ('Agreement on Confidence Measures and Development of Contacts between Republic of Moldova and Transdniestria') of 20 March 1998, is available at https://www.osce.org/ (accessed 14 December 2017).
272 Ministry of Foreign Affairs of the Russian Federation, 'Comment of the Information and Press Department of the MFA of Russia in Connection with the 15th Anniversary since Signing Memorandum on the Bases for Normalization of Relations between the Republic of Moldova and Transnistria', 15 May 2012 (975-15-05-2012). Available at http://www.mid.ru/en/main_en (accessed 29 November 2017).
273 These words have appeared multiple times in Moldovan discussions and presumably were coined by Oazu Nantoi, politician and analyst at the Institute for Public Policy in Chisinau.
274 Interview of Victor Osipov, Deputy Prime Minister of Moldova, with *European Dialogue* ('Moldovan Deputy PM: Transnistria Is a European Problem', by Georgi Gotev), 30 April 2010. Available at http://eurodialogue.org/Moldova-Deputy-PM-Transnistria-Is-A-European-Problem (accessed 24 November 2017).
275 'Igor Dodon Predicts Early Parliamentary Elections in Moldova', *Infotag*, 30 January 2015. Available at http://www.infotag.md/politics-en/198765/ (accessed 24 November 2017).
276 The Socialist Party of the Republic of Moldova, 'Concept Paper on the Fundamental Principles of the Moldovan Federation', 2013. Available at www.scribd.com/fullscreen/233369176?access_key=key-atkRfWTbvf3vD4kUQzqZ&allow_share=true&escape=false&view_mode=scroll (accessed 14 December 2017).
277 Both Russian and Moldovan languages have the status of a language of inter-ethnic communication; but Moldovan, in addition, is the only national language. See Pål Kolsto, *Political Construction Sites: Nation-Building in Russia and the Post-Soviet States*, pp. 138–51.
278 In an interview with *Ekho Moskvy* radio in May 2010, Yuri Lyanke, Moldova's Minister of Foreign Affairs and European Integration, stated that Moldova is 'a neutral non-bloc state' (*neitral'noe vneblokovoe gosudarstvo*). See transcript in *Press obozrenie* ('Moldova vystupaet za transformatsiiu mirotvorcheskogo kontingenta na Dnestre v Mezhdunarodnuiu missiiu grazhdanskikh nabliudatelei'), 28 May 2010. Available at http://press.try.md/item.php?id=113318 (accessed 7 December 2017).
279 An opinion poll in spring 2010 indicated that 19 per cent of Moldova's population supported joining NATO and 62 per cent supported joining the EU. See 'Most Moldovans Favor Accession to EU, Oppose NATO', *Moldova.Org*, 12 May 2010. Available at http://www.moldova.org/en/most-moldovans-favour-accession-to-eu-oppose-nato-208905-eng/ (accessed 25 November 2017). According to a barometer of public opinion in the end of 2017, 38 per cent were in favour of membership in the EU while 32 per cent supported

joining the EAEU (*Synthesis and Foreign Policy Debates, APE/ FES, Newsletter* 12, December 2017, p. 1).

280 The word 'compatriot' (*sootechestvennik za rubezhom*) combines a sense of togetherness with patriotism: a love with the fatherland (*otechestvo*) to be defended. (When the reference, by contrast, is the land of ancestors and home the word is *rodina*.)

281 The Mihail Kogalniceanu Air Base annexed to the US 86th Air Base is the central hub of a network of bases and training grounds for air, ground and naval forces. It is located on the grounds of the Soviet-time 34th Mechanized Brigade Base near the city of Constanta on the Black Sea Coast. It has functioned as a major centre for the US forward military operations, including the operations in Afghanistan after the US base in Kyrgyzstan was closed in spring 2014.

282 'Nado nashim vlastiam podumat', prezhde chem prinimat' kakie-to rezkie shagi v otnoshenii Pridnestrov'ia. Zhelaiushchie "obmeniat'" nepriznannuiu respubliku v ocherednoi raz nastupiat na grabli' (*Kommersant Plus*, 'Pridnestrov'e – forpost dlia protivodeistviia okruzheniiu Rossii', 13 May 2011. Available at http://www.km.press.md/index.php/russia/3638-2011-05-13-20-23-20.html (accessed 1 June 2011) (link no longer working).

283 In 2012, Moldova and Romania signed an agreement about military cooperation, which deals with a range of activities, including joint participation in exercises, training and cooperating in information sharing.

284 Moldova joined the North Atlantic Cooperation Council in 1992 and the Partnership for Peace program in 1994. Beginning 2014, it participated in the NATO force in Kosovo.

285 'Moldova: Transnistria Welcomes Russian Missiles', *Vox europ* (original source: *Jurnalul de Chisinau*), 16 February 2010. Available at http://www.voxeurop.eu/en/content/news-brief/191551-transnistria-welcomes-russian-missiles (accessed 14 December 2017).

286 Russia confirmed the permanent deployment of nuclear-capable Iskander-M missiles in Kaliningrad in early 2018. See Bruce Jones, 'Russian Duma Confirms Iskander-M Kaliningrad Deployment', *IHS Jane's Defence Weekly*, 8 February 2018. Available at http://www.janes.com/article/77745/russian-duma-confirms-iskander-m-kaliningrad-deployment (accessed 8 May 2018).

287 See 'Transdniestrian Leader: NATO Drills in Moldova Threaten Regional Stability', *TASS*, 20 May 2016. Available at http://tass.com/world/877290 (accessed 25 November 2017). Verbal conflict over military incidents has intensified after the war in Ukraine started in spring 2014. Tiraspol's protests against the visits of international inspection groups to the security zone on the basis of international agreements in the OSCE frame expressed the political sensitivities that were included in the participation of NATO member states in the visits to the security zone. The visits tasked

with inspection and exchange of information were claimed 'to penetrate into PMR military objects' and to be 'uncoordinated' because the consent of the PMR to carry out them was not asked. In February 2012, the visit of a Canadian group together with Moldovan military officers in the security zones prompted such protest. See 'Transnistrian Foreign Ministry Frowns on Uncoordinated Inspection Attempts', *Infotag*, 9 February 2012. Available at http://www.infotag.md/news-en/593384/ (accessed 25 November 2017).

288 Other examples of the same communication pattern are the suggestions that the number of Russia's peacekeepers should be raised and the military equipment increased in Transnistria. Oleg Belyakov, the Transnistrian co-chairman in the Joint Control Commission (JCC) for the Transnistrian Conflict Settlement (until July 2016), made such arguments in May 2010 and again in May 2011 with reference to the need to keep the conflict local. See, for example, 'While Chisinau Asks Russia to Pull Out Its Troops from Moldova, Tiraspol Demands More'.

289 'Most Citizens of Moldova's Breakaway Region Call for Joining Russia – Poll', *TASS*, 17 June 2016. Available at http://tass.ru/en/world/882892 (accessed 14 December 2017).

290 See 'In Chisinau Considered Populism the Decree of the President of PMR on Implementation of the Outcome of the Referendum on Independence in Transnistria', *Last News from Russia*, 10 September 2016. Available at http://en.news-4-u.ru/in-chisinau-considered-populism-the-decree-of-the-president-of-pmr-on-implementation-of-the-outcome-of-the-referendum-on-independence-in-transnistria.html (accessed 14 December 2017).

Chapter 9

291 See 'Kommunal'nye platezhi v Pridnestrov'e snachitel'no vyrastut', *Dniester*, 18 May 2011. Available at http://dniester.ru/content/kommunalnye-platezhi-v-pridnestrove-znachitelno-vyrastut (accessed 14 December 2017).

292 The foreign policy concept of the PMR, ready to be adopted at the time of Gubarev's visit in Tiraspol in October 2012, mentions that 'integration processes in the CIS area, including involvement in the Customs Union of the Russian Federation, the Republic of Belarus and the Republic of Kazakhstan' is among the policy objectives of the PMR. See Ministry of Foreign Affairs of the Pridnestrovian Moldavian Republic, 'Foreign Policy Concept of the Pridnestrovian Moldavian Republic', 20 November 2012. Available at http://mfa-pmr.org/en/(accessed 26 November 2017).

293 'Transdniestrian President Thanks Russia for Humanitarian Aid', *TASS*, 6 July 2016. Available at http://tass.com/world/886673 (accessed 25 November 2017). About 'ANO "Evraziiskaia integratsiia"' (Autonomous

Nonprofit Organization Eurasian integration). Available at http://www.eurasianintegration.ru/?q=node/71 (accessed 25 November 2017).
294 In spring 2012, Farit Mukhametshin was appointed Russia's ambassador in Moldova. Mukhametshin's previous position was Director of the Federal Agency for the Commonwealth of Independent States, Compatriots Living Abroad and International Humanitarian Cooperation (commonly known in its abbreviation 'Rossotrudnichestvo').
295 Russia's Ministry of Foreign Affairs announced that a large number of the passports of the approximately 160,000 Russian citizens in Transnistria waited for renewal. Measures to open the consulate were taken in the next autumn ('Briefing of the Spokesman of Foreign Affairs of Russia A.K. Lukashevich, November 22, 2012' (2196-22-11-2012). Available at http://www.mid.ru/en/main_en (accessed 25 November 2017.)
296 Vladimir Socor, 'Rogozin Details Preconditions to Transnistria Conflict-Resolution'.
297 Ibid.
298 Jeffrey Mankoff rightly argues that the emphasis of multipolarity in Russian foreign policy is an expression of the 'concert' idea (Jeffrey Mankoff, *Russian Foreign Policy: The Return of Great Power Politics*, pp. 19–20).
299 When the goal of developing a joint conflict management process between the EU and Russia intensified the efforts to resolve the Transnistrian conflict in the summer of 2010, Russia gained a new possibility to see if this top-level political process – launched as the Medvedev–Merkel dialogue – would help it to establish political parity in Europe. Merkel introduced the metaphor of the 'Common European House' as a launch concept, an echo of Gorbachev's 'Common European Home'. Political parity in European security has been the persistent goal of Russian and previously Soviet foreign and security policy. The CSCE Act (the Helsinki Act) of 1975 was the first milestone in this respect. In February 1994, Yeltsin presented an idea of an all-European security architecture, in which European organizations would be responsible for geographical spheres under the auspices of the CSCE. The proposal was published in May 1994 in view of the CSCE session in Budapest in October 1994, but was not pressured further because it failed to receive support from the Western states. Much later, in June 2008, President Medvedev's proposal about a European Security Treaty (EST) argued that a legal frame was needed, because the experience of the past decades shows that a political consensus – the approach of the OSCE – is not sufficient.
300 'From Vancouver to Vladivostok' repeated the words of the vision about a zone of peace and security launched by the US Secretary of State James Baker at the OSCE Ministerial Council in June 1991 in Berlin. The decision of the Obama administration to place Standard SM-3 interceptor missiles in Romania and a radar system in Turkey (instead of the GBI interceptor missiles in full systems in Poland and a radar system in the Czech

Republic, which was the plan of the George W. Bush administration) reduces the threat of these systems for Russia, but simultaneously a new threat is presented by the development of the Prompt Global Strike system, which means that any target in the world is within one hour's reach for the United States.

301 'Lavrov Urges Discussion on Transdniestria Status as Part of United Moldova', *TASS*, 4 April 2016. Available at http://tass.ru/en/politics/866973 (accessed December 2017).

302 Organization for Security and Co-operation in Europe, 24th Meeting of the Ministerial Council, 'Ministerial Statement on the Negotiations on the Transdniestrian Settlement Process in the "5+2" Format' (MC.DOC/1/17), 8 December, 2017. Available at https://www.osce.org/ (accessed 24 June 2018).

303 United Nations General Assembly, 72nd session, 98th plenary meeting, A/RES/72/282 ('Resolution adopted by the General Assembly on 22 June 2018, Complete and unconditional withdrawal of foreign military forces from the territory of the Republic of Moldova', 26 June 2018). Available at http://www.un.org/en/ga/72/resolutions.shtml (accessed 7 August 2018).

304 Ibid. See also United Nations, Meetings Coverage and Press Releases, 'General Assembly Adopts Texts Urging Troop Withdraw from Republic of Moldova, Strengthening Cooperation in Central Asia' (GA/12030), 22 June 2018. Available at https://www.un.org/press/en/2018/ga12030.doc.htm (accessed 24 June 2018).

305 Stenogramma parlamentskikh slushanii Komiteta po delam SNG i sviaziam s sootechestvennikami na temu: 'O sostoianii uregulirovaniia konfliktov na territorii SNG i obrashcheniiakh k Rossiiskoi Federatsii o priznanii nezavisimosti Respubliki Abkhaziia, Respubliki Iuzhnaia Osetiia i Pridnestrovskoi Moldavskoi Respubliki'. Zdanie Gosudarstvennoi Dumy. Malyi zal. 13 marta 2008 goda. 15 chasov. Predsedatel'stvuet predsedatel' Komiteta po delam SNG i sviaziam s sootechestvennikami A.V. Ostrovskii. (The State Duma Committee for CIS Affairs and Relations with Compatriots, 'Verbatim Records of Parliamentary Hearings'.(document no longer accessible).

306 Vladimir Yastrebchak, Foreign Minister of the PMR, quoted in 'Transnistria's Appeal for Recognition to United Nations Is Illogical', *All Moldova*, 4 August 2010. Available at http://www.allmoldova.com/en/moldova-news/politics/1249047918.html (accessed 5 August 2010) (link no longer working). The title of the article reflects the opinions of Victor Osipov, Deputy Prime Minister of the Republic of Moldova, who also is quoted in the article. About the PMR's position, see also Ministry of Foreign Affairs of Pridnestrovian Moldavian Republic, 'Statement of the Foreign Ministry of the Transdniestrian Moldavian Republic in view of the Decision of the International Court of Justice on Kosovo', 26 July 2010. Available at http://mfa-pmr.org/en (accessed 15 December 2017).

307 'Member of Duma: Russia Shall Never Let Down Transnistria', *Moldova.Org* [April 2010], no date. Available at http://www.moldova.org/en/member-of-duma-russia-shall-never-let-down-transnistria-208503-eng/(accessed 25 November, 2017).
308 Igor Smirnov, cited in *Kommersant Plus*, 6 May 2011. Available at http://www.km.press.md/index.php/pridnestrovye/3576-1-r-.html (accessed 1 June 2011 (link no longer working). The original quote is: 'Rossiia ne predast Pridnestrov'e'.
309 Konstantin Kosachev quoted in 'Konstantin Kosachev: Pridnestrov'e nyzhdaetsia v modernizatsii', *All Moldova*, 16 May 2011. Available at http://www.allmoldova.com/ru/news/konstantin-kosachev-pridnestrove-nuzhdaetsya-v-modernizacii (accessed 1 December 2017).
310 'RF mozhet priznat'' Pridnestrov'e v sluchae utraty Moldaviei suvereniteta', *RIA Novosti*, 13 October 2012. Available at https://ria.ru/politics/20121013/773361328.html (accessed 1 December 2017). See also Wojciech Kononczuk and Witold Rodkiewicz, 'Could Transnistria Block Moldova's Integration with the EU?', *OSW Commentary* 95 (23 October 2012), p. 3 Available at www.osw.waw.pl (accessed 25 November 2017).
311 See, for example, Ministry of Foreign Affairs of the Russian Federation, 'Remarks by Foreign Minister Sergey Lavrov during an open Lecture on Russia's Current Foreign Policy, Moscow, 20 October' (video, in Russian), 20 October 2017 (2432-20-10-2014). Available at http://www.mid.ru/en/main_en (accessed 1 December 2017). In April 2009, Lavrov argued in more abstract terms, saying that should Moldova lose its 'identity' the Transnistrians, consequently, would have to decide their future independently. See 'Transcript of Russian Minister of Foreign Affairs Sergey Lavrov's Interview with RIA Novosti, the Voice of Russia Radio Station and the Russia Today TV Channel, Moscow, April 9, 2009', 10 April 2009 (566-10-09-2009). Available at http://www.mid.ru/en/main_en (accessed 22 March 2018).
312 A conclusion that can be made on the bases of several polls is that since the first years of independence in the early 1990s, not more than 13 per cent of the population in the Republic of Moldova has supported unification with Romania.
313 Marta Jaroszewicz and Kamil Calus, 'Moldova: A Year after the Introduction of the Visa-free Regime', *OSW (Analyses)*, 6 May 2015. Available at https://www.osw.waw.pl/(accessed 23 November 2017); 'Around 1 Million Moldovans Acquire Romanian Citizenship in Past Years', *Publika*, 27 March 2018. Available at https://en.publika.md/around-1-million-moldovans-acquire-romanian-citizenship-in-past-years-_2647124.html (accessed 5 November 2018).
314 'If Kyiv has pretensions concerning the return of Transdniestria to Ukraine, then officials there should not forget about the return to Chisinau of Southern Bessarabia and Northern Bukovina [Chernivtsi region of

Ukraine – addition by the author], territories which the former Ukrainian SSR received after the Second World War' (President Train Basescu, quoted in Paul Goble, 'Further Amputation of Bessarabia by Russia and Ukraine in the Making?' *Moldova.Org*, 25 May 2010. Available at https://www.moldova.org/en/further-amputation-of-bessarabia-by-russia-and-ukraine-in-the-making-209226-eng/) (accessed 5 November 2018).

315 Nationalist sentiments in Moldova burst out with protest marches when Chisinau in spring 2009 ceded the Palanca area to Ukraine on the basis of a border treaty signed with Kiev in 1999 and ratified in summer 2001. The joint statement by Moscow and Kiev on 17 May 2010 prompted rumours about a secret protocol, which would prepare the 'annexation' of Transnistria to Ukraine with some kind of autonomous status. The Ukrainian government soon dismissed the rumours about 'annexation' as a provocation.

316 The authors of the initiative argued: 'The white-blue-red flag is the state symbol of the Russian Federation – the successor to the USSR, the country acting as a guarantor, the country which the Transnistrian people strive so strongly for' ('Transnistria Considers Broadening its State Symbols', *Moldova.Org* [May/June 2009], no date. Available at http://www.moldova.org/en/transnistria-considers-broadening-its-state-symbols-200548-eng/(accessed 2 December 2017).

317 In April 2017, the Supreme Soviet of the PMR approved a law which allowed the use of the Russian flag alongside with the PMR flag. See 'VPMR rossiiskii flag razreshili ispol'zovat' naravne s gosudarstvennym', *RIA Novosti*, 12 April 2017. Available at https://web.archive.org/web/20170413093740/https://ria.ru/world/20170412/1492102043.html (accessed 2 December 2017).

318 'Transnistria Appeals to Putin to Act as Guarantor', *Armedia*, 26 May 2015. Available at https://armedia.am/eng/news/18639/transnistria-appeals-to-putin-to-act-as-guarantor.html (accessed 12 November 2018). Originally published by *Sputnik News*, 26 May 2015. Available at https://sptnkne.ws/jYY6 (accessed 12 November 2018).

319 Russia's policy is to continue to emphasize that it will be ready to act as a mediator in the conflict over Transnistria and 'to guarantee compliance with agreements that may be reached by the parties'. President of Russia, 'Joint News Conference with President of Moldova Igor Dodon', 17 January 2017. Available at http://en.kremlin.ru/events/president/news/53744 (accessed 13 November 2018).

320 The addition to the pension – US$15 per month, which increases the sums paid to the 130,000 pensioners (of the total population of 555,000) in the PMR by 45 per cent – is an oft-mentioned example of Moscow's support for the people in Transnistria.

321 Jeffrey Mankoff describes *derzhavnost'* as 'great power ideology'. He argues that although the term *velikaia derzhava* (great power) is already old in Russia, the notion of striving for great power status remains an important

part of Russian policy (Mankoff, *Russian Foreign Policy*, pp. 16-7 and 63). The term *velikoderzhavnost'* refers to the specifically imperial character of being a great power (Irina Isakova, *Russian Governance in the Twenty-First Century: Geo-strategy, geopolitics and governance*, p. 13).

322 This unity is depicted in paintings that show the emperor (*samoderzhets*, the autocrat) holding the duality of the sceptre-and-derzhava, the signs of rule and the realm endowed by God. In the old imperial tradition, the royal sceptre symbolizes the power to rule in the temporal domain while the orb – which in Russian is called *derzhava* and alternatively *mir* – is about the moral obligation to bear in heart the idea of Christian peace and harmony in this undertaking. The religious content of *mir* (peace, world) is about a peace of mind projected upon the world.

323 See also Legvold, 'Russian Foreign Policy', p. 116.

324 Stenogramma parlamentskikh slushanii Komiteta po delam SNG i sviaziam s sootechestvennikami (see endnote 305).

325 Deputy Prime Minister Victor Osipov, 'Transnistrian Conflict Settlement: Towards a Genuine Reintegration of Moldova', presentation at the Center for Strategic and International Studies, Washington, DC, 3 May 2010. Available at https://www.csis.org/ (accessed 26 November 2017).

326 The diplomatic episode which in summer 2016 was prompted by the appeal of Minister of Defense Anatolie Salaru (Liberal Party) for the support of NATO in transforming the peacekeeping mission in Transnistria into a civilian mission is an example of such sensitivities. See 'Moldova Asks NATO to Kick Russian Peacekeepers Out of Transnistria', *Sputnik News*, 11 July 2016. Available at https://sptnkne.ws/fjpP (accessed 2 December 2017).

Chapter 10

327 Speech of Mihail Formuzal, Bashkan (governor) of Gagauzia, at the first congress on the International Security and Strategy, organized by the National Center for Security and Strategy at the Istanbul Aydin University (Turkey). See 'Glava Gagauzii: Rossiia i Turtsiia dolzhny vystupit' stranami-garantami sushchestvovaniia gagauzov', *Regnum*, 25 March 2013. Available at http://regnum.ru/news/polit/1640299.html#ixzz2PZcIwnZW (accessed 22 November 2017, transl. by the author).

328 The income level in Gagauzia is lower than the Moldovan average, and the population is not growing: in 2011, it was reported to be 160,000.

329 The Gagauz were ruled by the Russian Empire during 1812–1917, Romania during 1920–40 and 1941–4, the Soviet Union during 1940–1 and 1944–91, and Moldova since 1991 (also shortly during 1917–8).

330 During the Soviet rule the Gagauz, of which 70 per cent were settled in Moldova, were the largest Turkic group without a national territorial formation of their own, i.e. they were recognized as an ethnic group only.

331 The Legal Code of Gagauzia is available at www.gagauzia.md (accessed 15 September 2017). This law stipulates that the status of Gagauzia 'cannot be changed without the agreement of its people,' and that 'if the status of the Republic of Moldova as an independent state changes, the people of Gagauzia shall have the right of external self-determination' (Article 7). External self-determination makes general reference to the right of the Gagauz to retain the idea and practice of their special status. The reference to Moldova's change of status is originally to a possible unification with Romania. In effect, the same is stated in the Moldovan Constitution (29 July 1994, Article 111) which acknowledges Gagauzia's special status as part of the Republic of Moldova. Gagauz-Yeri has its own tribunal (a second-order court), its own legislature for local laws, executive authorities and budget. It has external affairs in its own matters (with emphasis on a cultural frame of cooperation) but cannot act independently of Chisinau.
332 In Gagauz-Yeri, the Communist Party of Moldova has 60 per cent of the votes and is more pro-Russian than it is in other parts of the country.
333 The Gagauz language has its own alphabet but according to the legal code of Gagauzia (1994) as an official language it is written based on the Latin script.
334 See, for example, 'Posol Turtsii v Moldove: V Gagauzii net armii, poetomu ne nado ikh boiat'sia', *Gagauzyeri.md*, 29 November 2017. Available at http://gagauzyeri.md/(accessed 4 December 2017).
335 See pp. 63–4 (in Part One) in this book.

Chapter 11

336 Ministry of Foreign Affairs of the Russian Federation, 'Foreign Policy Concept of the Russian Federation (approved by President of the Russian Federation Vladimir Putin on November 30, 2016)', Article 58 (2232-01-12-2016). Available at http://www.mid.ru/en/main_en (accessed 15 December 2017).
337 Ibid.
338 Ministry of Foreign Affairs of the Russian Federation, 'Speech and Answers to Questions of Mass media by Russian Foreign Minister Sergey Lavrov during Joint press Conference Summarizing the Results of Negotiations with Foreign Minister of Azerbaijan Elmar Mammadyarov, Moscow, 21 May 2013', 21 May 2013 (1005-21-05-2013). Available at http://www.mid.ru/en/main_en (accessed 15 December 2017).
339 Ministry of Foreign Affairs of the Russian Federation, 'Concept of the Foreign Policy of the Russian Federation (Approved by President of the Russian Federation V. Putin on 12 February 2013)', 18 February 2013, Article 46. Available at http://www.mid.ru/en/main_en (accessed 15 December 2017). The description of Russia's policies in

340 Thomas de Waal, *Black Garden: Armenia and Azerbaijan through Peace and War*. In its Persian–Turkic etymology of the word 'karabakh' means 'black garden'. The 'black' presumably refers to the colour of the mountains and the same word ('karabakh') also has the connotation of 'beautiful'. 'Nagorno' (nagornyi) is the Russian word for mountainous and highland area.
341 Ibid., pp. 189–90. The conflicting parties had both set the town in fire in 1905. In March 1920, the Azerbaijani army burnt the Armenian quarter in the town; in May 1992, the Armenians took their turn to destroy the town when driving out its Azeri population. The town, once a central place along the Silk Road route, still today, has great significance for the historical and cultural identity of both parties in the war.
342 Ibid., p. 123.
343 The pogroms occurred during 26 February–1 March 1988, in Sumgait 30 kilometres north of Baku. Sumgait is an industrial city burdened with social problems and in 1988 had an Armenian population of 7–8 per cent of the total of 223,000. Official reports apparently give too low numbers of the dead: 26 Armenians and 6 Azeri, although it is also recognized that hundreds were injured.
344 The peace plan was signed on 23 September 1991. Nazarbayev made a second attempt to mediate in the following year.
345 President of Azerbaijan, 'Ilham Aliyev was Interviewed by the Influential British Magazine "The Business Year"', 4 April 2013. Available at http://en.president.az/articles/7708 (accessed 29 November 2017).
346 In the same vein of logic, Azerbaijan has not recognized Kosovo and argues that the Western reaction to the annexation of Crimea is so much louder than its condemnation of Nagorno-Karabakh's takeover by Armenia.
347 From the time of the establishment of the NKAO in 1923 till 1939, Armenians composed 88–89 per cent of the population in Karabakh. At the time of the 1989 All-Union Census, Armenians were recorded to constitute 76.9 per cent of Karabakh's population.
348 The Karabakh Committee was a group of intellectuals and political leaders formed in 1988 with the objective of the unification of Karabakh and Armenia.
349 The term 'Azeri' does not emerge until the 1930s, as an effect of the existence of the Azerbaijani SSR.
350 During the last years of the Soviet Union, the banned Armenian nationalist party (the 'Dashnaks') apparently provided weapons to the Karabakh Armenians. The goals of these two groups were mutually different, although they were interlinked.

(Note: entry starting with "relation to the conflicts in Transnistria and in Nagorno-Karabakh is essentially the same in the 2013 Foreign Policy Concept (see Article 49) and the 2016 Foreign Policy Concept quoted in this book." precedes note 340 as continuation from previous page.)

351 See Laurence Broers, 'Introduction' and Thomas de Waal, 'The Nagorny Karabakh conflict: origins, dynamics and misperceptions'.
352 Artsakh is a historical name which refers to an ancient Armenian province (assumed to have developed between 200 BCE and the fourth century CE) and, later, to an Armenian principality and kingdom which, from the eleventh to the fourteenth centuries CE resisted Turkic invasions.
353 Sergey Minasyan, 'Armenia in Karabakh, Karabakh in Armenia: The Karabakh factor in Armenia's foreign and domestic policy', p. 8.
354 'Pashinyan Unveils Details of His Meeting with Russian Ambassador', *Armenia News–News.am*, 26 April 2018. Available at https://news.am/eng/news/448364.html (accessed 26 April 2018). After two five-year terms as the president, Sargsyan's plan was to continue in power as the prime minister. A constitutional reform concentrated power in the prime minister's office. However, popular opposition with mass demonstrations in April 2018 compelled not only Sargsyan but also the government to resign and new parliamentary elections to be held during the same spring. See also Thomas de Waal, 'Sometimes Armenian Protests Are Just Armenian Protests: Not Every Post-Soviet Revolution Is about the Geopolitics of Russia'.
355 According to Azerbaijani sources (2016), the almost 1 million refugees in Azerbaijan include 40,000 people from Karabakh, 750,000 from the seven occupied regions and 200,000 from Armenia. 'Ilham Aliyev: "A reasonable compromise on Karabakh is possible"', *Vestnik Kavkaza*, 18 October 2016. Available at http://vestnikkavkaza.net/interviews/Ilham-Aliyev-A-reasonable-compromise-on-Karabakh-is-possible.html (accessed 3 December 2017). The numbers reported by the UNHCR are lower but well above half a million.
356 The requirement of such referendum has two variations in the peace negotiations: a nation-wide referendum in Azerbaijan and a referendum in Nagorno-Karabakh after the return of the former Azeri inhabitants. See Vadim Romashov and Helena Rytövuori-Apunen, 'Russia's Karabakh policy', p. 163.

Chapter 12

357 'Russian official: "My Deputy Konstantin Zatulin Takes Sides in Nagorno-Karabakh conflict"', *Trend*, 23 September 2010. Available at http://en.trend.az/news/karabakh/1755440.html (accessed 21 November 2017); 'Why Did Russian MP Decide Baku Enjoys Support of the Whole World in Karabakh Issue?', *PanArmenian Net*, 23 September 2010. Available at http://www.panarmenian.net/eng/world/news/53994/ (accessed 21 November 2017).

358 Ministry of Foreign Affairs of the Russian Federation, 'Transcript of Remarks and Response to Media Questions by Russian Minister of Foreign Affairs Sergey Lavrov at Joint Press Conference of Foreign Ministers from CSTO Member States and of the CSTO Secretary General', Moscow, 4 September 2008. Available at http://www.mid.ru/en/main_en (1303-04-09-2008) (accessed 1 December 2017).

359 Russia's Ministry of Foreign Affairs stated: 'With the signing of the tripartite Declaration in Moscow on 2 November 2008, by the Presidents of Russia, Azerbaijan and Armenia new possibilities have opened up in this field. Russia welcomes the continued intensive negotiation process to untangle the Karabakh knot in a mutually acceptable way, and as an OSCE Minsk Group Co-Chair, will help this in every way' ('Russian MFA Spokesman Andrei Nesterenko, Interview with RIA Novosti Concerning Russian Minister of Foreign Affairs Sergey Lavrov's Upcoming visit to Azerbaijan', 10 March 2009 (372-10-03-2009). Available at http://www.mid.ru/en/main_en, accessed 30 November 2017).

360 Arguing about the balance of relations between the conflict parties, Sergey Minasyan emphasizes that the Moscow Declaration (2 November 2008), which committed Armenia and Azerbaijan to settle the conflict 'by peaceful means', established 'a new *status quo*' which increased the restraints put on especially Azerbaijan (Sergey Minasyan, 'Nagorno-Karabakh After Two Decades of Conflict: Is Prolongation of the Status Quo Inevitable?', pp. 20–1).

361 The Azerbaijani and Armenian presidents had met in St Petersburg in June 2008, and the war in August did not change Russia's diplomatic mediation scheduled for the autumn. Since the Moscow Declaration (Moscow, 2 November 2008) the Kremlin has summoned annual tri-party meetings in Sochi. These meetings have prompted criticism by the two other co-chairs. Russia has explained that they are complementary to the processes in the frame of the OSCE Minsk Group.

362 The Minsk Group, named after a city in which a planned conference failed to realize because of intense battles in Karabakh, consists of the three co-chairs, the conflict parties and eight other and changing UN member states.

363 On 27 January 2011, the Parliamentary Assembly of the Council of Europe decided to create a subcommittee on Nagorno-Karabakh to continue the work of the temporary committee which had been established on 27 June 2005.

364 The United States postponed its participation until February 1997.

365 In May 1992 Armenian forces recaptured the town of Shusha (Shushi) and proceeded to open a corridor to Armenia by taking the Lachin district. Throughout the summer and autumn that followed Azerbaijani offensives established control over large parts of the north of the Karabakh area, including the Kelbajar (there exist various spellings, including Kalbajar,

Kelbadjar) district, which had been part of the Azerbaijani SSR. During March–April 1993 the combined Armenian forces—the Karabakh Armenians and the military of the Armenian Republic—in turn gained control of the entire Kelbajar district, through which another corridor to Armenia was opened. During summer and autumn 1993, when Azerbaijan had fallen into internal disarray, Armenian forces advanced to take the main part of Agdam and the western part of Fizuli. By the winter they had also taken the Jabrayil (also spelled Jebrail), Qubadli and Zangelan districts (see Map 3 on p. 157).

366 According to Trenin Heydar Aliyev's rise to power in Baku had an indirect involvement from Moscow, which, however, does not make Aliyev Moscow's 'puppet'; rather, he was the best choice from the candidates available. Elchibey was known for his pro-Ankara attitudes (Trenin, 'Russia's Security Interests', pp. 99–100). Aliyev's presidency prevented the military commander Suret Husseinov from taking this office (he became prime minister instead) when president Elchibey had fled to Nakhchivan.

367 UNHCR, 'Some 65,000 Refugees from Azerbaijan Gain Armenian Citizenship', 6 February 2004. Available at www.unhcr.org (accessed 30 November 2017). 360,000 people are reported to have fled from Azerbaijan to Armenia during 1988–93.

368 During the early 1990s, when military command structures had become confused, Russian soldiers served as mercenaries on both sides of the conflict, but it was the Azerbaijani side that had a dire need for skilled military personnel because they had been trained to a much lesser extent than their Armenian counterparts in the defunct Soviet army. Azerbaijan benefitted from the skills of especially the Russian and Ukrainian pilots, who were contracted to fly air offensives with equipment from a major Soviet-time air base near Baku. During the first years of the war Karabakh had no air defence systems. See de Waal, *Black Garden*, pp. 195–7.

369 United Nations, Security Council, S/RES/822 (30 April 1993). Available at http://www.un.org/en/sc/documents/resolutions/1993.shtml (accessed 30 November 2017).

370 The Bishkek Protocol (5 May 1994). Available at https://peacemaker.un.org/sites/peacemaker.un.org/files/ArmeniaAzerbaijan_BishkekProtocol1994.pdf (accessed 30 November 2017).

371 Dmitri Danilov, 'Russia's search for an International Mandate in Transcaucasia', p. 147.

372 In July (1994), a further ceasefire agreement was signed to legalize the one signed earlier in May.

373 Danilov, 'Russia's search', p. 145.

374 Additionally, during the Soviet time in Azerbaijan there were artillery and rocket regiments. Azerbaijan supplied the Soviet army with about 60,000 conscripts.

375 The Special Caucasian Border District (KOPO) had been created by the Russian government in March 1994 to guard both the Russian border with the states in the South Caucasus and the Armenian and Georgian borders.
376 CSCE Budapest Document 1994, 'Towards a Genuine Partnership in a New Era' (21 December 1994). Available at https://www.osce.org/ (accessed 30 November 2017).
377 United Nations, Security Council, S/RES/822 (30 April 1993). Available at http://www.un.org/en/sc/documents/resolutions/1993.shtml (accessed 30 November 2017).
378 United Nations, Security Council, S/RES/853 (29 July 1993). Available at http://www.un.org/en/sc/documents/resolutions/1993.shtml (accessed 30 November 2017).
379 Robert Kocharian served as the president of the Nagorno-Karabakh Republic (1994–7), as the prime minister of Armenia (1997–8) and as the president of Armenia (1998–2008).
380 Viacheslav Trubnikov quoted in Jane Sutton, 'Key West Peace Talks called Serious, Open', Reuters, 4 April 2001, posted on *Azerbaijan International*. Available at http://www.azer.com/aiweb/categories/karabakh/media/key_west/media_reuters_sutton.html (accessed 30 November 2017).
381 International Crisis Group, 'Nagorno-Karabakh: A Plan for Peace' (2005) and 'Nagorno-Karabakh: Risking War' (2007).
382 The Minsk Group proposals known as the 'Madrid principles' (presented to the Armenian and Azerbaijani foreign ministers by the OSCE Minsk Group co-chairs at the OSCE ministerial meeting in Madrid, 29 November 2007) laid the basis for the 'basic principles' for the renewed negotiations geared towards the conclusion of a comprehensive peace agreement. These principles were outlined in six main points: Return of the territories surrounding Nagorno-Karabakh to Azerbaijan's control; an interim status for Nagorno-Karabakh providing guarantees for security and self-governance; a corridor linking Armenia to Nagorno-Karabakh; future determination of the final legal status of Nagorno-Karabakh through a legally binding expression of will; the right of all internally displaced persons and refugees to return to their former places of residence; and international security guarantees that would include a peacekeeping operation. (See, for example, Anna Hess Sargsyan, 'Nagorno-Karabakh: Obstacles to a Negotiated Settlement', p. 3.) The work began in Madrid has been continued by the Minsk Group co-chairs in the sidelines of G8 conferences since 2009.
383 President of Azerbaijan, 'Speech by Ilham Aliyev at the Fourth Meeting of the Heads of Diplomatic Service', 21 September 2012. Available at http://en.president.az/articles/6304 (accessed 29 November 2017).
384 During 25–26 February 1992, Armenian separatists, assisted by military personnel who formerly were a part of the 366th infantry regiment of the

Soviet troops, killed more than 600 civilian Azeri fleeing from their home town of Khojaly.
385 The official Armenian position is that the mass killing was a plot by the Azerbaijani officers for propaganda purpose. See, for example, 'The Interview of the Armenian Deputy Foreign Affairs Minister Shavarsh Kocharian to the "Haylur" Program', 1 April 2011. Available at http://www.mfa.am/en/interviews/item/2011/04/01/haylur/ (accessed 30 November 2017).
386 International Crisis Group, 'Nagorno-Karabakh: Risking War'.
387 Laurence Broers, 'The Nagorny Karabakh Conflict: Defaulting to War' is a comprehensive analysis of the war in April 2016.
388 On 16 May 2016, the co-chairing countries of the OSCE Minsk Group held a meeting with the presidents of Armenia and Azerbaijan. The co-chairs issued a joint statement, according to which the presidents agreed 'to finalize in the shortest possible time an OSCE investigative mechanism' and that they also agreed 'to the expansion of the existing Office of the Personal Representative of the OSCE Chairperson in Office' ('Joint Statement of the Minister of Foreign Affairs of the Russian Federation, Secretary of State of the United States of America and State Secretary for Europe Affairs of France', Vienna, 16 May 2016. Available at https://www.osce.org/ (accessed 29 November 2017).

Chapter 13

389 National Assembly of the Republic of Armenia, Standing Committee on Foreign Relations, 'Conclusion of the 29-30.03.2005 Parliamentary Hearings on the theme "The Nagorno-Karabakh Problem: Means of Settlement"', 3 February 2006. Available at www.parliament.am (accessed 1 December 2017).
390 Ministry of Foreign Affairs of the Russian Federation, 'Russian MFA Spokesman Andrei Nesterenko, Interview with RIA Novosti Concerning Russian Minister of Foreign Affairs Sergey Lavrov's Upcoming visit to Azerbaijan', 10 March 2009 (372-10-03-2009). Available at http://www.mid.ru/en/main_en (accessed 30 November 2017).
391 Ministry of Foreign Affairs of the Russian Federation, 'Russian Foreign Minister Sergey Lavrov, Interview Granted to Leading Azerbaijan News Agencies, 10 March 2009'. Available (in Russian) at http://www.mid.ru/en/main_en (accessed in its English translation at http://www.ln.mid.ru 13 March 2009).
392 Ministry of Foreign Affairs of the Russian Federation, 'Speech and answers of the Minister of Foreign Affairs of the Russian Federation S.V. Lavrov to questions of Russian mass media at the end of the meetings of the CSTO and CIS Ministers of Foreign Affairs, Astana, 6 April 2012' (711-06-04-

2012) and 'Briefing of the Official Representative of the Ministry of Foreign Affairs of Russia A.K. Lukashevich, 20 July 2012' (1416-20-07-2012); both available at http://www.mid.ru/en/main_en (accessed 18 December 2017).

393 The bilateral treaty signed in 1995 was ratified by the Armenian and Russian parliaments in 1997. By the early 2010s, the equipment at the Russian 102nd military base in Gyumri near the Turkish border included 201 armoured combat vehicles (of which 74 main battle tanks), 84 artillery systems, two SAM S-300V missile batteries and one SAM SA-6 missile battery. An air defence unit with about 18 MIG-29 fighter aircraft is located near Yerevan. The combined strength of the Russian base and border guard in Armenia is about 5,000 military (Sergey Minasyan, 'Foreign and Security Policy of Armenia: "Complementarism" and "Pragmatism"', p. 80; the author's personal communications with Armenian researchers, 5 June 2013).

394 'Treaty on Friendship, Cooperation and Mutual Assistance', signed by presidents Boris Yeltsin and Levon Ter-Petrosian on 29 August 1997. Available at the website *Genocide.ru*, http://www.genocide.ru/lib/treaties/22.htm (accessed in Russian and in English, 21 November 2008).

395 Ibid.

396 Ibid.

397 The joint protection of the borders towards Turkey and Iran is based on an agreement signed in September 1992. Joint service is the practice also elsewhere, including the Zvartnots International Airport.

398 Amendment 2690 to the Fiscal Year 1989 Foreign Operations Appropriations bill, cited at the website of the Armenian National Committee of America (https://anca.org/, accessed 18 December 2017). During 2013–4, the California and Louisiana State Senates announced recognition of Artsakh's independence.

399 Vartan Oskanian served as foreign minister during the presidency of Robert Kocharian (1998–2008). About Armenia's 'complementarist' policy, see Minasyan, 'Foreign and Security Policy of Armenia', p. 69.

400 Ministry of Defence of the Republic of Armenia, 'The Military Doctrine of the Republic of Armenia', Chapter V. Available at http://www.mil.am/media/19192015/07/825.pdf (accessed 2 December 2017); See also Minasyan, 'Foreign and Security Policy of Armenia'.

401 Armenia signed an accession treaty to the Eurasian Economic Union (EAEU) on 9 October 2014. This treaty came into force on 2 January 2015, i.e. one day after the treaty establishing the union and signed by Belarus, Kazakhstan and Russia on 29 May 2014, entered into force. Later, at the occasion of the EU's 5th Eastern Partnership Summit on 24 November 2017, Armenia signed a new agreement (Comprehensive and Enhanced Partnership Agreement) with the EU. The purpose of this new agreement is to keep alive the reforms already started in Armenia by focusing on

projects in the fields of business and trade relations and cooperation among civil society organizations.

402 The heavy costs of the war in the early 1990s made Armenia's economy dependent on Russian loans (in the mid-1990s 60 per cent of the budget revenues came from Russia). Because the border towards Turkey was closed since 1993, fuel and food items are imported from mainly Russia. For the supply of natural gas, Armenia is completely dependent on Russia, which provides gas at a considerable discount (US$150 per one thousand cubic meters since 2013) and is in full control of ArmRosGaz in Armenia. Since 2014, Gazprom owns 100 per cent of this company, of which previously 20 per cent was Armenian. Like for gas, export taxes have been abolished for petroleum as a special favour. Additionally, Armenia's nuclear power plants are being modernized by mainly Russia.

403 Azerbaijan had only nominally participated in the EU's Eastern Partnership and was reluctant to proceed with anything less than a bilateral 'strategic partnership' with the EU.

404 Unlike Moldova, Ukraine and Georgia, Armenia has not asked about a membership perspective to be included in the preamble of the association agreement.

405 Ministry of Defence of the Republic of Armenia, 'The Military Doctrine of the Republic of Armenia', Preface. Available at http://www.mil.am/media/192015/07/825.pdf (accessed 2 December 2017).

406 The National Security Strategy of the Republic of Armenia (approved by the National Security Council on 26 January 2007), section III, states: 'The just and peaceful resolution of the Nagorno Karabakh conflict is a key issue for the National Security Strategy of the Republic of Armenia, which is the guarantor of the safety and security of the population of the Republic of Nagorno Karabakh (Artsakh)'. Available at the website of the Ministry of Foreign Affairs of the Republic of Armenia, http://www.mfa.am/en/security/ (accessed 2 December 2017).

407 The notion of the Armenian nation whose identity is very different from the 'Turkic world' had already begun to develop during the rule of Tsarist Russia, and this idea was not conducive to a power-sharing agreement which could transport the historical practice of joint rule into the modern era. In the last six decades of the eighteenth century, when the Ottoman and Persian powers had eased their grip on the region and Russia was not yet in control of it, Karabakh had existed as a khanate based on marriage arrangements between Azeri nobility and Armenian ruling families. According to the historical narrative of the region, Karabakh was set up as a khanate around 1740 through such arrangements. Karabakh became a Russian province in 1805, and Russia's control of the region was established through the treaties of Gulistan (1813) and Turkmenchai (1823).

408 See Alexander Iskandaryan, 'Armenia–Russia Relations: Geography Matters'; Minasyan, 'Foreign and Security Policy of Armenia', 80–2. Based

on a trust management agreement concluded in 2008, Armenia's railroads are modernized by the Russian Railroads company.
409 Since 1998 the annual sums have ranged from $12.5 to 3 million (see Artak Beglaryan's Personal Website, 'The History of U.S. Financial Direct Aid to Nagorno-Karabakh Republic with Statistics', 10 July 2015. Available at http://beglaryan.info/the-history-of-u-s-financial-direct-aid-to-nagorno-karabakh-republic-with-statistics/ [accessed 2 December 2017]).
410 See *Soiuz Armian Rossii* (Union of Armenians in Russia). Available at http://www.sarinfo.org/ideology/goals.shtml (accessed 2 December 2017).
411 Ibid.
412 After 2008, the main border-crossing points from Georgia (which in August 2008 denounced its membership in the CIS) to Armenia have been modernized with the financial support of the European Union and through projects implemented by the UNDP. From Russia's point of view, such modernization facilitates the transit of Russian goods through Georgia to Armenia and harmonizes border management practices between the EU and the EAEU.
413 'Russia and Azerbaijan establish AzRusTrans company', *Vestnik Kavkaza*, 10 October 2016. Available at http://vestnikkavkaza.net/news/Russia-and-Azerbaijan-establish-AzRusTrans-company.html (accessed 22 November 2017); 'Ilham Aliyev: "A Reasonable Compromise on Karabakh Is Possible"', *Vestnik Kavkaza*, 18 October 2016. Available at http://vestnikkavkaza.net/interviews/Ilham-Aliyev-A-reasonable-compromise-on-Karabakh-is-possible.html (accessed 22 November 2017).
414 President of Russia, 'Press Statement and Answers to Journalists' Questions Following Russian–Armenian Talks', 2 December 2013. Available at http://en.kremlin.ru/events/president/transcripts/19741 (accessed 22 November 2017). See also Romashov and Rytövuori-Apunen, 'Russia's Karabakh policy'.
415 Vage Davtyan, 'Transportno–politicheskaia situatsiia na yuzhnom kavkaze: zhelecnodorozhnye voiny', Part I, *Ia Rex*, 27 July 2017. Available at http://www.iarex.ru/articles/54287.html and Part II, *Ia Rex*, 28 July 2017. Available at http://www.iarex.ru/articles/54289.html; both articles accessed 2 December 2017).
416 Earlier in October, 1992, President Elchibey had signed a friendship treaty with Russia. This treaty called for mutual assistance in the case of an aggression directed at either of the signatories and agreed about the mutual protection of the rights of the resident citizens of the other country. Because Elchibey was ousted from power in 1993 and the relationship with Russia became firmer during the rule of Heydar Aliyev, a new treaty was negotiated in 1997. Since the conclusion of the FCMS treaty in 1997, Russia and Azerbaijan have reconfirmed their relationship with declarations on strategic partnership (2001, 2008).

417 The Treaty of Friendship, Cooperation and Mutual Security between the Russian Federation and the Republic of Azerbaijan, 3 July 1997 (ratified in Moscow and in Baku in January and in February 1998, respectively). Available at CIS Legislation database, http://cis-legislation.com/(accessed 19 December 2017).
418 Article 4.29 of the Military Doctrine of the Republic of Azerbaijan, cited by The Center of Military Analyses and Research in an article titled 'Military Doctrine of the Republic of Azerbaijan', website of 'Doctrine' Journalists' Military Research Center, 3 November 2012. Available at https://azdoctrine.wordpress.com/2012/11/03/military-doctrine-of-the-republic-of-azerbaijan/ (accessed 2 December 2017); 'Military doctrine "flexible and long-term"', interview of Fuad Alasgarov, head of the department for work with law-enforcement agencies in the Presidential Administration, with News.Az–Latest News from Azerbaijan, 4 June 2010. Available at http://news.az/articles/politics/16895 (accessed 2 December 2017).
419 Azerbaijan: Law of 1993 on Armed Forces of Azerbaijan Republic, 26 November 1993, Article 2. Available at Refworld.org, http://www.refworld.org/docid/451a72394.html (accessed 16 August 2017, link no longer working).
420 After independence, Azerbaijan added to the normative weight of its demand about Russia's military exit from its territory by joining the Treaty on Conventional Armed Forces in Europe (CFE) in July 1992. Azerbaijan was later, when its defence budget grew rapidly with the revenues earned from energy exports, argued to violate the CFE treaty.
421 During the Western coalition's war in Afghanistan (active phase 2001–14) Azerbaijan was part of the transit country network for the Northern Distribution Network. Roughly 40 per cent of the US and the coalition's supplies to Afghanistan went through Azerbaijani territory.
422 Azerbaijan joined NATO's Partnership for Peace (PfP) in May 1994. The cooperation with NATO developed with partnership mechanisms such as the Individual Partnership Program (IPP), the Planning and Review process (PARP), and the Individual Partnership Action Plan (IPAP). The PARP and the Partnership Goals of Azerbaijan are meant to increase military interoperability in a broad sense which also includes border security. See 'NATO to Assist in Preparation of Strategic Defense Review on Azerbaijan', Today.Az, 24 June 2008. Available at http://www.today.az/news/politics/45925.html (accessed 3 December 2017); Ministry of Foreign Affairs of the Republic of Azerbaijan, 'Overview of Azerbaijan–NATO Partnership', 30 April 2013. Available at http://www.mfa.gov.az/ (accessed 3 December 2017).
423 A new cooperation agreement between Azerbaijan and the European Union was negotiated during 2017–8 with emphasis on trade issues. It is expected to be ratified during 2019.

424 'Caspian States Adopt Declaration on Repelling Aggressors – 2', *Sputnik News*, 16 October 2007. Available at https://sptnkne.ws/fjWp (accessed 3 December 2017); 'Ekspert: SSHA vtiagivaiut Azerbaidzhan v svoiu voennuiu orbitu', *Rosbalt*, 5 February 2013. Available at http://www.rosbalt.ru/exussr/2013/02/05/1090058.html (accessed 3 December 2017). The declaration was signed by the five Caspian Sea littoral states, i.e. Azerbaijan, Iran, Kazakhstan, Russia and Turkmenistan in Tehran on 16 October 2007.

425 President of Azerbaijan, 'Ilham Aliyev was Interviewed by the Influential British Magazine "The Business Year"', 4 April 2013. Available at http://en.president.az/articles/7708 (accessed 29 November 2017).

426 President of Azerbaijan, 'Official Dinner Reception was Hosted in Honor of Ilham Aliyev in Singapore', 21 November 2012. Available at http://en.president.az/articles/6681 (accessed 29 November 2017). In March 2008 Azerbaijan introduced a declaration to the UN General Assembly 62nd session in which it demanded 'the immediate, complete and unconditional withdrawal of all Armenian forces from all the occupied territories of the Republic of Azerbaijan'. This declaration was approved by 39 countries in favour and 7 against while a total of 100 countries abstained from voting (Resolution A/62/L.42, 14 March 2008). See also Rasim Musabayov, 'Nagorno-Karabakh: a factor in Azerbaijan's foreign and domestic policy'.

427 An example is the Final Document of the 16th Summit of the Heads of State or Government of the Non-Aligned Movement (Tehran, 26–31 August 2012), which supports the principle of territorial integrity but also mentions non-use of force. Article 391 of this document states: 'The Heads of State or Government *expressed* their regret that the conflict between Armenia and Azerbaijan remains unresolved and continues to endanger international and regional peace and security. They *reaffirmed* the importance of the principle of non-use of force enshrined in the Charter of the United Nations, and encouraged the parties to continue to seek a negotiated settlement of the conflict within the territorial integrity, sovereignty and the internationally recognized borders of the Republic of Azerbaijan'. Available at http://www.namiran.org/Files/16thSummit/FinalDocument(NAM2012-Doc.1-Rev.2).pdf (accessed 29 November 2017).

428 Cavid Veliev, 'The Role of the Turkic Council for the Future of Eurasian Politics'.

429 President of Azerbaijan, 'Opening Speech by Ilham Aliyev at the Meeting of the Cabinet of Ministers', 10 October 2012. Available at http://en.president.az/articles/6439 (accessed 29 November 2017).

430 Embassy of the Russian Federation in Azerbaijan, 'Deklaratsiia o druzhbe i strategicheskom partnerstve mezhdu Azerbaidzhanskoi Respublikoi i Rossiiskoi Federatsiei', Baku, 3 July 2008. Accessed at http://embrus-az.

com/66-deklaracija-o-druzhbe-i-strategicheskom.html, 3 March 2009 (link no longer working), transl. by the author; See also President of Russia, 'Strategic Partners Russia and Azerbaijan Will Continue Developing Their Equal, Mutually Advantageous and Constructive Relations in a Multifaceted Way', 3 July 2008. Available at http://en.kremlin.ru/events/president/news/651 (accessed 20 November 2017).

431 'Military Doctrine of the Republic of Azerbaijan – Analyse', *Military and Political Review* (Belarus), 22 November 2011. Available at http://www.belvpo.com/en/4641.html (accessed 3 December 2017).

432 Rasim Musabekov, 'Where Fields of Attraction Overlap: Azerbaijan between Turkey and Russia'.

433 The parade of the Armenian military forces in September 2016 demonstrated that Armenia had at least four 9K720 Iskander missiles. See 'Armenian Parade Reveals Iskander Ballistic Missiles', *Pakistani Defence*, 24 September 2016. Available at https://defence.pk/pdf/threads/armenian-parade-reveals-iskander-ballistic-missiles.451126/ (accessed 3 December 2017). Original article at http://www.janes.com/article/64044/(link no longer working).

434 John C. K. Daly, 'Azerbaijan's Defense Spending Hits $ 4.8 Billion', *Liverostrum News Agency*, 2 December 2014. Available at https://www.liverostrum.com/azerbaijans-defence-spending-hits-4-8-billion/12095.html (accessed 3 December 2017). Originally published at http://www.silkroadreporters.com/2014/11/25/(link no longer working). Armenia in its turn has announced an increase of 17 per cent in its defence budget for 2018.

435 'Azerbaijan to buy Iron Dome Anti-Missile System from Israel', *Azeri News Agency APA*, 17 December 2016. Available at www.en.apa.az (accessed 3 December 2017). The Iron Dome system is installed in Baku and Ganja.

436 Heidi Kjaernet, 'The Energy Dimension of Azerbaijani–Russian Relations: Maneuvering for Nagorno-Karabakh'.

437 Unlike in many countries in Central and Southeastern Europe, Gazprom has little previous influence in these regions. The purchase by SOCAR of 66 per cent of a Greek gas operator DESFA, formerly a public company, in June 2013 pushed the competition between the Trans-Adriatic Pipeline (TAP) and the Nabucco pipeline to favour the first-mentioned. These two pipeline projects were the two, in the foreseeable future mutually alternative ways in which Azerbaijan's Shah Deniz gas field producer consortium (which includes British Petroleum and the Norwegian Statoil) in Europe was planned to connect with European markets. The Nabucco-West route was planned to run from Turkey through Bulgaria, Romania and Hungary to Austria and the TAP from Turkey through Greece, Albania and the Adriatic seabed to Italy. Nabucco-West would decisively reduce the dependence of Central and Southeastern European countries on Gazprom. Romania, which has Gazprom-dependent Moldova as its

neighbour, has been one of the main advocators of the Nabucco project, which competes for markets with Gazprom's South Stream.
438 Gulmira Rzaeva, 'The Southern Gas Corridor: Who Stands Where?' Likewise, also Uzbekistan and Turkmenistan have stayed out of the CIS 2010 Transit Agreement.
439 President of the Republic of Azerbaijan, 'Ilham Aliyev Was Interviewed by Russia-24 TV Channel', 25 December 2012. Available at http://en.president.az/articles/6938 (accessed 3 December 2017).
440 Azerbaijan signed the Alma-Ata Declaration in December 1991 to establish the CIS but its parliament refused to ratify the membership and participation remained on an observer status. President Heydar Aliyev pressured the parliament to ratify the CIS Charter in January 1993.

Chapter 14

441 About the Hayastan All Armenian Fund see http://www.himnadram.org/(accessed 19 December 2017).
442 'Rosssiiskie platezhnye sistemy Contact i Vlizko lisheny prava na deiatel'nost' v Armenii', *Regnum*, 27 December 2012. Available at http://www.regnum.ru/news/1609290.html (accessed 22 November 2017).
443 When the Russian Vneshtorgbank (VTB), in which the Russian state holds 77.5 per cent of the shares, prepared to buy 51 per cent of the Azerbaijani AF-Bank, The National Bank of Azerbaijan set the condition that the Karabakh branch of the VTB Armenia must be closed down. The bank's office in Stepanakert was closed down in September 2008, but operations were continued through other Armenian banks cooperating with the VTB on Armenian territory. When Azerbaijan bans the operations of those Russian banks that operate in Karabakh, Armenia's response is to ban the money transfer systems which under Baku's pressure close down their operations in Karabakh. The VTB case in 2008 shows that a Karabakh branch weighs little when Russian banks have to trade it for their access to Azerbaijani markets, and that Armenia's revenge measures do not ease the situation in Karabakh. See 'VTB (Armenia) Bank to Close Stepanakert Bank, Says Ready to Continue Investment Programs in Karabakh', *Arka*, 9 September 2008. Available at http://www.arka.am/en/news/economy/11050/ (accessed 22 November 2017).
444 After the rule of the Russian Empire was consolidated in 1823 by the treaty of Turkmenchai between Russia and Iran, Karabakh became a part of Russia's Elizavat province. At that time a Governor General represented the Tsar in the region, but this did not lift it up from being a remote and peripheral part of the empire.
445 Examples include cooperation of Russian state and Armenian non-state universities in Karabakh, such as the cooperation between the Southern

Federal University (Rostov-on-Don) and the Mesrop Mashtots University (Yerevan) in Stepanakert, as well as the co-financing which Russian business provides for educational projects through Armenian foundations (such as the Ayb Educational Foundation) for developing basic education in both Armenia and Karabakh.
446 Minasyan, 'Armenia in Karabakh'.
447 Foreign Minister Edward Nalbandian quoted in Arshaluys Mghdesyan, 'NKR Recognition Issue in Focus', *PanArmenian Net*, 18 September 2010. Available at http://www.panarmenian.net/eng/politics/details/53752/ (accessed 21 November 2017).
448 'Aram Safaryan: "We are against Discussing the Issue of Recognition of Artsakh Now"', *Armenpress*, 13 December 2010. Available at https://armenpress.am/eng/news/632360/aram-safaryan-'we-are-against-discussing-the-issue-of-recognition-of-artsakh-now'.html (accessed 21 November 2017).
449 'V Gosdume prizyvaiut ob"edinit' usiliia dlia skoreishego uregulirovaniia nagorno-karabakhskogo konflikta', *Regnum*, 12 February 2013. Available at http://www.regnum.ru/news/1624286.html (accessed 22 November 2017); 'Pereizbranie Sargsiana pozvolit sokhranit' vector v peregovornom protsesse no Nagornomu Karabakhu – glava komiteta Gosdumy', *Regnum*, 19 February 2013. Available at http://www.regnum.ru/news/1627052.html (accessed 22 November 2017); 'Azerbaidzhan predstavil notu protesta Rossii', *Regnum*, 26 February 2013. Available at http://www.regnum.ru/news/1629947.html (accessed 22 November 2017).
450 'Karabakh's Combat Readiness Has Been Supplemented by One More Component – Pashinyan Meets with Bako Sahakyan', *Armenia News–News.am*, 9 May 2018. Available at https://news.am/eng/news/450450.html (accessed 18 May 2018).
451 Ministry of Foreign Affairs of the Russian Federation, 'Transcript of Remarks and Response to Media Questions by Russian Minister of Foreign Affairs Sergey Lavrov at Joint Press Conference of Foreign Ministers from CSTO Member States and of the CSTO Secretary General'.
452 'Press-sekretar' Minoborony Armenii: Baku ne shutit, obeshscaia sbivat' grazhdanskie samolety', *Regnum*, 31 January 2013. Available at https://regnum.ru/news/1619862.html (accessed 1 December 2017).
453 'Gensek ODKB ne vosprinimaet vser'ez ugrozy Baku sbivat' grazhdanskie samolety nad Karabakhom', *Regnum*, 29 January 2013. Available at https://regnum.ru/news/1618531.html (accessed 1 December 2017).
454 'Sekretar' Sovbeza Armenii osudil "srednevekovyi" obraz myshleniia Baku', *Regnum*, 31 January 2013. Available at http://www.regnum.ru/news/1619822.html (accessed 3 December 2017).
455 Nanore Barsoumian, 'Artsakh, Armenia React to Downed Helicopter', *The Armenian Weekly*, 14 November 2014. Available at http://armenianweekly.com/2014/11/14/artsakh-armenia-react/ (accessed 3 December 2017);

'President Sarkisian Flies to Karabakh, Attends Joint Military Exercises', *MassisPost*, 13 November 2014. Available at https://massispost.com/2014/11/president-sarkisian-flies-to-karabakh-attends-joint-military-exercises/ (accessed December 2017). The airport near Stepanakert, which had been built in 1974, ceased to operate in 1992. Its reconstruction started in 2009.

456 Although the Soviet state did not allow the people of Azerbaijan to entertain trans-border contacts, especially the early Soviet decades saw the use of Azerbaijani diplomats to increase Soviet influence in the Middle East through missions to Iran, Turkey and Afghanistan. In the post–Second World War period, the Azerbaijani Ministry of Foreign Affairs could issue limited visas for travel to Iran, and Iran maintained a consulate in Baku.

457 Paul Goble, 'Re-Opening the Talysh Question in Azerbaijan: Armenian, Iranian and Russian "Traces"'.

458 Nakhchivan's (5,500 square kilometres) border with Armenia is 221 kilometres long.

459 'Sergey Markov: Nagorno-Karabakh Conflict Will Be Resolved through "Kazan" formula', *Vestnik Kavkaza*, 22 April 2016. Available at http://vestnikkavkaza.net/news/Sergey-Markov-Nagorno-Karabakh-conflict-will-be-resolved-through-Kazan-formula.html (accessed 23 November 2017). This proposal immediately brings in the enduring problems: the number of regions from which Armenia would withdraw, the question of the width of the corridors (in particular in Lachin), as well as the form and timing of the referendum about the status of Karabakh and the return of the internally displaced population.

Chapter 15

460 'Ilham Aliyev: "A Reasonable Compromise on Karabakh Is Possible"'. See endnote 413 (chapter 13), p. 290.

461 In this connection it is worth noting that Armenia's initial willingness to sign the Association Agreement with the EU, including the Deep and Comprehensive Free Trade Agreement (DCFTA), prompted opinions in the media according to which Russia should reconsider its support of Armenia in the economic sector; some experts even raised the question of whether Russia would not be best served by re-evaluating its cooperation in the field of security. For a summary of these discussions, see Emil Danielyan, 'European Integration Unlikely To End Armenia's Alliance With Russia', RFE/RL, 6 August 2013. Available at https://www.rferl.org/a/armenia-russia-european-integration/25068199.html (accessed 23 November 2017).

462 'Rossiiskie zhurnalisty v Stepanakerte obsuzhdaiut vozmozhnosti uregulirovaniia Karabakhskogo konflikta', *Kavkazkii Uzel*, 28 August

2013. Available at http://www.kavkaz-uzel.ru/articles/229162 (accessed 23 November 2017).

Conclusion

463 Reality is 'hard' in the pragmatist sense when it does not yield to realize – make real in their practical implications – the concepts by which it is framed. See, for example, Peirce, 'On Reality' (MS 194: Fall 1872) in Charles S. Peirce, *Writings of Charles S. Peirce: A Chronological Edition, Volume 3, 1872-1878*, pp. 28-32.
464 Martin Wight, *Power Politics*, pp. 57-8.
465 The domestic armies in Abkhazia and South Ossetia serve infrastructural tasks for state functions and the military cooperation with Russia. The number of Abkhazia's military is about 5,000 troops; another 5,000 people are spread between the interior ministry, security forces, border guard and customs officers. South Ossetia's military is about 1,250 and, in addition, about 900 are in the border service. The reservists number 40,000-50,000 and 16,000, respectively. About the types of armaments, see, for example, Boris Sokolov, 'Po forme – armiia, a po suti – karikatura', *Voenno-promyshlennyi kur'er (VPK)* 22/490 (12 June 2013). Available at https://vpk-news.ru/articles/16286 (accessed 23 November 2017).
466 During the Cold War Abkhazia's mountains were the key location from which to monitor air space in the Middle East and the Mediterranean.
467 About Abkhazia's participation in the construction works of the 2014 Winter Olympics in Sochi, see Revaz Tchantouria, 'Abkhazia and the Preparations for the Sochi Games: Possibilities and Conditions', pp. 222-5.
468 The CISFTA agreement was signed on 18 October 2011, between Russia, Moldova, Ukraine, Belarus, Armenia, Kazakhstan and Kyrgyzstan. It is based on earlier agreements signed in September 1993 and April 1994 in the CIS frame.
469 See pp. 33-4 (in Part One) in this book.
470 Already in 2002, when the diplomatic conflict with Georgia was fully manifest and a visa regime had been introduced for Georgia in December 2000, Russia eased the previously complicated application procedure.
471 The number given in Transnistria about residents in the region with Ukrainian passports is around 90,000 ('Serghei Gherasimciuk: At the high level, there is a lack of confidence between Chisinau and Kiev', *Synthesis and Foreign Policy Debates, APE/FES, Newsletter* 8 October 2017, p. 5). According to the sources of the Republic of Moldova, 315,000 people in Transnistria have Moldovan passports ('George Balan: We need a roadmap for development of a special legal status for the Transnistrian region', *Synthesis and Foreign Policy Debates, APE/FES, Newsletter* 11 December 2016).

472 A few years after Romania in 2007 became a member state of the European Union, it started to grant its passports, which enable visa-free travel within the European Union, to people who lived in Bessarabia during Romania's rule (1918–40) as well as to their descendants. The growth of the numbers of Moldovans owning a Romanian passport stabilized after 2014, which was the year when Moldovan citizens holding a biometric passport were granted visa-free travel to the Schengen area. See pp. 127–8 (in Part Two) in this book.

473 According to the Ministry of Foreign Affairs of the Russian Federation, the number of Russian citizens in Transnistria is 160,000 ('Briefing of the Spokesman of Foreign Affairs of Russia A.K. Lukashevich, November 22, 2012' (2196-22-11-2012). Available at http://www.mid.ru/en/main_en (accessed 25 November 2017).

474 In contrast to Georgia's separatist regions, both the NKR and the PMR started to issue certificates of citizenship (to be attached to the Soviet/ Russian, Armenian or another passport) to its residents already in 1994, and since 2001 the PMR has had its own passport.

475 After the last Soviet census in 1989, Moldova's Russian population was reduced from 13 to 5.9 per cent in 2004. In Armenia, the decline was from 1.6 to 0.5 per cent in 2001 and in Azerbaijan from 5.6 to 1.8 per cent in 1999. In Georgia, it was from 6.3 to 1.6 per cent in 2002. See Trenin, *Post-Imperium*, pp. 194–5.

476 This approach became manifest in the Constitution of the Russian Federation (1993), which provides Russia with much space in policies over defining the groups to whom it, as the successor state of the Soviet Union, is prepared to grant citizenship. While stating that citizenship is attained through procedures stipulated in federal law, this Constitution mentions that 'foreign nationals and stateless persons' enjoy the rights and bear the obligations of citizens, except in cases regulated by federal law or international agreements by the Russian Federation (Article 62, 3). The Constitution (1993) is available at http://www.constitution.ru/en/10003000-03.htm (accessed 3 December 2017).

477 'Federal'noe agentstvo po delam Sodruzhestva Nezavisimykh Gosudarstv, sootechestvennikov, prozhivaiushchikh za rubezhom, i po mezhdunarodnomu gumanitarnomu sotrudinchestvu'.

478 See endnote 171 (chapter 5), pp. 260–1.

479 'Historic Church Unification Act Signed in Moscow-1', *Sputnik International*, 17 May 2007. Available at https://sptnkne.ws/gf3w (accessed 3 December 2017).

480 Trenin, *Post-Imperium*, pp. 200–9.

481 The 'Russian (national) idea', which was composed for the purposes of Russia's European approaches under Nikolai I, includes three basic elements: the trinity of the Orthodox religion, God-endowed autocracy and the idea of the unique character of the people (*narod*), which meant

the capability to sense the sentiments of the people (*narodnost'*) as a feature of the rule.
482 In the analytical perspective offered by John R. Searle, the establishment of the *Rossotrudnichestvo* is a performative act from which it follows that the endemic connection that intertwines the people and culture becomes an 'institutional fact'. See John R. Searle, *The Construction of Social Reality*.
483 'Endemic', from the Greek en-demos, in-population.
484 President of Russia, 'Address to the Federal Assembly', 12 December 2012. Available at http://en.kremlin.ru/events/president/news/17118 (accessed 16 December 2018).
485 Kolossov and Turovsky demonstrate how geopolitical determinism in Russia simplifies Halford Mackinder's 'classical' ideas about the control of the Eurasian 'heartland' as the means to control the balance of power in world politics and serves the nationalist-patriotic political discussion in the context of the neo-Eurasianist discourse. See Vladimir Kolossov and Rostislav Turovsky, 'Russian Geopolitics at the Fin-de-siecle'.
486 See, for example, Sergey Karaganov, 'Russian Foreign Policy Finding New Bearings'.
487 President of Russia, 'Presidential Address to the Federal Assembly' on December 3, 2015, and 1 December 2016. Available at http://en.kremlin.ru/events/president/news/50864 and http://en.kremlin.ru/events/president/news/53379, respectively; both accessed 3 December 2017).
488 'For centuries, Russia developed as a multi-ethnic nation (from the very beginning), a civilization-state bonded by the Russian people, Russian language and Russian culture native for all of us, uniting us and preventing us from dissolving in this diverse world' (President of Russia, 'Address to the Federal Assembly'. About the significance of the Victory Day in contemporary Russia, see Walker, *The Long Hangover*, pp. 30–41.
489 Personal letter by Vasilii A. Zhukovskii (Russian poet, 1783–852) quoted in Iver B. Neumann, *Russia and the Idea of Europe: A Study in Identity and International Relations*, p. 43–4, from Michael Cherniavsky's '"Holy Russia": A Study in the History of an Idea'(*American History Review* 63/3, 1958, p. 630).
490 *Soglashenie* is about coming to agreement, whereas *dogovor* suggests an already negotiated agreement (which consequently can be or has been formalized by signing).
491 Helge Blakkistrud, 'The Russian regionalisation process: Decentralisation by design or disintegration by default?' p. 63; Kahn, *Federalism*, 151–88 and 234–84; Sakwa, *Russian Politics and Society*, pp. 259–83. The bilateral treaty, signed on 15 February 1994, spoke about Tatarstan as being 'united' with the Russian Federation. Article 1 of the Constitution of the Republic of Tatarstan (from November 1992, with several amendments) defines the constitutional order in the following way: 'The Republic of Tatarstan is a democratic constitutional State associated with the Russian Federation by the Constitution of the Russian Federation, the Constitution of the

Republic of Tatarstan and the Treaty between the Russian Federation and the Republic of Tatarstan "On Delimitation of Jurisdictional Subjects and Mutual Delegation of Powers between the State Bodies of the Russian Federation and the State Bodies of the Republic of Tatarstan", and a subject of the Russian Federation. The sovereignty of the Republic of Tatarstan shall consist in full possession of the State authority (legislative, executive and judicial) beyond the competence of the Russian Federation and powers of the Russian Federation in the sphere of shared competence of the Russian Federation and the Republic of Tatarstan and shall be an inalienable qualitative status of the Republic of Tatarstan.' The Constitution of Tatarstan (without date) is available at http://tatarstan.ru/file/ Constitution%20of%20the%20Republic%20of%20Tatarstan.pdf (accessed 3 December 2017).

492 'The President of the Russian Federation shall have the right to suspend acts of the Bodies of executive power of the subjects of the Russian Federation in case these acts contradict the Constitution of the Russian Federation and the federal laws, international commitments of the Russian Federation or violate the rights and freedoms of man and citizen until the issue is solved by a corresponding court' (Constitution of the Russian Federation, 1993, Article 85, 2. Available at http://www.constitution.ru/en/10003000-05.htm, accessed 20 November 2017).

493 Kahn, *Federalism*, pp. 245–52, esp. pp. 250–1. Kahn quotes a Bashkortostani senior official whose name is kept anonymous.

494 About a specific Asian approach to integration see Elnara Bainazarova, 'Kazakhstan gaining ground as a prominent regional actor'.

495 Andrey Pertsev argues that such 'islands' of relative autonomy in using political power and economic resources can be found in regional administration (his examples include Tatarstan and the Moscow, Kaluga and Ulyanovsk regions), in some of the large state corporations (Rosneft, Rostech) and in also the organization of the dominant party, United Russia, specifically in its work in the State Duma. See Andrey Pertsev, 'Svoi miry: kak nachala razrushat'sia vertikal' vlasti'. Pertsev's conclusion that these developments are signs of the 'crumbling' of the power vertical seems short-sighted; instead, they may be signs of the system becoming more settled after the reforms of the 2000s.

496 If we consider totalitarianism as a form of government or a political system that recognizes no limits to its authority and exercises centralized control that pertains to all aspects of public and private life, Stalin's rule is not a good example. Although it established a governmental machinery which generated totalitarian features in society, it was less a concept or a system than an arbitrary use of power connected with Stalin as a person.

497 Karaganov, 'Russian Foreign Policy'.

498 Hans J. Morgenthau, *Politics Among Nations: The Struggle for Power and Peace*, p. 28. About repressive and emancipatory power, see Berenice A. Carroll, 'Peace Research: The Cult of Power'.

499 Jeffrey Mankoff argues that *derzhavnost'* (which he describes as great power ideology) and *gosudarstvennost'* (which he describes as etatism) are the two major components of the geopolitical worldview among the Russian elite since the 1990s. He also emphasizes that both terms, which have a long history in Russia, appear in many shades of emphasis in the elite's world view (Jeffrey Mankoff, *Russian Foreign Policy: The Return of Great Power Politics*, pp. 62–5). While the present book cannot but agree with the broad lines of this argument, its approach is different (methodological holism instead of individualism) and its argument more specific, pertaining to the semantic logic of the practices which are historically 'inbuilt' in the two terms and help us to make sense of contemporary Russian policies.

500 By contrast to most other former Soviet subjects, which upon independence adopted a territorial concept of citizenship, the emphasis in Estonia and Latvia was ethnonational.

501 The first years of the Russian Federation gave emphasis to the civic identity of the citizens (*rossiianin*) irrespective of their ethnic features. Issues about Russian ethnic identity (*russkii*) started to impact the official discourse in 1993–4. See Vera Tolz, 'Politicians' Conceptions of the Russian Nation'.

502 'Soft power' is meant to be the opposite of hard, coercive power ('command power'). Soft power draws from the resources of cultural attraction, shared values and the perceived legitimacy and morality of policies (Joseph S. Nye, *Soft Power*, pp. 11–15). While coercion can be indirect and induce others to act according to one's wishes, soft power means shaping others' action based on what they already initially want, i.e. it is based on a preliminarily existing consensus.

503 Ibid., p. 7.

504 On 1 March 2017, Moldova's president Igor Dodon declared that Russia's migration authorities had decided to apply an amnesty to the Moldovan migrant workers whose illegal entry had recently been punished with a travel ban to Russia. This decision was understood to be a result of Dodon's negotiations in the Kremlin that January, which was his first month as president. See 'Igor Dodon: Russia to Grant Amnesty for Moldovan Migrant Workers', Moldova.Org [March 2017], no date. Available at http://www.moldova.org/en/igor-dodon-russia-grant-amnesty-moldovan-migrant-workers/ (accessed 23 August 2018).

505 The estimated number of the people who fled to Russia in autumn 2008 is 38,500. The estimated number of the people who fled to Georgia is 48,500. See Freedom House, Freedom in the World 2010/South Ossetia. Available at https://freedomhouse.org/report/freedom-world/2010/south-ossetia (accessed 17 December 2018).

506 Unification with Russia is the political agenda of especially the party *Edinaia Osetiia*. See 'South Ossetian Opposition Calls For Referendum on Unification', *RFE/RL*, 8 January 2014. Available at https://www.rferl.org/a/south-ossetia-unification/25224202.html (accessed 24 November 2017).
507 Based on census in 2013, Abkhazia's population is almost 216,000 people. Approximately 50 per cent are ethnic Abkhazians, 21 per cent Georgian (mostly Mingrelians or Svans), 20 per cent Armenians, and 11 per cent Russians. Georgia contests the results of the census, and many international sources report the population number to be closer to 175,000. More than half a million Abkhaz live in Turkey and smaller population groups exist in also Syria and Jordan. Written Abkhaz language, based on the Cyrillic alphabet, first appeared in 1862, though the Russian language also has been used since those times. Mingrelian and Georgian are widely spoken in the Gali district, where most of the Georgian people live.
508 Constitution of the Republic of Abkhazia (Apsny), 1994, Article 6. This Constitution was adopted by the Supreme Council of the Republic of Abkhazia in November 1994 and approved by national voting in October 1999 (amended in 1999, 2014 and 2016). Available (in Russian) at http://presidentofabkhazia.org/doc/const/(accessed 5 December 2017). For the official narrative of Abkhazia's history see the website of *Torgovo-Promyshlennaia Palata Respubliki Abkhaziia* (The Chamber of Commerce and Industry of the Republic of Abkhazia) at http://www.tppra.org/ru/Abkhazia (accessed 28 November 2017).
509 Besides Orthodox Christians, another significant religious affiliation in Abkhazia is Sunni Islam. In addition, there are followers of the Armenian Apostolic Orthodox Church and smaller numbers of Jews, Lutherans, Catholics and followers of traditional religions.
510 The autocephaly (self-governance) of the Georgian Orthodox Church (officially named the Georgian Apostolic Autocephalous Orthodox Church) was restored in 1990. In September 2009 the Sukhumi–Abkhazian Eparchy declared the re-establishment of the Catholicate of Abkhazia, which had functioned as an independent entity in western Georgia as a subdivision of the Georgian Orthodox Church from the 1470s until Russia took control of the church in Georgia in 1800–20. The revival of the Catholicate was a practical solution to the impasse caused by the Eastern Orthodox ecclesiastical organization's (and the Moscow Patriarchate's) continued recognition of Abkhazia as a canonical territory of the Georgian Orthodox Church. (See Giorgi Menabde, 'Russia and Georgia Agree to Unite Against "Church Separatism" in Abkhazia.') In May 2011, the path of separation was consolidated through the announcement of a new organization, the Holy Metropolis of Abkhazia, by the National Assembly of the Church, and an appeal was made to the heads and synods

of the Autocephalous Orthodox Churches, including Georgia, about its recognition for establishing the Orthodox Church of Abkhazia.
511 The Russian Orthodox Church was involved in ecclesiastical tasks in Abkhazia already in the early 1990s. During the years of intensive warfare (1992–3) the Georgian Orthodox Church lost control of the Sukhumi–Abkhazian Eparchy because the clergy had fled Abkhazia and the diocese there was only able to run the affairs of the Orthodox population – which at that time required large numbers of funerals – with support from the clergy of the Russian Orthodox Church.
512 In Transnistria (the 'left bank') cultural conflict is not openly expressed, but the population is also more homogenous than that of the 'right bank'. The connection to the Moscow Patriarchate remains unquestioned but religion plays hardly any role in the lives of the people in this region, which is historically the industrialized part of Moldova.
513 The Romanian Church, which like the Russian Church has a history in Moldova that stretches back to 1812 (the time when the Russian Empire extended its control over Bessarabia), was registered in 2004 after legal disputes.
514 The independence from Constantinople which the Romanian Orthodox Church declared in 1865 was recognized by the ecclesiastical community in 1885. About the developments in 2018, see Daniel McLaughlin, 'Churches on Guard as Ukraine Seeks Spiritual Split from Russia', *The Irish Times*, 27 November 2018. Available at https://www.irishtimes.com/news/world/europe/churches-on-guard-as-ukraine-seeks-spiritual-split-from-russia-1.3711032 (accessed 28 November 2018).
515 The Moldovan language also has this legal status, but this has little significance because it is also the sole national language. During the five years of the pro-EU government that followed the change of power in summer 2009, especially the recruitment to higher positions in the state administration has prioritized the Moldovan culture affiliated to Romania and exacerbated the issues of the cultural hierarchy in Moldovan society.
516 Nadine Gogu, 'Media Outlets in Moldova', *Balkanmedia, Konrad-Adenauer-Stiftung*. Available at http://www.kas.de/wf/en/71.13615/ (accessed 3 December 2017).
517 Culturally and in terms of population flow, Armenia is more present in Russia than vice versa. After independence in 1991 almost 1 million Armenians moved abroad and first of all to Russia.
518 Because Armenia has a history of being a 'diaspora nation', it is natural for it to approach the problems of such cooperation with the requirement of symmetry: the cooperation between the Russian Orthodox Church and the Armenian Apostolic Church must fuse religious boundaries and, consequently, Armenia will build its own church in Moscow.
519 The Moldovan government made the final decision about a NATO liaison office in Chisinau in early December 2016, a few weeks before Igor Dodon

became president. Dodon immediately required that the establishment of the office must be combined with its recognition of Moldova's neutral position. The issue was turned off from the side of NATO by referring to the anomalous nature of the issue in the procedural sense. However, when the liaison office was opened on 8 December 2017, NATO's Deputy Secretary-General Rose Gottemoeller mentioned in her speech in Chisinau that the alliance 'fully respects Moldova's neutrality, independence and sovereignty'. See Interview of Igor Dodon, President of Moldova, with *RT TV* (formerly *Russia Today TV*) by Sophie Shevardnadze, 23 January 2017. Transcript available at https://www.rt.com/shows/sophieco/374739-moldova-eu-economic-crisis/(accessed 3 December 2017); *Synthesis and Foreign Policy Debates*, APE/FES, Newsletter 11 December 2017, p. 1.

520 Uzbekistan's foreign policy is based on a law, which the late President Islam Karimov introduced to the Parliament in August 2012. According to the concept expressed by this law, Uzbekistan 'is not involved in military-political blocs, reserves the right to withdraw from any interstate organization if it transforms into a military-political bloc, does not allow the deployment of foreign military bases and facilities on its territory, and takes political, economic and other measures to prevent its involvement in armed conflicts and tensions in neighboring states' (cited in Arkady Dubnov, 'Tashkent goes, problems stay. Will the CSTO overcome the conceptual crisis?'). See also Romashov, 'Uzbekistan's Balancing Act: A Game of Chance for Independent External Policies', 170–4.

521 Tajikistan, Kyrgyzstan and Kazakhstan are militarily allied with Russia, whereas Uzbekistan and Turkmenistan are under pressure to accept external assistance – not only from Russia and the United States but increasingly from also China – for encountering the multifaceted threat which comes from Afghanistan and intertwines with their own submerged domestic insurgency. Together with the weight of their oil and gas reserves, this situation invites external rivalries and can also exacerbate separatist conflicts. Karakalpakstan in northern Uzbekistan is a possible case. In Turkmenistan, a similar threat relates mainly to the border areas towards Afghanistan and Iran. See Romashov, 'Uzbekistan's Balancing Act'; Slavomír Horák and Jan Šír, 'Turkmenistan's Afghan border conundrum'.

522 Roy Allison (*The Soviet Union and the Strategy of Non-Alignment in the Third World*) and Bo Petersson (*The Soviet Union and Peacetime Neutrality in Europe: A Study of Soviet Political Language*) demonstrate how the Soviet scholars tried to develop general theory based on Moscow's policy interests and to adjust neutrality to the Soviet ideology. The contrast made between 'traditional' and 'contemporary' or 'positive' neutrality illustrates the inspiration which Soviet discussion drew from the 'neutralist' policies declared by the formerly colonized countries in the Movement of Non-Aligned Countries (later renamed Non-Aligned Movement) where the main idea was to stay outside the East–West conflict. In addition, Allison

shows how ideas about neutrality already around the mid-1950s in Moscow were considered to offer solutions to post–Second World War Europe.
523 The FCMA treaty was concluded in 1948 and formally in force until January 1992, when a new treaty – a conventional neighbourhood treaty – with the Russian Federation was almost ready to replace it.
524 When Finland in the early 1960s began to engage step by step in multilateral economic cooperation with the West, the Soviet Union did not object in so far as this cooperation was limited to free trade (in its classical form) and Finland also was able to assure Moscow about the continuity of its neutral policy. After Finland concluded a free trade agreement with the EEC (European Economic Community) in 1973, it also agreed with the Comecon (the organization for economic cooperation between the former Eastern European countries) to conclude bilateral free trade agreements with five of its member states. Such 'parallelism' furnished the guarantees that Finland gave about the continuity of its neutral policy in its bilateral relations with the Soviet Union.
525 Because the classical neutrality is limited to wartime only it is also called 'occasional neutrality'. Impartiality towards all parties in the war is strictly required.
526 Samuel Charap argues correctly that Russia's use of military force in current international conflicts from Ukraine to Syria can be described through 'compellence', i.e. that Russia uses military force to coerce political outcomes (rather than simply annihilating the 'opponent', which would be the plain military logic for action). See Samuel Charap, 'Russia's use of military force as a foreign policy tool: Is there a logic?' In his book *The Strategy of Conflict* (pp. 187–99) Thomas C. Schelling distinguishes two forms of such coercive diplomacy and bargaining which uses military means: compellence and deterrence, which refer to forcing to do and forcing to refrain from doing something, respectively.
527 The Treaty on Friendship, Cooperation and Mutual Security between Russia and Azerbaijan (ratified 1998) states that the parties to the treaty undertake 'not to participate in any actions or activities' 'directed against' the other party, and do not allow their territories to be used against 'aggression or other violent acts' against the other party (Article 6). See pp. 177–82 (in Part Three) in this book.
528 See pp. 105–10 (in Part Two) in this book.
529 Lynch, *The Conflict in Abkhazia*, p. 15.
530 Neighbouring Gagauzia is Taraclia, a region with a total population of 40,000 where Bulgarians are the main ethnic group. Like these regions also Balti, the second largest city of 'right-bank' Moldova (102,500 inhabitants), is politically pro-Russian.
531 About Russia's assessment of its relationship with Austria, see Ministry of Foreign Affairs of the Russian Federation, Comment by the Information

and Press Department on a working visit to Russia by Federal Minister for Europe, Integration and Foreign Affairs of the Republic of Austria Karin Kneissl, 18 April 2018 (732-18-04-2018). Available at http://www.mid.ru/en/ (accessed 6 September 2018).

532 Nora Bensahel, 'Darker Shades of Gray: Why Gray Zone Conflicts Will Become More Frequent and Complex'. 'Gray zone security challenges' are in the US military practice defined as 'existing short of a formal state of war'. 'They are characterized by ambiguity about the nature of conflict, opacity of the parties involved, or uncertainty about the relevant policy and legal frameworks'. See United States Special Operations Command, White Paper, The Gray Zone, 9 September 2015, p. 1. Available at https://info.publicintelligence.net/USSOCOM-GrayZones.pdf (accessed 5 December 2017).

533 Hal Brands ('Paradoxes of the Gray Zone', Foreign Policy Research Institute, 5 February 2016) cited in Bensahel, 'Darker Shades of Gray'.

534 Package of Measures for the Implementation of the Minsk Agreements, 12 February 2015 ('Minsk II'). Available (in Russian) at http://www.osce.org/cio/140156 (accessed 6 December 2017).

535 Ibid., paragraph 9. This paragraph is a political compromise which leaves the process in a gridlock: it states that the restoration of the full control of the border by Ukraine will start immediately after the local elections, but that the process will be *completed* after a 'comprehensive political settlement' has been reached. An additional clause in brackets indicates that the denotation of this term is the local elections, which will be organized according to a specific Ukrainian law, and the constitutional reform. Whereas the organization of local elections is a definable phase in the process, the condition about the constitutional reform makes it possible for Russia to postpone its withdrawal from the border until a reform exists which is acceptable to both itself and the rebel regions.

536 Ibid., footnote 1, provides a preliminary outline of the decentralization.

537 'Withdrawal first' is the point of departure consistently emphasized by President Poroshenko. See, for example, NATO, 'Joint press conference with NATO Secretary General Jens Stoltenberg and the President of Ukraine, Petro Poroshenko', Kiev, 10 July 2017. Available at http://www.nato.int/cps/en/natohq/opinions_145865.htm (accessed 6 December 2017). Ukraine supports Moldova in its objection to any federal solution and emphasizes the need to implement the OSCE 1999 Istanbul requirements on the withdrawal of Russian troops, weapons and ammunition from the territory of the Republic of Moldova. See 'Ukrainian ambassador to Chisinau, Ivan Gnatisin: Ukraine is a good neighbour and friend of Moldova', *Synthesis and Foreign Policy Debates, APE/FES, Newsletter* 2 March 2017.

538 The Budapest Memorandum was signed by presidents Bill Clinton, Boris Yeltsin and Leonid Kutchma and the British prime minister John Major in

December 1994. Until 30 April 2018, Ukraine's armed action in Donbas was carried out as an 'anti-terrorist operation'. On this date, it became a joint-forces operation under the authority of Ukraine's armed forces and included the police, the security service, the National Guard and the border guards deployed in the war zone.

539 See also Charap, 'Russia's use of military force'.

540 President of Russia, 'Transcript of Meeting with the Leaders of the News Agencies of G8 Member Countries', Novo-Ogaryovo, 2 June 2006. Available at www.en.kremlin.ru/events/president/transcripts/23613 (accessed 20 November 2017).

541 Karaganov, 'Russian Foreign Policy'.

542 On the local dynamics of the separatist conflict in the Donbass region, see Walker, *The Long Hangover*, pp. 185–232.

543 President Putin argues: 'There are people who hold radical nationalist views both in Russia and in Ukraine. But overall, for the majority, we are one people, a people who share a common history and culture and are ethnically close.' President of Russia, 'Meeting of the Valdai International Discussion Club', 27 October 2016. Available at http://en.kremlin.ru/events/president/news/53151 (accessed 13 November 2018). A working paper of the Council for Foreign and Defence Policy, which was published by *Nezavisimaya Gazeta* on 23 May 1996, stated that Ukraine and Belarus are the most important states for Russia and, consequently, key parts of a union without which the formation of Russian national statehood is not possible. (See Tolz, 'Politicians' Conceptions', pp. 357–8.) Although this position reflects the rise of Russian nationalism in the mid-1990s it is a clear statement of the endemic connection which in Russia is seen to exist between the two countries.

544 The proclamation of 'Malorossiya' by Alexander Zakharchenko, head of the separatist Donetsk People's Republic, in July 2017 (*The Washington Post*, 19 July 2017) arguably is a 'trial balloon' from Moscow to emphasize federal structure as the key element of a compromise solution. See also Zakharchenko's interview with *Der Spiegel* ('Donetsk Separatist Leader: We Are Not Citizens of Ukraine', by Christian Neef), *Spiegel Online International*, 29 April 2015. Available at http://www.spiegel.de/international/(accessed 6 December 2017). Zakharchenko was killed in an explosion in a café in Donetsk in August 2018.

545 'Ukrainian President Petro Poroshenko Has Signed A Law Ending His Country's Non-Aligned Status', *SBS News*, 29 December 2014. Available at http://www.sbs.com.au/news/article/2014/12/30/ukraine-president-suggests-nato-referendum (accessed 6 December 2017).

546 An opinion poll in December 2016 suggested that 44 per cent of the population (excluding Crimea and the rebel regions) supported joining NATO (in 2013 this number was 16), and in July 2017 President Poroshenko made a broad-brush summary of the trend by arguing that

'more than 60 per cent of Ukrainians support Euro Atlantic integration for Ukraine'. NATO, 'Joint press conference with NATO Secretary General Jens Stoltenberg and the President of Ukraine, Petro Poroshenko', Kiev, 10 July 2017 (see endnote 537). See also: 'Poll shows most Ukrainians favor joining NATO', *KyivPost*, 28 December 2016. Available at https://www.kyivpost.com/ukraine-politics/poll-shows-ukrainians-favor-joining-nato.html (accessed 6 December 2017); 'Poroshenko Says He Plans Referendum on Ukraine's NATO Membership', *TASS*, 2 February 2017. Available at http://tass.com/world/928572 (accessed 6 December 2017).

547 See, for example, 'Russia – Ukraine Sea Clash in 300 Words', *BBC News*, 26 November 2018. Available at https://www.bbc.com/news/world-europe-46345697 (accessed 29 November 2018).

548 See, for example, 'Ukraine Bars Russian Men Aged 16–60 from Entry', *BBC News*, 30 November 2018. Available at https://www.bbc.com/news/world-europe-46397644 (accessed 1 December 2018).

549 'Dividing Ukraine' is a threat image which emerged already earlier and was considerably strengthened by the events in 2009, when the peaceful settlement by a ruling of the International Court of Justice of the decades-long dispute between Romania and Ukraine about the Serpent Island near the Danube delta gave 80 per cent of the disputed area to Romania. Although this solution had the consent of Ukraine (at the time led by President Yushchenko), many observers considered it as a sign of a negative course of developments. See, for example, 'Moldavskii ekspert: Reshenie suda OON polozhilo iuridicheskoe nachalo razdelu Ukrainy, initsiirovannumu Rumyniei', *Regnum*, 3 February 2009. Available at https://regnum.ru/news/polit/1119970.html (accessed 15 December 2017).

550 The political, cultural and economic dividing lines are discussed in depth in Richard Sakwa, *Frontline Ukraine: Crisis in the Borderlands*, pp. 1–25.

Bibliography

1. Monographs, journal articles and reports

Alexandrova-Arbatova, Nadia, 'Framework for a New European Security Architecture', in A. Kaliadine and A. Arbatov (eds), *Russia: Arms Control, Disarmament and International Security: IMEMO Supplement to the Russian edition of the SIPRI Yearbook 2009* (Moscow: Russian Academy of Sciences, Institute of World Economy and International Relations, 2010).

Allison, Roy, *The Soviet Union and the Strategy of Non-Alignment in the Third World* (Cambridge: Cambridge University Press, 1988).

Apunen, Osmo, 'The Principles of Relations between the States of Europe', in *Yearbook of Finnish Foreign Policy 1975*, pp. 36–47 (Helsinki: The Finnish Institute of International Affairs, 1975).

Asmus, Ronald D., *A Little War that Shook the World: Georgia, Russia, and the Future of the West* (New York: Palgrave Macmillan, 2010).

Austin, John L., *How to Do Things with Words* (Cambridge, MA: Harvard University Press, 1962).

Bainazarova, Elnara, 'Kazakhstan Gaining Ground as a Prominent Regional Actor', in H. Rytövuori-Apunen, H. Palu, S. Khatlamajyan and N. Iskandaryan (eds), *Security and Development in a Complex Policy Environment: Perspectives from Moldova, Armenia, Tajikistan and Kazakhstan* (Yerevan: Limush, 2012).

Baranovsky, Vladimir and Anatoly Mateiko, 'Responsibility to Protect: Russia's Approaches', *The International Spectator* 51/2 (2016), pp. 49–69. Available at http://dx.doi.org/10.1080/03932729.2016.1176648.

Bellamy, Alex J., *Responsibility to Protect: The Global Effort to End Mass Atrocities* (Cambridge, UK: Polity Press, 2009).

Bensahel, Nora, 'Darker Shades of Gray: Why Gray Zone Conflicts Will Become More Frequent and Complex', *Center for Security Studies (ETH, Zürich), Resources*, 20 February 2017. Available at http://www.css.ethz.ch/en/services/digital-library/articles/article.html/9e160cb2-a285-475f-9b82-3963d7488a0f (accessed 5 December 2017).

Black, Cyril E. 'The Pattern of Russian Objectives', in Ivo J. Lederer (ed.), *Russian Foreign Policy: Essays in Historical Perspective* (New Haven: Yale University Press, 1962).

Blakkistrud, Helge, 'The Russian Regionalisation Process: Decentralisation by Design or Disintegration by Default?', in G. Honneland and H. Blakkistrud (eds), *Centre-Periphery Relations in Russia: The Case of the Northwestern Regions* (Aldershot: Ashgate, 2001).

Blandy, Charles W., 'Provocation, Deception, Entrapment: The Russo-Georgian Five Day War', *Advanced Research and Assessment Group, Caucasus Series* 09/01 (Shrivenham: Defence Academy of the United Kingdom, March 2009). Available at http://www.da.mod.uk/publications/Provocation-Deception-Entrapment-The-Russo-Georgian-Five-Day-War (accessed 31 August 2017).

Boian, Victoria, 'Republic of Moldova's Security Context: Challenges and Future Perspectives', in H. Rytövuori-Apunen, H. Palu, S. Khatlamajyan and N. Iskandaryan (eds), *Security and Development in a Complex Policy Environment: Perspectives from Moldova, Armenia, Tajikistan and Kazakhstan* (Yerevan: Tampere Peace Research Institute – Caucasus Institute – Institute for Civil Society and Regional Development, 2012).

Bolton, Grace and Gezim Visoka, 'Recognizing Kosovo's Independence: Remedial Secession or Earned Sovereignty?' *South East European Studies at Oxford* (St Antony's College), *Occasional Papers* 11/10 (Oxford: University of Oxford, 2010).

Broers, Laurence, 'Introduction', in L. Broers (ed.), 'The Limits of Leadership: Elites and societies in the Nagorny Karabakh Peace Process', *Accord* 17 (2005), pp. 8–11.

Broers, Laurence, 'The Nagorny Karabakh Conflict: Defaulting to War', in *Research Paper, Russia and Eurasia Program* (London: The Royal Institute of International Affairs, July 2016).

Burton, John W., *Violence Explained: The Sources of Conflict, Violence and Crime and their Provention* (Manchester: Manchester University Press, 1997).

Caputo, John D., *Heidegger and Aquinas: An Essay on Overcoming Metaphysics* (New York: Fordham University Press, 1982).

Carr, E.H., *The 20 Years' Crisis 1919–1939: An Introduction to the Study of International Relations* (London: Macmillan, 1978). (First Edition 1939.)

Carroll, Berenice A., 'Peace Research: The Cult of Power', *Journal of Conflict Resolution* 16/4 (1972), pp. 585–616. Available at http://journals.sagepub.com/doi/10.1177/002200277201600409.

Clunan, Anne L., *The Social Construction of Russia's Resurgence* (Baltimore: Johns Hopkins University Press, 2009).

Charap, Samuel, 'Russia's Use of Military Force as a Foreign Policy Tool: Is There a Logic?' *Ponars Eurasia*, Policy Memo 443 (19 October 2016). Available at http://www.ponarseurasia.org/policy-memos/2016 (accessed 8 December 2017).

Chirila, Victor, 'Moldova: More Focus, Flexibility, and Visibility for the European Neighbourhood Policy', in A. Inayeh and J. Forbrig (eds), *Reviewing the European Neighbourhood Policy: Eastern Perspectives*, Europe Policy Paper (Washington, DC: German Marshall Fund of the United States, 2015).

Coyle, James J., *Russia's Border Wars and Frozen Conflicts* (Cham: Springer International, 2017).

Dale, Catherine, 'The Case of Abkhazia (Georgia)', in L. Jonson and C. Archer (eds), *Peacekeeping and the Role of Russia in Eurasia* (Boulder, CO: Westview Press, 1996).

Danilov, Dmitri, 'Russia's search for an international mandate in Transcaucasia', in B. Coppitiers (ed.), *Contested Borders in the Caucasus* (Brussels: VUBPRESS, 1996).

Dubnov, Arkady, 'Tashkent Goes, Problems Stay. Will the CSTO Overcome the Conceptual Crisis?', *Russia in Global Affairs*, No. 3, 2012 (7 October). Available at http://eng.globalaffairs.ru/ (accessed 31 August 2017).

Dzutsati, Valery, 'Signs of Balkanization Emerge in the North Caucasus', *Eurasia Daily Monitor* 10/42 (6 March The Jamestown Foundation 2013). Available at www.jamestown.org (accessed 31 August 2017).

Felgenhauer, Pavel, 'Putin Confirms the Invasion of Georgia Was Preplanned', *Eurasia Daily Monitor* 9/152 (9 August The Jamestown Foundation 2012). Available at www.jamestown.org (accessed 8 November 2017).

Filippova, Olga, 'Dimensions of Transnistrian Identity in Present-day Political Developments', in H. Rytövuori-Apunen, H. Palu, S. Khatlamajyan and N. Iskandaryan (eds), *Security and Development in a Complex Policy Environment: Perspectives from Moldova, Armenia, Tajikistan and Kazakhstan* (Yerevan: Tampere Peace Research Institute – Caucasus Institute – Institute for Civil Society and Regional Development, 2012).

Francis, Céline, *Conflict Resolution and Status: The Case of Georgia and Abkhazia (1989–2008)* (Brussels: VUBPRESS, 2011).

Ghinea, Cristian and Victor Chirila, 'EU–Moldova negotiations: What is to be discussed, what could be achieved?' *Romanian Center for European Policies* (CRPE) and *Foreign Policy Association of Moldova* (APE), Policy memo 12, May 2010. Available at http://www.crpe.ro/ (accessed 12 December 2017).

Goble, Paul, 'Re-Opening the Talysh Question in Azerbaijan: Armenian, Iranian and Russian "Traces"', *Eurasia Daily Monitor* 10/76 (23 April The Jamestown Foundation 2013). Available at www.jamestown.org (accessed 15 September 2017).

Gomart, Thomas, *Russian Civil-Military Relations: Putin's Legacy* (Washington, DC: Carnegie Endowment for International Peace, 2008).

Gromyko, Alexei, 'Russia's Conundrum in the Post-Soviet Space', *Institute of Europe* (Russian Academy of Sciences), *Working Paper* 10 (Moscow, 2015).

Hajizadeh, Hikmet, 'Azerbaijan: Regional Integration in an Explosive Region and the Next Ten Years of the South Caucasus', in A. Iskandaryan (ed.), *Caucasus Neighborhood: Turkey and the South Caucasus* (Yerevan: Caucasus Institute, 2008).

Hast, Susanna, *Beyond the Pejorative: Sphere of Influence in International Theory*. Acta Universitatis Lapponiensis 239 (Rovaniemi: University of Lapland Printing Centre, 2012).

Hellberg-Hirn, Elena, *Soil and Soul: The Symbolic World of Russianness* (Aldershot: Ashgate, 1998).

Hess Sargsyan, Anna, 'Nagorno-Karabakh: Obstacles to a Negotiated Settlement', *CSS Analysis in Security Policy* No. 131 (April 2013). Center for Security Studies (ETH, Zürich). Available at http://www.css.ethz.ch/ (accessed 30 November 2017).

Hewitt, George B., 'Abkhazia: A Problem of Identity and Ownership', *Central Asian Survey* 12/3 (1993), pp. 267–323.

Hill, William H., *Russia, the Near Abroad, and the West: Lessons from the Moldova–Transdniestria Conflict* (Washington, DC: Woodrow Wilson Center Press – Baltimore: Johns Hopkins University Press, 2012).

Hoffman, Aaron M., 'A Conceptualization of Trust in International Relations', *European Journal of International Relations* 8/3 (2002), pp. 375–401.

Horák, Slavomír and Jan Sír, 'Turkmenistan's Afghan border Conundrum', in H. Rytövuori-Apunen (ed.), *The Regional Security Puzzle Around Afghanistan: Bordering Practices in Central Asia and Beyond* (Opladen: Barbara Budruch, 2016).

van Houtum Henk, Oliver Kramsch and Wolfgang Zierhofer (eds), *B/ordering Space* (Aldershot: Ashgate, 2005).

ICISS, *The Responsibility to Protect: Report of the International Commission on Intervention and State Sovereignty* (Ottawa: International Development Research Centre, December 2001). Available at https://www.idrc.ca (accessed 23 November 2017).

Independent International Fact-finding Mission on the Conflict in Georgia, *Report*, Vol. I (September, 2009). Available at http://news.bbc.co.uk/2/shared/bsp/hi/pdfs/30_09_09_iiffmgc_report.pdf (accessed 14 August 2017).

International Crisis Group, 'Nagorno-Karabakh: A Plan for Peace', Europe Report No. 167 (11 October 2005).

International Crisis Group, 'Nagorno-Karabakh: Risking War', Europe Report No. 187 (14 November 2007).

Isakova, Irina, *Russian Governance in the Twenty-First Century: Geo-strategy, Geopolitics and Governance* (London: Frank Cass, 2005).

Iskandaryan, Aleksander, 'Armenia–Russia Relations: Geography Matters', in A. Hug (ed.), *Spotlight on Armenia* (London: The Foreign Policy Centre, 2011). Available at https://fpc.org.uk (accessed 18 December 2017).

Jackson, Robert H., *Quasi-States: Sovereignty, International Relations, and the Third World* (Cambridge: Cambridge University Press, 1990).

Jonson, Lena and Clive Archer, 'Russia and Peacekeeping in Eurasia', in L. Jonson and C. Archer (eds), *Peacekeeping and the Role of Russia in Eurasia* (Boulder, CO: Westview Press, 1996).

Kahn, Jeffrey, *Federalism, Democratization, and the Rule of Law in Russia* (Oxford: Oxford University Press, 2002).

Kanet, Roger E., 'The Return of Imperial Russia', in M. Sussex (ed.), *Conflict in the Former USSR* (Cambridge: Cambridge University Press, 2012).

Karaganov, Sergey, 'Russian Foreign Policy Finding New Bearings', *Russia in Global Affairs*, 7 June 2016. Available at http://eng.globalaffairs.ru/ (accessed 8 December 2017). Published originally in *Rossiyskaya Gazeta* 6980/112 (2016).

Katchanovski, Ivan, *Cleft Countries: Regional Political Divisions and Cultures in Post-Soviet Ukraine and Moldova* (Stuttgart: *ibidem*-Verlag, 2006).

Khramchikhin, Aleksandr, 'Iuzhnyi okrug: Protivniki na Kavkaze Rossii ne strashny', *Politika*, 7 October 2013. Available at http://rusplt.ru/policy/yujnyiy-okrug-protivniki-na-kavkaze-rossii-ne-strashnyi.html (accessed 20 November 2017).

Kjaernet, Heidi, 'The Energy Dimension of Azerbaijani–Russian Relations: Maneuvering for Nagorno-Karabakh', *Russian Analytical Digest* 56/3 (March 2009), pp. 2–5.

Kolossov, Vladimir and Rostislav Turovsky, 'Russian Geopolitics at the Fin-de-siecle', in A. H. Dawson and R. Fawn (eds), *The Changing Geopolitics of Eastern Europe* (London: Frank Cass, 2002).

Kolsto, Pål, *Political Construction Sites: Nation-Building in Russia and the Post-Soviet States* (Boulder, CO: Westview Press, 2000).

Kosachev, Konstantin, 'Rezhimy prikhodiat i ukhodiat … Mif, budto Rossiia oderzhima zhelaniem vernut' Gruziiu v sferu svoego vliianiia', *Rossiyskaya Gazeta* No. 4859 (3 March 2009). Available at https://rg.ru/2009/03/03/kosachev-gruzia.html (accessed 20 November 2017).

Kotlyarov, Ivan, 'The Logic of South Ossetia Conflict', *Russia in Global Affairs*, No. 4, 2008 (16 November). Available at http://eng.globalaffairs.ru/ (accessed 8 December 2017).

Kryshtanovskaya, Olga and Stephen White, 'The Formation of Russia's Network Directorate', in V. Kononenko and A. Moshes (eds), *Russia as a Network State: What Works in Russia When State Institutions Do Not?* The Finnish Institute of International Affairs (Basingstoke: Palgrave Macmillan, 2011).

Lavrov, Sergey, 'Face to Face with America: Between Non-Confrontation and Convergence', *Russian Politics and Law* 47/3 (May 2009), pp. 45–60. Available at https://www.researchgate.net/publication/265180885_Face_to_Face_with_America (accessed 20 November 2017).

Ledeneva, Alena V., *How Russia Really Works: The Informal Practices That Shaped Post-Soviet Politics and Business* (Ithaca: Cornell University Press, 2006).

Legvold, Robert, *Return to Cold War* (Cambridge: Polity Press, 2016).

Legvold, Robert, 'Russian Foreign Policy During Periods of Great State Transformation', in R. Legvold (ed.), *Russian Foreign Policy in the 21st Century and The Shadow of the Past* (New York: Columbia University Press, 2007).

Lukyanov, Fyodor, 'Uncertain World: 5 Years After the 5-Day War, Everyone's Learned Their Lessons', *Russia in Global Affairs*, 9 August 2013. Available at http://eng.globalaffairs.ru/ (accessed 8 December 2017).

Lynch, Dov, *The Conflict in Abkhazia: Dilemmas in Russian 'Peacekeeping' Policy*. Russia and Eurasia Programme, Discussion Paper 77 (London: The Royal Institute of International Affairs, 1998).

Lynch, Dov, *Engaging Eurasia's Separatist States: Unresolved Conflicts and De Facto States* (Washington, DC: United States Institute of Peace Press, 2004).

Mankoff, Jeffrey, *Russian Foreign Policy: The Return of Great Power Politics* (Lanham, MD: Roman & Littlefield, 2012).

Markedonov, Sergey, 'Unfreezing Conflict in South Ossetia: Regional and International Implications', in Annie Jafalian (ed.), *Reassessing Security in the South Caucasus: Regional Conflicts and Transformation* (Surrey: Ashgate, 2011).

Menabde, Giorgi, 'Russia and Georgia Agree to Unite Against "Church Separatism"', Abkhazia, *Eurasia Daily Monitor* 14/143 (7 November The Jamestown Foundation 2017). Available at www.jamestown.org (accessed 8 November 2017).

Minasyan, Sergey, 'Armenia in Karabakh, Karabakh in Armenia: The Karabakh factor in Armenia's foreign and domestic policy', in A. Iskandaryan (ed.), *Caucasus Neighborhood: Turkey and the South Caucasus* (Yerevan: Caucasus Institute, 2008).

Minasyan, Sergey, 'Nagorno-Karabakh After Two Decades of Conflict: Is Prolongation of the Status Quo Inevitable?' *Research Papers* 2 (Yerevan: Caucasus Institute, 2010).

Minasyan, Sergey, 'Foreign and Security Policy of Armenia: "Complementarism" and "Pragmatism"', in H. Rytövuori-Apunen, H. Palu, S. Khatlamajyan and N. Iskandaryan (eds), *Security and Development in a Complex Policy Environment: Perspectives from Moldova, Armenia, Tajikistan and Kazakhstan* (Yerevan: Tampere Peace Research Institute – Caucasus Institute – Institute for Civil Society and Regional Development, 2012).

Morgenthau, Hans J., *Politics Among Nations: The Struggle for Power and Peace*. Fifth Edition (New York: Alfred A. Knopf, 1973). (First Edition 1948.)

Musabayov, Rasim, 'Nagorno-Karabakh: A Factor in Azerbaijan's Foreign and Domestic Policy', in A. Iskandaryan (ed.), *Caucasus Neighborhood: Turkey and the South Caucasus*. (Yerevan: Caucasus Institute, 2008).

Musabekov [Musabayov], Rasim, 'Where Fields of Attraction Overlap: Azerbaijan Between Turkey and Russia', *Russia in Global Affairs*, No. 3, 2011 (24 September). Available at http://eng.globalaffairs.ru/ (accessed 8 December 2017).

Möllering, Guido, 'The Nature of Trust: From Georg Simmel to a Theory of Expectation, Interpretation and Suspension', *Sociology* 35/2 (2001), pp. 403–420.

Neumann, Iver B., *Russia and the Idea of Europe: A Study in Identity and International Relations* (London: Routledge, 1996).

Nicol, James P., *Diplomacy in the Former Soviet Republics* (Westport, CT: Praeger, 1995).

Niedermaier, Ana K. (ed.), *Countdown to War in Georgia: Russia's Foreign Policy and Media Coverage of the Conflict in South Ossetia and Abkhazia* (Minneapolis, MN: East View Press, 2008).

Nye, Joseph S., Jr., *Soft Power: The Means to Success in World Politics* (New York: PublicAffairs, 2004).

Peirce, Charles S., 'Logic as Semiotic: The Theory of Signs' (1931, selections written during 1897–1903), in R. E. Innis (ed.), *Semiotics: An Introductory Reader* (London: Hutchinson, 1986).

Peirce, Charles S., *Writings of Charles S. Peirce: A Chronological Edition, Volume 3, 1872–1878*. Edited by Christian J.W. Kloesel et al. (Bloomington: Indiana University Press, 1986).

Peirce, Charles S., 'How to Make Our Ideas Clear' (1878), in *Charles Sanders Peirce: Collected Papers*. Charlottesville: InteLex, 1992. CD-ROM Databases. Also in L. Menand (ed.), *Pragmatism: A Reader* (New York: Vintage Books, 1997).

Pertsev, Andrey, 'Svoi miry: kak nachala razrushat'sia vertikal' vlasti', *Carnegie Moscow Center*, 18 January 2017. Available at https://carnegie.ru/commentary/67705 (accessed 18 November 2017).

Pertsev, Andrey, 'Volodin vs. Kiriyenko: The Battle for Influence in Russia's Power Vertical', *Carnegie Moscow Center*, 16 June 2017. Available at https://carnegie.ru/commentary/71280 (accessed 9 June 2018).

Petersson, Bo, *The Soviet Union and Peacetime Neutrality in Europe: A Study of Soviet Political Language*. The Swedish Institute of International Affairs (Gothenburg: MH Publishing, 1990).

Petrov, Nikolai, 'Who is Running Russia's Regions?', in V. Kononenko and A. Moshes (eds), *Russia as a Network State: What Works in Russia When State Institutions Do Not?* The Finnish Institute of International Affairs (Basingstoke: Palgrave Macmillan, 2011).

Pipes, Richard E., 'Domestic Politics and Foreign Affairs', in Ivo J. Lederer (ed.), *Russian Foreign Policy: Essays in Historical Perspective* (New Haven: Yale University Press, 1962).

Pouliot, Vincent, *International Security in Practice: The Politics of NATO–Russia Diplomacy*. Cambridge Studies in International Relations 113 (Cambridge, UK: Cambridge University Press, 2010).

Primakov, Evgenii, *Mir bez Rossii? K chemu vedet politicheskaia blizorukost'* (Moskva: Rossiyskaya Gazeta, 2009).

Prozorov, Sergei, 'Ethos Without Nomos: The Russian–Georgian War and the Post-Soviet State of Exception', *Ethics & Global Politics* 3/4 (2010), pp. 255–75.

Riasanovsky, Nicholas V., *A History of Russia*. Fifth Edition (Oxford: Oxford University Press, 1993). (First Edition 1963.)

Ricoeur, Paul, *Hermeneutics & the Human Sciences: Essays on Language, Action & Interpretation*. Ed. and trans. J. B. Thompson (Cambridge: Cambridge University Press, 1982).

Romashov, Vadim, 'Uzbekistan's Balancing Act: A Game of Chance for Independent External Policies', in H. Rytövuori-Apunen (ed.), *The Regional Security Puzzle Around Afghanistan: Bordering Practices in Central Asia and Beyond* (Opladen: Barbara Budruch, 2016).

Romashov, Vadim and Helena Rytövuori-Apunen, 'Russia's Karabakh Policy: New Momentum in Regional Perspective', Caucasus Survey 5/2 (2017), pp. 160–176. Available at http://www.tandfonline.com/doi/full/10.1080/2376 1199.2016.1231491 (published online 23 September 2016).

Rosca, Alla, 'The US Factor in the Transnistrian Conflict's Settlement', in V. Teosa and C. Morari (eds), *Moldovan Peace Dialogues: Societal Integration, Accommodative Policies and Strategies, from an Academic Perspective* (Chisinau: Moldova State University, 2015).

Roshchin, Evgeny, 'The Concept of Friendship: From Princes to States', *European Journal of International Relations* 12/4 (2006), pp. 599–624.

Rytövuori-Apunen, Helena, 'Forget "Post-Positivist" IR! The Legacy of IR Theory as the Locus for a Pragmatist Turn', *Cooperation and Conflict* 40/2 (2005), pp. 147–177.

Rytövuori-Apunen, Helena, 'Abstractive Observation as the Key to the "Primacy of Practice"' (section in 'Pragmatism and International Relations', Forum edited by Günther Hellmann), *International Studies Review* 11/3 (2009), pp. 641–645.

Rytövuori-Apunen, Helena, 'Disputed Frontiers: Abkhazia in Russia's Sochi 2014 Project', in B. Petersson and K. Vamling (eds), *The Sochi Predicament: Contexts, Characteristics and Challenges of the Olympic Winter Games in 2014* (Newcastle upon Tyne: Cambridge Scholars Publishers, 2013).

Rytövuori-Apunen, Helena and Furugzod Usmonov, 'Tajikistan's Unsettled Security: Borderland Dynamics of the Outpost on Russia's Afghan Frontier', in H. Rytövuori-Apunen (ed.), *The Regional Security Puzzle Around Afghanistan: Bordering Practices in Central Asia and Beyond* (Opladen: Barbara Budruch, 2016).

Rytövuori-Apunen, Helena, 'The Depth of Borders Beyond the State: Analytical, Normative and Epistemic Challenges of Study', in C. Günay and N. Witjes (eds), *Border Politics: Defining Spaces of Governance and Forms of Transgressions* (Cham: Springer, 2017).

Rzaeva, Gulmira, 'The Southern Gas Corridor: Who Stands Where?' *Natural Gas Europe*, 17 June (2013). Available at www.naturalgasworld.com.

Sakwa, Richard, *Russian Politics and Society*, Fourth Edition (London: Routledge, 2008).

Sakwa, Richard, 'Great Powers and Small Wars in the Causasus', in M. Sussex (ed.), *Conflict in the Former USSR* (Cambridge: Cambridge University Press, 2012).

Sakwa, Richard, *Frontline Ukraine: Crisis in the Borderlands* (London: I.B. Tauris, 2015).

Schelling, Thomas C., *The Strategy of Conflict* (Cambridge, MA: Harvard University Press, 1960).

Schoen, Douglas E., with Evan Roth Smith, *Putin's Master Plan: To Destroy Europe, Divide NATO, and Restore Russian Power and Global Influence* (New York: Encounter Books, 2016).

Searle, John R., *The Construction of Social Reality* (Middlesex: Allen Lane, 1995).

Secrieru, Stanislav, 'Transnistria Zig-zagging towards a DCFTA', Policy Paper 4/145 (Warsaw: *The Polish Institute of International Affairs*, 2016).

Socor, Vladimir, 'Moldova's New Electoral Law Could Be Fatal to Pro-Western Parties', Part One and Part Two, *Eurasia Daily Monitor* 15/98 (25 July, The Jamestown Foundation 2017). Available at www.jamestown.org (accessed 15 August 2017).

Socor, Vladimir, 'Moscow Meeting Fails to Re-Launch 5+2 Negotiations on Transnistria Conflict', *Eurasia Daily Monitor* 8/120 (22 June The Jamestown Foundation 2011). Available at www.jamestown.org (accessed 15 August, 2017).

Socor, Vladimir, 'Rogozin Details Preconditions to Transnistria Conflict-Resolution', *Eurasia Daily Monitor* 9/79 (20 April, The Jamestown Foundation 2012). Available at www.jamestown.org (accessed 15 August 2017).

Strausz-Hupé, Robert, William R. Kintner, James E. Dougherty and Alvin J. Cottrell, *Protracted Conflict* (New York: Harper & Brothers, 1959).

Strategic and Security Studies Group, *Transnistrian Problem: a view from Ukraine*, Edited by S. Gerasymchuk (Kyiv, 2009).

Sussex, Matthew, 'Introduction: Understanding Conflict in the Former USSR', 'The Shape of the Security Order in the Former USSR' and 'Conclusions: The Future of Conflict in the Former USSR', in M. Sussex (ed.), *Conflict in the Former USSR* (Cambridge: Cambridge University Press, 2012).

Tchantouria, Revaz, 'Abkhazia and the Preparations for the Sochi Games: Possibilities and Conditions', in B. Petersson and K. Vamling (eds), *The Sochi Predicament: Contexts, Characteristics and Challenges of the Olympic Winter Games in 2014* (Newcastle upon Tyne: Cambridge Scholars Publishers, 2013).

Tolz, Vera, 'Politicians' Conceptions of the Russian Nation', in A. Brown (ed.), *Contemporary Russian Politics: A Reader* (Oxford: Oxford University Press, 2001).

Trenin, Dmitri, 'Russia's Security Interests and Policies in the Caucasus Region', in Bruno Coppiters (ed.), *Contested Borders in the Caucasus* (Brussels: VUBPRESS, 1996).

Trenin, Dmitri, *Post-Imperium: A Eurasian Story* (Washington, DC: Carnegie Endowment for International Peace, 2011).

Veliev, Cavid, 'The Role of the Turkic Council for the Future of Eurasian Politics', *Eurasia Daily Monitor* 11/124 (9 July, The Jamestown Foundation 2014). Available at www.jamestown.org (accessed 15 August 2017).

de Waal, Thomas, *Black Garden: Armenia and Azerbaijan through Peace and War* (New York: New York University Press, 2003).

de Waal, Thomas, 'The Nagorny Karabakh Conflict: Origins, Dynamics and Misperceptions', in Laurence Broers (ed.), The limits of leadership: Elites and societies in the Nagorny Karabakh peace process, *Accord* 17 (2005), pp. 12–17.

de Waal, Thomas, 'Sometimes Armenian Protests Are Just Armenian Protests: Not Every Post-Soviet Revolution is about the Geopolitics of Russia', *Foreign Policy*, 23 April 2018 (Op-Ed). Available at http://foreignpolicy.com/2018/04/23/sometimes-armenian-protests-are-just-armenian-protests/ (accessed 27 April 2018).

Walker, Shaun, *The Long Hangover: Putin's New Russia and the Ghosts of the Past* (New York: Oxford University Press, 2018).

Waltz, Kenneth N., *Theory of International Politics* (Reading, MA: Addison-Wesley, 1979).

Wight, Martin, *Power Politics*. Edited by H. Bull and C. Holbraad (Leicester: Leicester University Press, 1978).

Yanov, Alexander, 'The Birth of Pan-Slavism', Part One and Part Two (*Institute of Modern Russia*, August 2013). Available at https://www.imrussia.org/en/analysis (accessed 18 November 2017).

2. Internet websites used to access official policy documents, press releases, news material and blogs

Full references of the sources cited in this category are given in the endnotes.
The Acronym Institute for Disarmament Diplomacy, http://www.acronym.org.uk/old/archive/index.htm;
All Moldova, http://www.allmoldova.com/ru/;
Apsnypress, http://apsnypress.info/en/;
Arka, http://arka.am/en/;
Armedia, https://armedia.am/eng/;
Armenia News–News.am, https://news.am/eng/;
Armenpress, https://armenpress.am/eng/news/;
Azerbaijan International–Azer.com, http://www.azer.com/aiweb/categories/karabakh/karabakh_index.html;
Azeri News Agency APA, www.en.apa.az;
BBC News, http://www.bbc.com/news/;
Charlierose.com, https://charlierose.com/videos/(transcripts);
Civil Georgia, civil.ge Daily News Online, http://www.civil.ge/eng/;
Dniester, http://dniester.ru/;
European Training Foundation (ETF), www.etf.europa.eu;
European Union External Action, https://eeas.europa.eu/headquarters/headquarters-homepage_en;
Foreign Policy Association of the Republic of Moldova, http://www.ape.md/en/;
Freedom House, https://freedomhouse.org/;
Gagauzyeri.md, http://gagauzyeri.md;

Gosudarstvennoe informatsionnoe agenstvo 'Res', Respublika Iuzhnaia Osetiia, http://cominf.org/en;
Government of the Russian Federation, http://government.ru/en/;
Ia Rex, http://www.iarex.ru/news/;
Infotag, http://www.infotag.md/politics-en/;
International Affairs, http://en.interaffairs.ru/;
International Alert, http://www.international-alert.org/;
International Organization for Migration, Mission to the Republic of Moldova, www.iom.md;
The Irish Times, https://www.irishtimes.com/;
Jane's 360, http://www.janes.com/;
Kavkazkii Uzel, http://www.kavkaz-uzel.eu/;
Lenta.ru, https://lenta.ru/news/;
Ministry of Foreign Affairs of Pridnestrovian Moldavian Republic, http://mfa-pmr.org/en/;
Ministry of Foreign Affairs of the Russian Federation, http://www.mid.ru/en/main_en [archiving code number mentioned when available];
Moldova.Org, http://www.moldova.org/;
The Moscow Times, https://themoscowtimes.com/;
NATO (North Atlantic Treaty Organization), http://www.nato.int/;
The New York Times, https://www.nytimes.com/;
News.Az–Latest News from Azerbaijan, https://news.az/;
News from Abkhazia, http://www.kapba.de/NewsAb.html;
Nezavisimaya Gazeta, http://www.ng.ru/;
OSCE (Organization for Security and Cooperation in Europe), https://www.osce.org/;
OSW (Centre for Eastern Studies), https://www.osw.waw.pl/en/;
PanArmenian Net, http://www.panarmenian.net/eng/politics/;
Permanent Mission of the Russian Federation to the United Nations, http://russiaun.ru/en;
Ponars Eurasia, http://www.ponarseurasia.org/;
President of Russia, http://en.kremlin.ru/;
Publika, https://en.publika.md/;
Radio Free Europe/Radio Liberty (RFE/RL), http://www.rferl.org;
RIA Novosti, https://ria.ru/world/;
Rossiyskaya Gazeta, https://rg.ru/;
RSO News, http://rsonews.org/ru/news/;
The Russian Government, http://government.ru/en/;
SBS News, http://www.sbs.com.au/news/;
Spiegel Online International, http://www.spiegel.de/international/;
Sputnik International, https://sputniknews.com/;
State Duma of the Russian Federation, http://www.duma.gov.ru;
TASS, http://tass.com/;

Trend News Agency, https://en.trend.az;
United Nations: General Assembly, http://www.un.org/en/ga/documents/index.shtml, https://www.un.org/press/en/content/general-assembly; *Security Council*, http://www.un.org/en/sc/meetings/.
Vestnik Kavkaza, http://vestnikkavkaza.net;

Index

Abkhazia: border with Georgia (2009–) 58; ceasefire and peacekeeping in (1992–2008) 17–18; in the Democratic Republic of Georgia (1918–21) 40; international relations of 36, 56–7, 62, 183; political leaders of 54, 56 n.128, 59 n.133; in the Russian Empire 40–1; relations with Russia 16, 44, 56–9, 207–9, 221–3; Soviet Socialist Republic (SSR) associated with the Georgian SSR and Autonomous Republic (ASSR) in the Georgian SSR 40–4; Soviet/Russian military base in Gudauta 44–9, 51–3, 59, 208, 229; separatist war (1991–2) 41–5, 51–3; as a political entity separate from Georgia 56–9, 221–2; *See also* war, Russo-Georgian

Adjara, Autonomous Republic of (in Georgia) 53; Adjarian groups 234

Adyghe (ethnic groups) 41, 48

Akhalkalaki (in Georgia) 46–8

Alexander I, Tsar of Russia (1801–25) 40, 83

Aliyev, Heydar (President of Azerbaijan 1993–2003) 146–7, 154–5, 159–61, 195–6

Aliyev, Ilham (President of Azerbaijan 2003–) 144, 152, 161, 181

analogy (historical), uses in political argument 6–7, 19–21

Armenia, Republic of: diaspora relations 145, 172, 175; economy and society 172–7; ethnonationalism and statehood 144–7; in European integration and Transatlantic cooperation 172–3; relations with Iran 176; military alliance relationship with Russia and the CSTO 171–2, 183–4; participation in the OSCE Minsk Group 154, 162–3, 192, 199; treaties and cooperation with Russia 169–71, 231; in the Russian Empire and the Soviet Union 145; 'Velvet Revolution' (2018) 146, 192; war over Nagorno-Karabakh, *see under* war, Armenian–Azerbaijani

Artsakh, *see under* Nagorno-Karabakh Republic

Azerbaijan, Republic of: Constitution 145–6, 160, 163, 178; economy and energy resources 184–6; in European and Transatlantic cooperation 179–80; relations with Iran 195; military capability 183–4; multinational statehood 144–7; participation in the OSCE Minsk Group 159–64, 199; treaty relations with Russia and non-aligned security policy 177–83, 231; in the Russian Empire and the Soviet Union 145; relations with Turkey 142–5, 183–4, 195; war over Nagorno-Karabakh, *see under* war, Armenian–Azerbaijani

Barroso, José Manuel (President of the European Commission 2004–14) 73–5, 126

bashkan (Gagauz governor) 133–5, 200, 232

Bashkortostan 216; Bashkortostani 217

Batumi (in Georgia) 47–8, 53

Belavezhskaia Pushcha (in Belarus) 36; Belovezh Accords (December 1991) 36, 143–4, 149, 165
Bender (in Moldova) 81, 83, 89–92
Bessarabia (historical region) 83–7, 90, 127, 224
Black Sea, the 2, 20, 45–6, 53, 66, 117–18, 185, 208, 210–11, 239
Bolshevik groups: cooperation with against regional rulers (and Menshevik groups) in the South Caucasus region during 1917–21 39–40, 44, 195; power takeover during 1917–21 140, 214
border: Russia's post-Soviet border security dilemma 10–12, 56, 61, 67, 204–6, 226. *See also* deep borders, concept of
borderlines, as boundaries of sovereignty (conceived as the legal sphere of competence with linearly defined territorial borders) 1, 3, 5, 10, 14. *See also* sovereignty
Bordyuzha, Nikolai (Secretary General of the CSTO 2003–17) 193, 197
Budapest Memorandum (1994) 237, 240

Caspian Sea, the 196, 211; cooperation of the littoral states of 180–1; region 144, 150, 172
Caucasus: mountains 4, 39, 174, 221; wars of Tsarist Russia 40
ceasefire agreements: in Abkhazia 17–18; in Transnistria 18; in South Ossetia 17; in Nagorno-Karabakh 18, 156
Chechen: ethnic groups 41, 48; wars (1994–6, 1999–2000) 2, 10, 48, 52–3, 55, 186
Chernomyrdin, Viktor (Prime Minister of the Russian Federation 1992–98) 48, 105

Churkin, Vitaly (Permanent Representative of the Russian Federation to the United Nations 2006–17) 30–1, 31 n.62
Civic Chamber of the Russian Federation 62, 201
civil war: in the post-Soviet frozen conflicts 89, 154, 236; in Tajikistan 2, 11, 17
Cold War, the: mode of thinking 2; years of 25, 144, 149, 181, 208, 228, 240; post-Cold War normative order 96, 105, 124
Collective Security Treaty Organization (CSTO) 48, 53, 56, 150–2, 197, 201, 211; and Armenia 169–71; and Azerbaijan 179, 183, 193–4; Tashkent Treaty (1992) 47, 170, 183
colour revolutions 232; Orange Revolution (Ukraine 2004–5) 80, 99, 112, 216; Rose Revolution (Georgia 2003) 46, 54, 98, 107
common state, concept of (as used in conflict settlement) 106, 114, 160, 168. *See also* 'united', 'unified' state 106–7, 107 n.260; 'common house', 161
Commonwealth of Independent States (CIS), cooperation: economic 185, 210; in the Inter-Parliamentary Assembly 36, 156; in peacekeeping 18, 43, 53, 90, 156; in security issues 46, 229; and Azerbaijan 55; and Georgia 47–8, 52–5, 65, 226, 229; and Moldova 74–6, 90–1, 101
Communist: ideology 4; party and rule in Moldova 71, 74–82, 106, 127, 160; party in Russia 215; party and rule in the Soviet Union 85, 144–7
compellence, concept of, in Thomas C. Schelling's *The Strategy of Conflict* 230

Comrat (in Gagauzia, Republic of Moldova) 133–4
Confederation of Mountain Peoples 41, 48, 61
Conference on Security and Co-operation in Europe (CSCE, OSCE since 1995): Budapest summit (1994) 97, 154, 165; Helsinki Final Act of (1975) 144; peacekeeping issues 154–8. *See also* Organization for Security and Co-operation in Europe; OSCE Minsk Group
conflict settlement, Russian and Western approaches 96–105, 111–12, 124–5
Conventional Armed Forces in Europe (CFE) Treaty 97–8, 112
corridor (military): in the South Caucasus region 155, 159, 161–2, 167, 208; in the Transnistrian conflict 118, 210
corruption (political and economic) 72, 78, 241
Council of Europe 100, 107, 153, 163
Crimea 236, 238; annexation of to the Russian Federation (2014) 2, 6–7, 19–20, 23, 71, 87, 144, 206–7, 238

Dagestan: in Azerbaijan–Russia relations 186
deep borders, concept of 1–6, 15–16, 21; institutions and policies of 56, 67, 131, 147, 177, 187, 200; pattern(ness) of Russia's practices 204–7, 211–12, 231, 235–6
de facto states in the frozen conflicts 54–5, 57–8, 62–5, 73, 119, 139, 174, 203
derzhava (Russian 'imperial state') 14, 203, 214, 219; *derzhavnost'* (Russian 'great-power character') 130. *See also* protection, Russia's historical relationship of

diaspora: Abkhaz 33 n.74; Armenian 149–59; Azeri 149–59; Russian 45
Dniestr (the, river): as boundary 85–6; as frontier 83, 90; as military borderline 91; 'right' and 'left' bank of 73, 75, 86, 92, 107, 127, 131, 210
Dodon, Igor (party leader in Moldova, President of Moldova 2016–) 72, 75, 114, 118, 233; Dodon plan 114–16
domination: over territory and society 9, 34, 218
Donbass (Donetsk and Luhansk regions in eastern Ukraine) 2, 237–8
double standard, use in political argumentation 35, 219
Dubossary (in Transnistria) 89, 92

empire: Austrian 223; Austro-Hungarian 84; Ottoman 145, 164, 174, 223; Russian 13, 39–42, 83–6, 134, 140, 145, 215. *See also* imperial
endemic Russian connection 214, 224–5, 236
energy companies: Gazprom 76, 122, 184; Moldovagaz 76; Rosneft 218 n.495; SOCAR 184–5
energy pipelines: Baku-Novorossiysk, Baku–Tbilisi–Ceyhan, Baku–Tbilisi–Erzurum, Trans-Adriatic, Trans-Anatolia 184–6; Iasi–Ungheni 76 n.172
Erebuni (in Armenia) 171, 194
Eurasian integration: policies and processes 72–4, 122, 128, 174, 176–7, 214, 221, 231, 238; Customs Union of Russia, Belarus and Kazakhstan 74, 122, 173; Eurasian Economic Union (EAEU) 56, 72–4, 122, 173, 177
Eurasian region 128
Eurasianism, neo-Eurasianism 214–15, 238

European Security Treaty (EST) initiative 123–4, 210
European Union (EU): European Neighbourhood Policy (ENP) 23, 73, 173, 180; Eastern Partnership policies 72–5, 96, 173, 180, 210, 226, 241; and relations with Russia 234, 241
European Union Border Assistance Mission to Moldova and Ukraine (EUBAM) 80
Euroregion 128

Federal Agency for the Commonwealth of Independent States, Compatriots Living Abroad and International Humanitarian Cooperation of the Russian Federation (*Rossotrudnichestvo*) 213–14
federal structure of the state, proposals for (in conflict settlement) 51, 58–9, 105–15, 133–4, 233, 238. *See also* 'common state'
Federation Council of the Russian Federation 29, 64
Filat, Vladimir (Moldovan politician, Prime Minister 2009–13) 75, 78, 82, 116
'Five plus Two' negotiations on the settlement of the Transnistrian conflict ('Permanent Conference for Political Questions in the Framework of the Negotiating Process on the Transdniestrian Settlement') 93–6, 124
frontier: European 14; Russian 83, 144, 211, 223

Gabala radar station (in Azerbaijan) 157, 179
Gagauz, language and people 86–7, 114, 133–5, 234
Gagauzia, Gagauz-Yeri ('Autonomous Territorial Entity in the Republic of Moldova'): administrative status as outlined in the Kozak plan 108–9, 111; proclamation of independence (1990) 87; regional autonomy in the Republic of Moldova 114–15, 133–5; in the Russian Empire and the Soviet Union 86–7, 133. *See also* bashkan
Gamzakhurdia, Zviad (President of Georgia 1991–2) 30, 43, 49, 65
Geneva talks ('Geneva international discussions') 61–2
genocide: in political argumentation in the frozen conflicts 30–1, 37, 39–40, 43–4, 46, 65, 164
Georgia: borders, control of 52; Democratic Republic of (1918–21) 40; nationalism and independence 30, 42–4, 49–50, 66; Transatlantic cooperation 54–5; relationship with Russia 1992–2008 45–55; Soviet/Russian military bases in 44–9, 51–3, 59, 208, 229; in the Soviet Union 41–2. *See also* war, Russo–Georgian
Ghimpu, Mihai (Moldovan politician, Acting President 2009–10) 75–7, 113, 116
Gorbachev, Mikhail (General Secretary of the Communist Party of the Soviet Union 1985–91, Head of State of the Soviet Union 1988–91) 41–2, 44, 98, 105, 140–1, 172
gosudar' (Russian 'sovereign', noun); *gosudarstvo* (Russian 'state') 217–18, 219, 225
Grachev, Pavel (Minister of Defense of the Russian Federation 1992–6) 46–8, 90, 155–6, 159, 169, 189
Gryzlov, Boris (Speaker of the State Duma of the Russian Federation 2003–11, Chairman of the political party United Russia 2004–8) 63, 126

GUAM (organization formed by Georgia, Ukraine, Azerbaijan and Moldova) 112, 185
Gubarev, Sergei (Ministry of Foreign Affairs of the Russian Federation, special envoy for the negotiations on Transnistria) 122, 126
guberniia (Russian 'administrative district') 20, 83

horizontal international relations, concept of (states as formally equal units) 5–6. *See also* sovereignty, as the legal sphere of authority with linearly defined territorial borders
humanitarian: assistance and relations 122, 127, 172, 200–1, 213, 225; semantic content in Russian 55, 129, 185
Husseinov, Suret (Azerbaijani military commander, Prime Minister 1993–4) 154–5

ideology: great power 219; Soviet 79, 103, 216; universal political 14
imperial: neo-imperial (power, structures) 10, 219. *See also* empire
Inguri (the, river) 51–2
internally displaced persons 39, 61, 162, 165, 167
Iran, Islamic Republic of: as Russia's strategic border 52, 144–5, 157, 167, 170–1, 176–7, 183; and stability around Nagorno-Karabakh 195–8, 200, 211; transboundary relations with Azerbaijan 176, 195–6

Karabakh Committee 145, 160
Karaganov, Sergey (Russian foreign and security policy expert) 238, 240
Kazan 217; Kazan formula (conflict settlement in the Nagorno-Karabakh conflict)

Kazimirov, Vladimir (Russian diplomat, head of the Russian mediating mission for the Nagorno-Karabakh conflict 1992–6) 154, 156
Kelbajar (disputed area in the Nagorno-Karabakh conflict) 155–6, 159, 162, 169, 189
Key West, conflict resolution negotiations in (2001) 160–2
Kocharian, Robert (President of Nagorno-Karabakh 1994–7, Prime Minister of Armenia 1997–8, President of Armenia 1998–2008) 160–1, 191
Kodori Valley (in Abkhazia) 48, 56
Kosachev, Konstantin (Russian parliamentarian and head of *Rossotrudnichestvo* 2012–, see Federal Agency) 34, 126, 238
Kosovo, independence of 29, 32, 35–7, 63, 66, 125–6, 149, 191
Kozak, Dmitry (Russian official in the presidential administration, Deputy Prime Minister 2008–) 79; Kozak plan 98, 107–16, 121, 232–3
Kozyrev, Andrei (Minister of Foreign Affairs of the Russian Federation 1990–6) 46, 66, 91, 156
Krasnodar Territory (*Krasnodarskii Krai*) 48, 57, 122, 208, 222
Kutchma, Leonid (President of Ukraine 1994–2005) 98, 112

Lachin 159, 161–2, 169. *See also* corridor
language issues in the frozen conflicts 75, 85, 92, 108–9, 115, 140
Lavrov, Sergey (Minister of Foreign Affairs of the Russian Federation 2004–) 35–6, 56, 64, 75, 104–5, 108, 124, 152, 192
Lebed, Aleksandr (Russian General and politician, Commander-in

Chief of Russia's military units in Transnistria 1992-4) 90, 209
legitimacy: as a problem of Russia's interventions in the frozen conflicts 1, 5, 14, 16; as a problem of authoritarian rule 14–15, 129–35, 219. *See also* protection

Maidan (protest events in Kiev 2013-14) 64, 79
Medvedev, Dmitry (President 2008-12 and Prime Minister 2012- of the Russian Federation): and the war with Georgia (2008) 34–6, 57, 65–7; and relations with Moldova 76, 81, 101, 113, 118, 121–3; and the Nagorno-Karabakh conflict 152, 197; and European Security Treaty (EST) initiative 210
Merkel, Angela (Chancellor of Germany 2005–) 66, 114; 'Merkel–Medvedev dialogue' on the Transnistrian conflict (2010–12) 94, 99, 113–14
migration: and the dissolution of the Soviet Union 212–13; migrant workers 186, 213
Moldavism 85; 'Moldavist' culture 131
Moldova, Republic of: Constitution of 96, 103, 116, 124, 226–7; culture and linguistic issues 75, 85–6, 223–4; economy and energy issues 76–7, 80–1; in European integration and Transatlantic cooperation 72–5, 116–18; Kozak plan, responses to 79–80, 114–15; parliamentary elections in 71–2, 80, 118, 127; participation in the 'Five plus Two' negotiations 93–6, 124; reintegration policy of 73, 76, 93, 95, 112; relations with Russia 75–82, 105–7, 112–15; in the Russian Empire and the Soviet Union 83–7; in the war over Transnistria (1992) 89–93

Molotov–Ribbentrop Pact (1939) 77, 85
Moscow Patriarchate. *See* Orthodox Church, Russian
Muslim: and connections within the 'Russian world' 214; population and the multinational Russian state 44, 215–16; population in the Soviet Union 144–5

Nagorno-Karabakh, Republic of (NKR, Artsakh): Autonomous Oblast' (NKAO) of the Azerbaijan Soviet Socialist Republic (SSR) 140–3, 145; borders and territorial areas under control 154–9; declaration of independence 142–3; economy and society 189–92, 225; Line of Contact 7, 18, 147, 151, 154, 158, 193; participation in the Minsk Group negotiations 191–2; relations with Russia 189–92, 199–201, 211–12, 224–5; in violent conflict and war (1991–) 146–7, 154–64
Nakhchivan, Autonomous Republic of Azerbaijan 147, 154, 161, 183, 196, 199
Naryshkin, Sergei (Head of the Presidential Administration in Russia 2008–11, Speaker of the Russian State Duma 2011–16) 126, 191
nationalism, nationalist movement: Armenian 145, Azerbaijani 141–2, Georgian 30, 42–4, 49–50, 66, 221; Moldovan and Moldovan-Romanian 85–7, Romanian 223; Russian 131
Nazarbayev, Nursultan (President of Kazakhstan 1991–2019) 142, 165
neutrality: concept and policy of 16, 25, 204–9, 225–31, 238, 240–1; guarantees for 231–6; and

Abkhazia 67; and Azerbaijan 178, 192, 200; and Georgia 176; and Moldova 96-7, 103-11, 113-16, 121, 124, 126, 131, 139, 209, 227
Nicholas I, Tsar of Russia (1825-55) 214
non-alignment: military 25, 54, 113, 178, 191, 226, 231; Non-Aligned Movement 144, 163, 180-1, 227; 'non-bloc' ('beyond the blocs') policy 116
North Atlantic Treaty Organization (NATO): and Armenia 170, 173; and Azerbaijan 150, 163, 180-3, 196, 200, 208; and Georgia 55, 61, 63, 67, 171, 178, 208; and Moldova 116, 130, 209, 227, 234; and Romania 116-19; and Russia 1, 10-11, 15, 23, 29, 35-6, 64-7, 97-8, 113, 122-5, 131, 209, 223, 226-7; and Ukraine 239-40

oblast' (Russian administrative 'region', 'province') 41-2, 85, 140-1, 145
Obnovlenie (political party in Transnistria) 119, 128
Ochamchira (in Abkhazia) 59, 208
Odessa: Agreement (1998) 114; region 83, 85, 127
Organization for Security and Co-operation in Europe (OSCE): ceasefire monitoring activity 7, 18, 154, 158; in ceasefire negotiations 56, 61; 'Istanbul requirements' 97-9, 112; Istanbul summit (1999) 53, 125; policies and statements on the frozen conflicts 124, 164. *See also* Conference on Security and Co-operation in Europe (CSCE); 'Five plus Two' negotiations on the settlement of the Transnistrian conflict; OSCE Minsk Group

Orthodox Church: in Abkhazia 222-3; Armenian Apostolic 214, 225; Moldovan 223-4; Romanian 224; Russian 55, 214, 223-5; Ukrainian 224
OSCE Minsk Group 139, 152-4, 159-60, 164-5, 167-9, 182, 191-5, 232; Basic Principles, Madrid Principles 152-3, 162-3, 167-9
Ossetia-Alania, North 43-4, 57-9, 221; relations with Ingushetia 44 n.99
Ossetia, South: as an autonomous *oblast'* (region) in the Georgian Soviet Socialist Republic (SSR) 41-2; border with Georgia (2009-) 58; ceasefire and peacekeeping in (1992-2008) 17-18; international relations of 36, 56; political leaders of 58, 59 n.133; in the Russian Empire and collaboration with the Bolsheviks 39-40; connection with North Ossetia in the Soviet Union/Russian Federation 33, 42-4; relations with Russia 56, 221; Russian military base in 58, 207-8; separatist conflict and war (1991-2) 41-4, 54; as a political entity separate from Georgia 56-9. *See also* war, Russo-Georgian

Pan-Slavism: in political argument 22; historical movement 215
Pashinian, Nikol (Prime Minister of Armenia 2018-) 146, 192
passports policies in the frozen conflicts: Armenian 149; Russian 33, 55, 92, 212; Romanian 92, 127; Soviet practices, continuation of 212
Persia: Azeri ethnic groups in 145. *See also* Iran
Persian, linguistic connection of ethnic groups 44, 195

Plahotniuc, Vladimir (Moldovan politician and businessman) 72, 75
political conditionality of policies, concept of 5, 101–5, 204, 227–9, 231–2, 236. *See also* trusting relationship
Poroshenko, Petro (President of Ukraine 2014–19) 239–40
power, concept of: traditional in international relations 206; vertical 5–6, 13, 15–16, 21, 203, 206, 213–14, 218, 229; 'power vertical' 5, 13, 94, 122; vertical power and soft power 219–20; relations of vertical power in Georgia 34, 49, 56–9; relations of vertical power in Moldova 80, 94, 103, 116, 121–3; relations of vertical power in Armenia and Azerbaijan 168, 190, 201–2
pragma, concept of 16, 24, 204
pragmatism: 3, 8, 15–16, 21–5, 68, 204; as developed by C. S. Peirce 15 n.34, 21 n.39, 24 n.48, 203 n.463; and primacy of practice 25; and theory-centred approaches 21, 24–5
Pridnestrovian (Transnistrian) Moldavian Republic (PMR): Autonomous Soviet Socialist Republic (ASSR) 83–5, proclamation of independence 71, 86–7; economy and society 73, 85–6, 131, 223–4; international relations 71–3; political status as outlined in the Kozak plan 108; participation in the 'Five plus Two' negotiations 93–6; political leaders of 81–3, 86, 94, 106–7, 118–19, 121–2, 126; in the Russian Empire 83–7; relations with Russia 81–2, 121–32, 223–4; Russian military base in 89–92, 209–11; separatist war (1992) 89–93; security zone 91–2, 100, 114

Primakov, Evgenii (Minister of Foreign Affairs 1996–8 and Prime Minister 1998–9 of the Russian Federation) 53, 66, 91, 106; Primakov Memorandum (1997) 95, 103, 106, 114, 160
protection: Russia's historical relationship of 34, 38, 44, 54, 56, 129–32, 134
Prut (river), the 83, 85
Putin, Vladimir (President of the Russian Federation 2000–8, 2012–, Prime Minister 2008–12): and policies on the frozen conflicts 37, 52, 58, 63–4, 66, 81, 107, 139, 161; and policies to strengthen central control of the Russian state 13, 129, 214–17; and Russia's relations with the Western states 66, 105, 238

quasi-states: concept of 57; in Russia's deep border practices 56–9, 67, 204

realism, realist school of international relations 206; trivial interpretations of (quasi-realism) 22, 22 n.40, 208
referendum of March 1991 (Union-wide referendum on the future of the Soviet Union) 42–3, 87, 134, 142
reintegration: in Ukraine 237; in Moldova, *see under* Moldova, Republic of. *See also* reunification, unification
responsibility to protect: as an international norm 31–2; in Russian political tradition 37–8. *See also* protection, Russia's historical relationship of
reunification 107, 122, 131, 211, 229–30. *See also* reintegration, unification

Index

Rogozin, Dmitry (Russian politician, Deputy Prime Minister 2011–18) 35
Romania: in energy networks 180, 185; expansion of the Russian Empire over the lands of 83; and the Gagauz people 86, 134; 'Greater', 84–5; Moldova's integration with 75, 108, 111, 123, 127; passports policies of 92, 127, 212; as political memory about Moldova (Bessarabia) being part of the Kingdom of Romania (1920–1940) 84–5; and shared experience of the Soviet decades 77, 85; in the Soviet/Russian geopolitical contest over the control of the region 85, 90, 127, 135, 223; US military systems in 92, 117–18, 210
Romanian, culture and language of as political dividing line 75, 77, 85–6, 133, 209, 224
Romanticist interpretation of Russia 4, 22, 215
Russia, tsarist (until 1917) 25, 85, 134, 140, 144–5
Russian World (Russkii Mir) foundation 213–15

Saakashvili, Mikhail (President of Georgia 2004–13) 30, 33, 54
Samachablo. *See* Ossetia, South
Sargsyan, Serzh (President of the Republic of Armenia 2008–18) 146, 152, 156, 173, 175, 193
self-determination (national, the right of peoples to), principle of: as defined for the Gagauz people in Moldovan law 134; in political argumentation in the frozen conflicts 20, 29, 33–6, 62–4, 71, 126, 143–5, 168
Sevastopol (Crimean Peninsula) 19, 144, 208

Shevardnadze, Eduard (President of Georgia 1995–2003) 30, 43, 48–54
Shusha (Shushi by its Azerbaijani name, in Nagorno-Karabakh) 140–1
Slavic, ethnic population and culture 14, 22, 36, 45, 83, 126, 131, 214
Snegur, Mircea (President of the Republic of Moldova 1991–7) 86, 90–1, 94, 96
Sochi 62, 209, 222
Socialist: political party in Moldova 72, 75, 114, 233
sovereignty: as the legal sphere of authority with linearly defined territorial borders (boundaries of sovereignty) 3, 12, 203, 216; in political argumentation in the frozen conflicts 30, 101, 124, 158, 163, 165, 194
Soviet Constitution (Constitution of the Soviet Union): from the year 1925 51; from the year 1977 87, 140, 143, 146
Soviet Union, the (USSR): dissolution 42, 45–6, 145, 216. *See also* Belovezh Accords
speech acts (philosophy of language and society) 104–5, 129
Stalin, Joseph (1878–1953), rule of 41–2, 218
State Duma of the Russian Federation 29, 35, 45–7, 52, 62–3, 72, 101–2, 106, 125–6, 130, 136, 150; Committee for CIS Affairs and Compatriot Relations 149, 191
Stepanakert (Khankendi by its Azerbaijani name, in Nagorno-Karabakh) 141, 155, 165–6, 191–4, 197, 202, 225
Sukhumi (in Abkhazia) 43, 47, 53, 57; military district 40

Talysh ethnic group 195, 234
Tatar people 215–16
Tatarstan 13, 51, 216–17

Ter-Petrosian, Levon (President of Armenia 1991–8) 146, 159–60, 233
territorial integrity (principle of): as used in the conflict between Armenia and Azerbaijan 144–5, 149, 158, 163, 166, 170–2, 178, 182, 194; as used in Russia's relations with Georgia 33–4, 48–9, 52–3, 65; as used in Russia's relations with Moldova 90, 101–5, 113, 124, 130, 139, 237
titular nation 133, 140, 143, 241
Transcaucasian Federation (1922–36) 41–2
trusting relationship (political): concept of 5, 12; examples of 49–50, 58–9, 65–6, 75–8, 105, 111, 119, 181–2, 204, 229. *See also* political conditionality of policies
Tskhinvali (in South Ossetia) 19, 30–1, 42, 54, 57, 59, 63, 66, 192, 208, 239
Turkey: Armenia's closed border with 159, 176; close relations with Azerbaijan of 142–5, 183–4, 195; as a regional actor in conflict settlement 135, 200, 234; in Russia's regional economic cooperation 151, 177, 197–8; as Russia's strategic border 52, 117, 196–7, 200, 208, 211

Ukraine: and war in eastern Ukraine. *See* Donbass
unification 75, 94, 98, 105, 108, 141, 201, 221. *See also* reintegration, reunification
United Nations (UN): General Assembly 124–5, 144, 158, 181; observer mission in Georgia (UNOMIG) 18, 43; Security Council 30–2, 55, 91, 126, 155, 158, 164, 181

United Russia (political party) 63, 107 n.260; and power vertical 217–18, 218 n.495
United States of America (US) 1, 7, 11, 25, 195–6, 208–10, 220, 226, 239; and the conflict over Kosovo 29, 35, 55; and frozen conflicts 61, 93, 97–8, 100, 112, 152–5, 161; and defence systems in Europe 92, 116–18, 123–4; and relations with Armenia 172–5, 189; and relations with Azerbaijan 175, 183

Vaziani (in Georgia) 46–8
vertical international relations, concept of. *See* power, vertical
Voronin, Vladimir (Moldovan politician, President 2001–9) 74, 77–82, 100, 106–7, 112, 127, 130

war (between states): Armenian-Azerbaijani, active phase during 1991–4 142, 155, 169–72, 184; and recent phase in 2016 7, 135, 147, 151, 164, 167, 183, 195, 197, 199; Russo-Georgian (2008) 29–34; First World War (1914–18) 84; Second World War (1939–45) 215, 218, 235

Yanukovich, Viktor (President of Ukraine 2010–14) 81, 100–1, 113
Yeltsin, Boris (President of the Russian Federation 1991–99) 11, 13, 214, 216; and the Nagorno-Karabakh conflict 142–3, 154, 160–1, 165; and relations with Armenia and Azerbaijan 142; and relations with Georgia 30, 43–4, 46–7, 50; and relations with Moldova 89–91, 94, 106, 116, 119
Yushchenko, Victor (President of Ukraine 2005–10) 80, 112, 238